Halloween

CAPTURING THE SPIRIT OF NEW YORK CITY FOR FIFTY YEARS, 1974–2024

Larry Racioppo

FOREWORD BY KEVIN BAKER

castle

First published in 2026 by Castle Books, an imprint of The Quarto Group,
135 West 36th Street, 13th Floor, New York, NY 10018, USA
(212) 779-4972 www.Quarto.com

EEA Representation, WTS Tax d.o.o.,
Žanova ulica 3, 4000 Kranj, Slovenia.
www.wts-tax.si

10 9 8 7 6 5 4 3 2 1

ISBN: 978-1-57715-879-0

Digital edition published in 2026
eISBN: 978-1-57715-880-6

Library of Congress Cataloging-in-Publication Data

Names: Racioppo, Larry photographer
Title: Halloween : capturing the spirit of New York City for Fifty Years, 1974–2024 / Larry Racioppo.
Description: New York, NY : Castle Books, 2026. | Summary: "In Halloween, trace the evolution of this spooky holiday in NYC, especially Brooklyn, from the 1970s and beyond with renowned photographer Larry Racioppo's stunning collection of vintage street photography"-- Provided by publisher.
Identifiers: LCCN 2025053971 (print) | LCCN 2025053972 (ebook) | ISBN 9781577158790 hardcover | ISBN 9781577158806 ebook
Subjects: LCSH: Halloween--New York (State)--New York | New York (N.Y.)--History
Classification: LCC GT4965 .R25 2026 (print) | LCC GT4965 (ebook) | DDC 394.264609747--dc23/eng/20260226
LC record available at https://lccn.loc.gov/2025053971
LC ebook record available at https://lccn.loc.gov/2025053972

Publisher: Rage Kindelsperger
Creative Director: Laura Drew
Editorial Director: Erin Canning
Managing Editor: Cara Donaldson
Cover and Interior Design: Madeleine Kane

Printed in Huizhou City, Guangdong, China TT052026

I dedicate this book to my three grandchildren:
Nico Harvey, Rowan Harvey, and Noa Hampton.
They have been a sweet surprise and an

1970s and 1980s

8

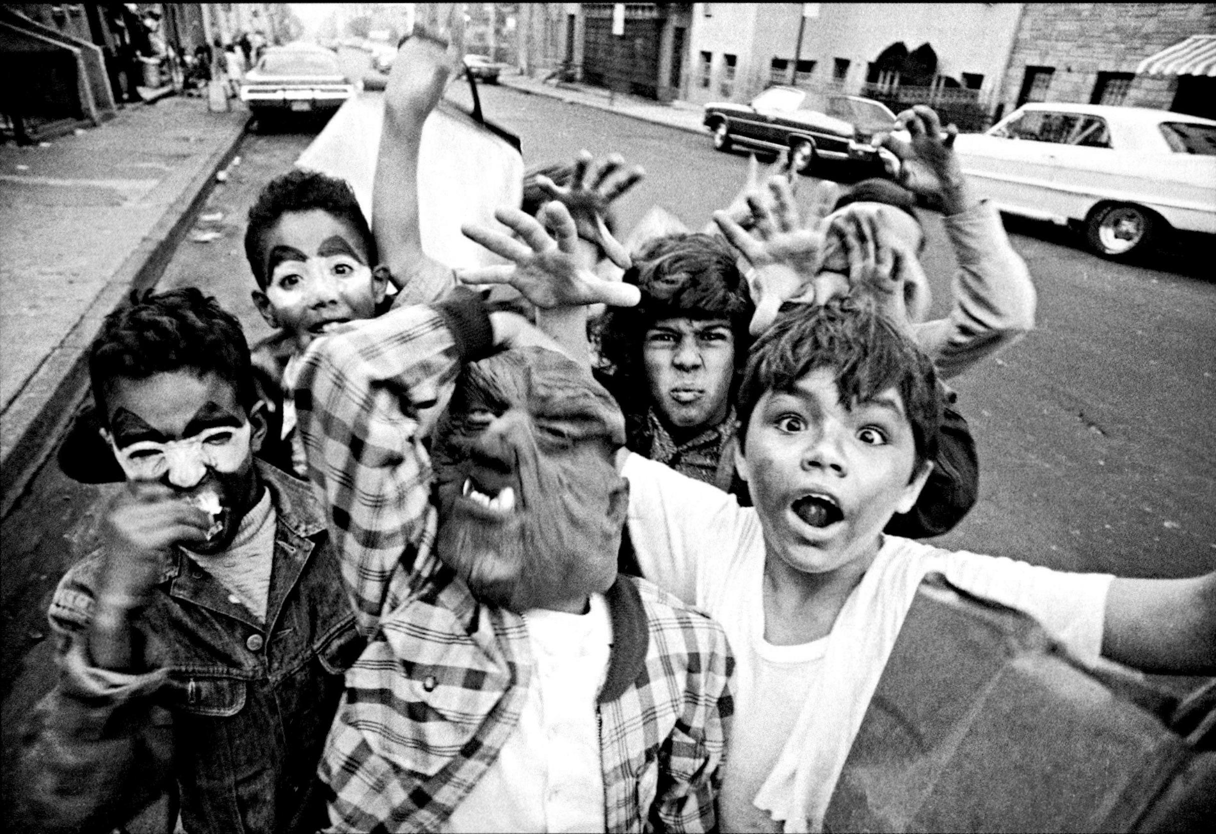

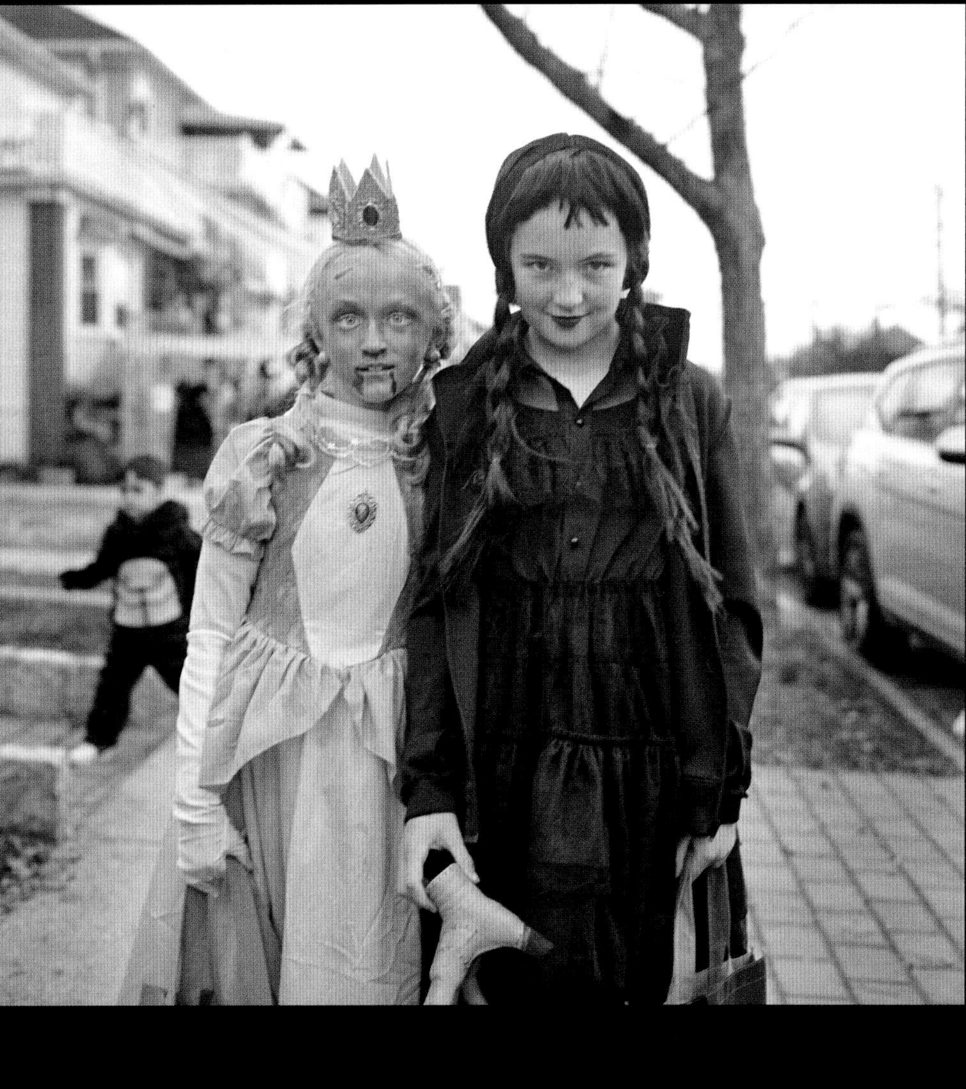

FOREWORD BY KEVIN BAKER

My family always loved Halloween. Maybe it was because my mother and father met at a church Halloween party. Maybe it was because we wanted to hide from each other, but I don't think so. We had, all of us, a performative streak. That is what Halloween is about, the chance for all of us to act out—to dress up, wear masks, hide our faces, melt into an alter ego. Play out a fantasy.

This is what Larry Racioppo, one of our most profound observers of urban life in America, brings across here. His pictures from the first section in *Halloween*, shot in the 1970s and '80s when he was just beginning and did not have enough money for a flash unit, bring this out in stark, startling black and whites snapped in the twilight hour. This is photography on the clock, taken between the hours when school lets out and the sun goes down at the end of October, with no time for second chances. Nonetheless, he got the pictures. He got more than the pictures.

What he brings out above all is the sheer humanity and joy of the children captured here. They are posed, for the most part, along Brooklyn streets that look as though they had just survived a war. It is a backdrop devoid of foliage or decoration. A cityscape of broken windows and crumbling concrete, of iron- and chain-link fencing. Of walls scarred with graffiti over graffiti, left by forgotten hands—or, in one instance, a child in a drooping skull mask, more sad than alarming, standing in front of a block association sign of a type that you once saw all over New York, honoring all those from the block who served and fell in World War II—"For God and Country"—and offering the apologetic addendum: "AND TO THE MANY DESERVING SERVICEMEN WHOM WE FORGOT WE ALSO OFFER OUR THANKS." We can't help but feel apologetic ourselves, for having forgotten this world.

But the children! They are obviously from families of limited means. Many wear the sorts of cheap, generic fright masks that used to be available in every five-and-dime, close and claustrophobic and reeking of plastic (I know). Some wear only a simple black mask across their eyes, like the Lone Ranger. Others rely on whatever might be left over from home. Old sheets pressed into service as ghosts, confirmation dresses converted to bridal gowns. (It is Halloween as the passage through youth to adulthood—and then death.) Sometimes the only costume is some adroitly placed face paint or makeup, applied by adults or the kids themselves: triangles of lipstick for vampire fangs, tracks of mascara for Frankenstein stitchings.

And yet, the children in these photos are far from forlorn. They look oblivious to the mean streets around them. Many beam at the camera, happy to lift their masks. *Surprise! Did you know it was me?* They link arms and hold hands, drape their arms protectively around the shoulders of friends and younger siblings. They are all together. Some look wonderfully daft in the way that only children can. Some seem to have imagined and put together their costumes out of who-knows-what, free of any adult sensibilities. A young girl with poignant dark eyes wears a skirt, a T-shirt with a cartoon character, a pair of foil wings, and a metal funnel hat like the Tin Man's. What is she supposed to be? Who knows? Who cares? It's Halloween!

Even the rare adults seem to be caught up in the spirit of the night. A young mother, wheeling her costumed trick-or-treater in a stroller, smiles coyly in front of a row of busted-up doorways and windows so ominous-looking that they might mark the entrance to a drug den. She is fearless. Everyone is out on the street tonight.

New York has long been a place that loves its *Walpurgisnachts*, its witches nights of real devilry, sometimes carried away to extremes of looting and arson and mayhem. Many of the immigrants who made the modern city came from cultures where everyone went to church on All Hallows' Eve. But even then, in the nineteenth century, New York had its own Ragamuffin Day, usually on or around Thanksgiving, when children dressed as hoboes roamed around the streets, aggressively demanding treats or money. Throughout our history, almost any excuse would serve for riot and revel: election nights, protests, ethnic parades—anything a reason for raw, sometimes terrifying violence.

There are hints of that older, darker tradition here, with the shaving cream-, and egg–, and chalk sock–wielders Larry captures (along with an actual guide to making a chalk sock!). But this, too, comes off more as innocent play than anything else. Most of the kids look delighted to be smeared with shaving cream and egg, the one day a year they are allowed such petty mischief.

This section is before Halloween was hijacked by the adults—before the professional costume shops began springing up like toadstools as early as August in our city. Larry captures this evolution as well. He even uses it to trace the gentrification of Brooklyn—to an extent. More experimental as a photographer, working in color as well as black and white, he gives us a taste of the fancier parties (and lifestyles) that would overrun much of the borough. But he doesn't linger there, seeming to share his brother's disdain for the pretensions of, say, the Park Slope Food Coop's Halloween party, or shindigs with real coffins, or dominatrixes.

He is drawn back again, to work where he lives, capturing the bar parties, and the entire trick-or-treating families out in the Rockaways, and even Coney Island. Is this the paradise we always dreamed the city could be? The compromise between grit and glitter? The place where whole families now seem . . . happy?

It could be. This is Larry Racioppo's New York. He has been here all his life, he knows it better than most people ever will, and he won't turn away from the thriving human spirit at its heart.

KEVIN BAKER is a novelist, historian, and journalist who lives in New York City, with his wife, the playwright Ellen Abrams. His most recent book is *The New York Game: Baseball and the Rise of a New City* (Knopf).

The Early Years, in Brooklyn

1970s

AND

1980s

In 1974 on Halloween, I decided, on a whim, to leave work early to photograph in my South Brooklyn neighborhood. I got to my apartment at about 3:30 p.m., loaded my camera, and went out into the fading light. I was standing in the street across from my apartment when a group of kids saw me and my camera. I photographed the first two, and then the rest as they charged at me. Little did I know that this would be the beginning of a fifty-year project.

Two masked boys,
1974, Brooklyn.

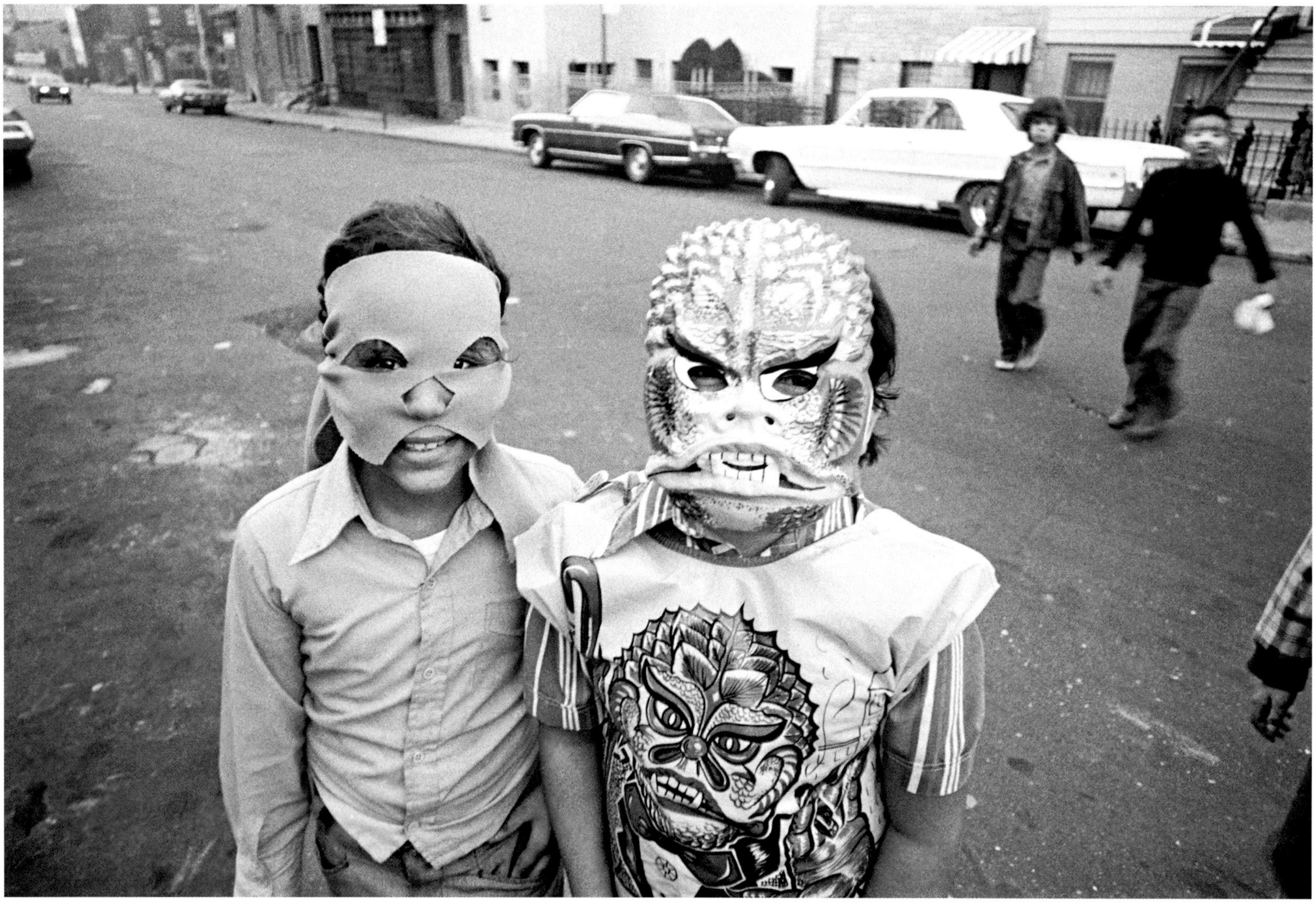

Excited boys,
1974, Brooklyn.

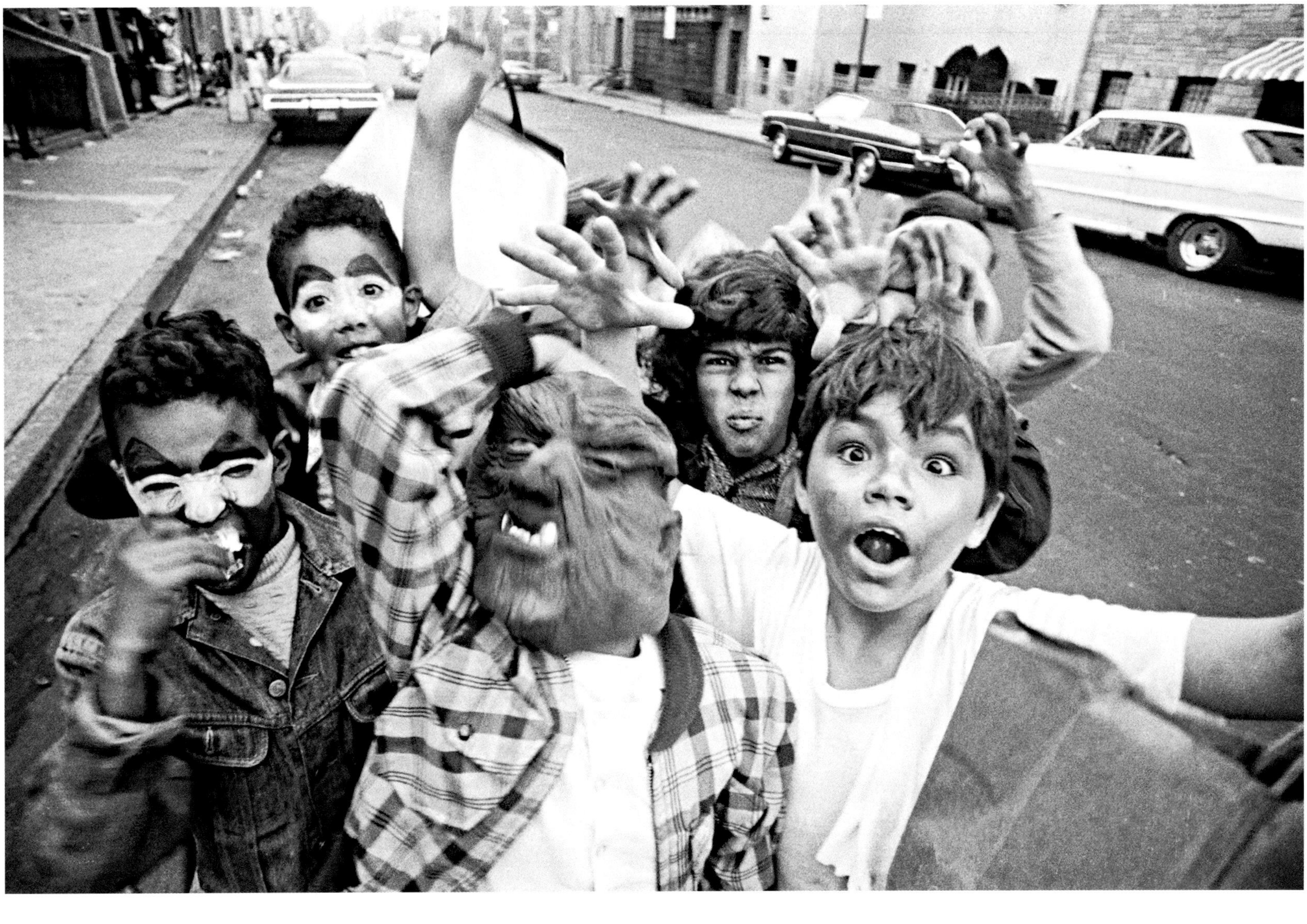

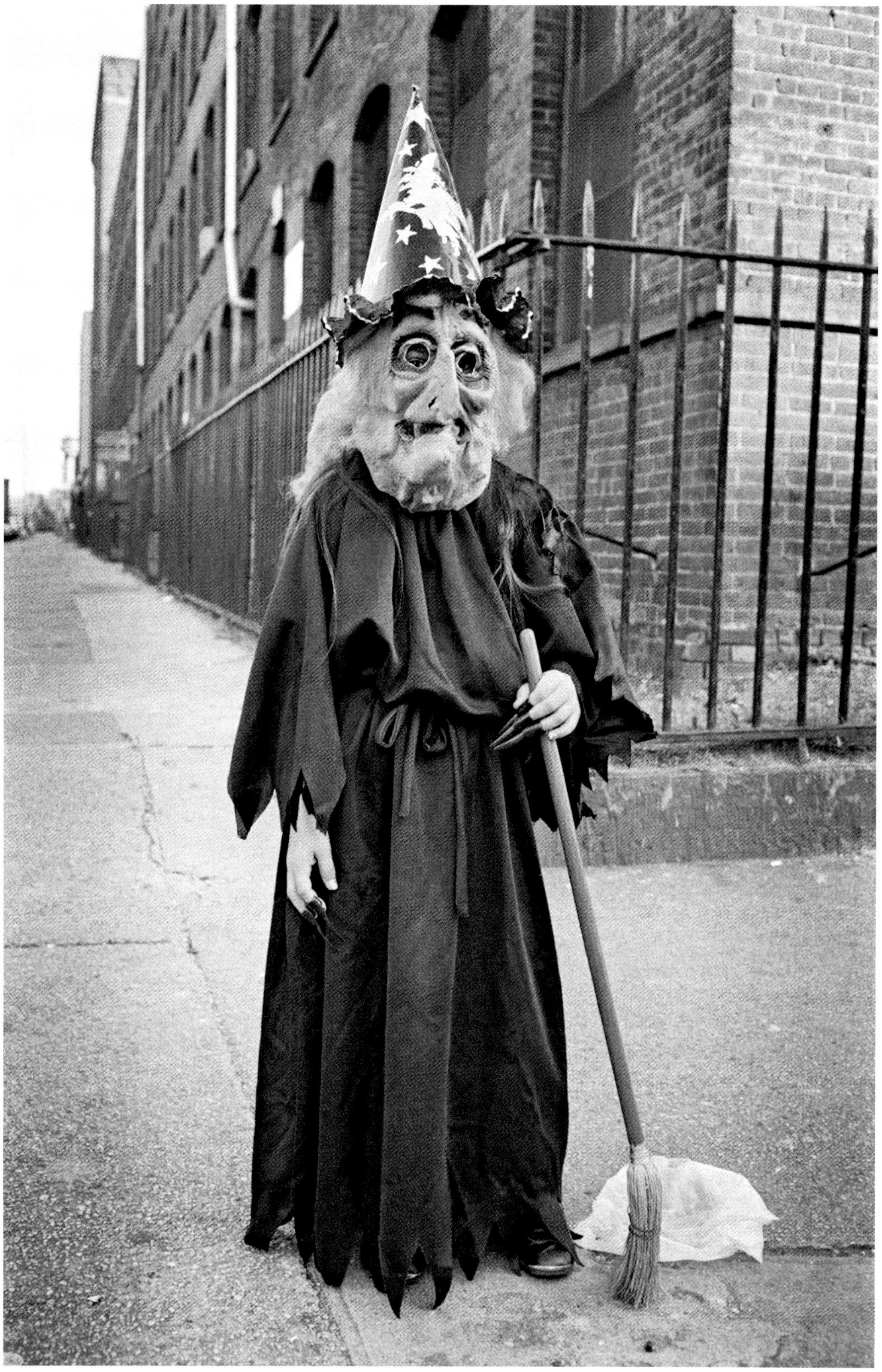

Left: Witch with broom, 1979, Brooklyn.

Opposite: Schoolyard ghost, 1978, Brooklyn.

As I photographed every year on Halloween, I began to distinguish between the "perennials," like ghosts and witches, pirates and princesses . . .

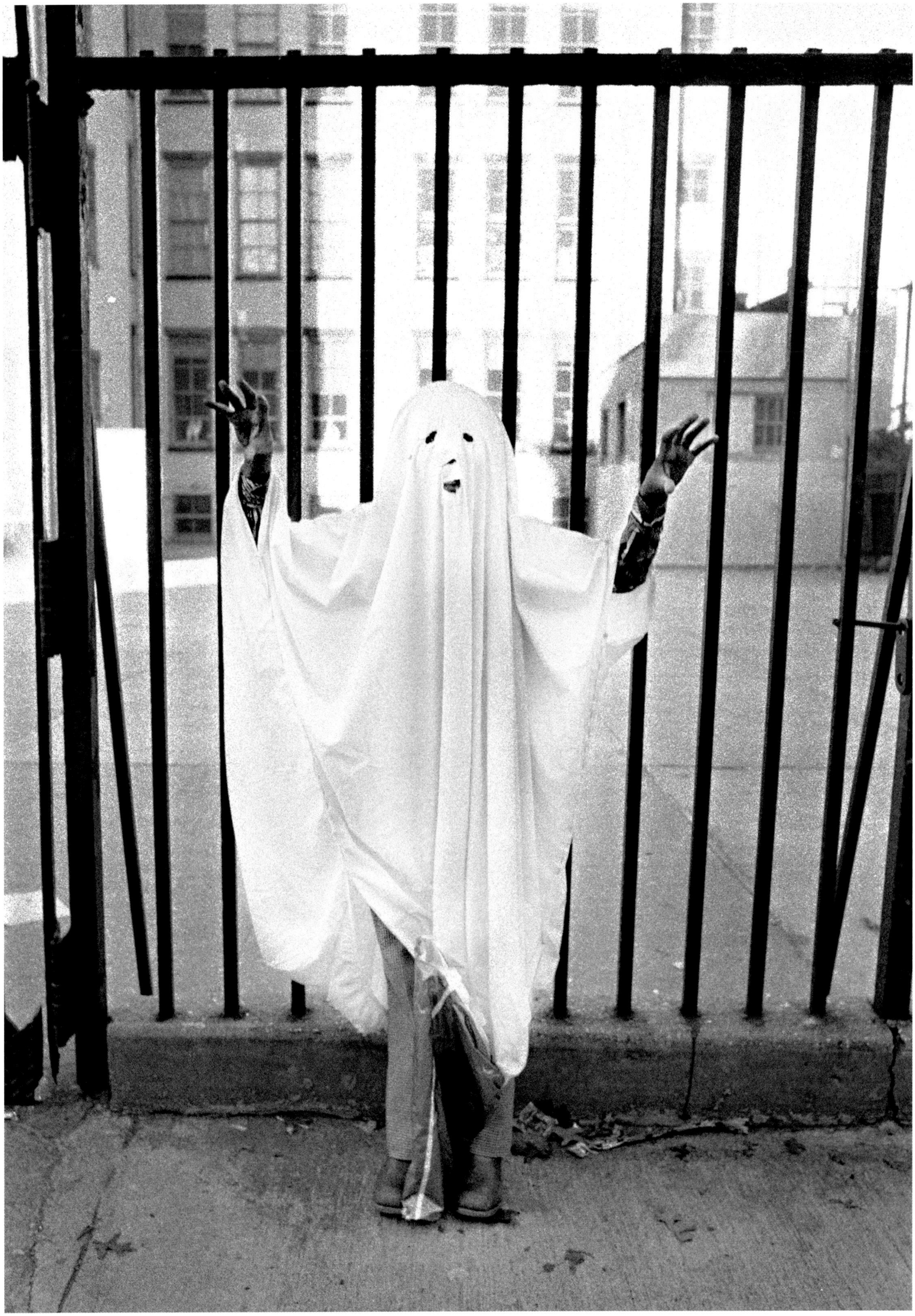

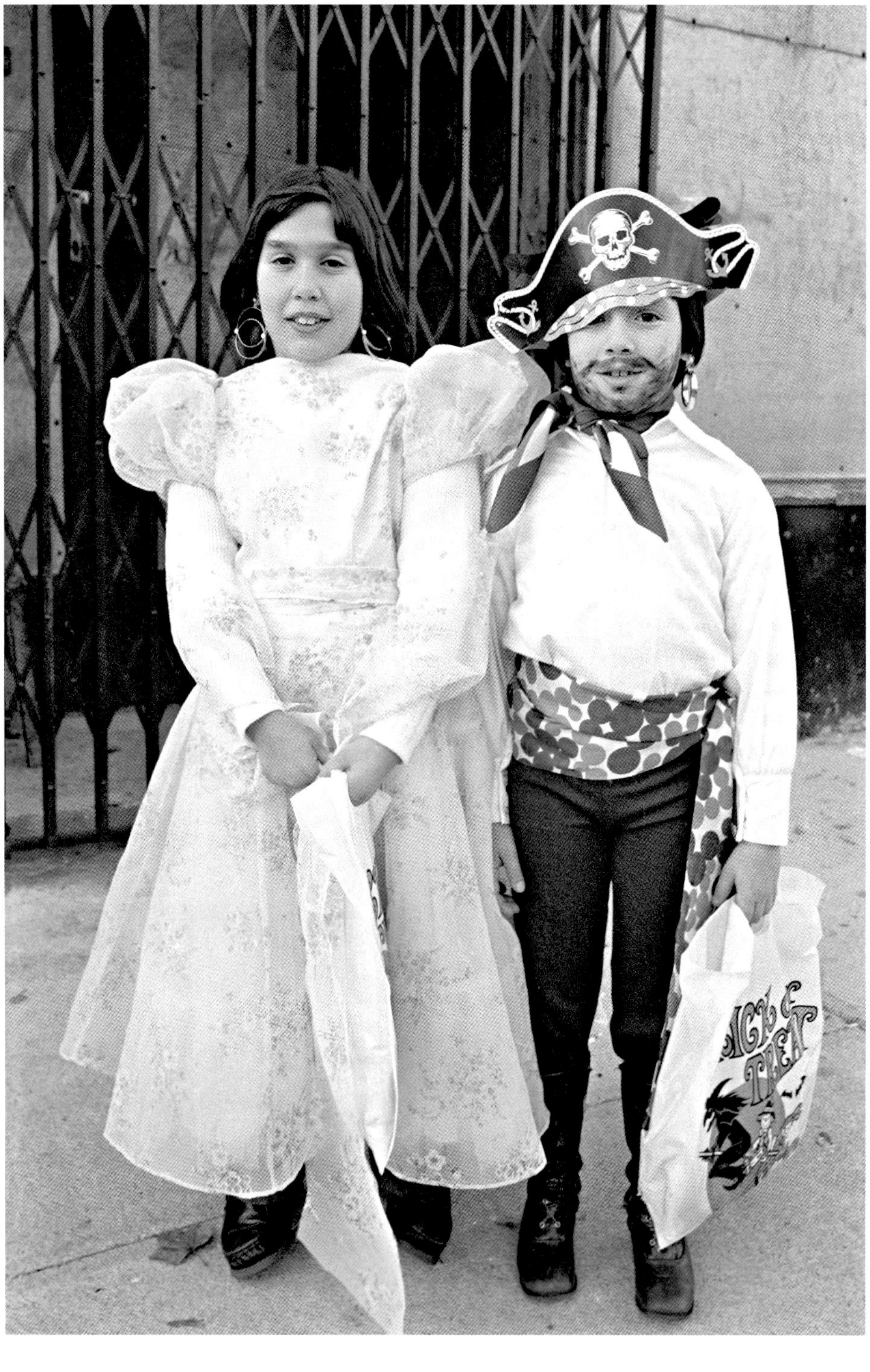

Bride and pirate,
1975, Brooklyn.

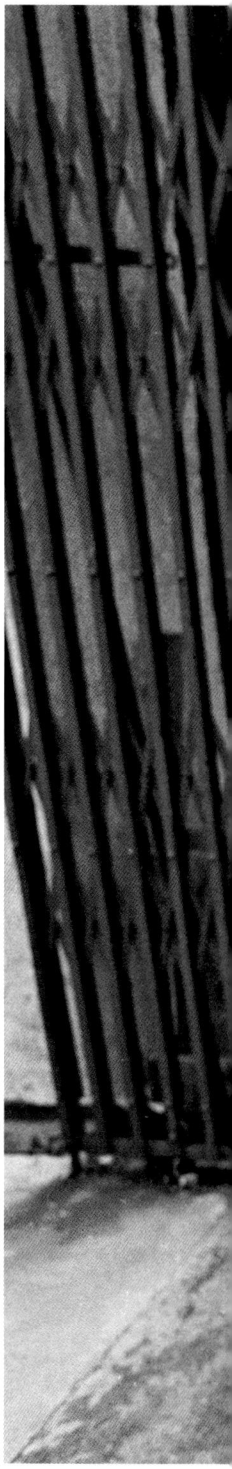

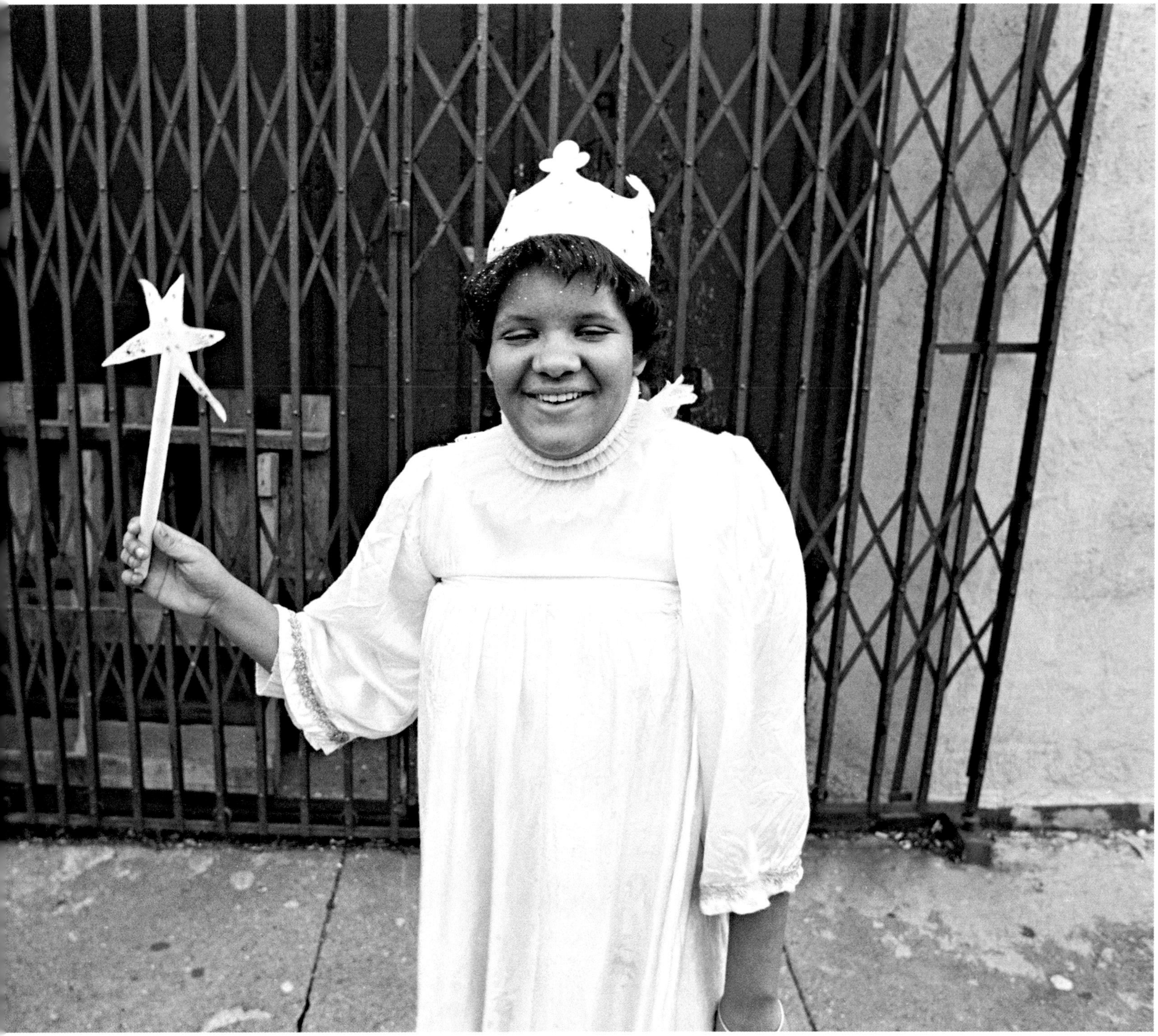

Princess with wand,
1976, Brooklyn.

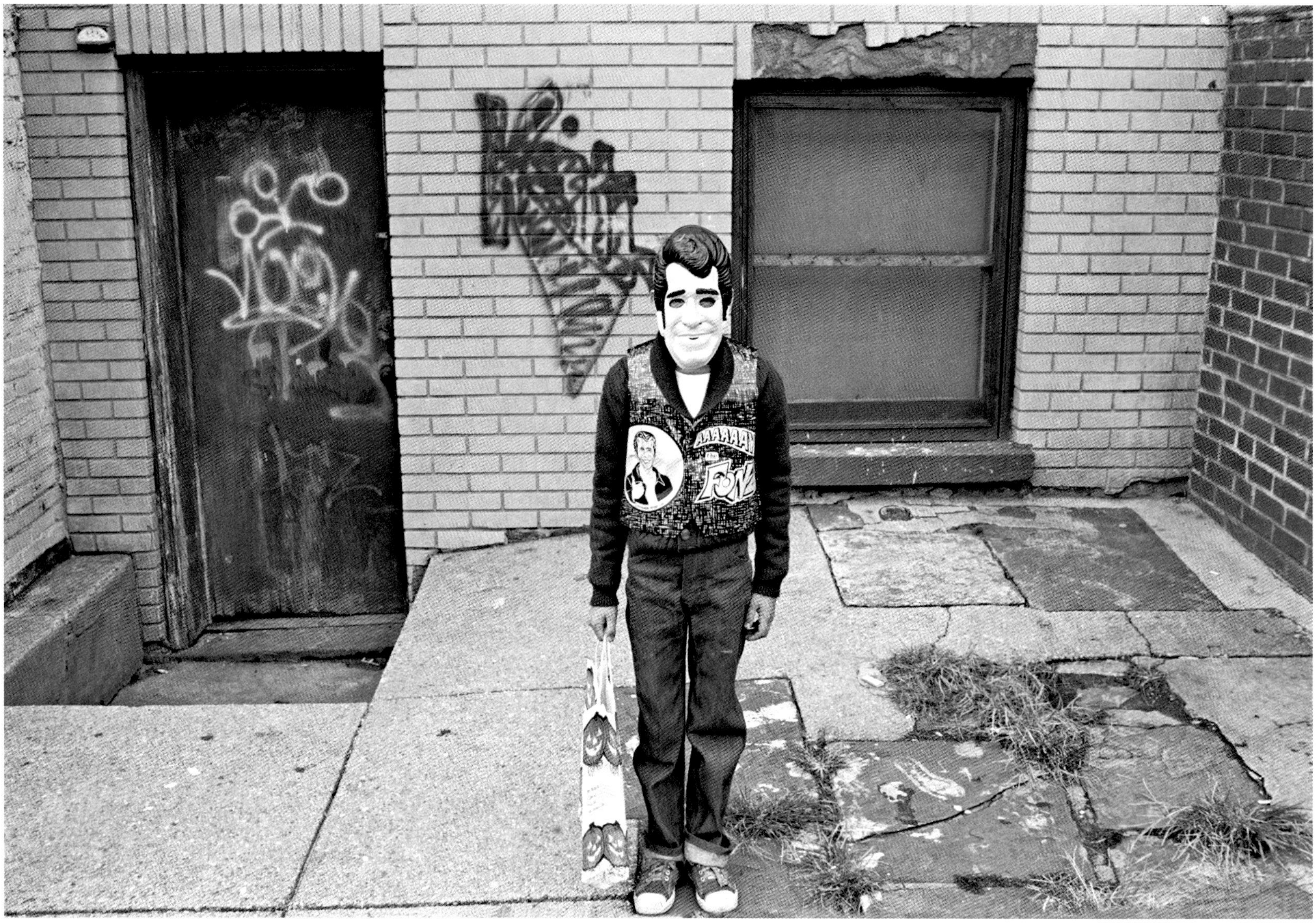

The Fonz, 1976, Brooklyn.

. . . and the "newcomers," who would appear for a year or two and sometimes were not seen again. These were often characters from popular TV shows and movies, like *Happy Days*, *Star Wars*, and *Jaws*.

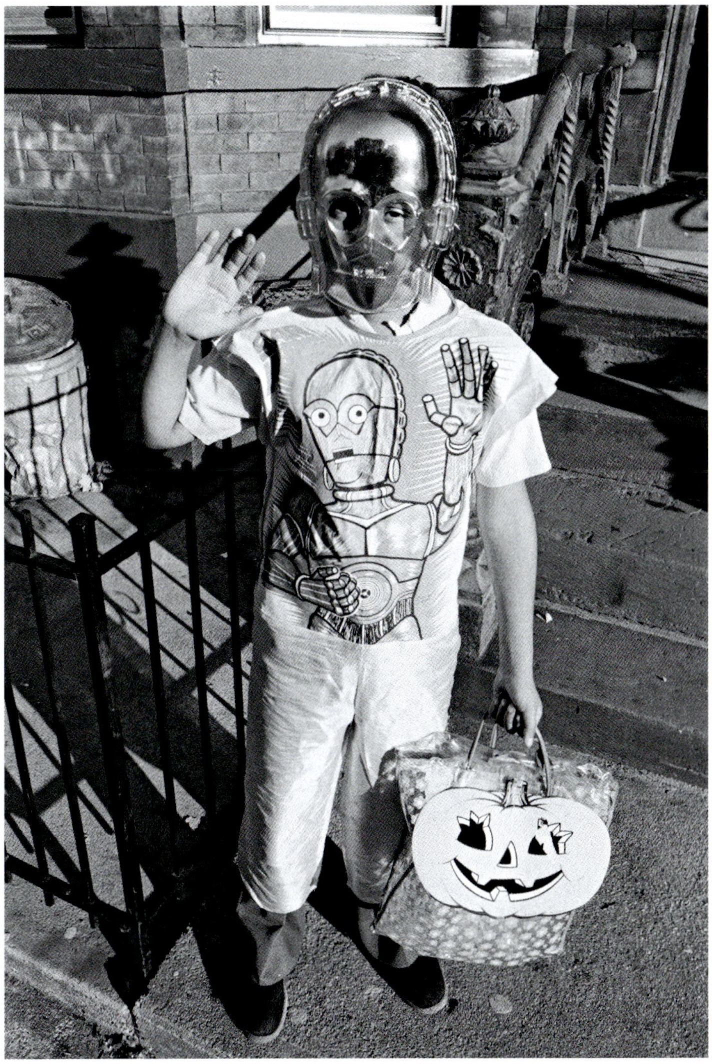

C-3PO, 1978, Brooklyn.

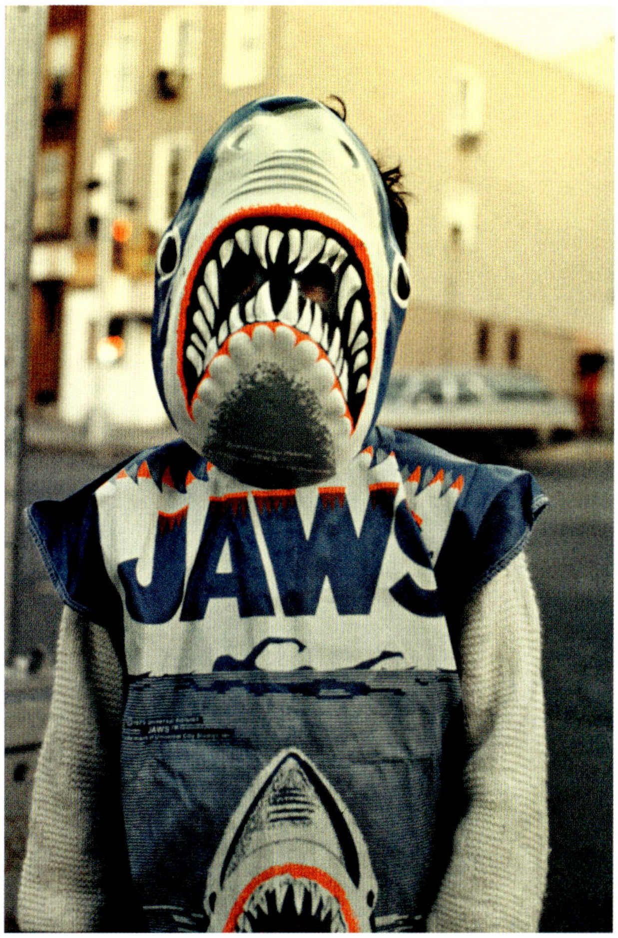

Boy in a *Jaws* costume, 1975, Brooklyn.

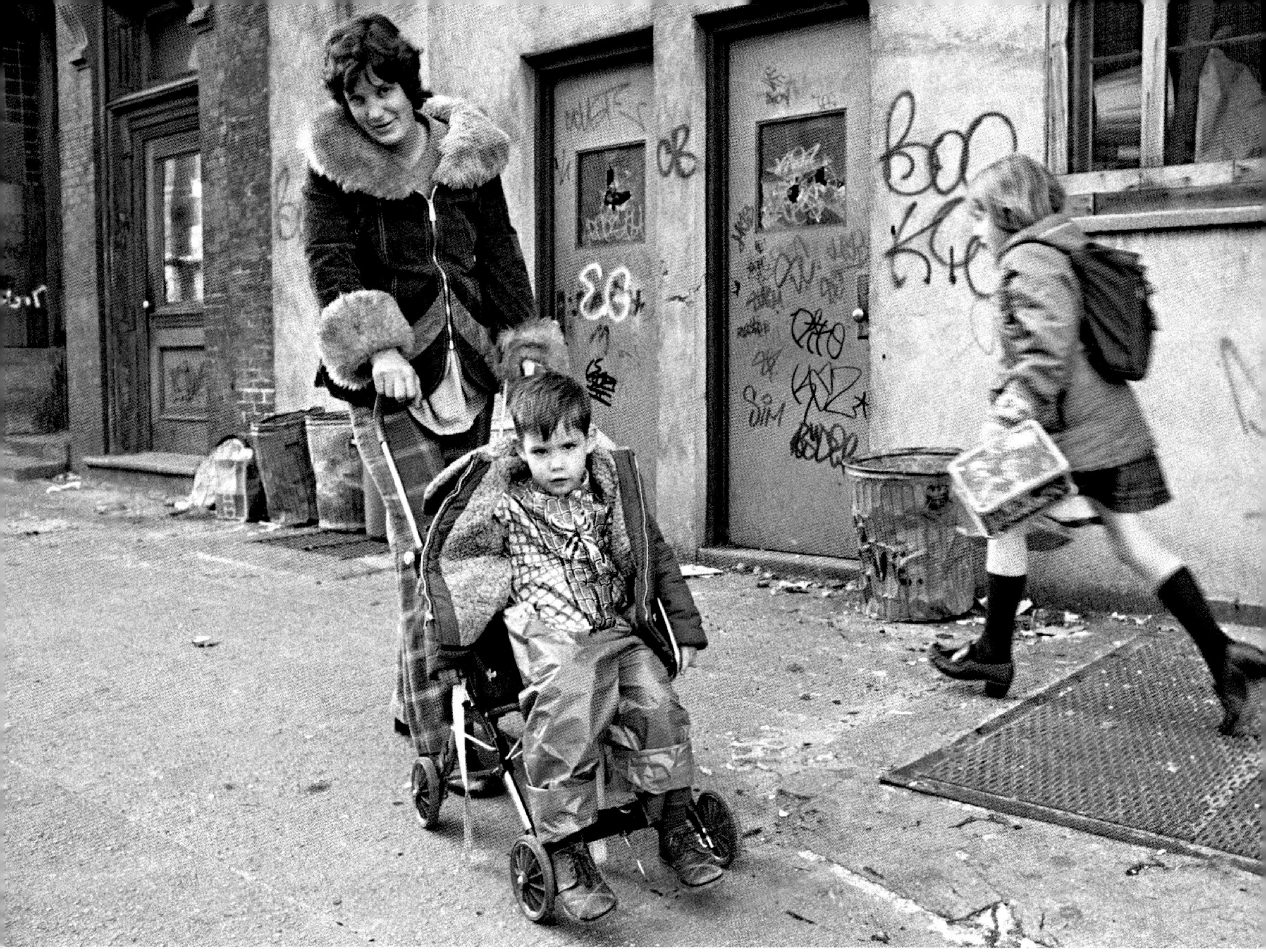

Back then, I photographed with a 35mm Nikon F and a 35mm lens. Because I did not own a flash unit, I photographed from the end of the school day (usually 3–3:30 p.m.) until dark (usually 5:30–6 p.m.).

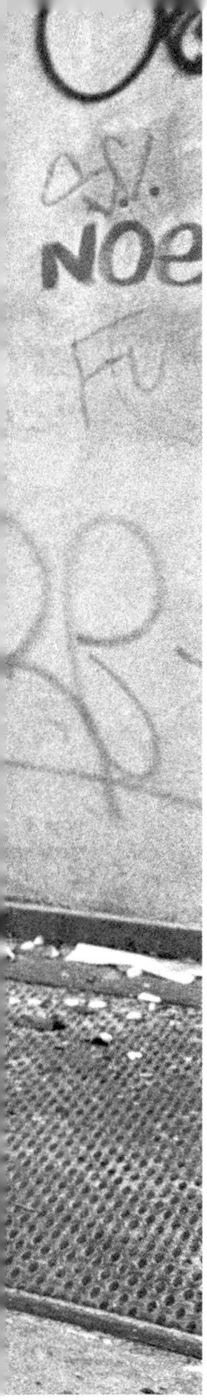

Woman and stroller, 1979, Brooklyn.

Bionic Woman, Bambi, and Cinderella, 1976, Brooklyn.

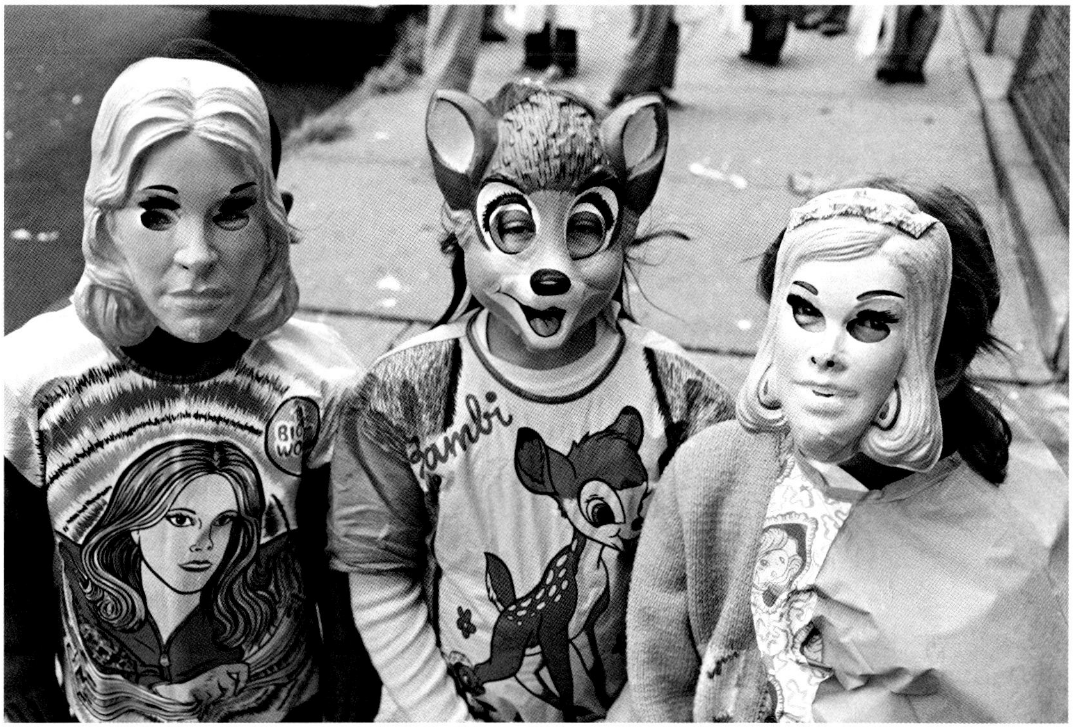

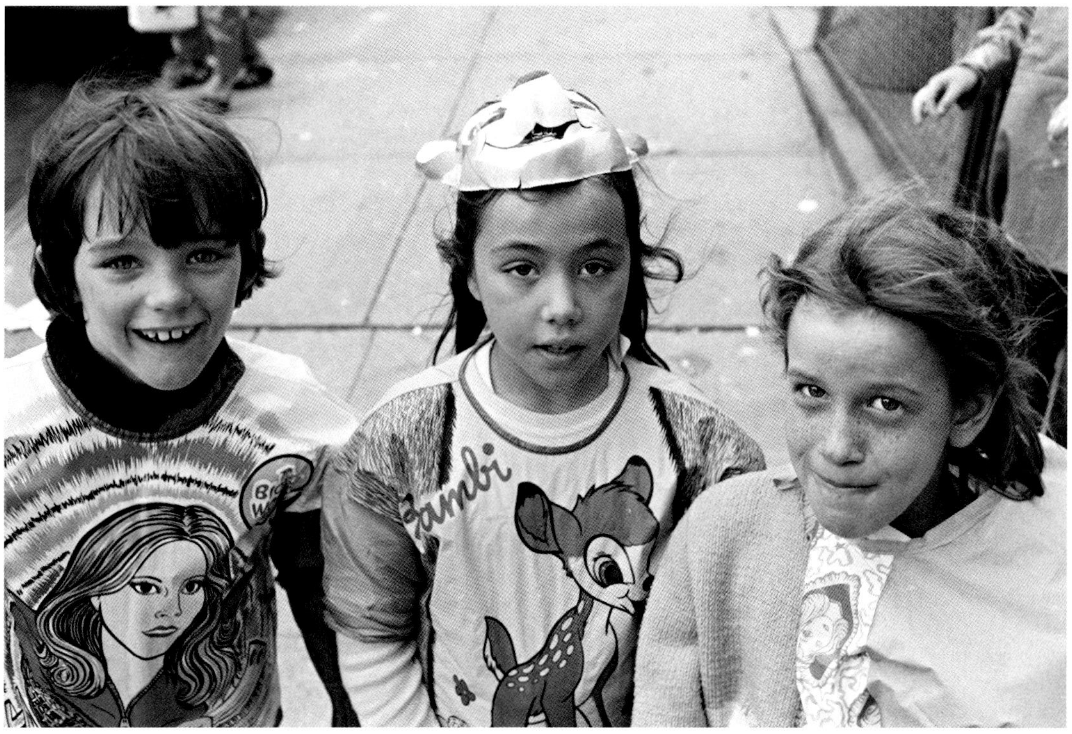

Bionic Woman, Bambi, and Cinderella (unmasked), 1976, Brooklyn.

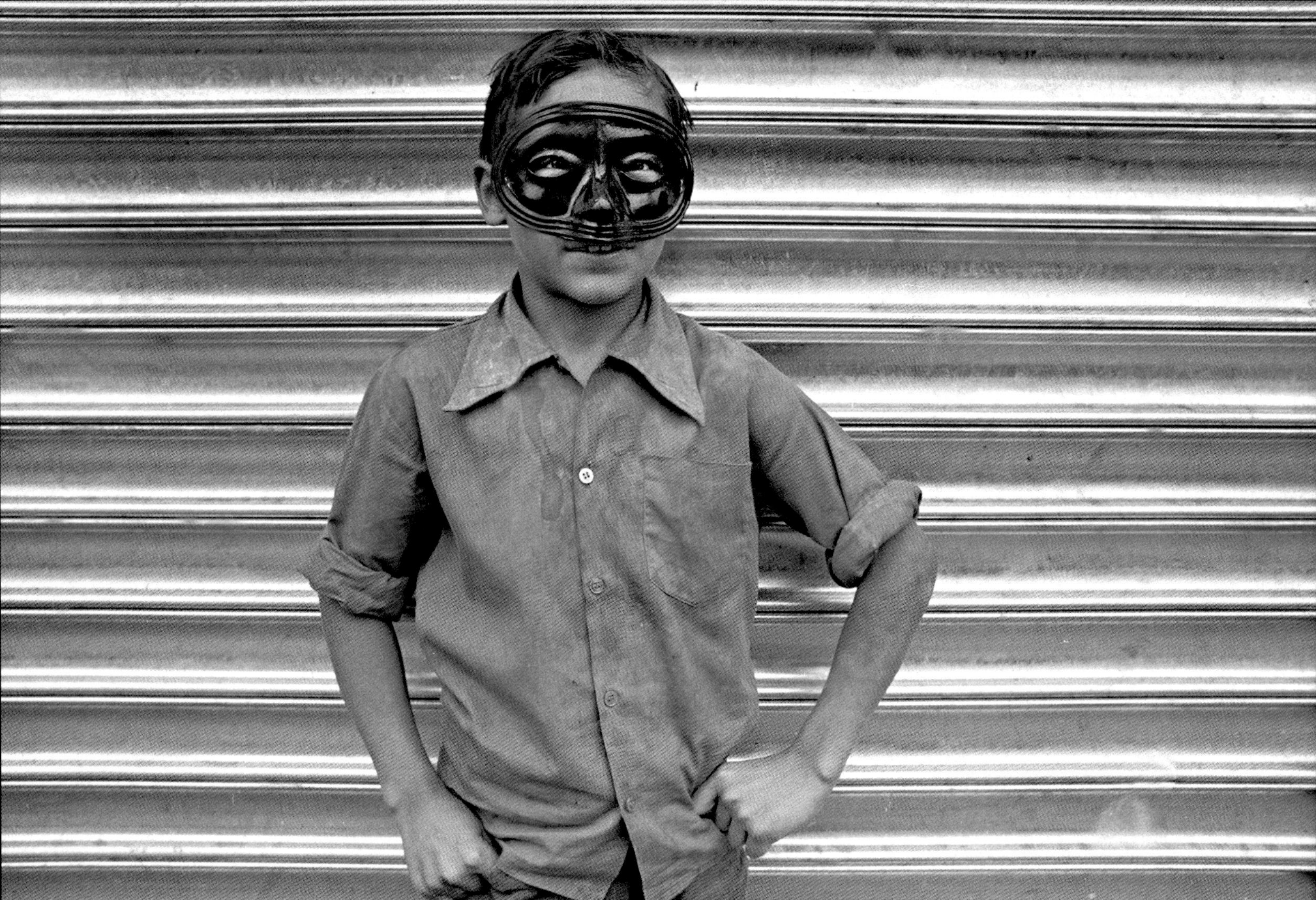

Boy with a black
mask, 1976, Brooklyn.

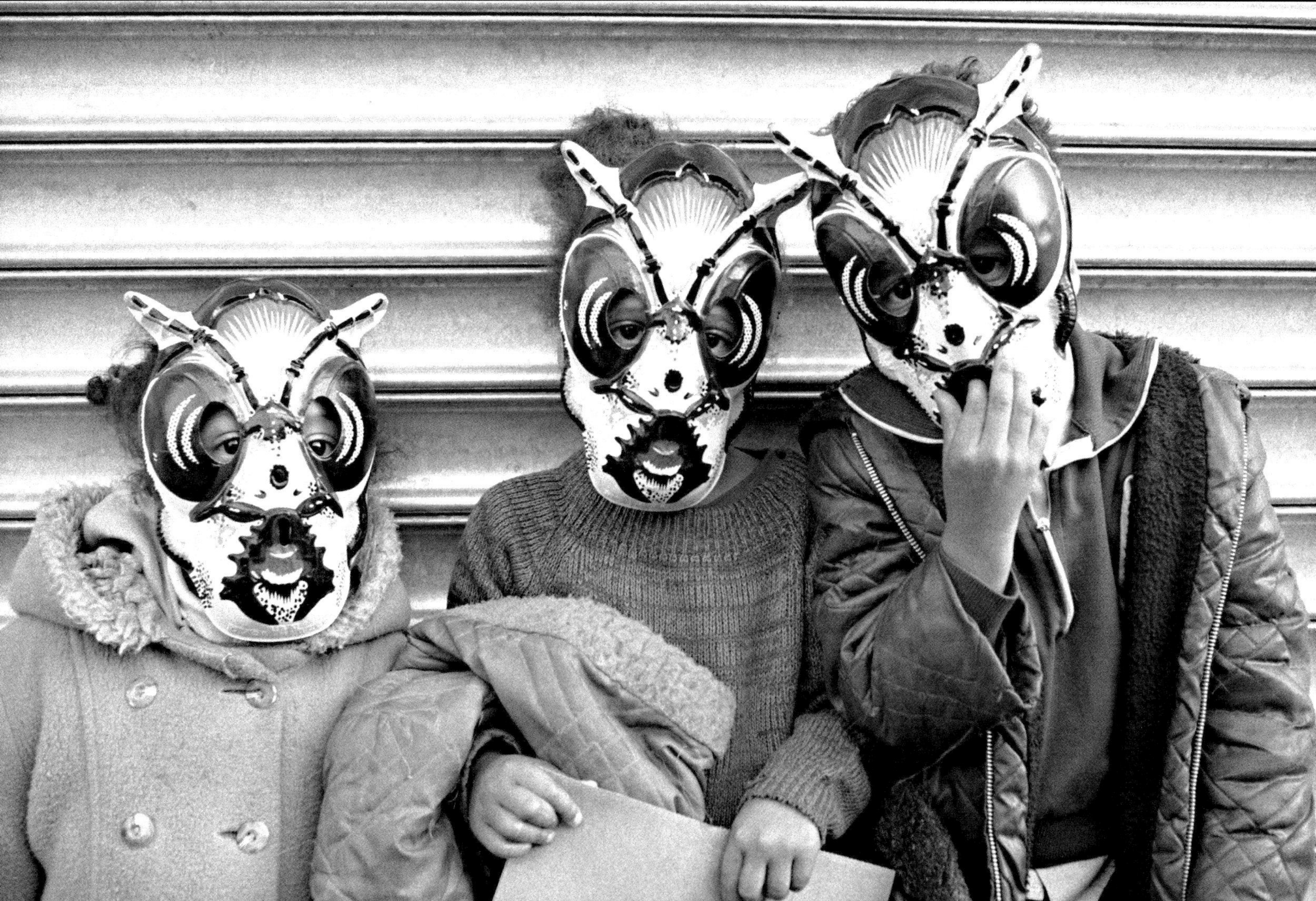

Three girls with bug
masks, 1979, Brooklyn.

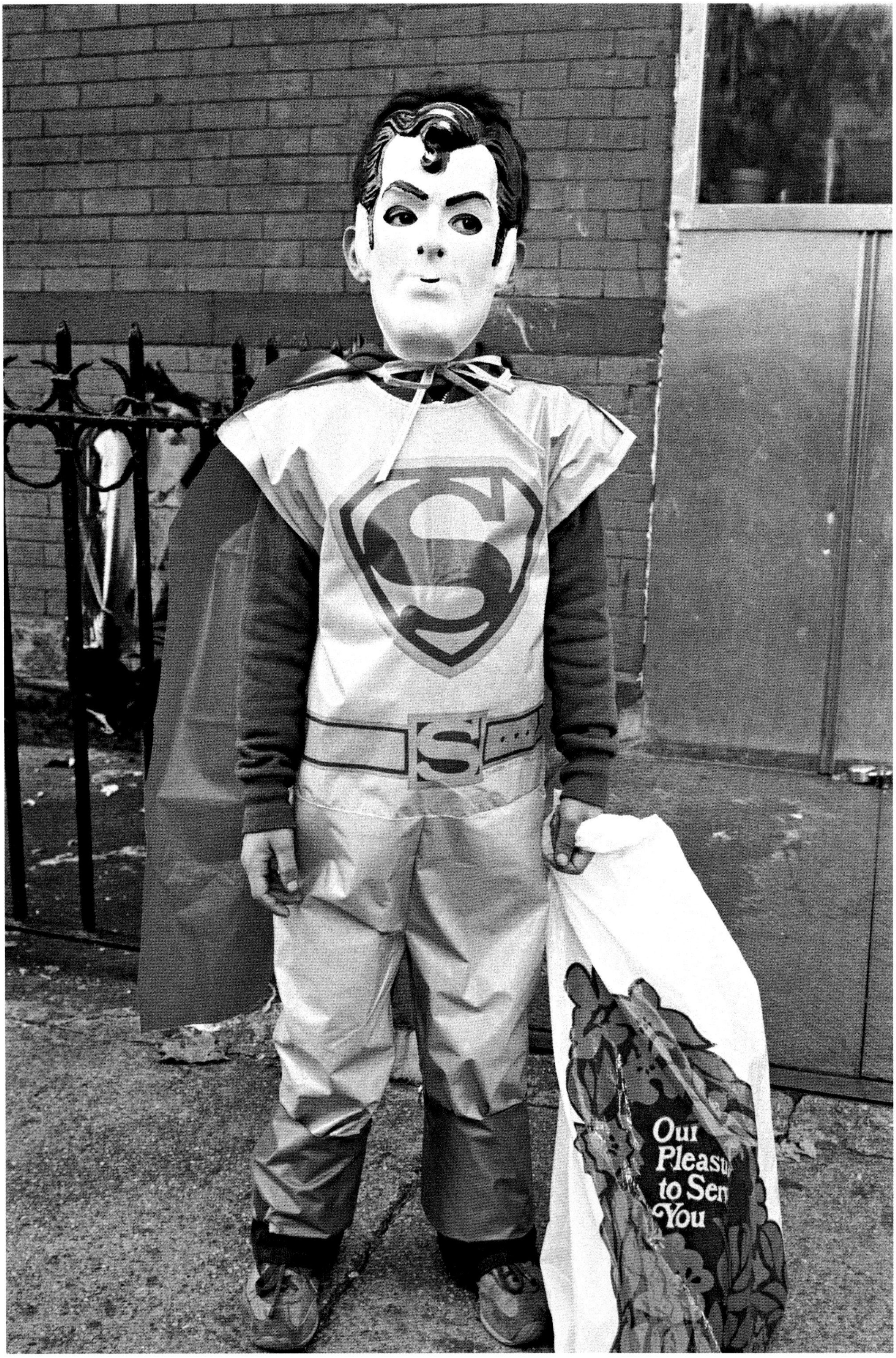
S
S
Our
Pleasu
to Serv
You

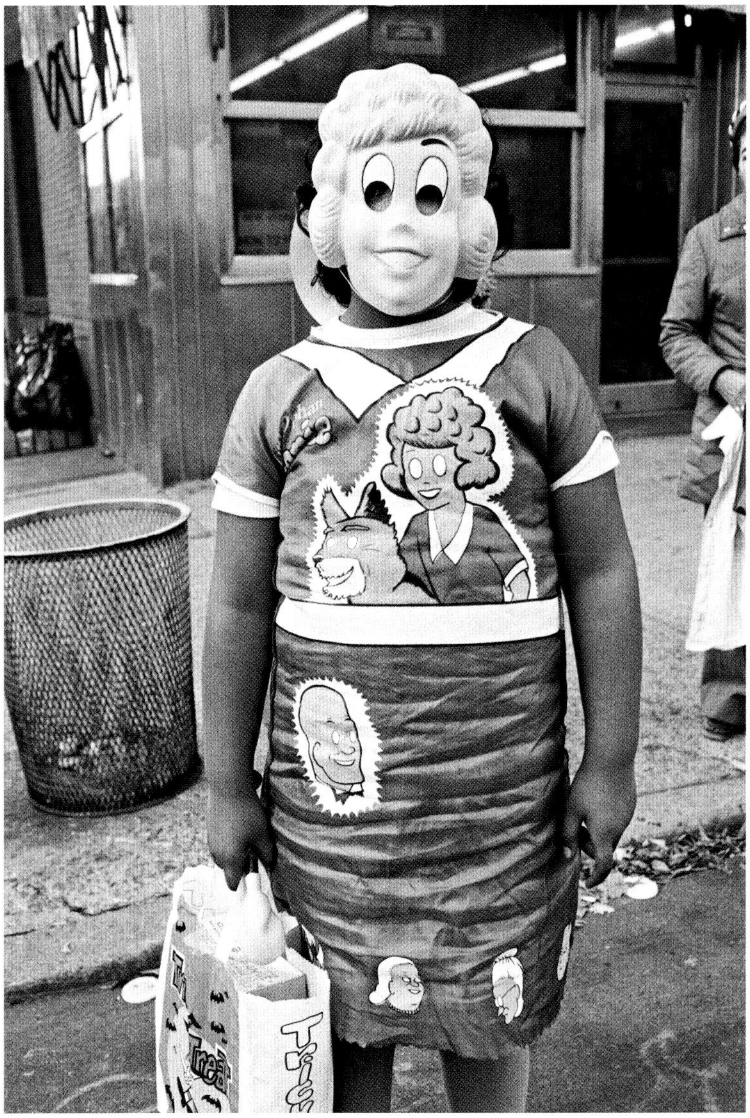

Little Orphan Annie, 1979, Brooklyn.

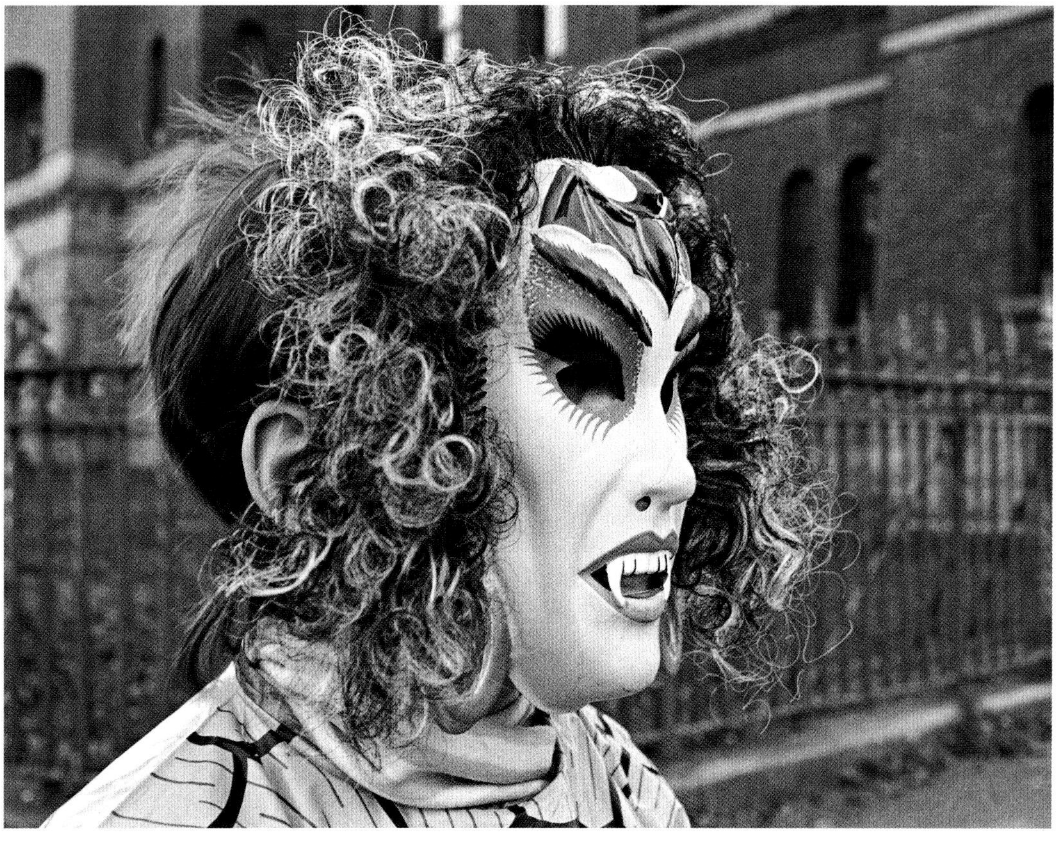

Right: Girl in a Vampira mask, 1979, Brooklyn.

Opposite: Superman, 1979, Brooklyn.

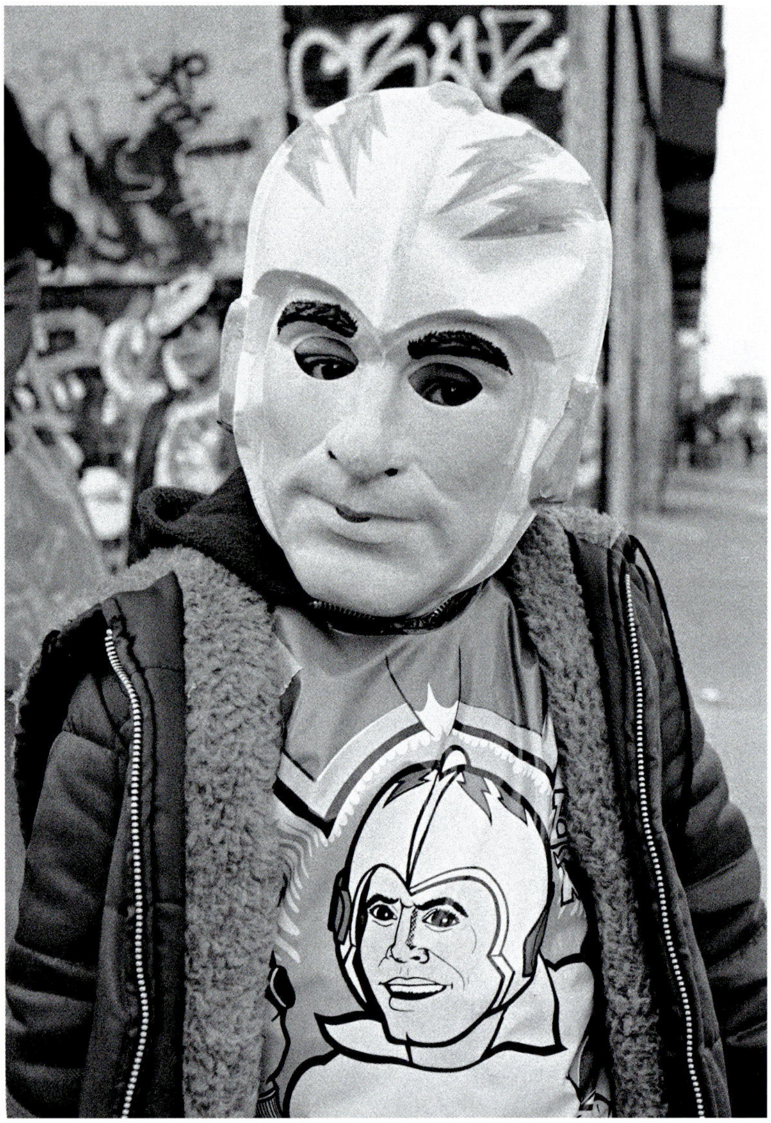

Lightning bolts, 1979, Brooklyn.

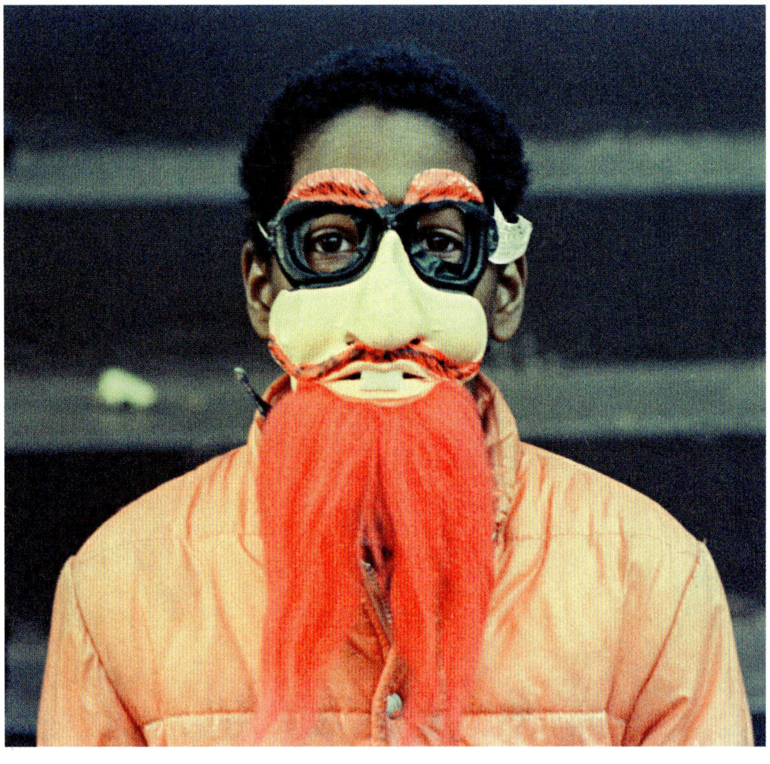

Boy in a red beard mask, 1979, Brooklyn.

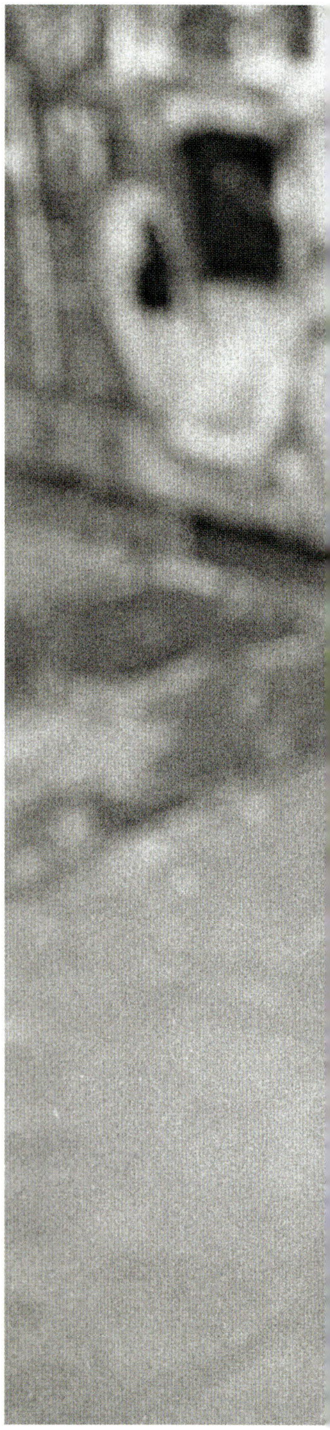

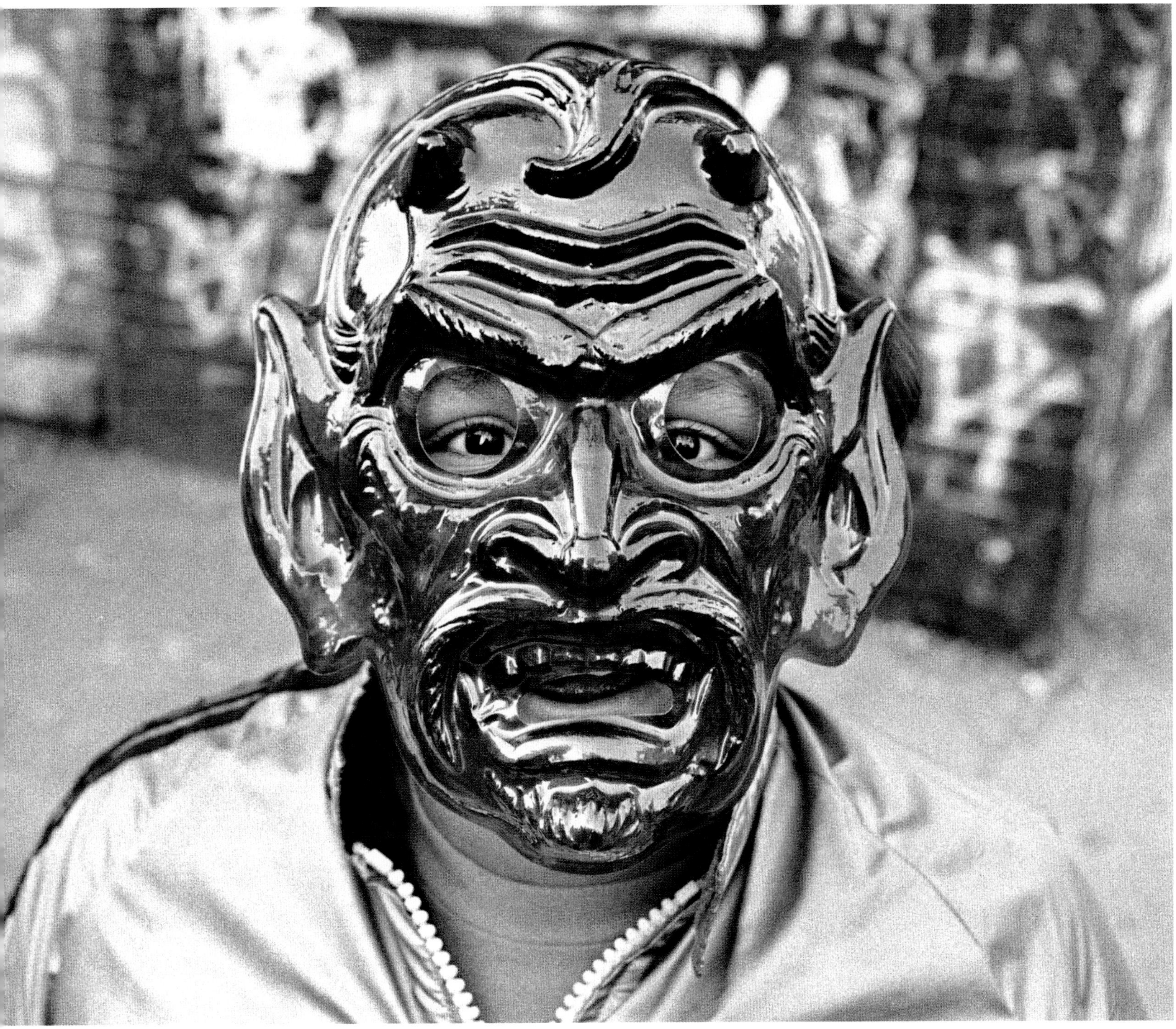

Boy in a gremlin
mask, 1979, Brooklyn.

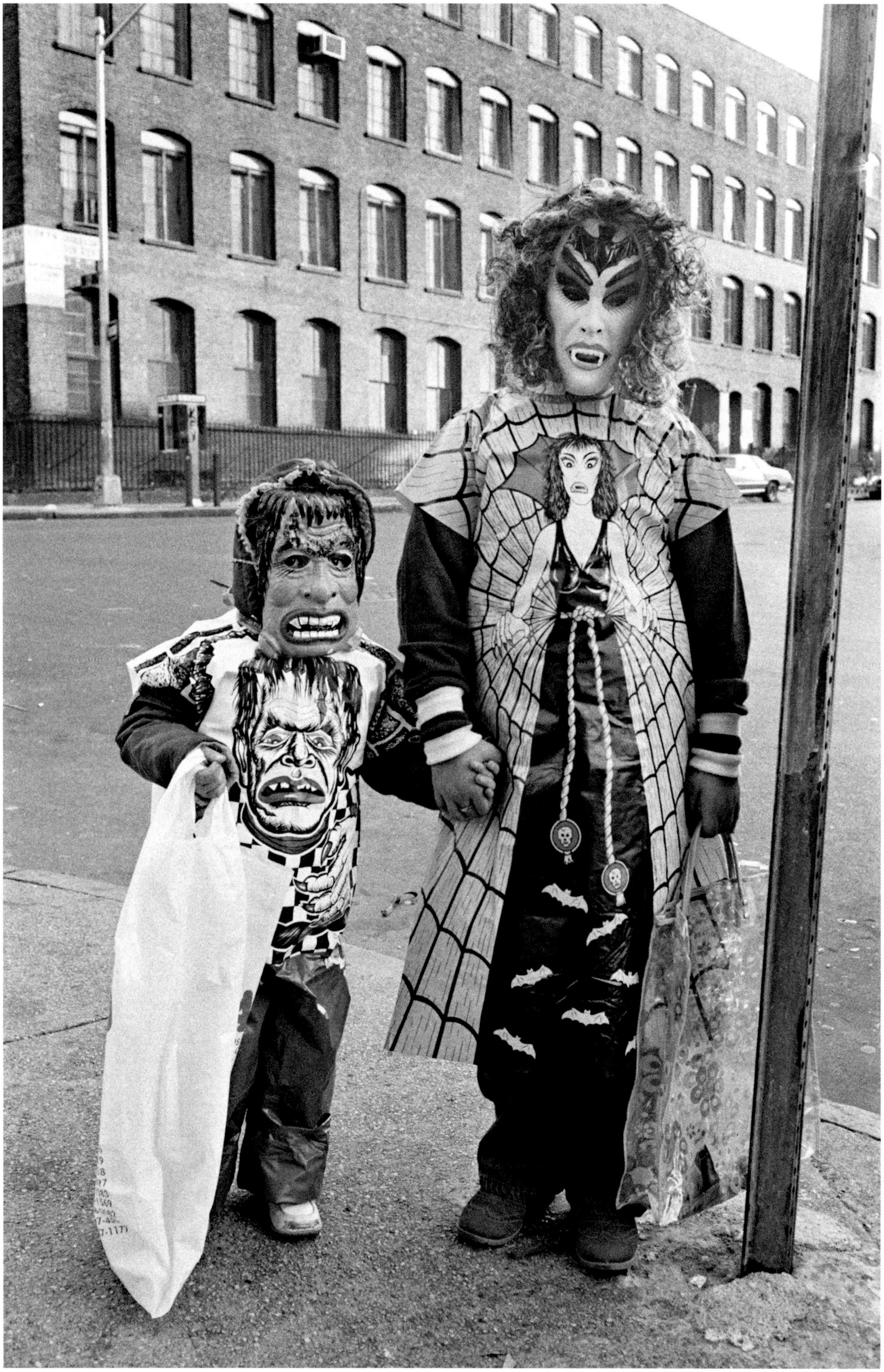

Frankenstein and Vampira, 1979, Brooklyn.

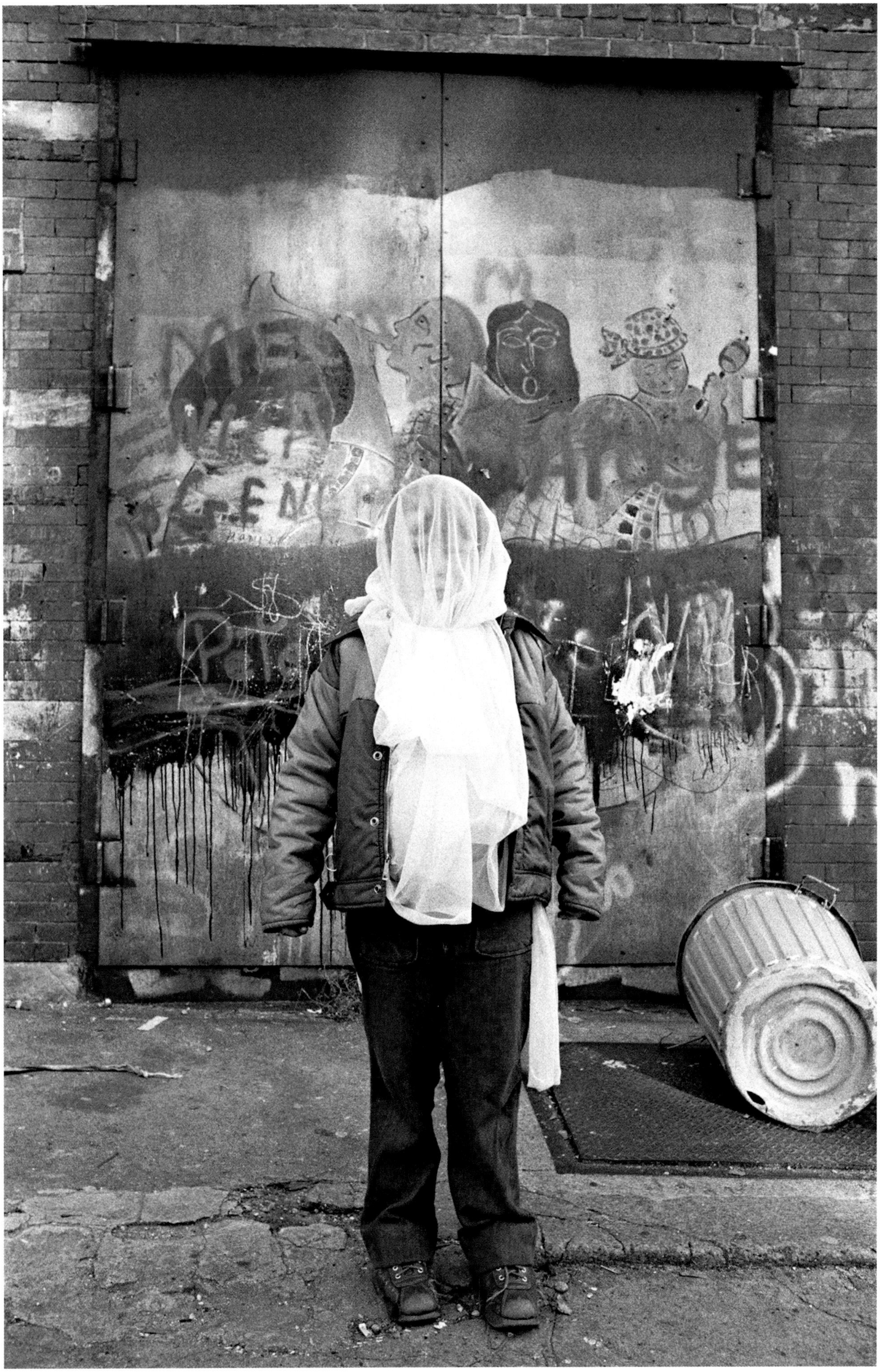

The Ghost,
1979, Brooklyn.

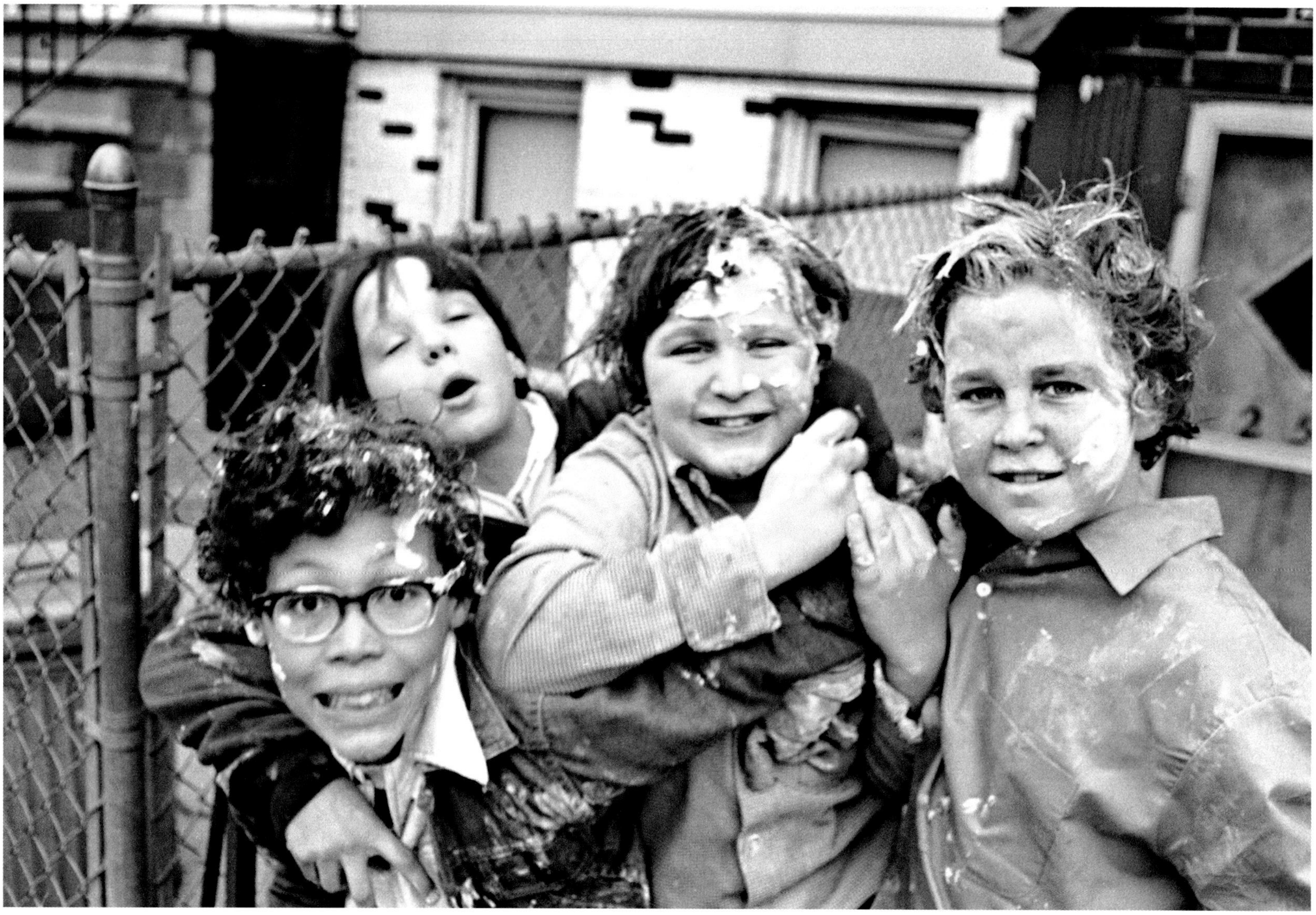

Shaving cream boys,
1976, Brooklyn.

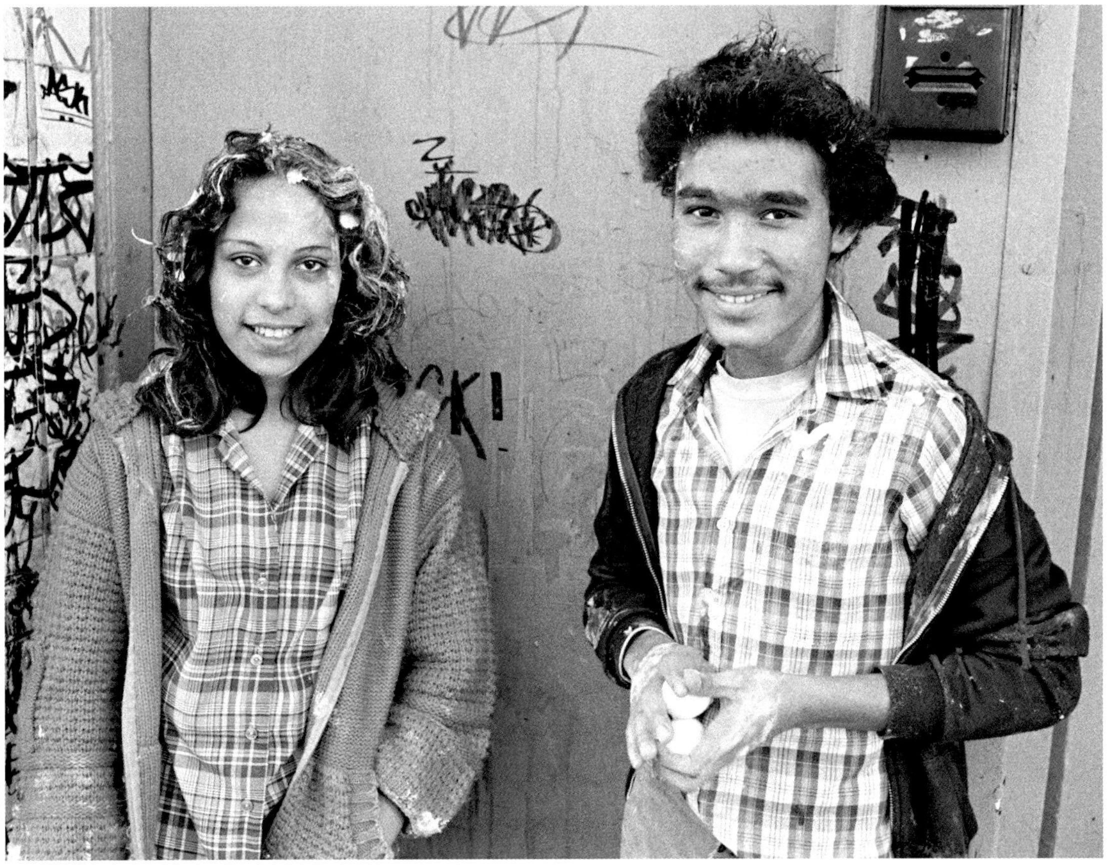

Shaving cream teens with eggs, 1980, Brooklyn.

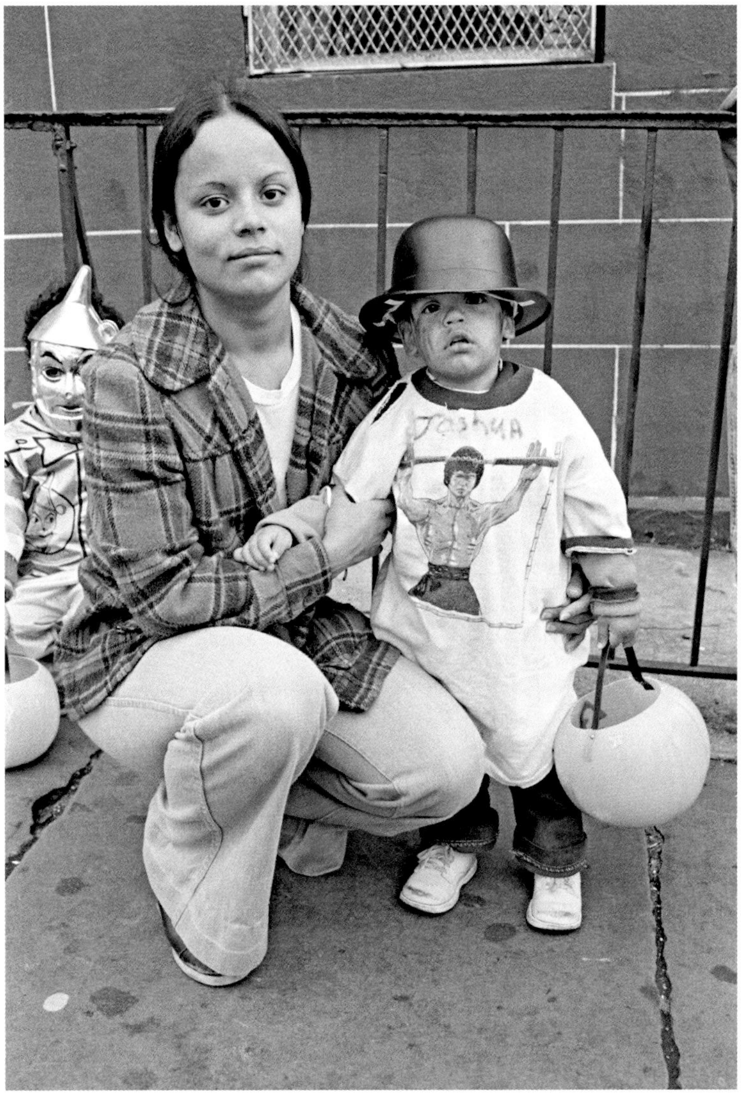

Woman with Bruce Lee boy, 1976, Brooklyn.

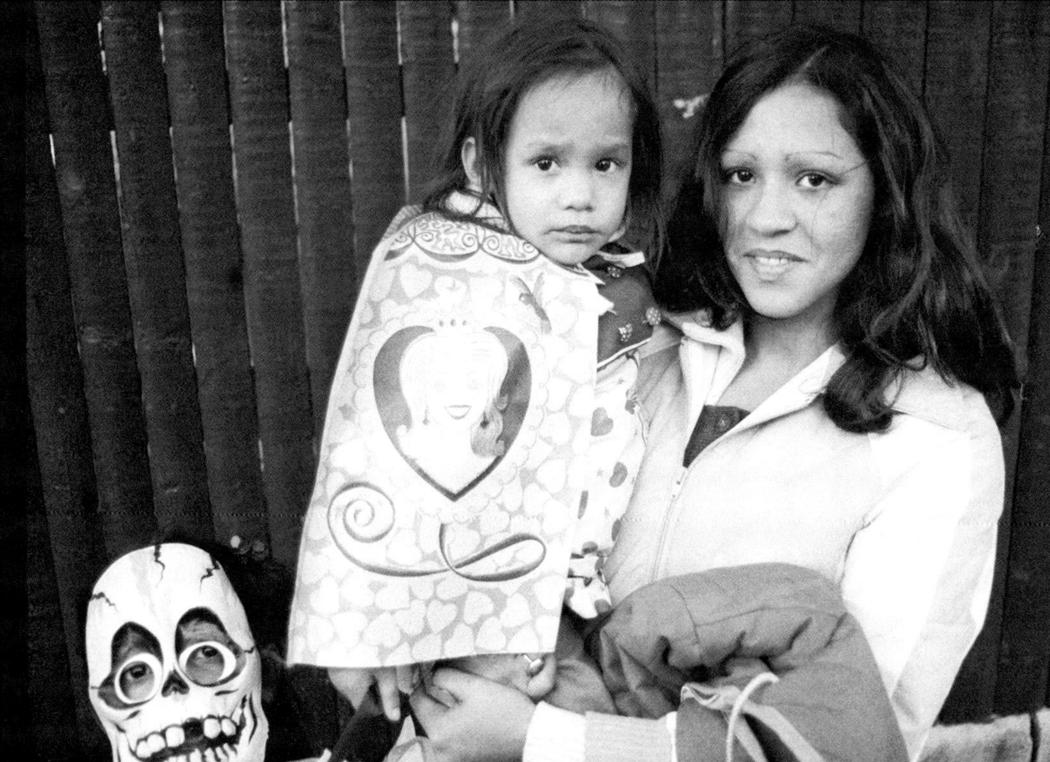

Woman with princess and skull, 1980, Brooklyn.

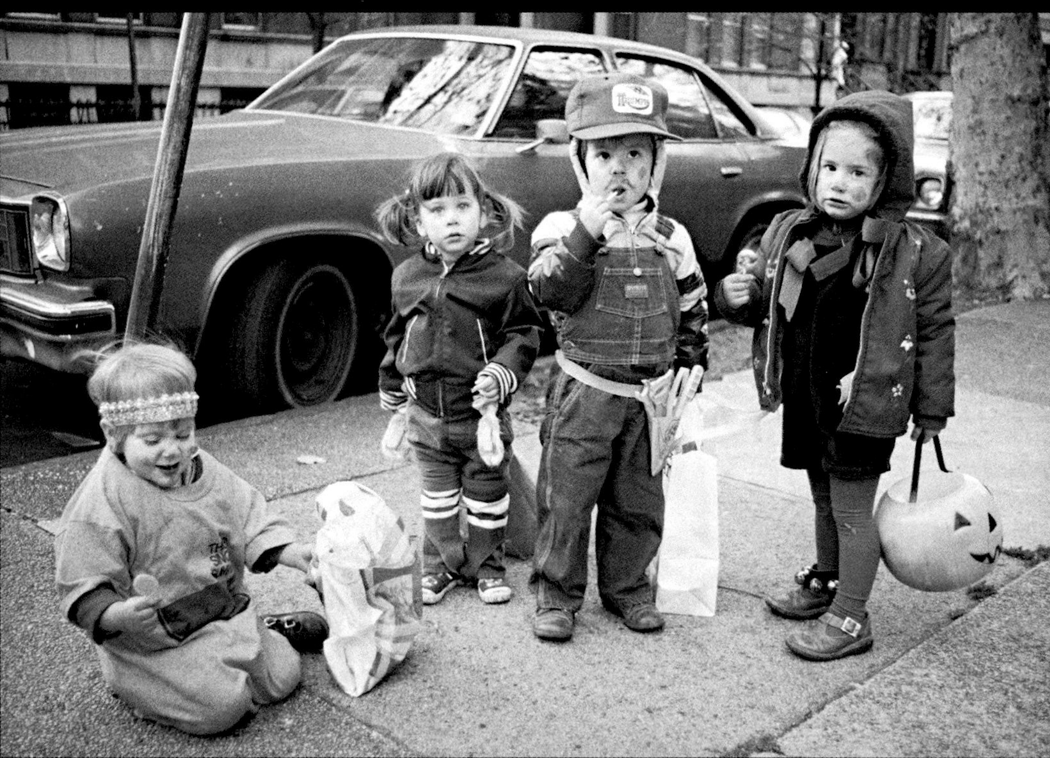

Costumed kids on sidewalk, 1980, Brooklyn.

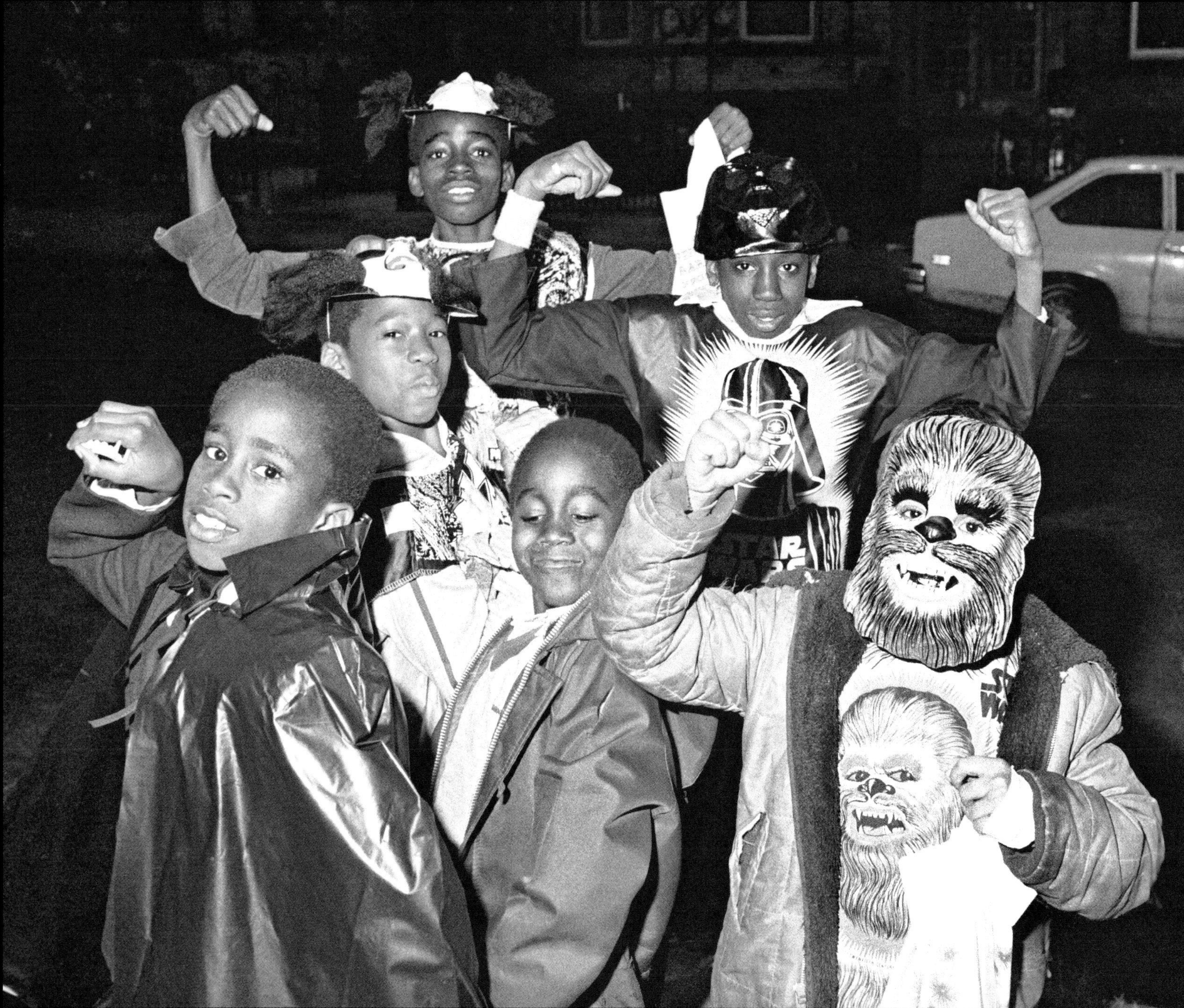

Costumed kids at night, 1980, Brooklyn.

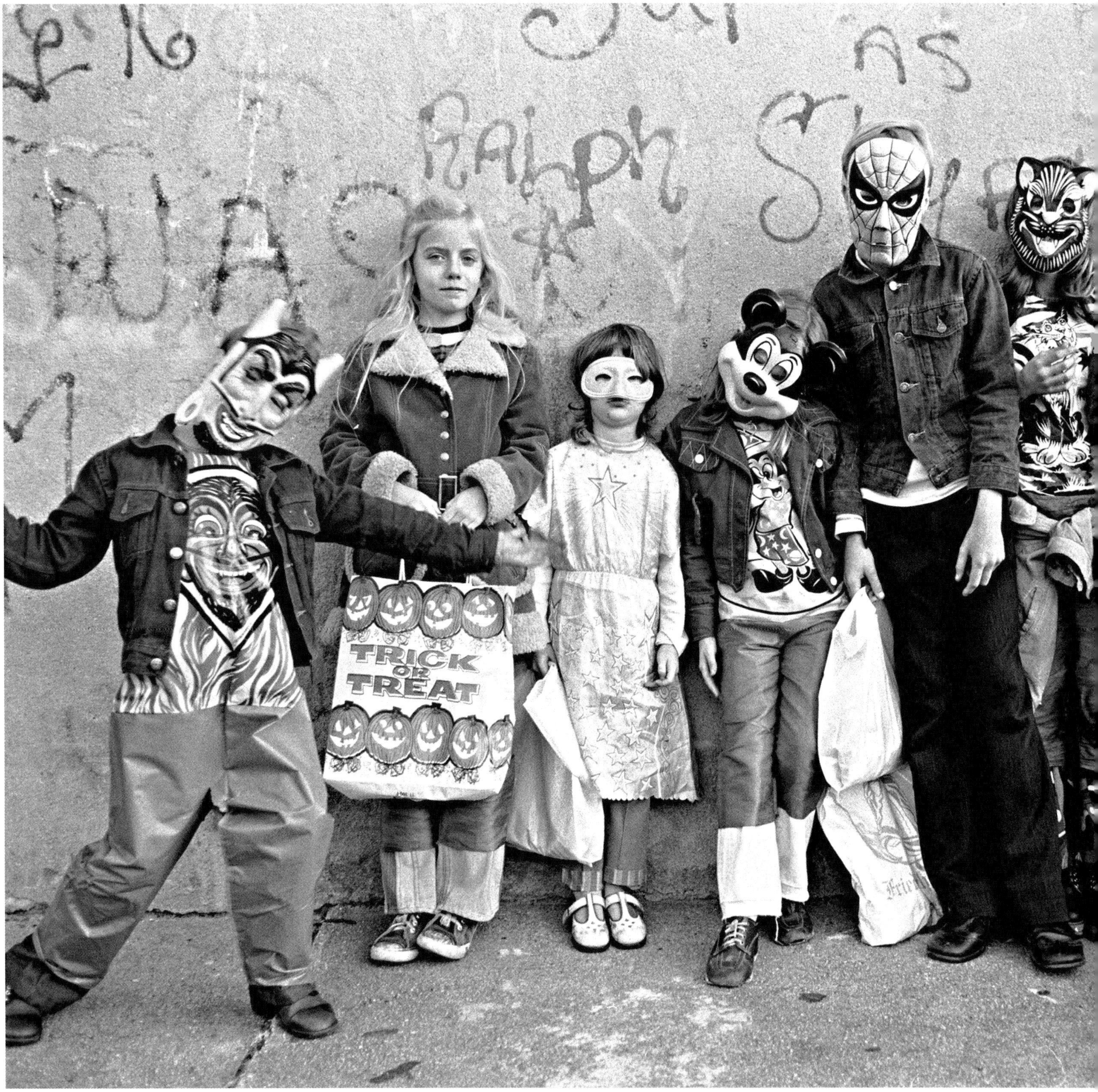
Ralph
TRICK OR TREAT

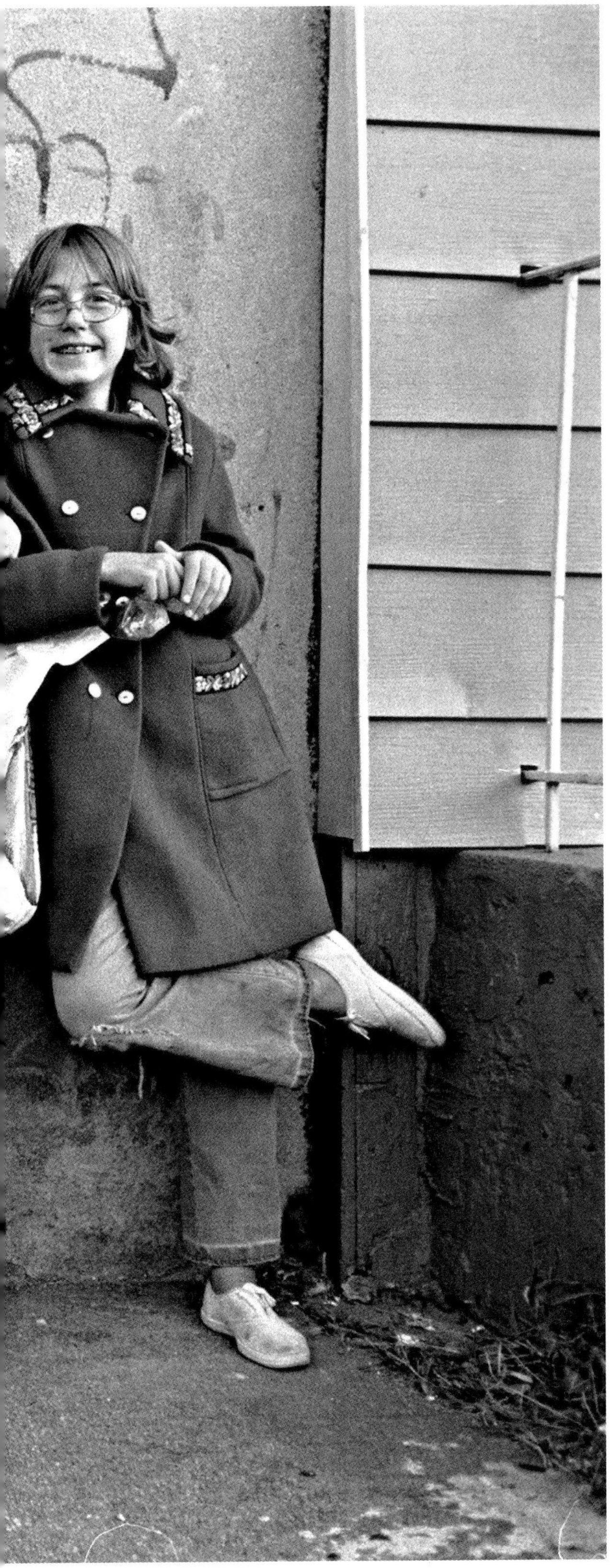

Trick-or-treaters relaxing,
1975, Brooklyn.

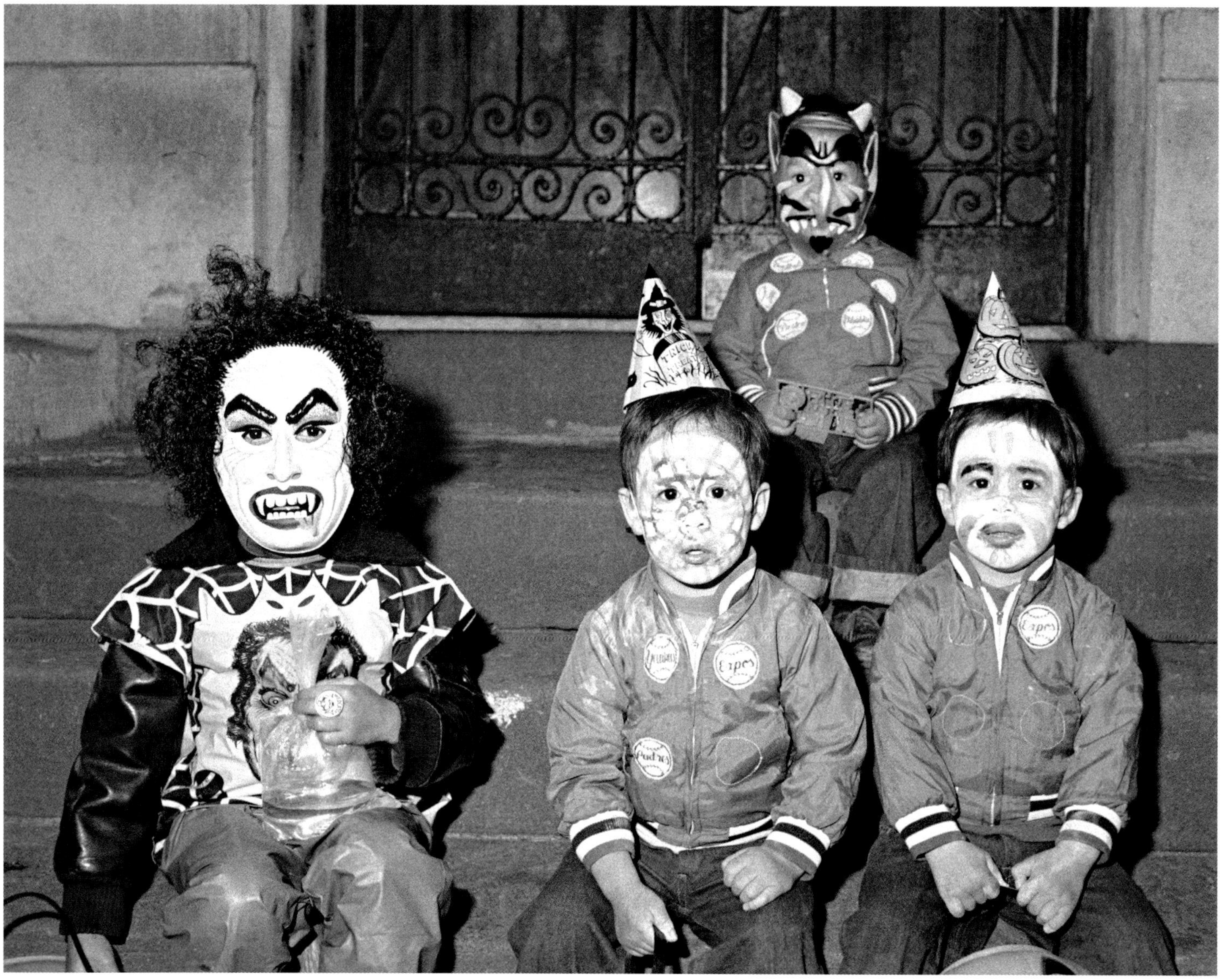

Four boys on a stoop,
1980, Brooklyn.

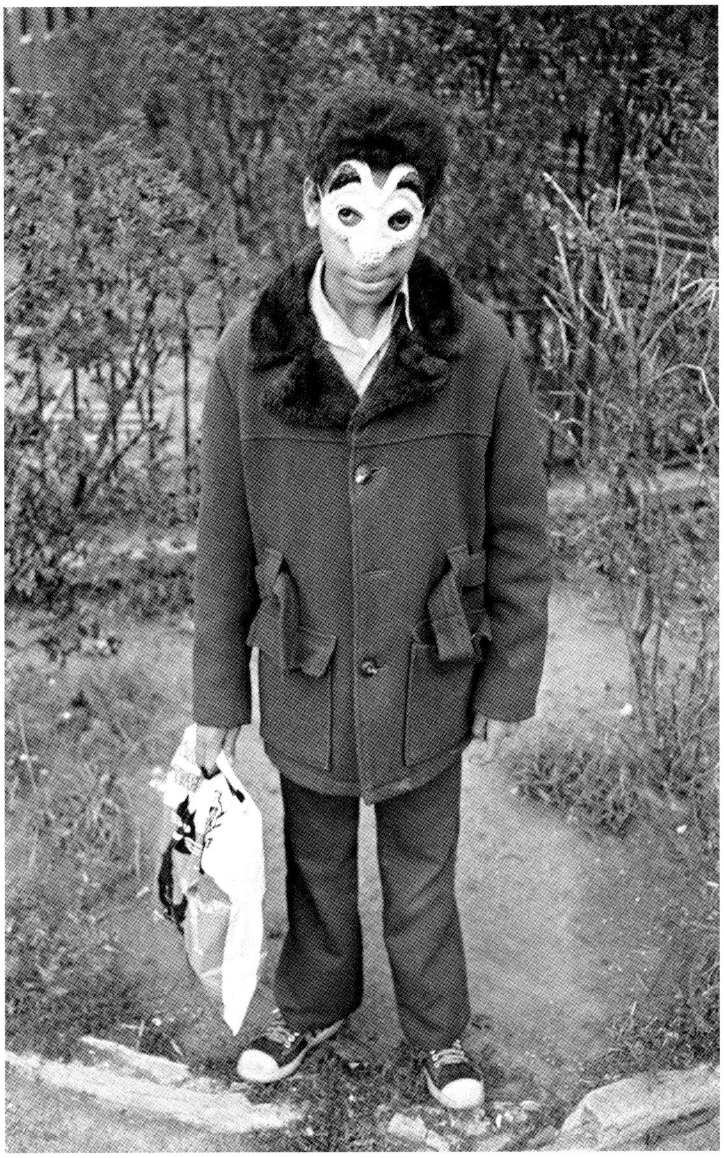

Masked boy,
1980, Brooklyn.

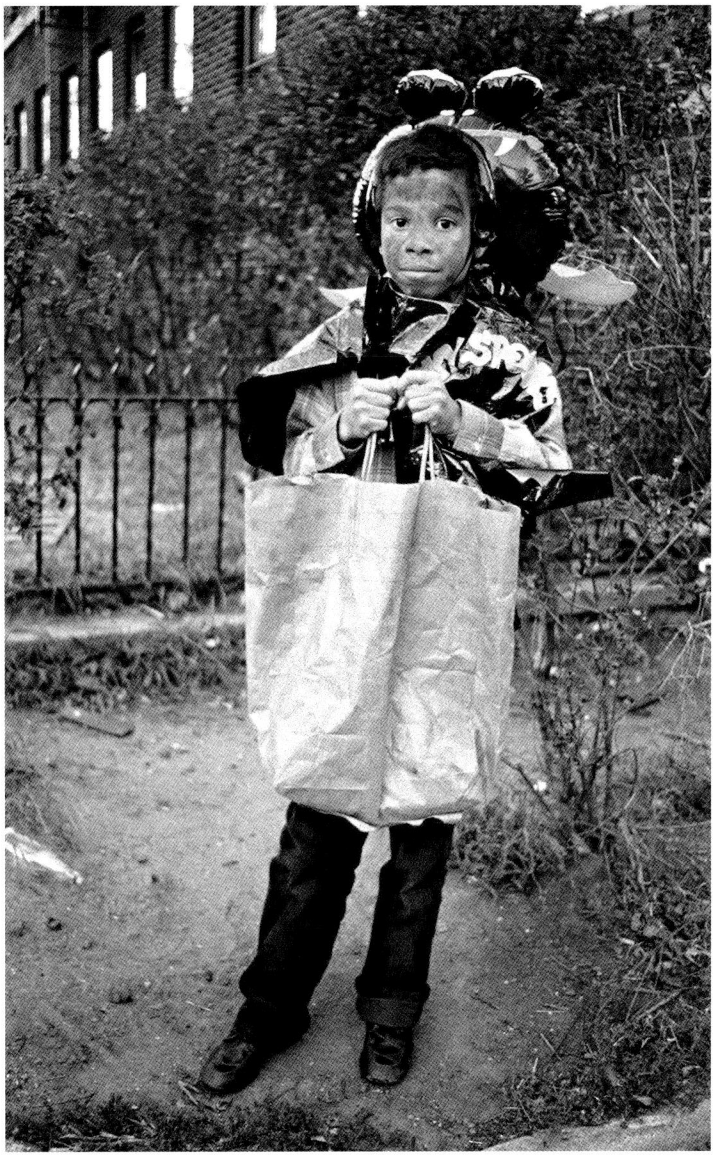

Boy with large shopping
bag, 1980, Brooklyn.

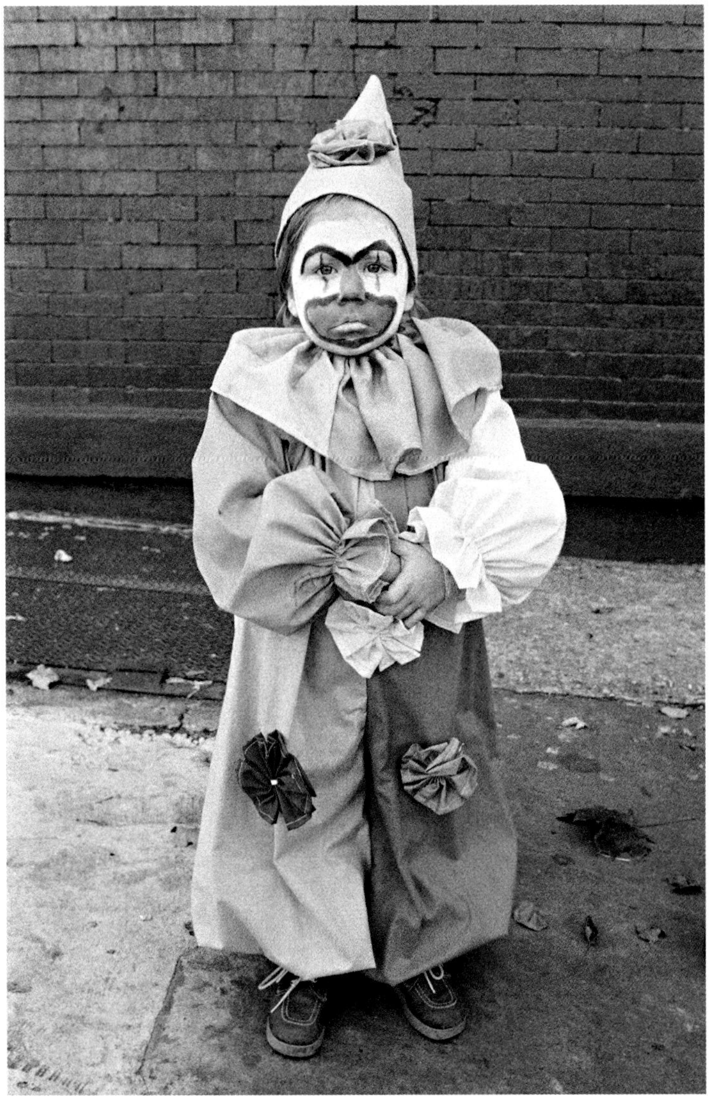

Clown, 1980, Brooklyn.

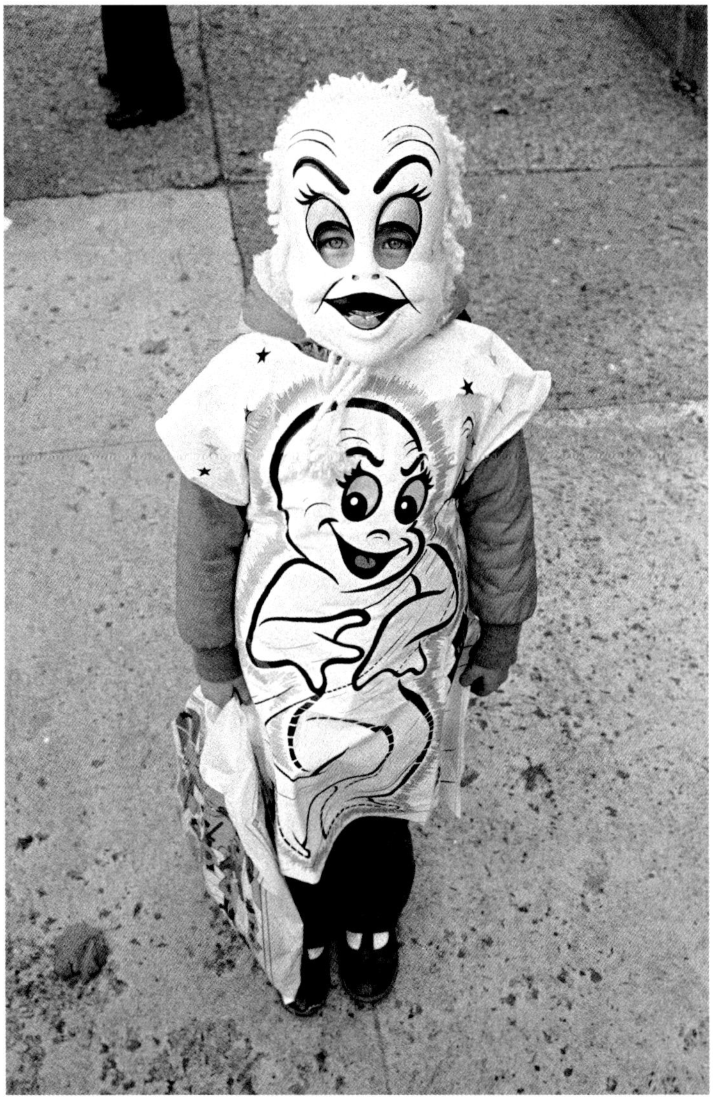

Casper (the Friendly Ghost), 1980, Brooklyn.

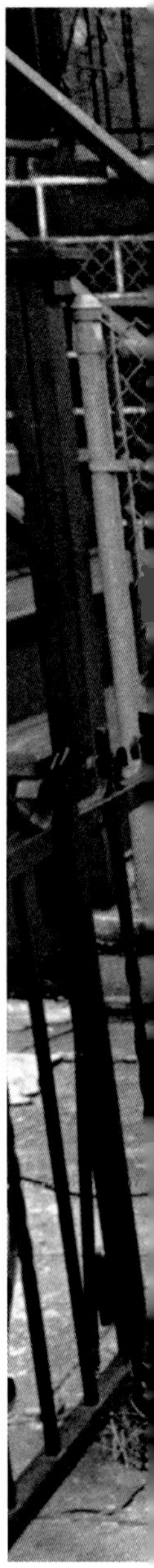

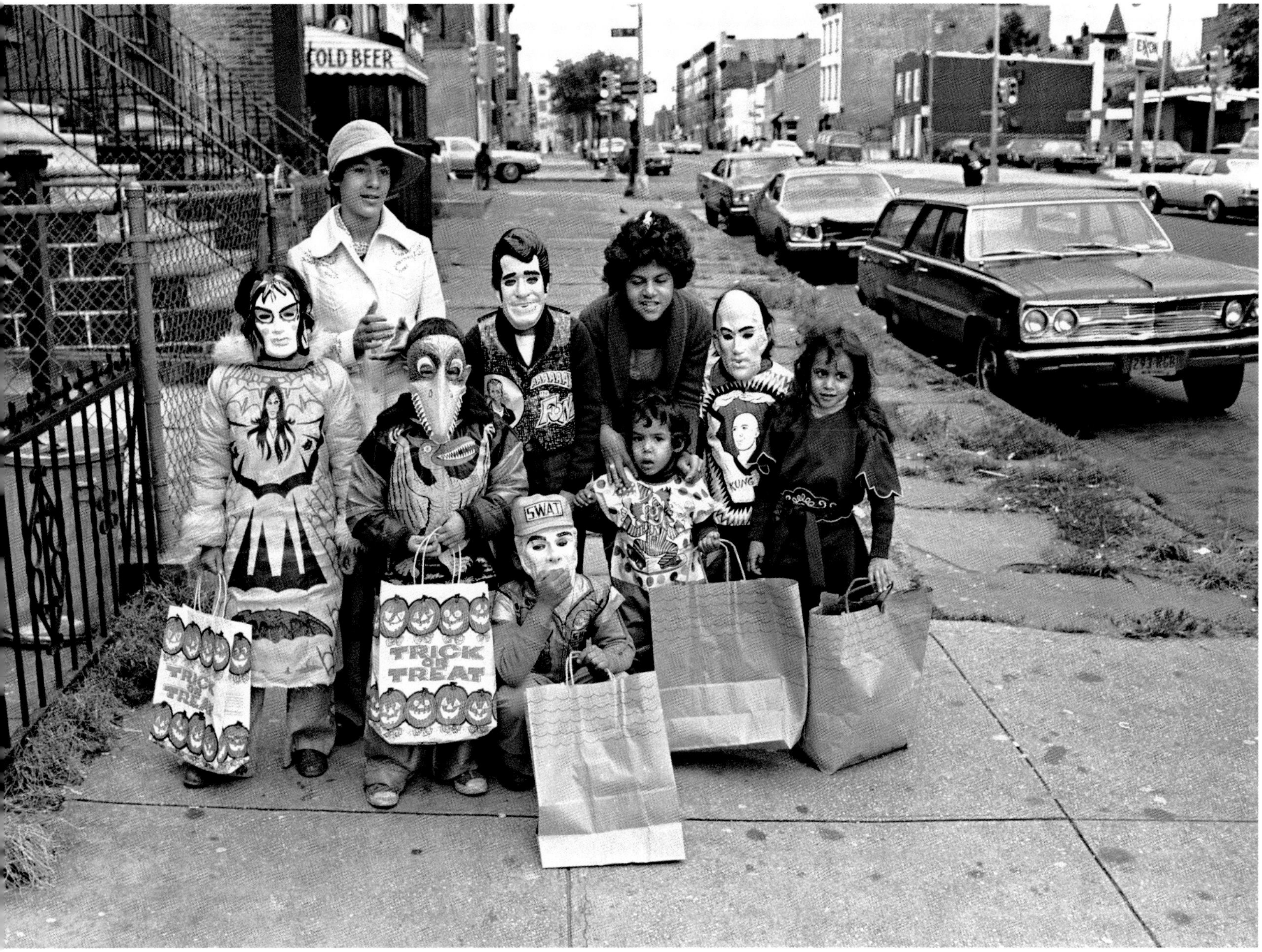

Group of trick-or-treaters, 1976, Brooklyn.

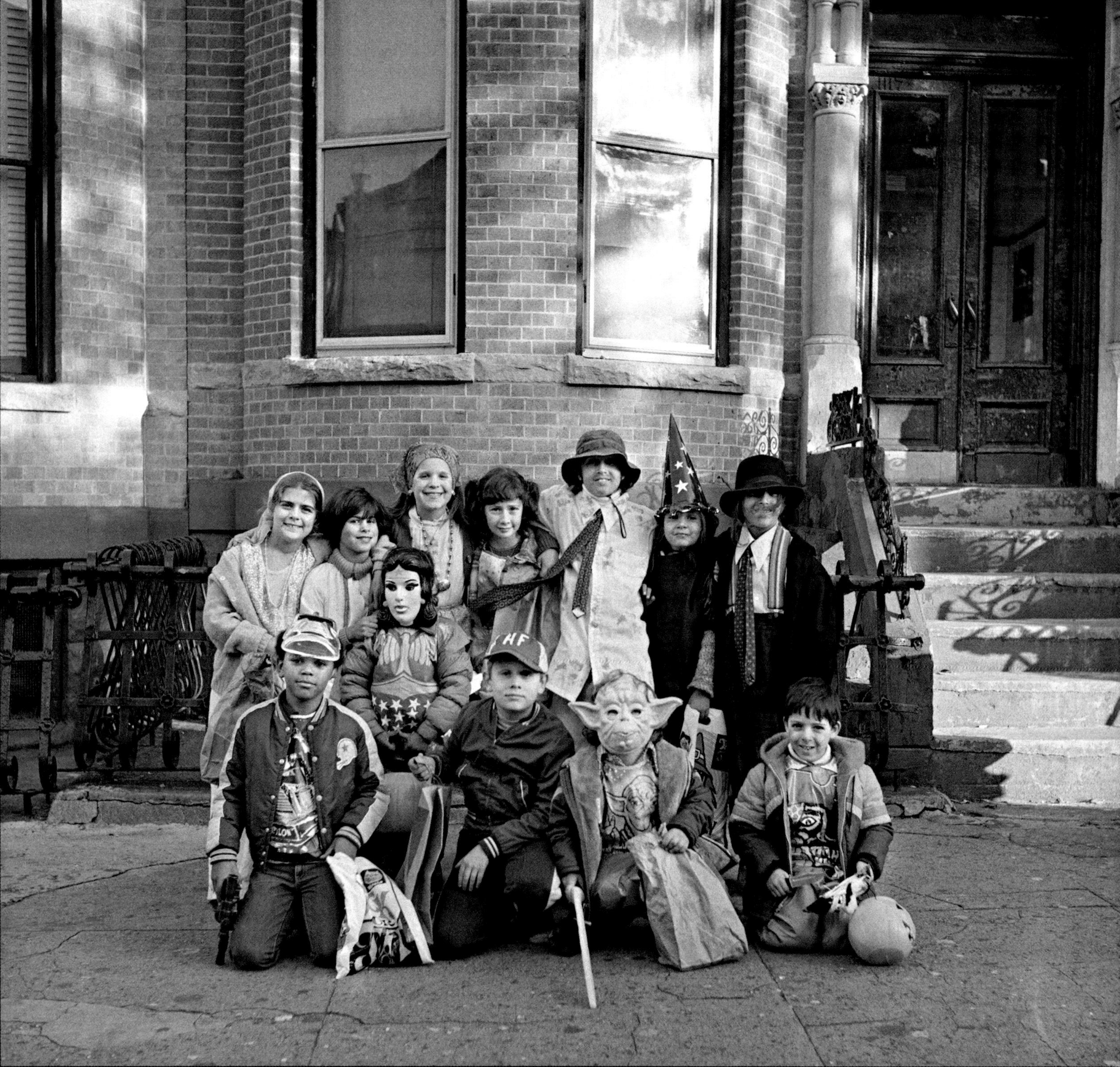

Above: Group of trick-or-treaters, 1980, Brooklyn.

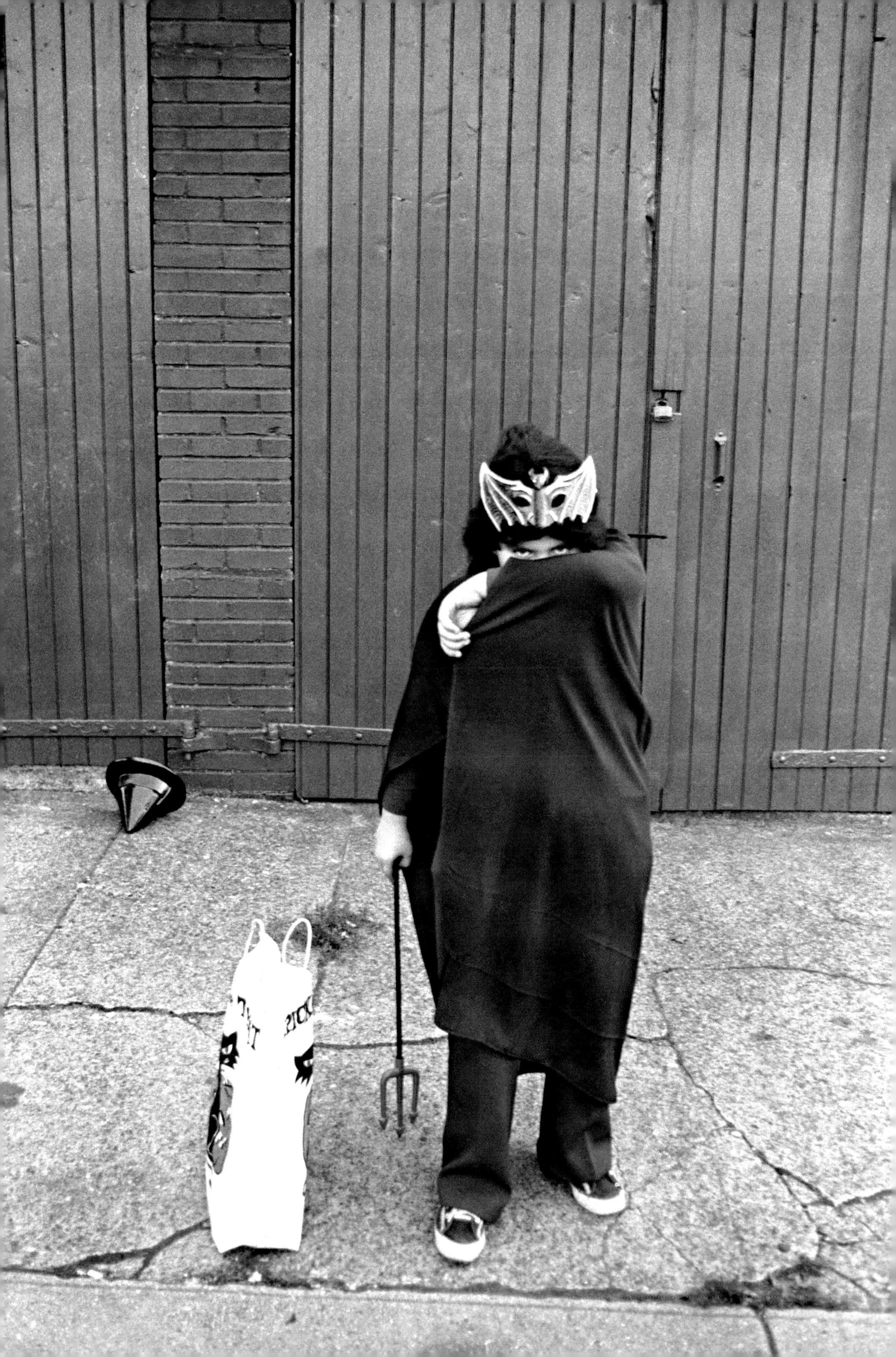

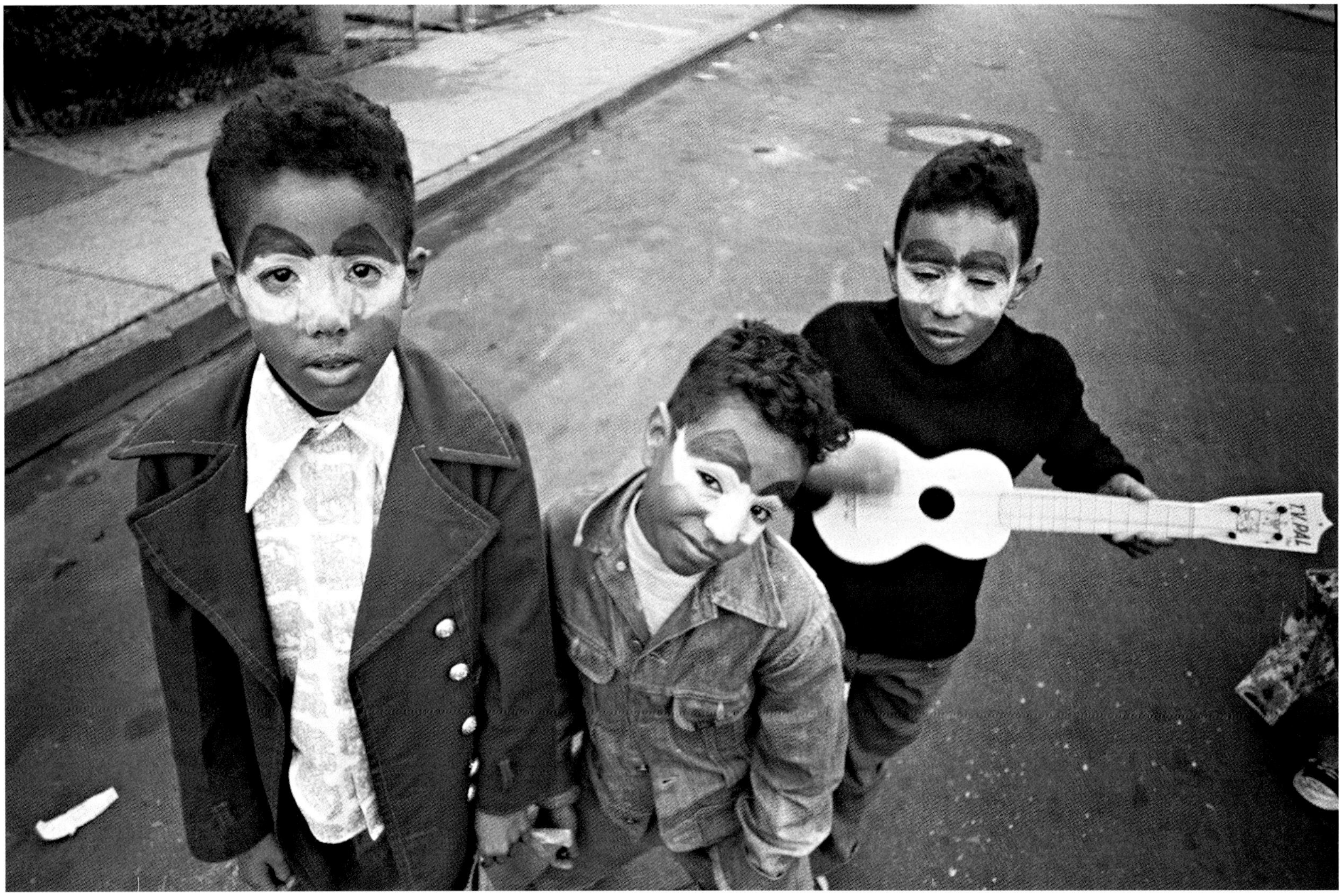

Three boys with tear
makeup, 1974, Brooklyn.

Ghost and two costumed girls, 1979, Brooklyn.

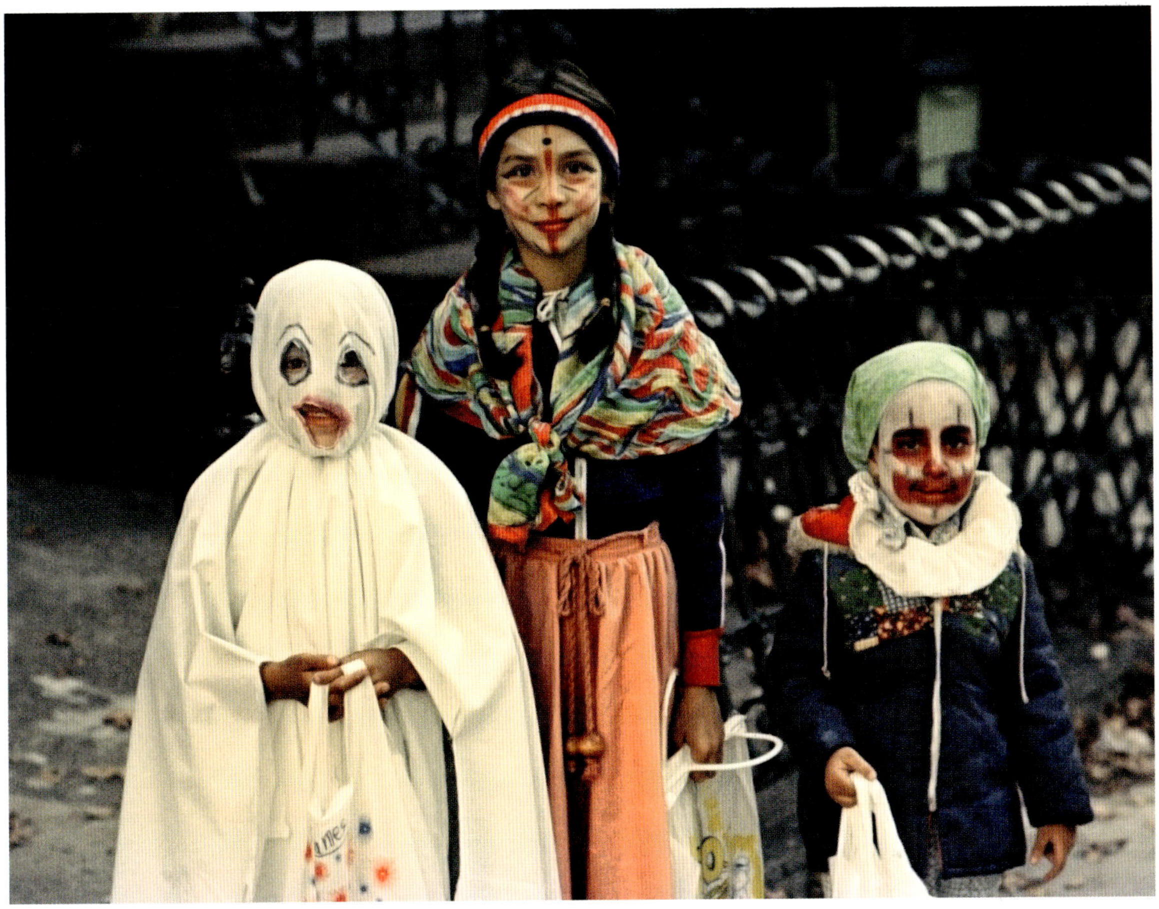

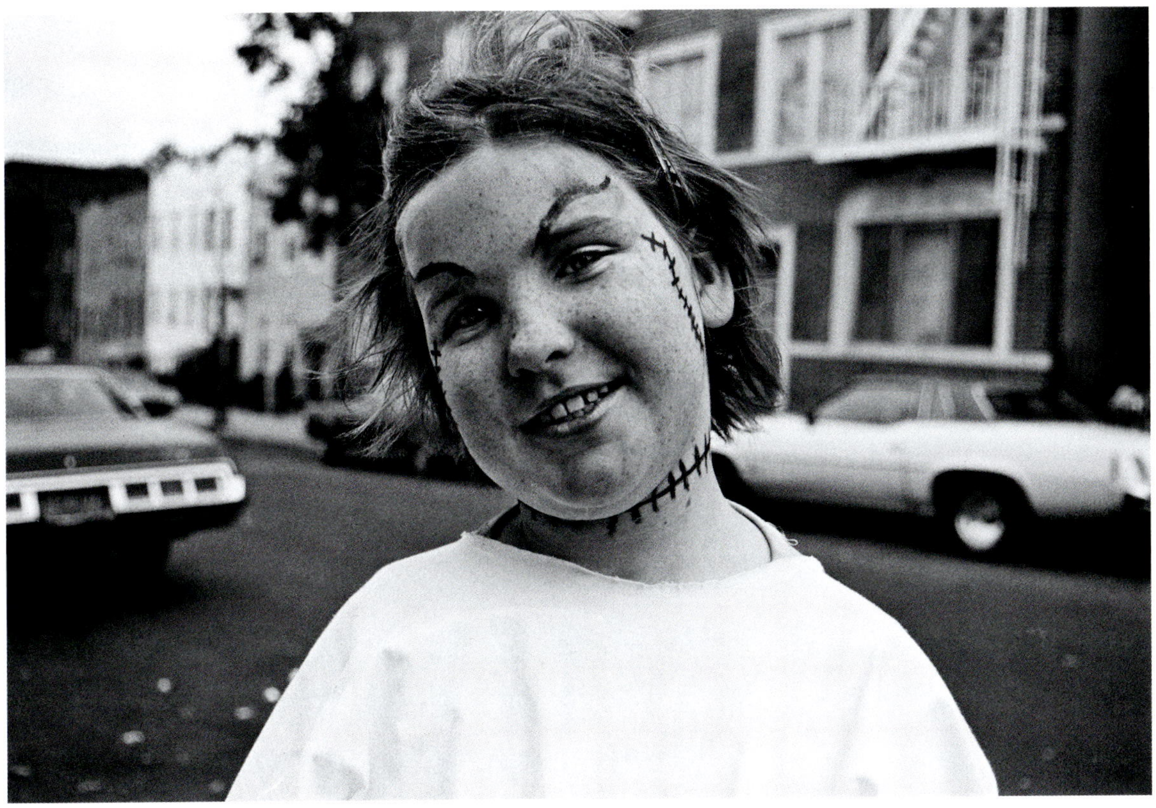

Bride of Frankenstein, 1976, Brooklyn.

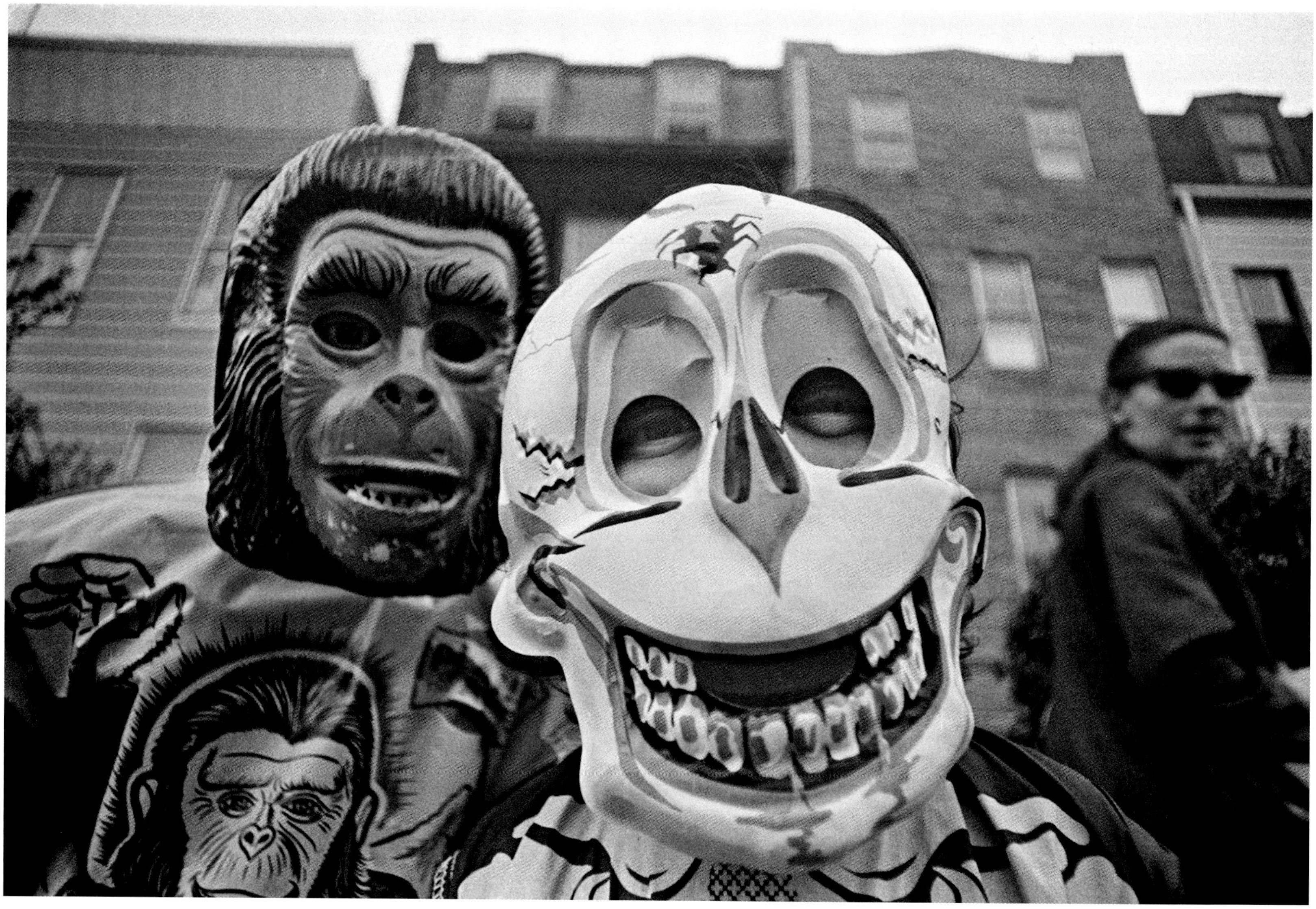

Skull, ape, and passerby,
1974, Brooklyn.

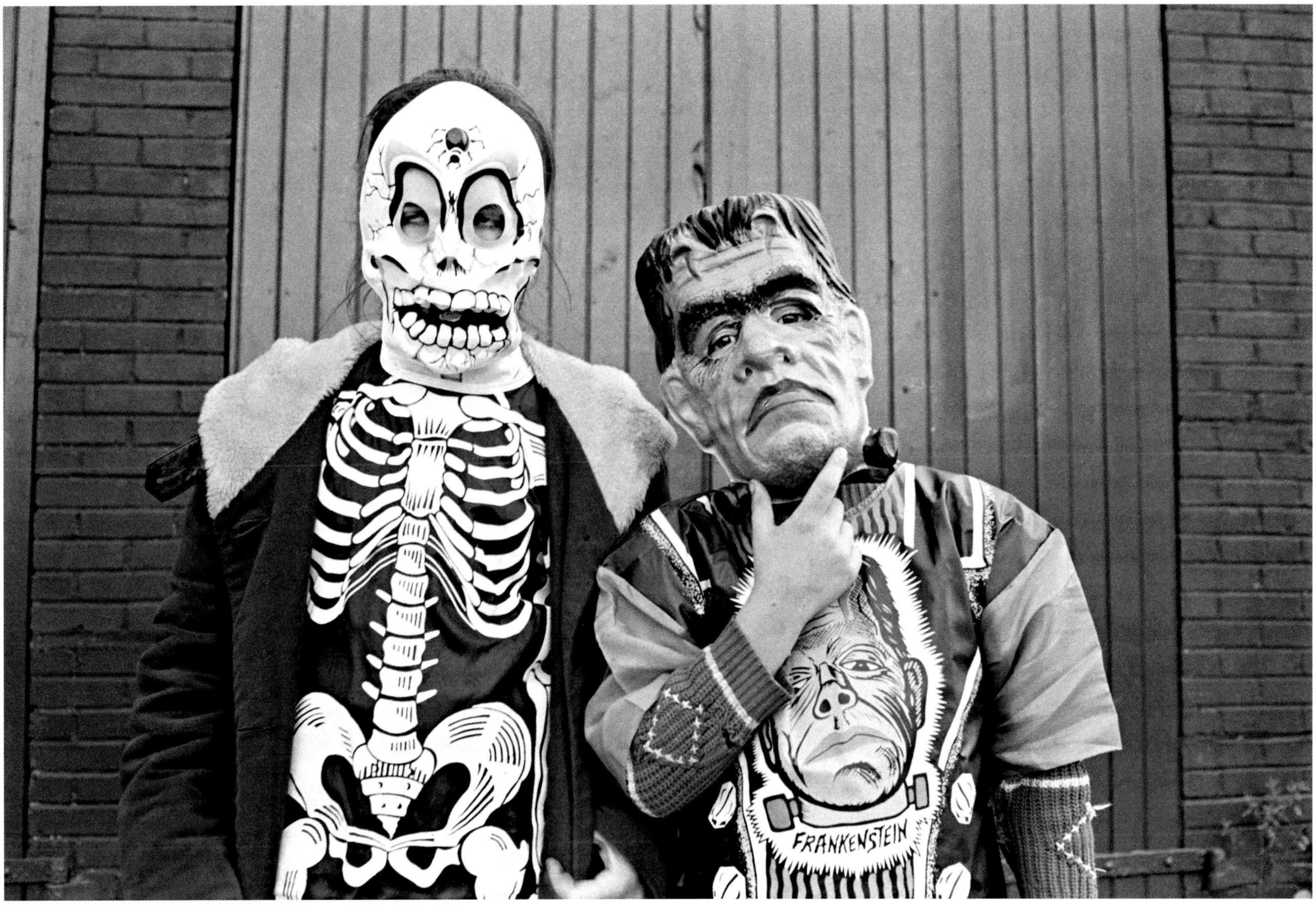

Skeleton and Frankenstein,
1975, Brooklyn.

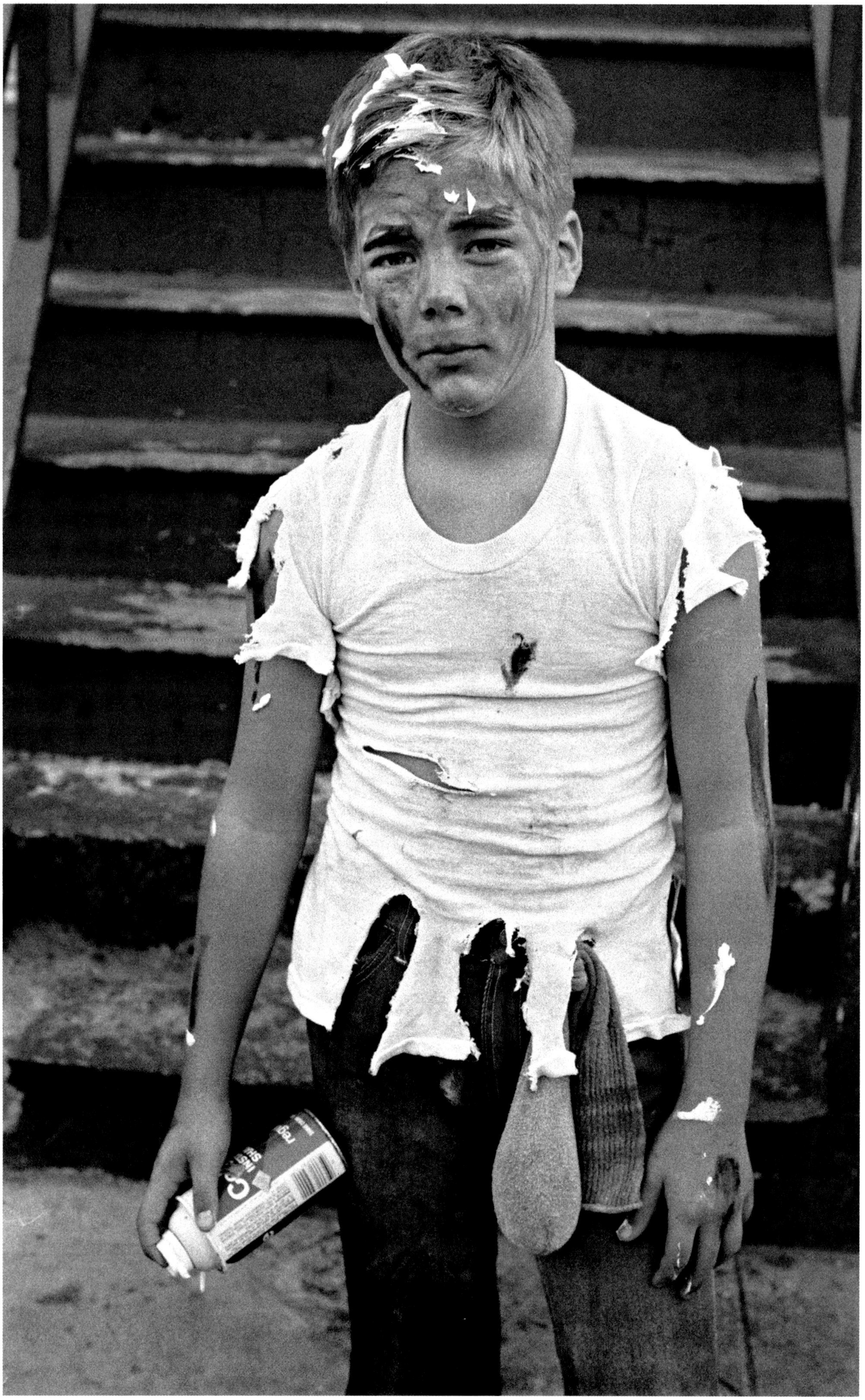

Shaving cream fighter
with chalk sock,
1978, Brooklyn.

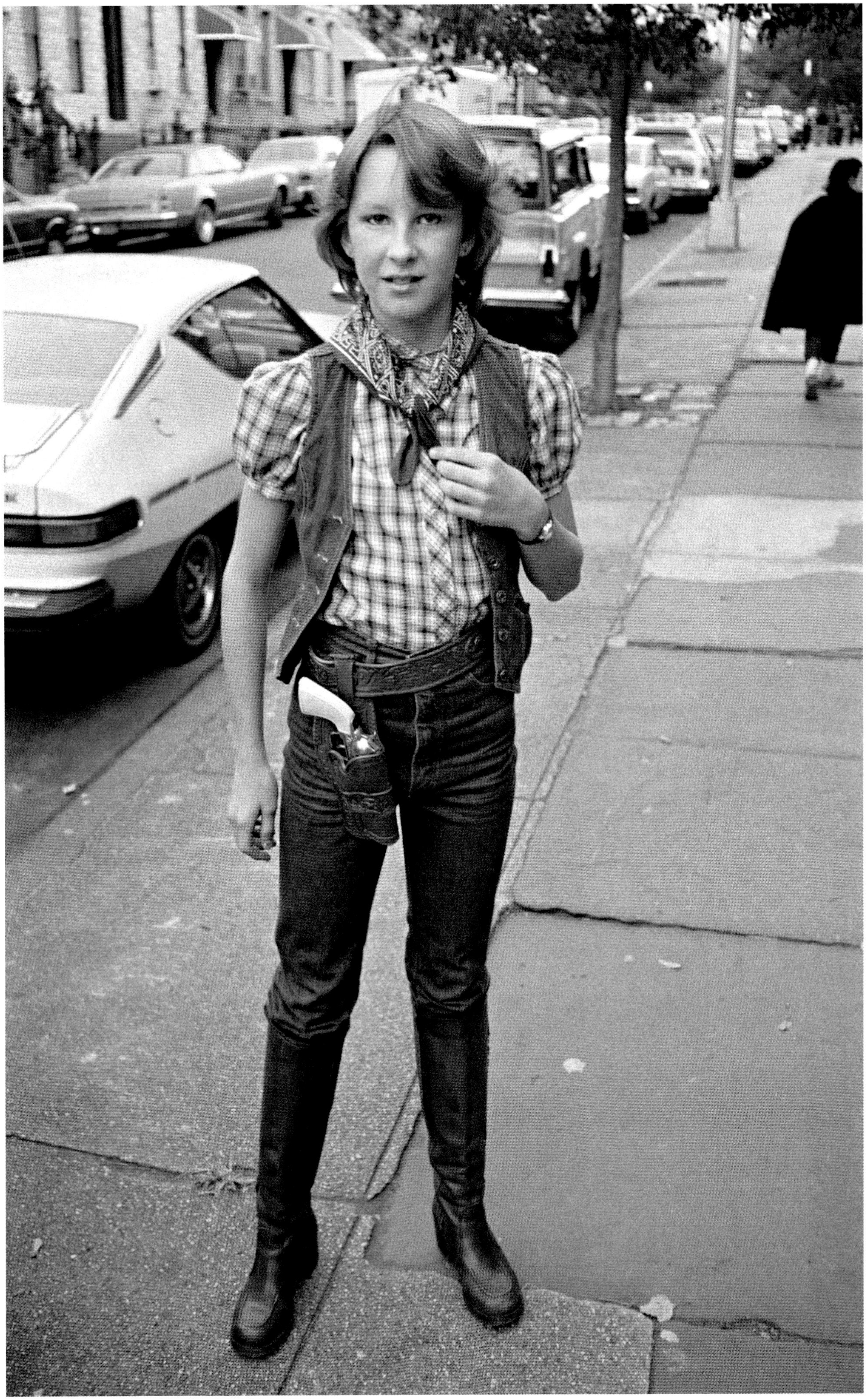

Cowgirl with a pistol,
1980, Brooklyn.

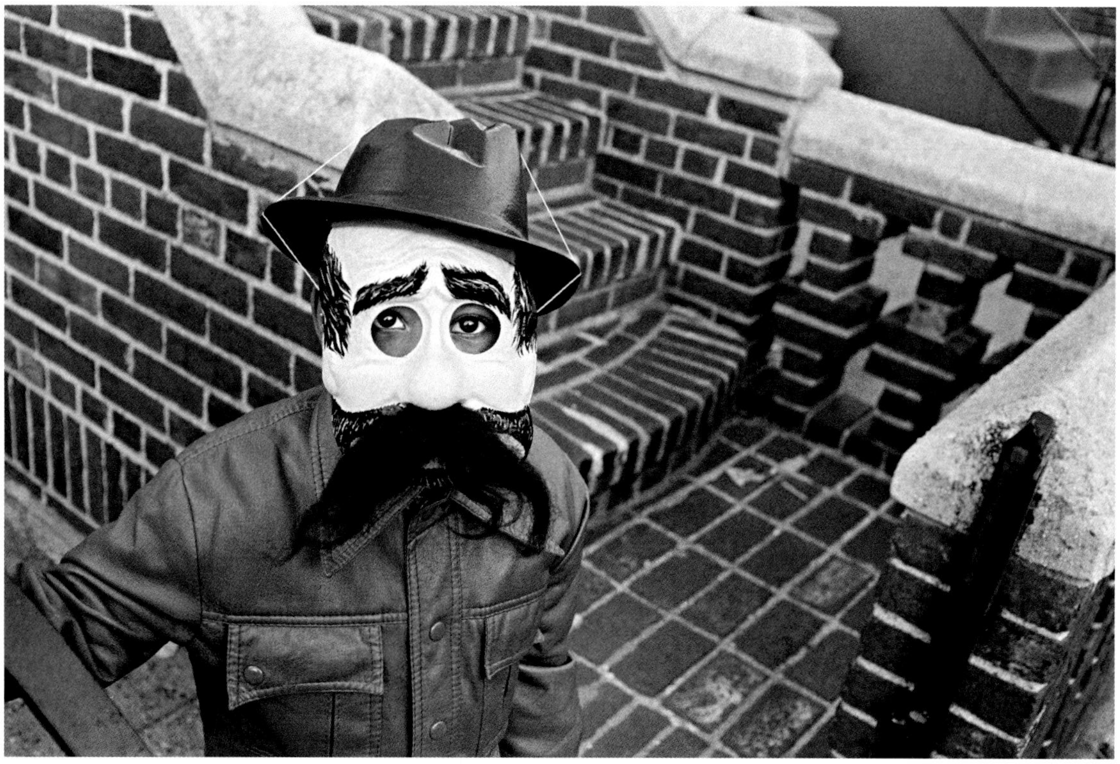

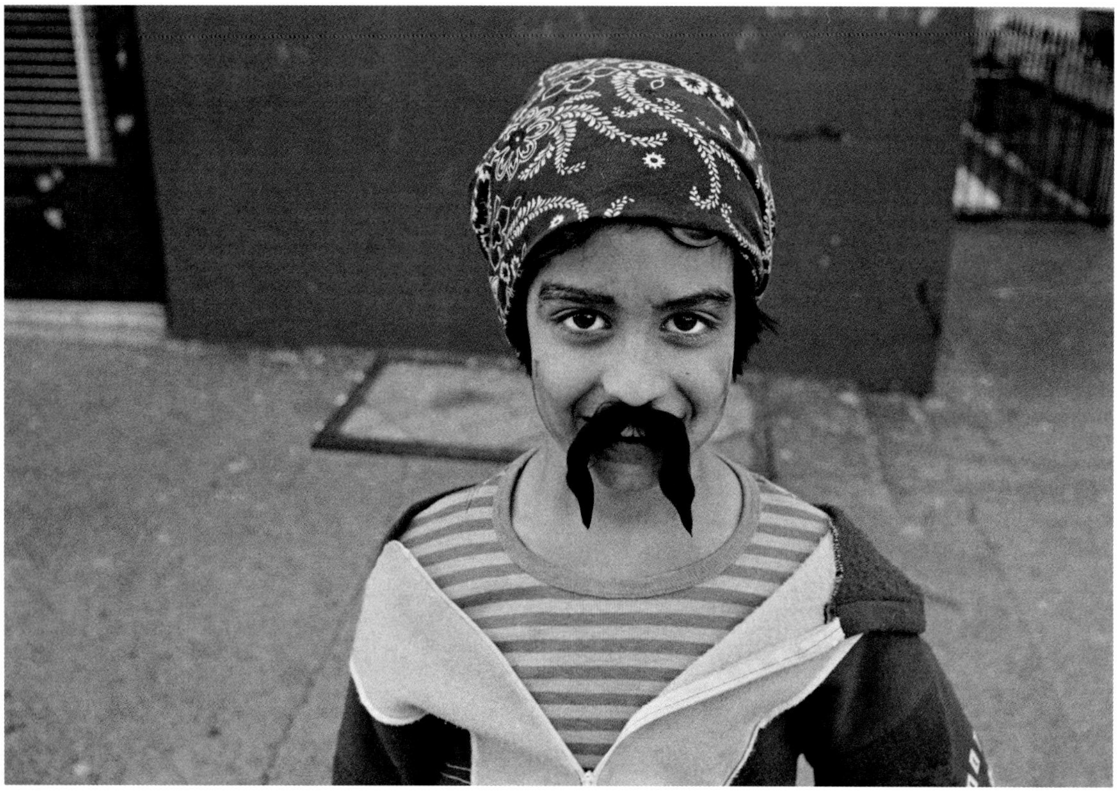

Above (top): "Bacigolup," 1975, Brooklyn.

Above (bottom): Pirate, 1979, Brooklyn.

Opposite: Cowboy with a gun, 1975, Brooklyn.

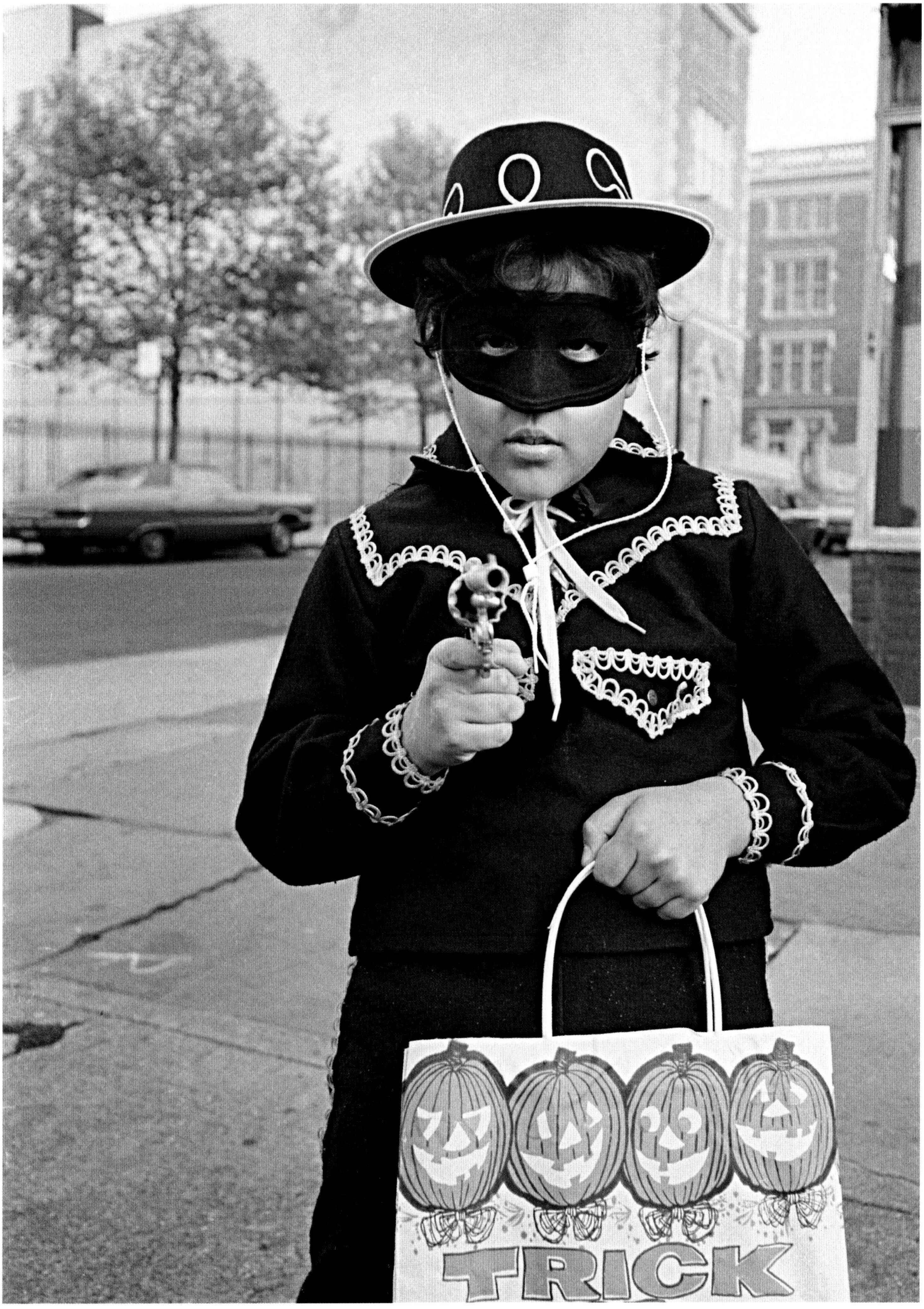
TRICK

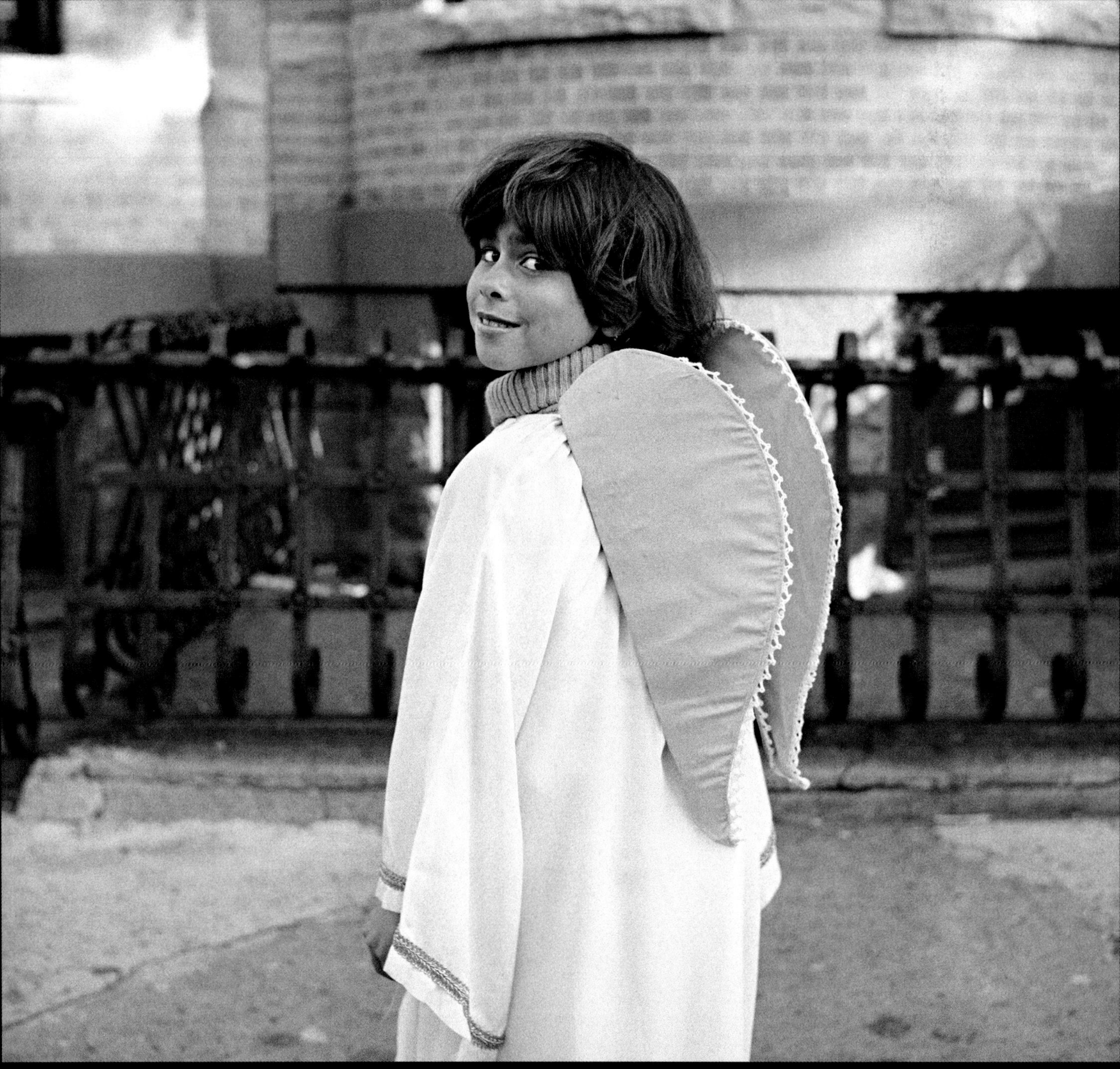

The Angel,
1980, Brooklyn.

The Skull, 1978,
Brooklyn.

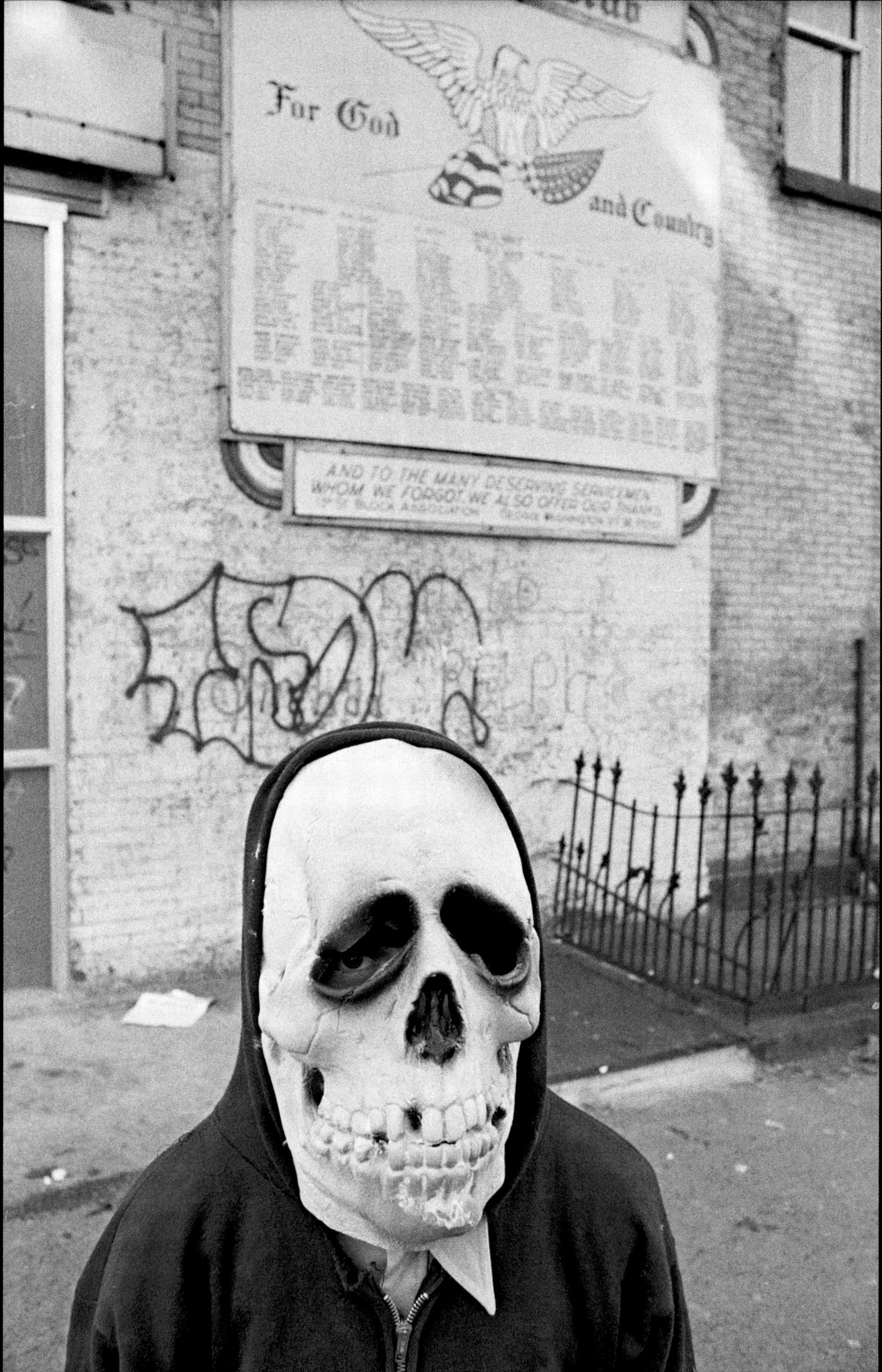

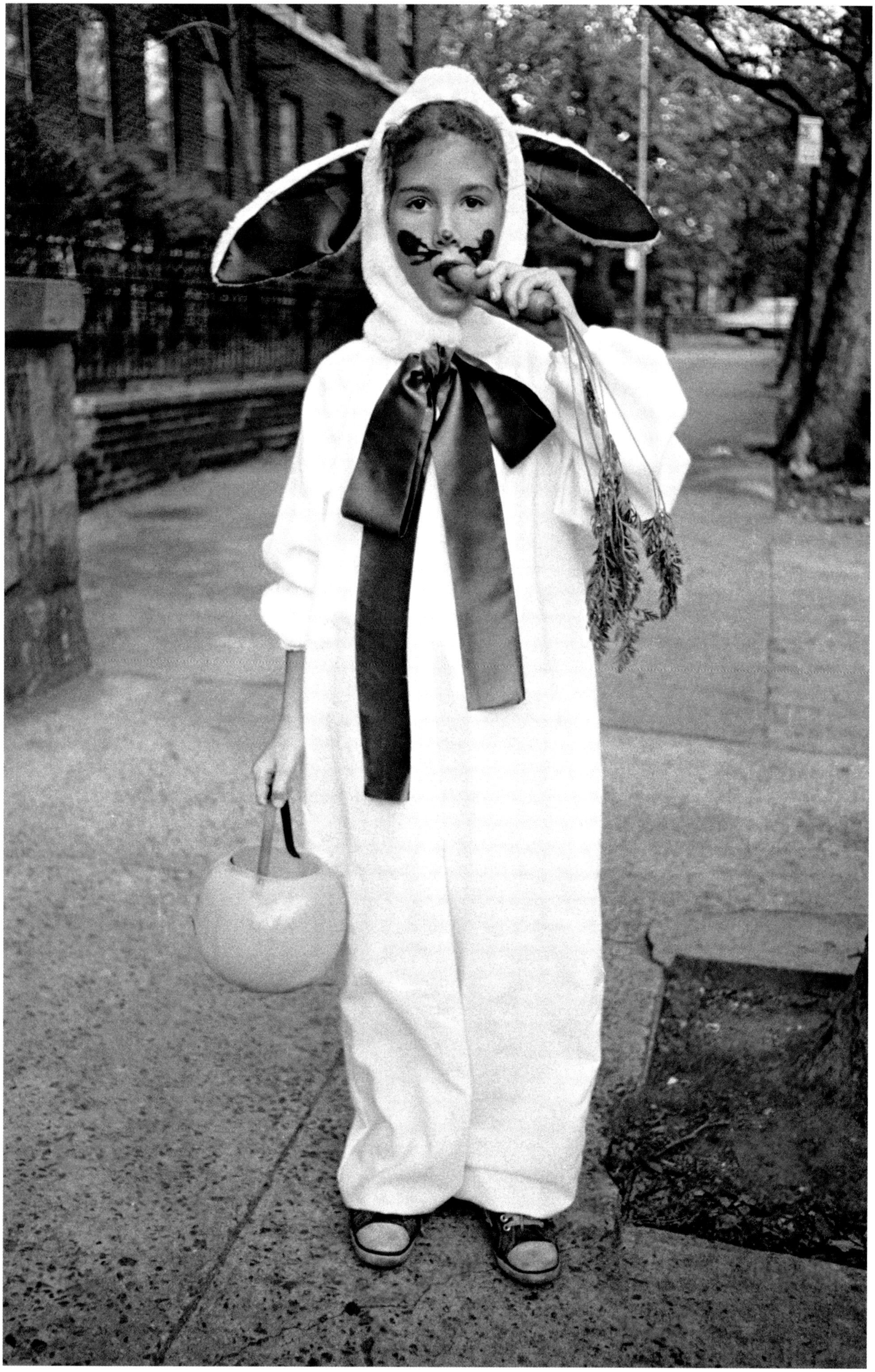

Bunny with a carrot, 1980, Brooklyn.

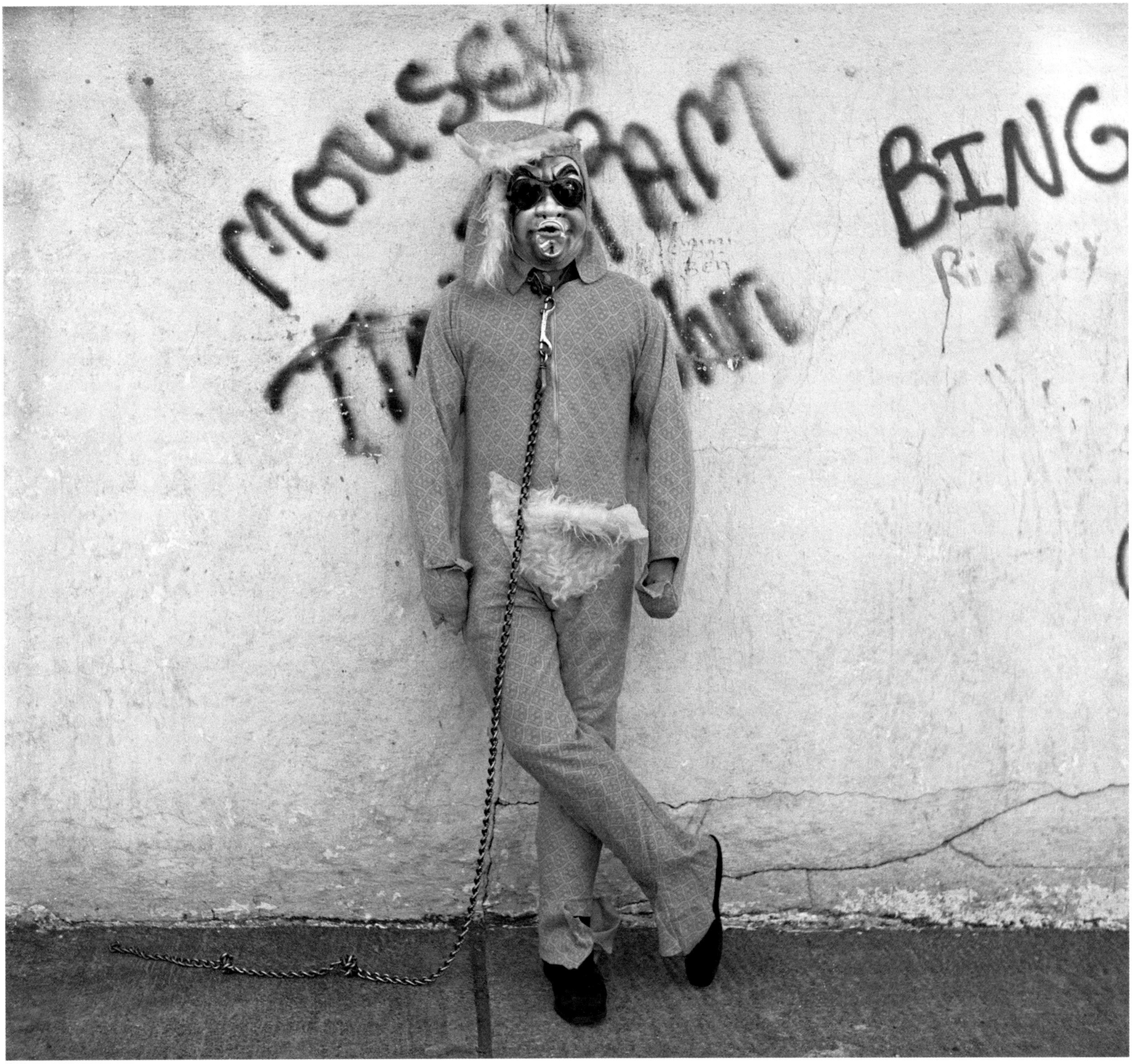

Chained rabbit,
1977, Brooklyn.

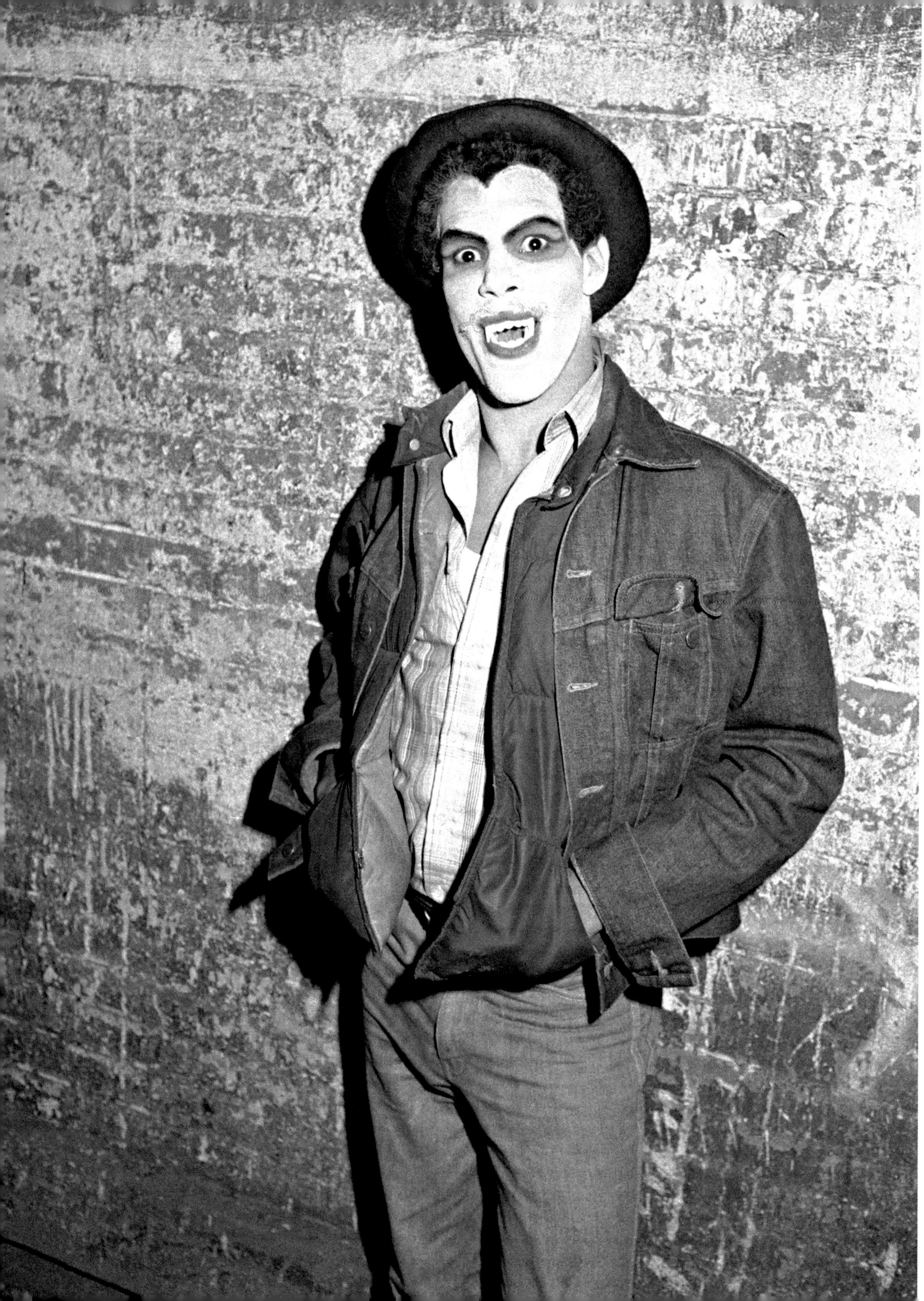

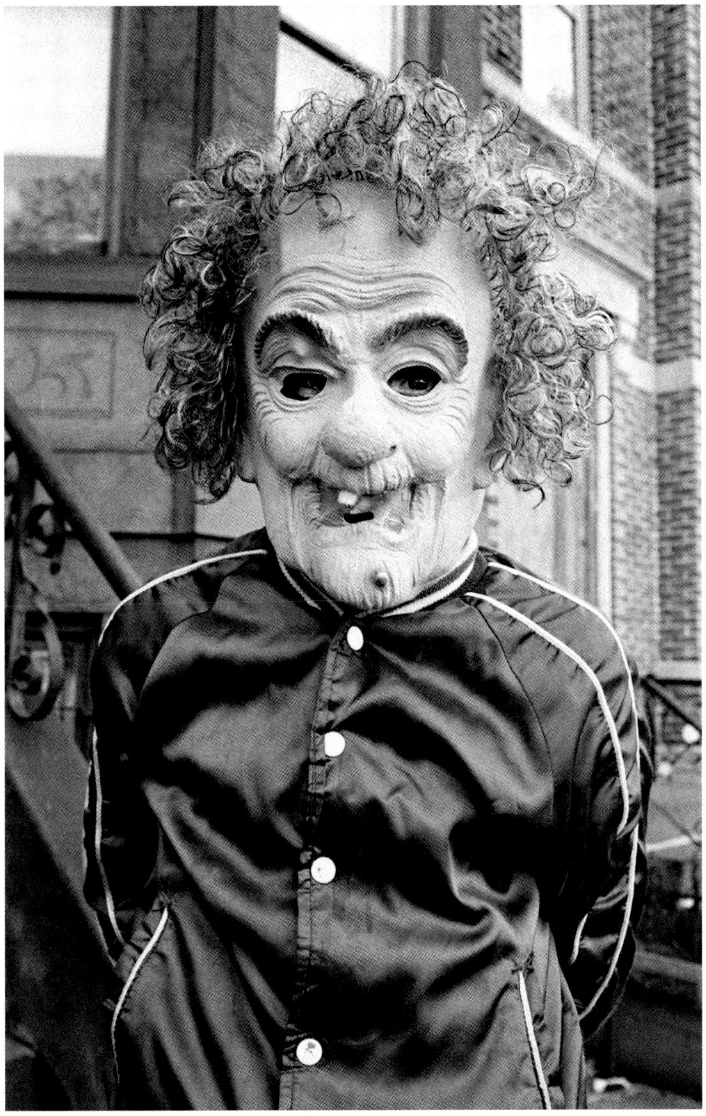

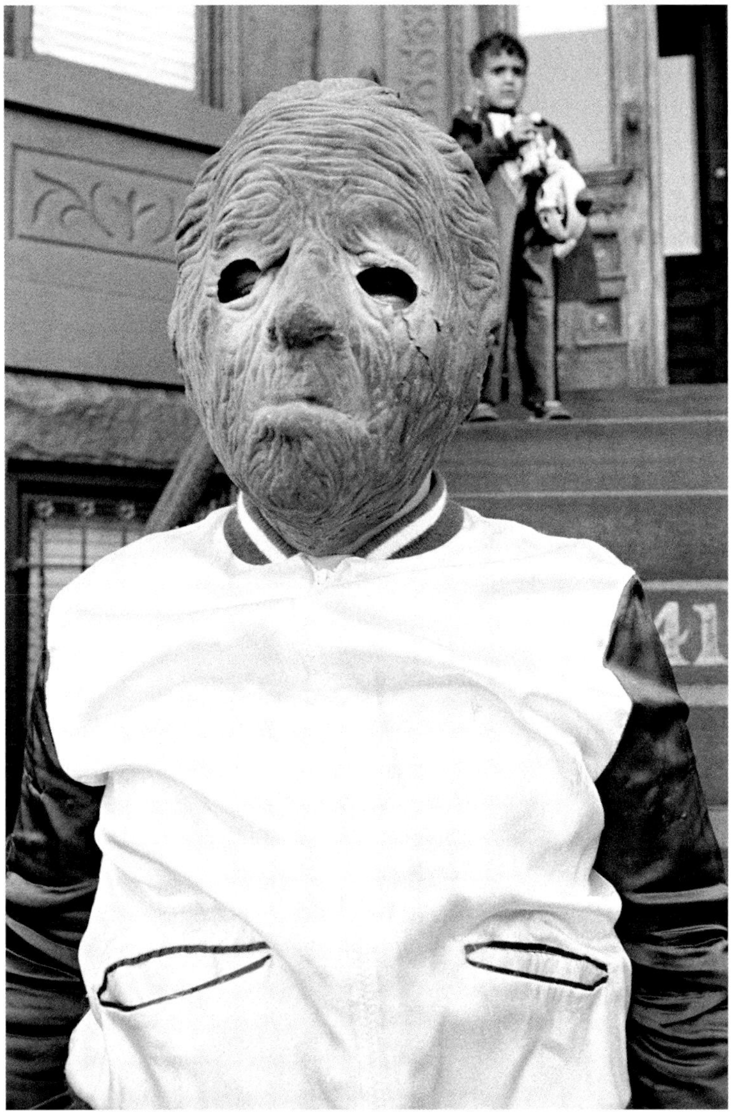

Above: Old man mask,
1980, Brooklyn.

Opposite: Vampire at
night, 1980, Brooklyn.

Werewolf mask,
1980, Brooklyn.

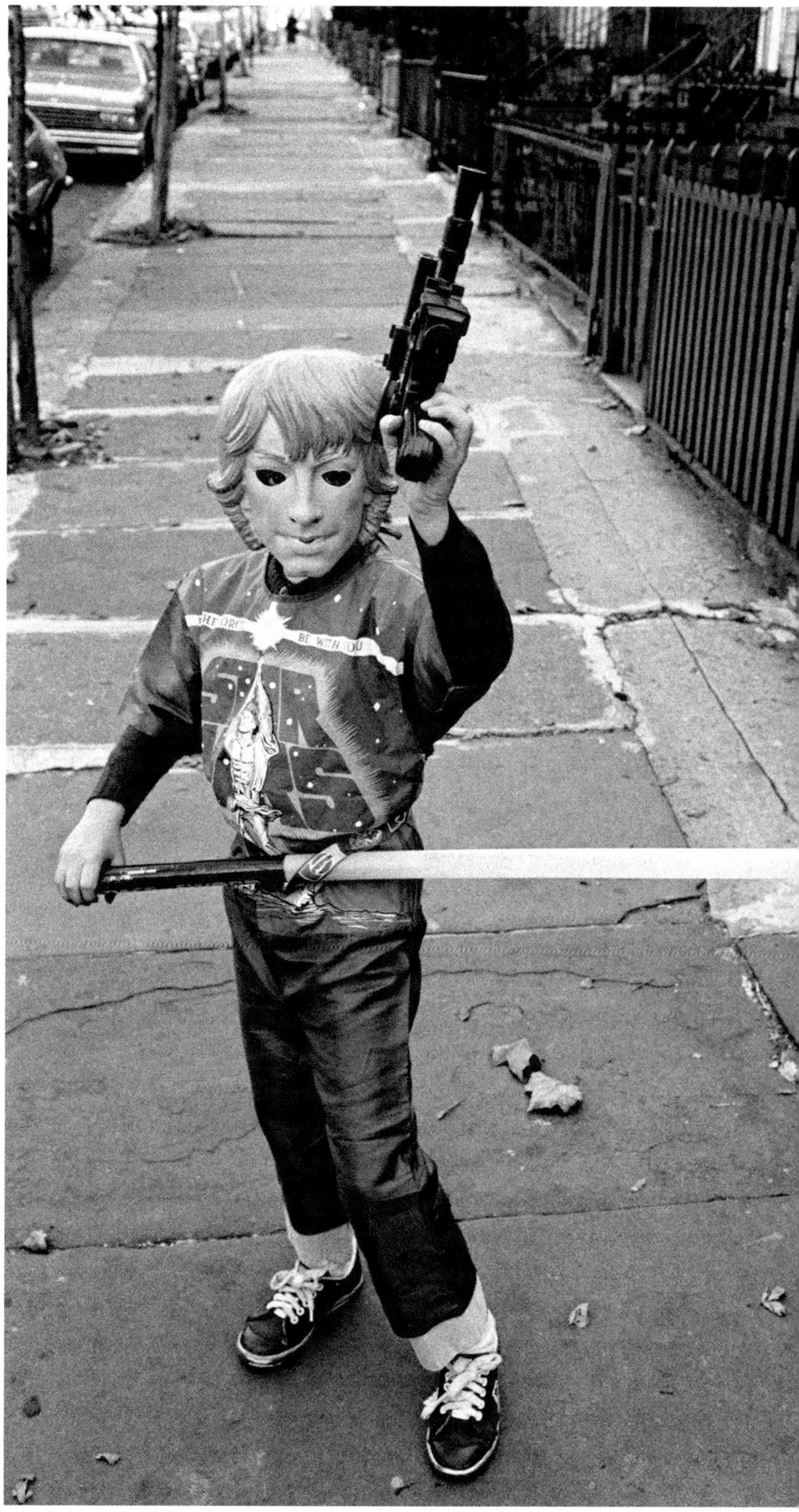

Luke Skywalker with lightsaber, 1980, Brooklyn.

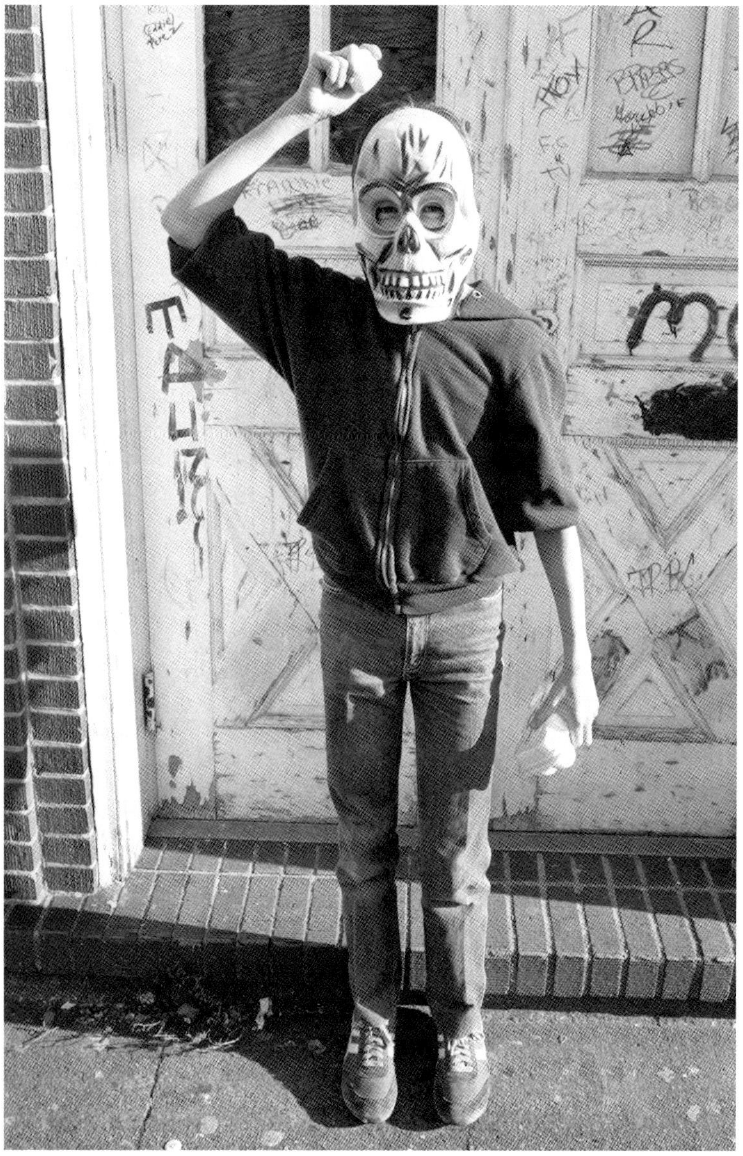

Egg thrower in a skull mask, 1980, Brooklyn.

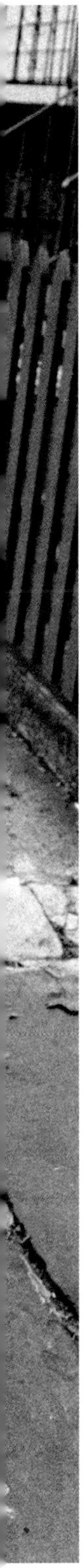

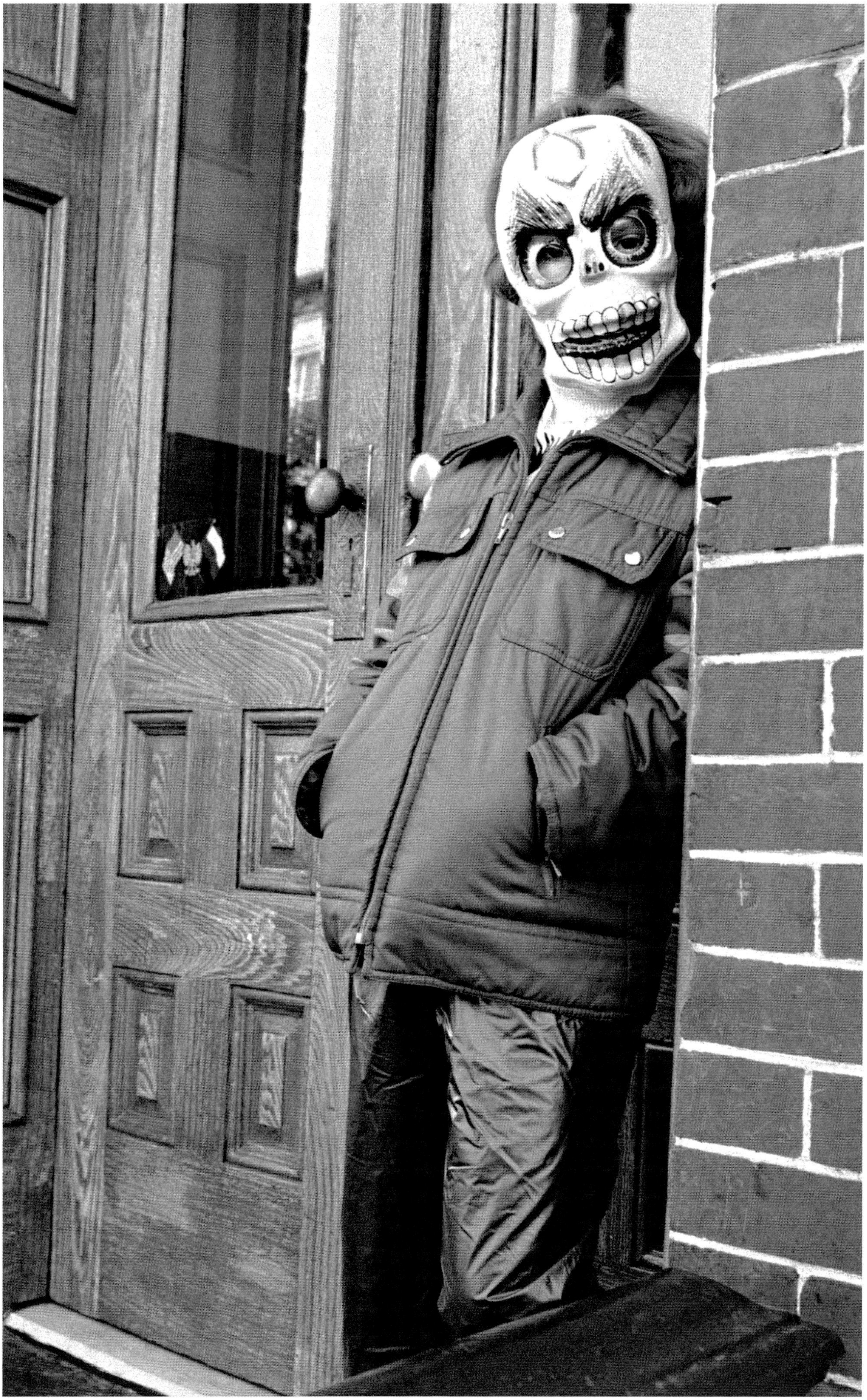

Skull on the lookout,
1980, Brooklyn.

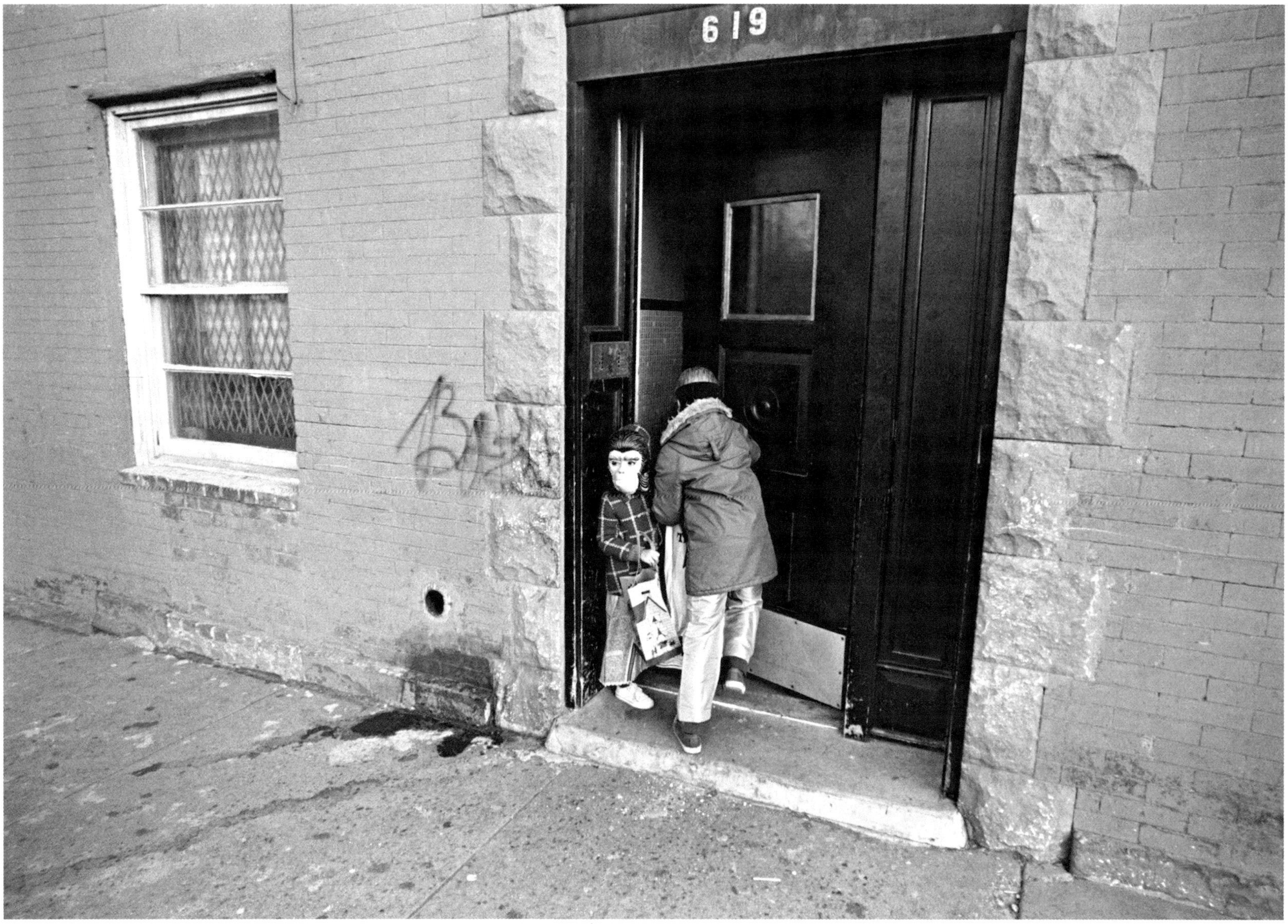

Doorway trick-or-treaters,
1975, Brooklyn.

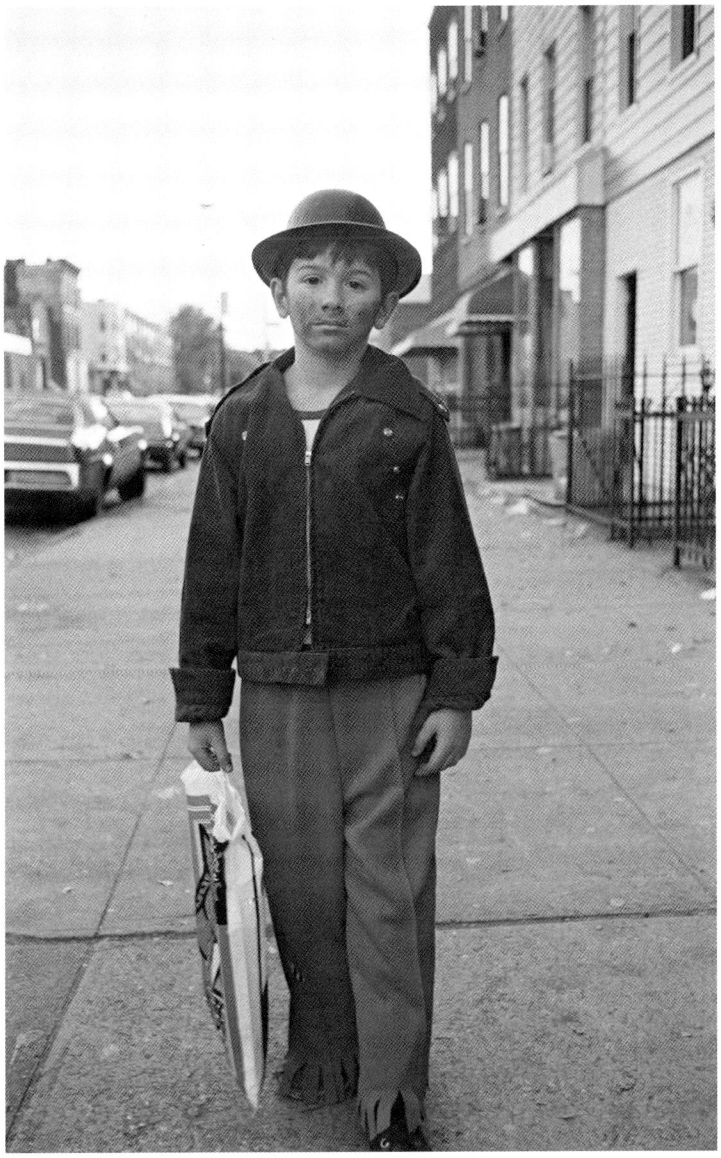

The Tramp, 1975, Brooklyn.

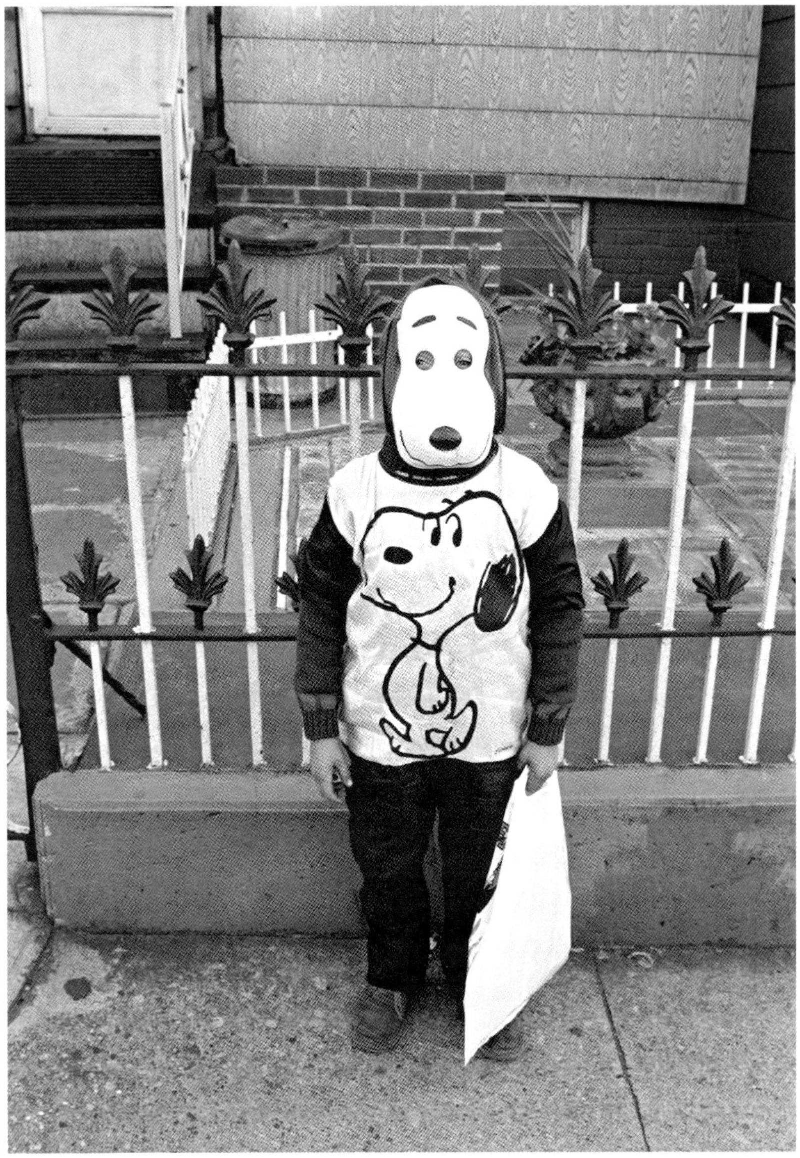

Snoopy, 1975, Brooklyn.

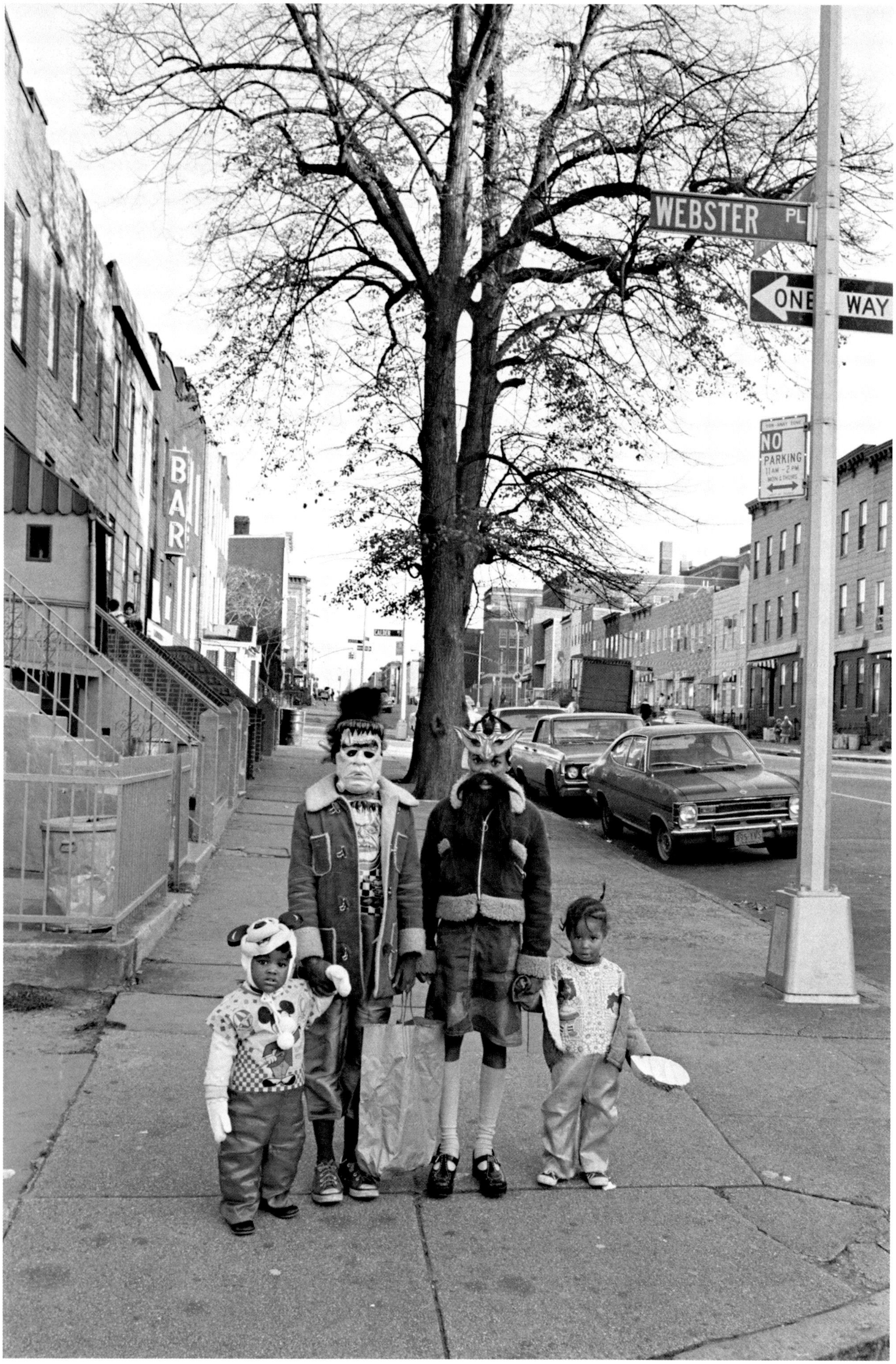

Left: Four girls with masks, 1975, Brooklyn.

Opposite: Indian and cowboy, 1980, Brooklyn.

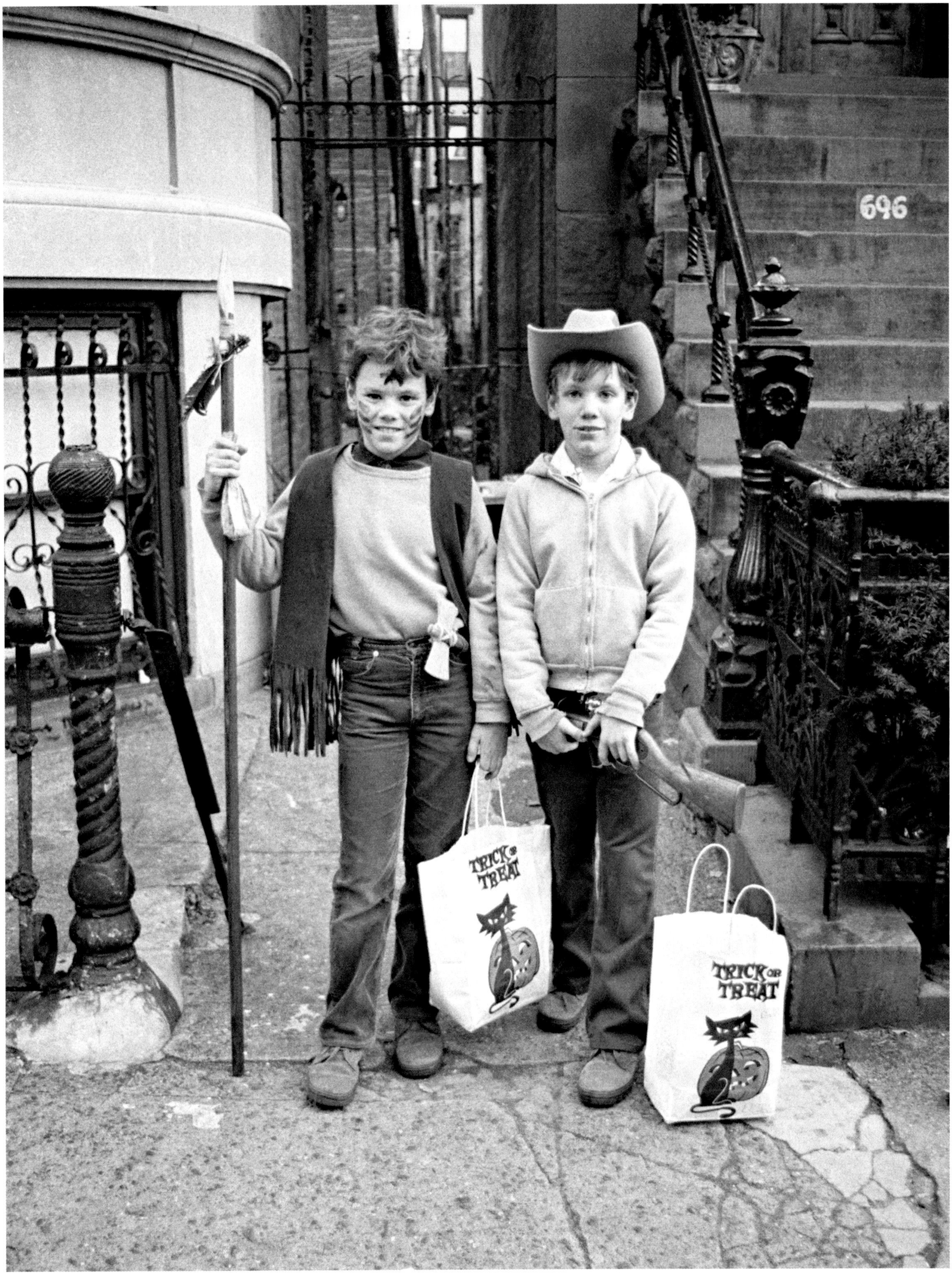
696
TRICK OR TREAT
TRICK OR TREAT

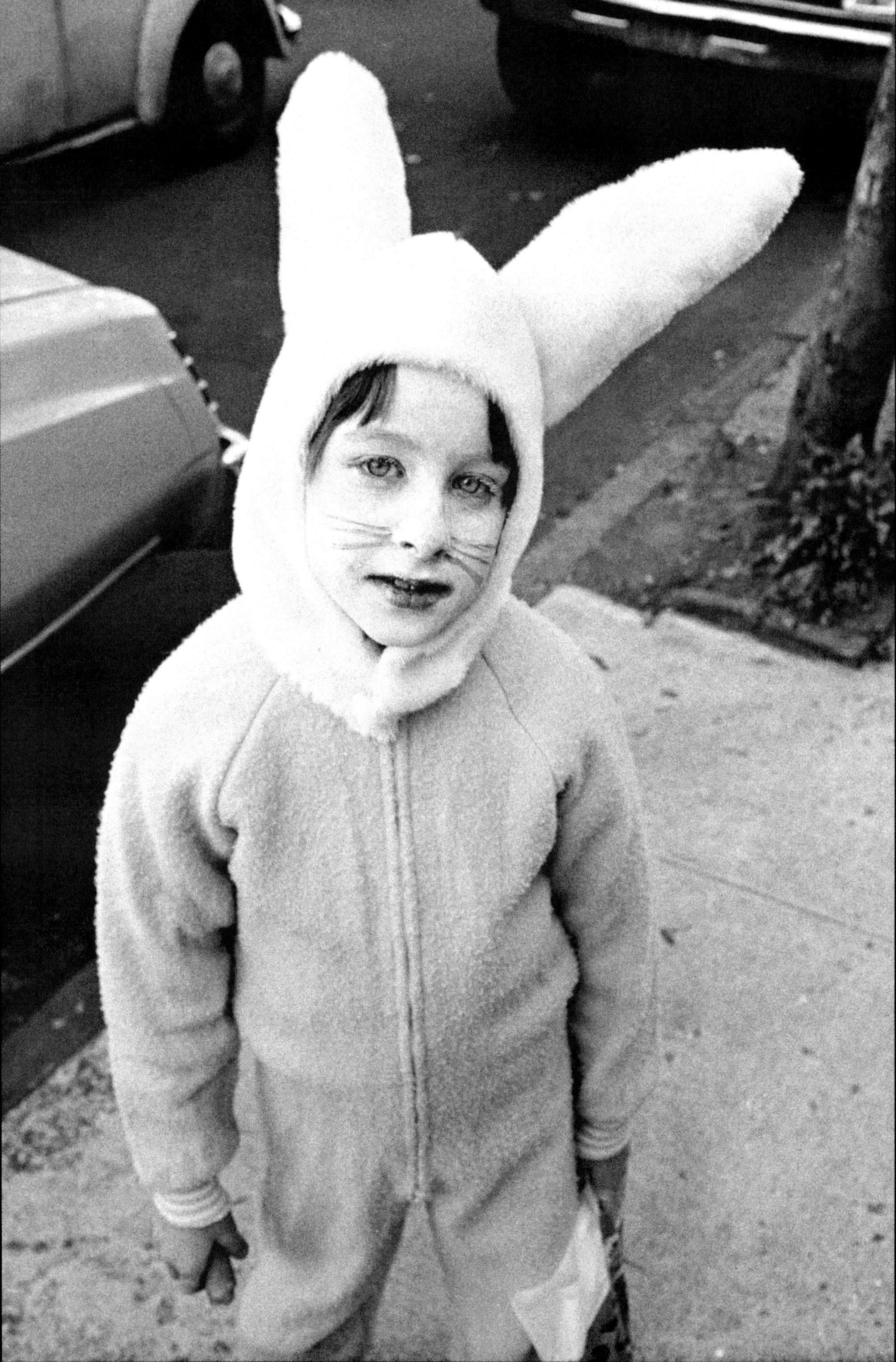

Bunny, 1980
Brooklyn.

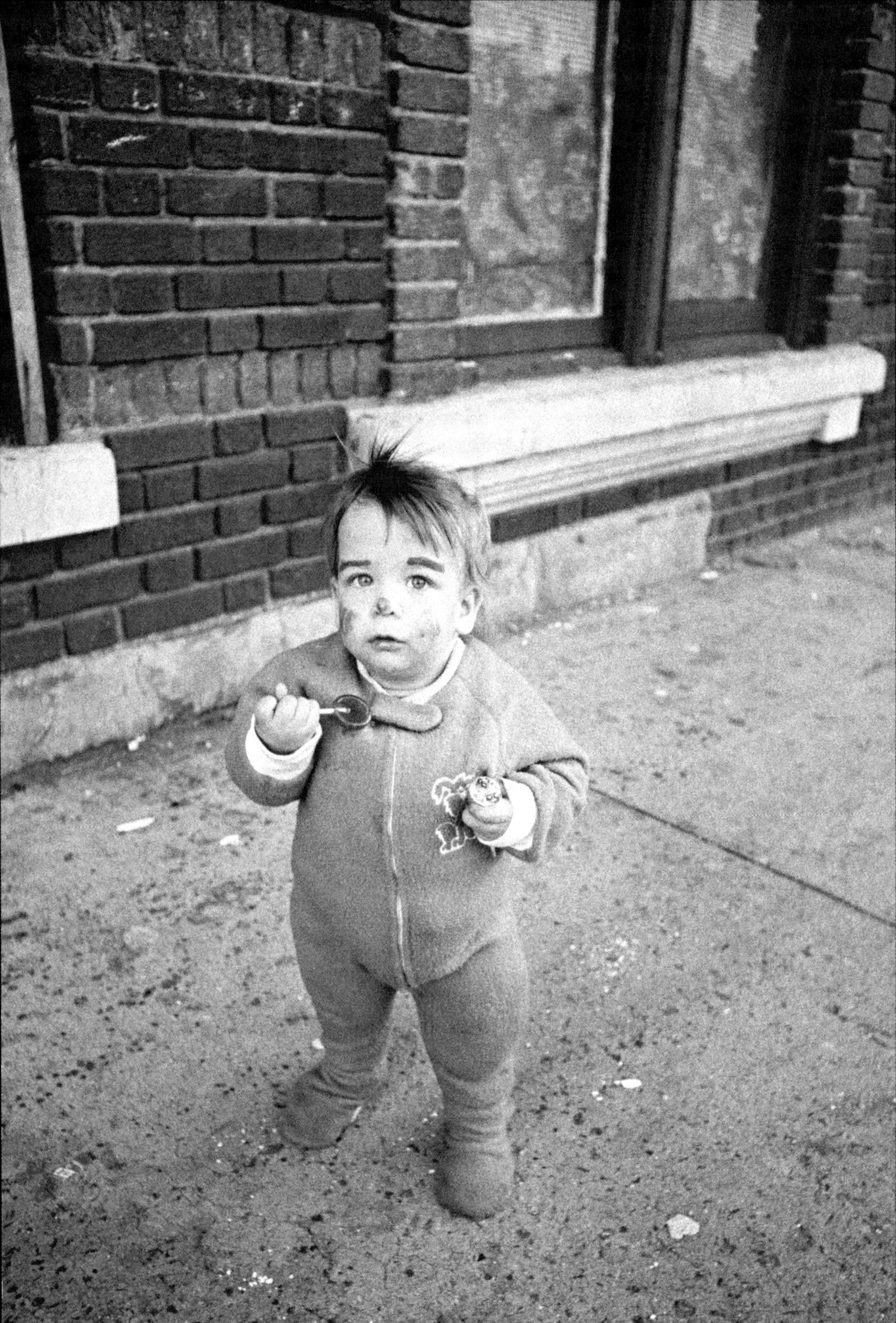

Toddler with lollipop,
1978, Brooklyn.

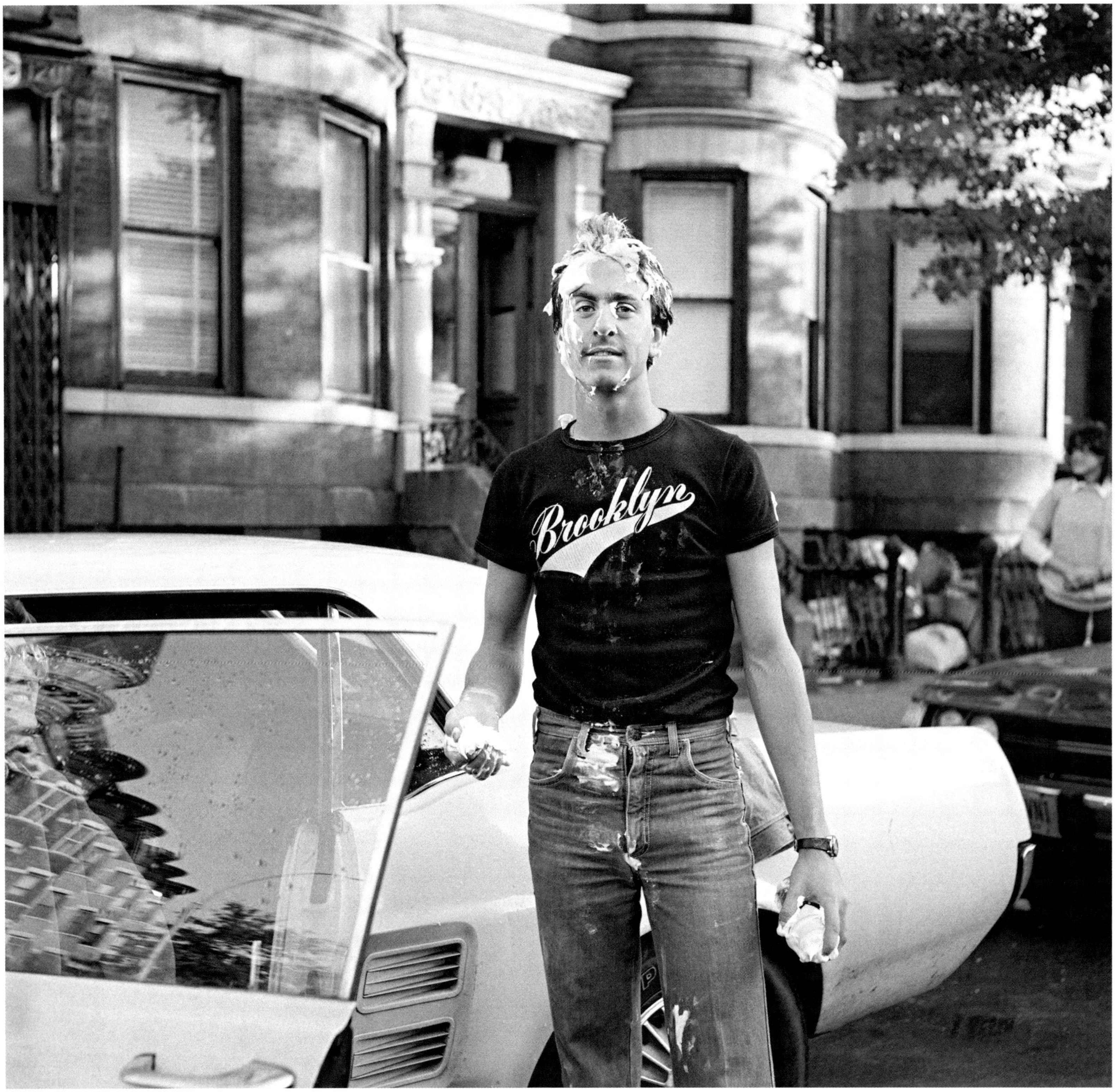

Shaving cream man and
car, 1980, Brooklyn.

Boy, Frankenstein, and Vampira, 1979, Brooklyn.

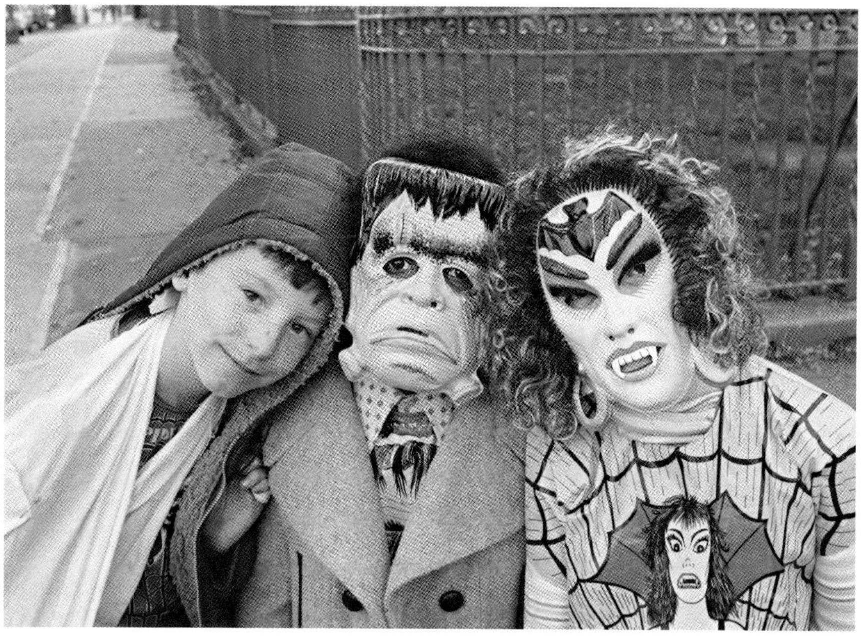

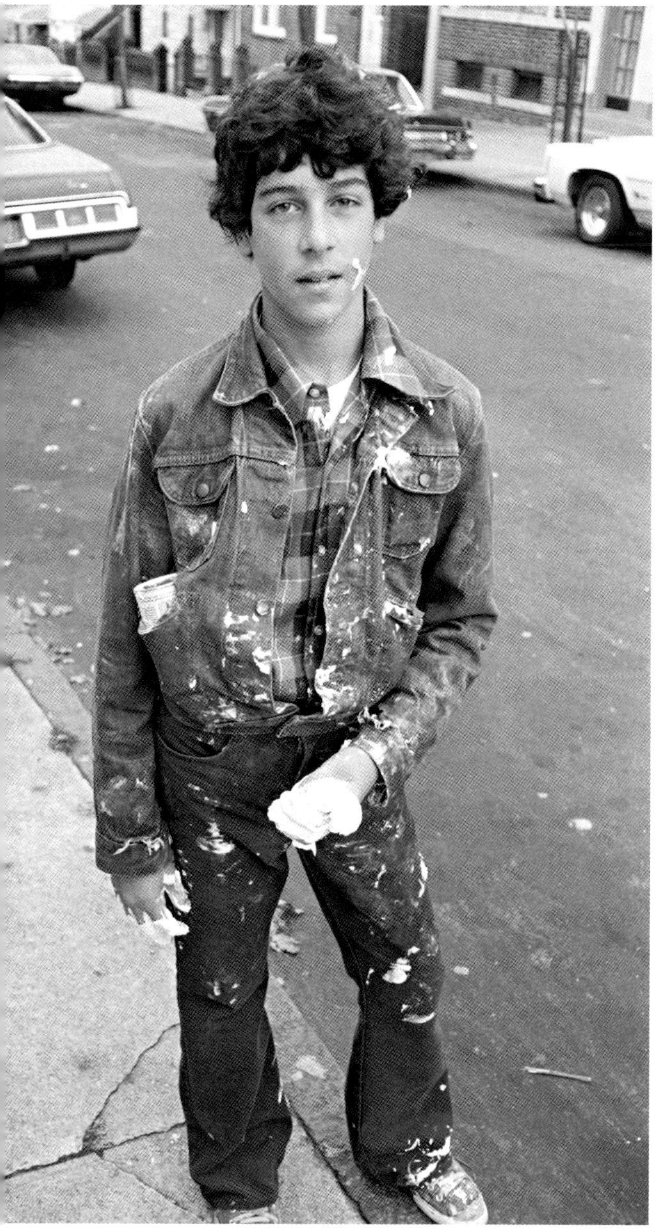

Shaving cream fighter, 1976, Brooklyn.

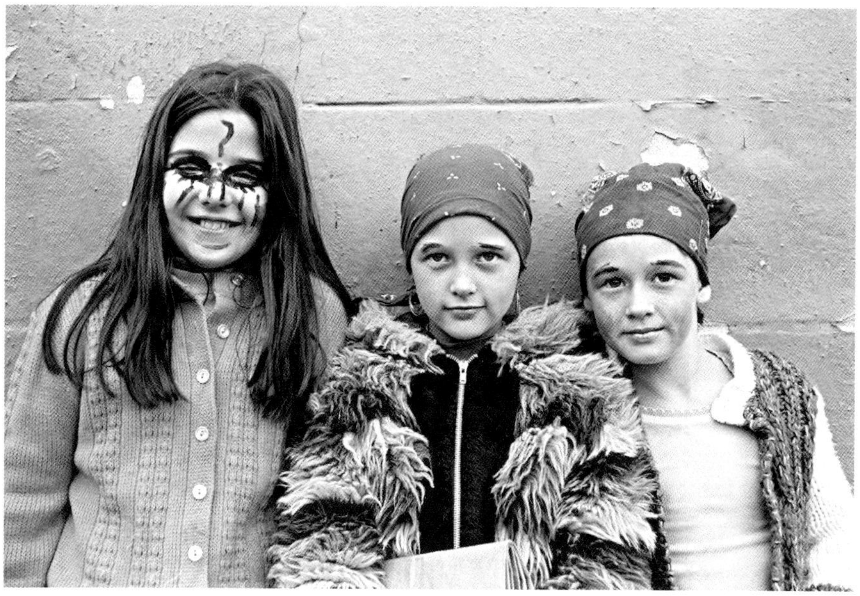

Two girls with a question, 1976, Brooklyn.

In 1978, I photographed a young girl dressed as St. Ann (below, center). When I saw her the following year, she was a shaving cream toughie (opposite, far right), who laughed when I asked if she had been St. Ann the year before.

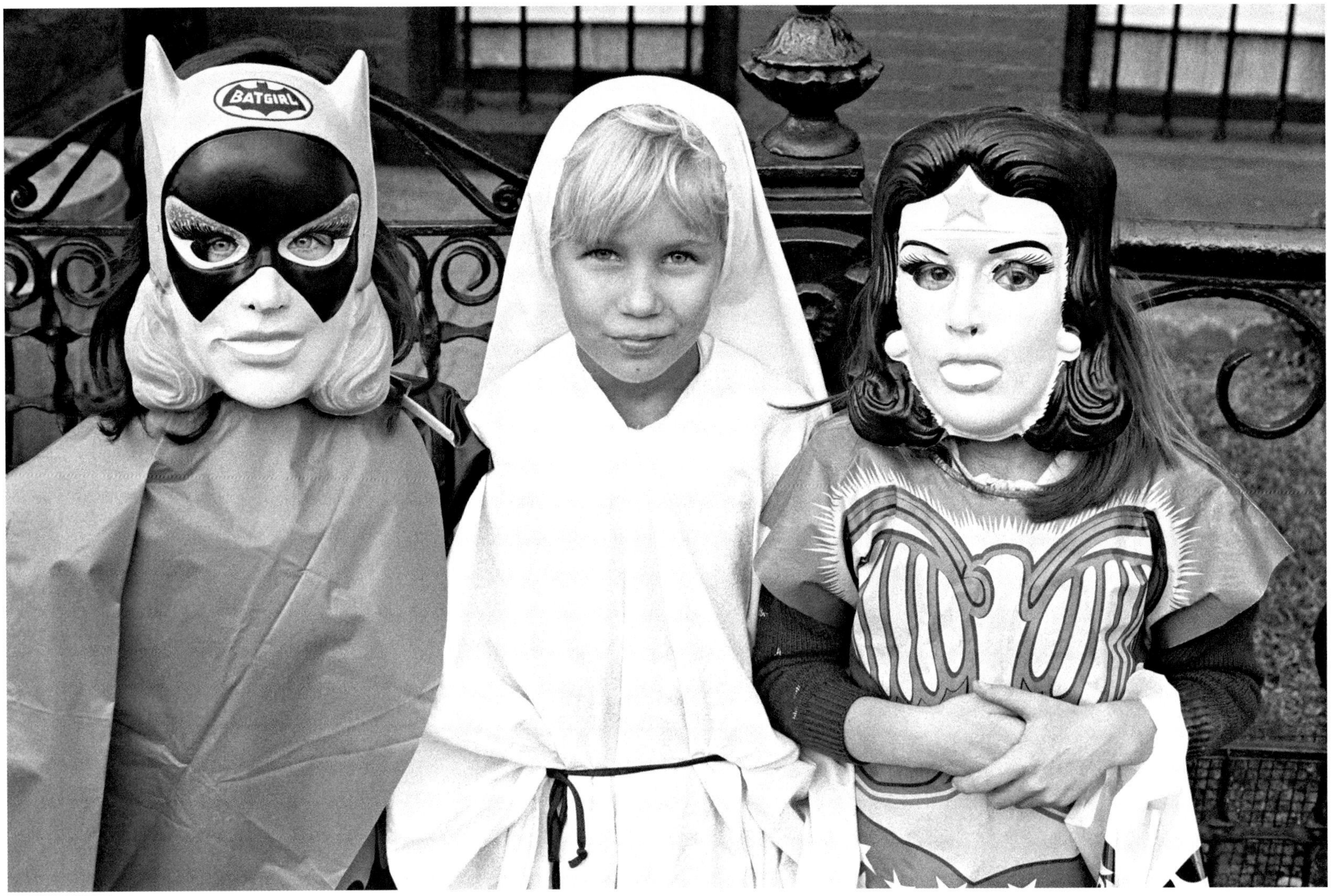

Batgirl, St. Ann, and Wonder Woman, 1978, Brooklyn.

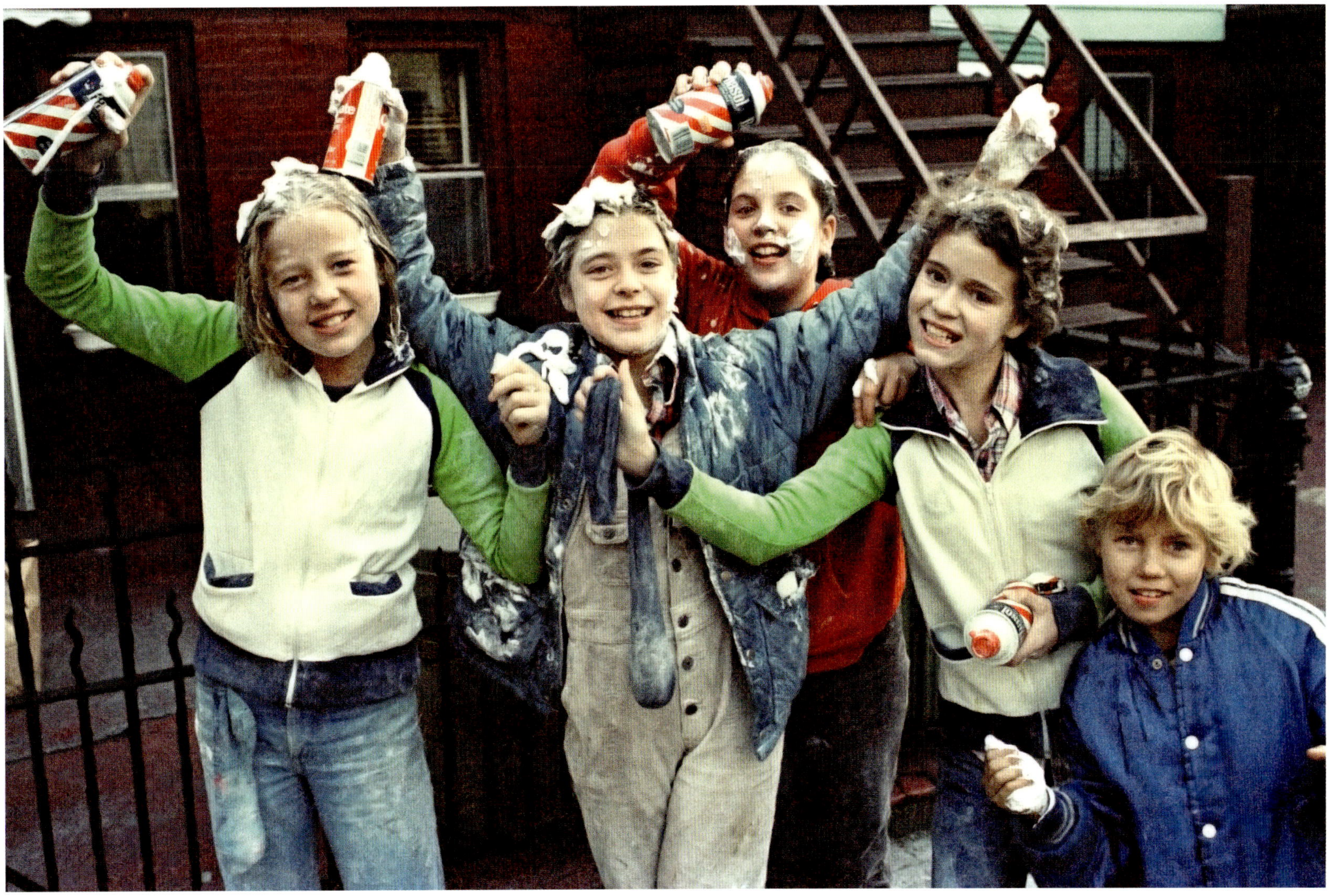

Shaving cream fighting girls, 1979, Brooklyn.

I continued to photograph on the street in my usual way from 1974 until 1980.

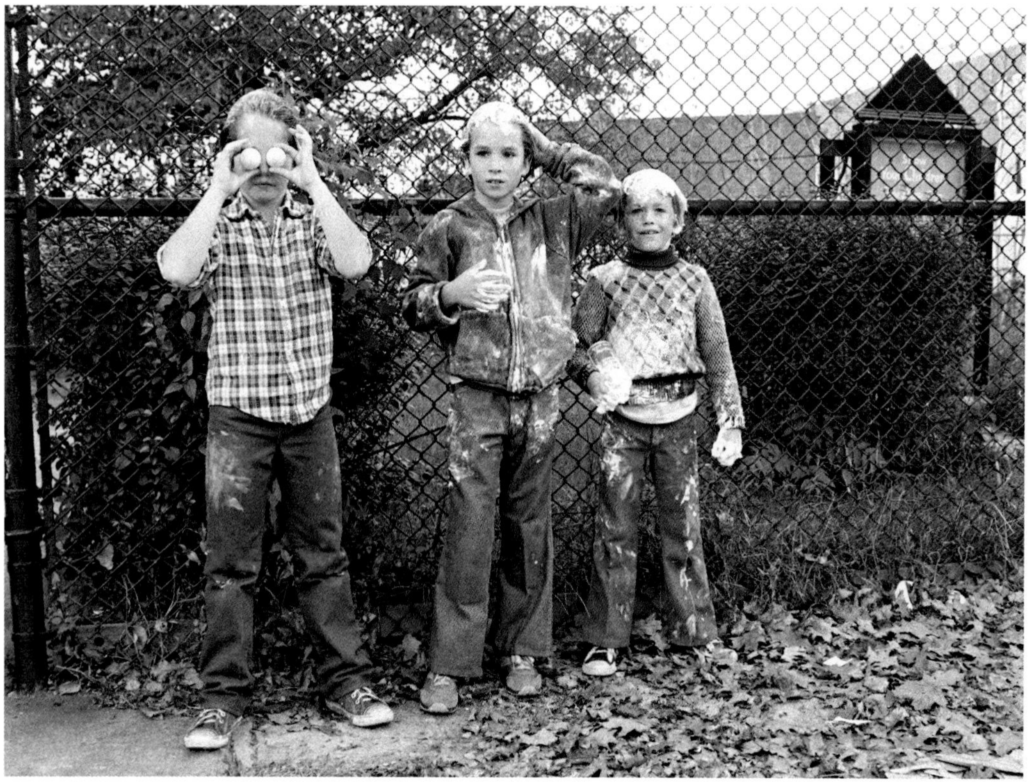

Boys with eggs and shaving cream, 1979, Brooklyn.

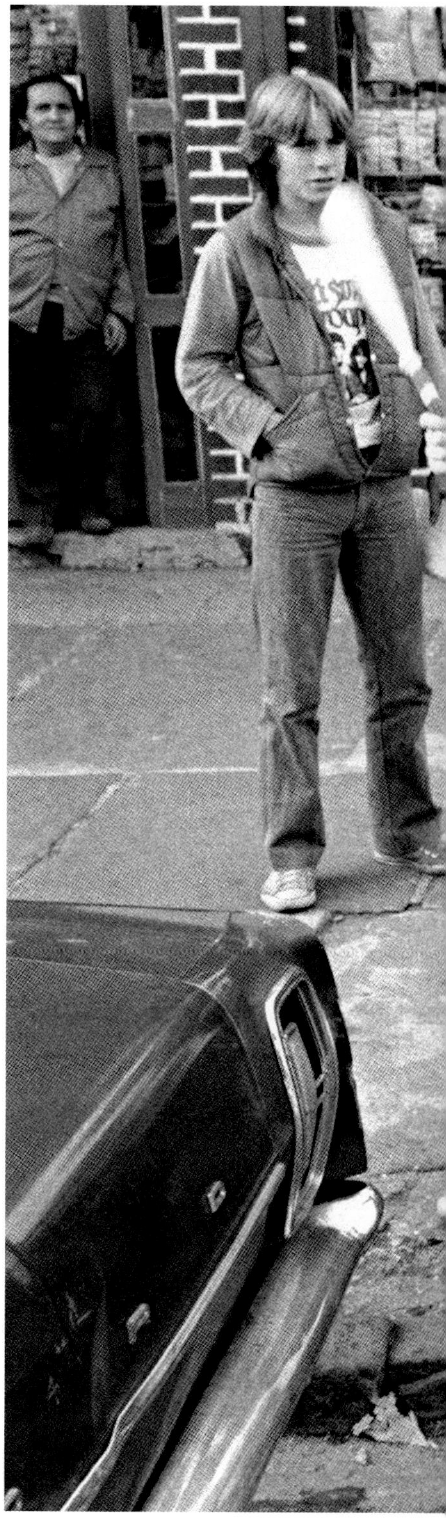

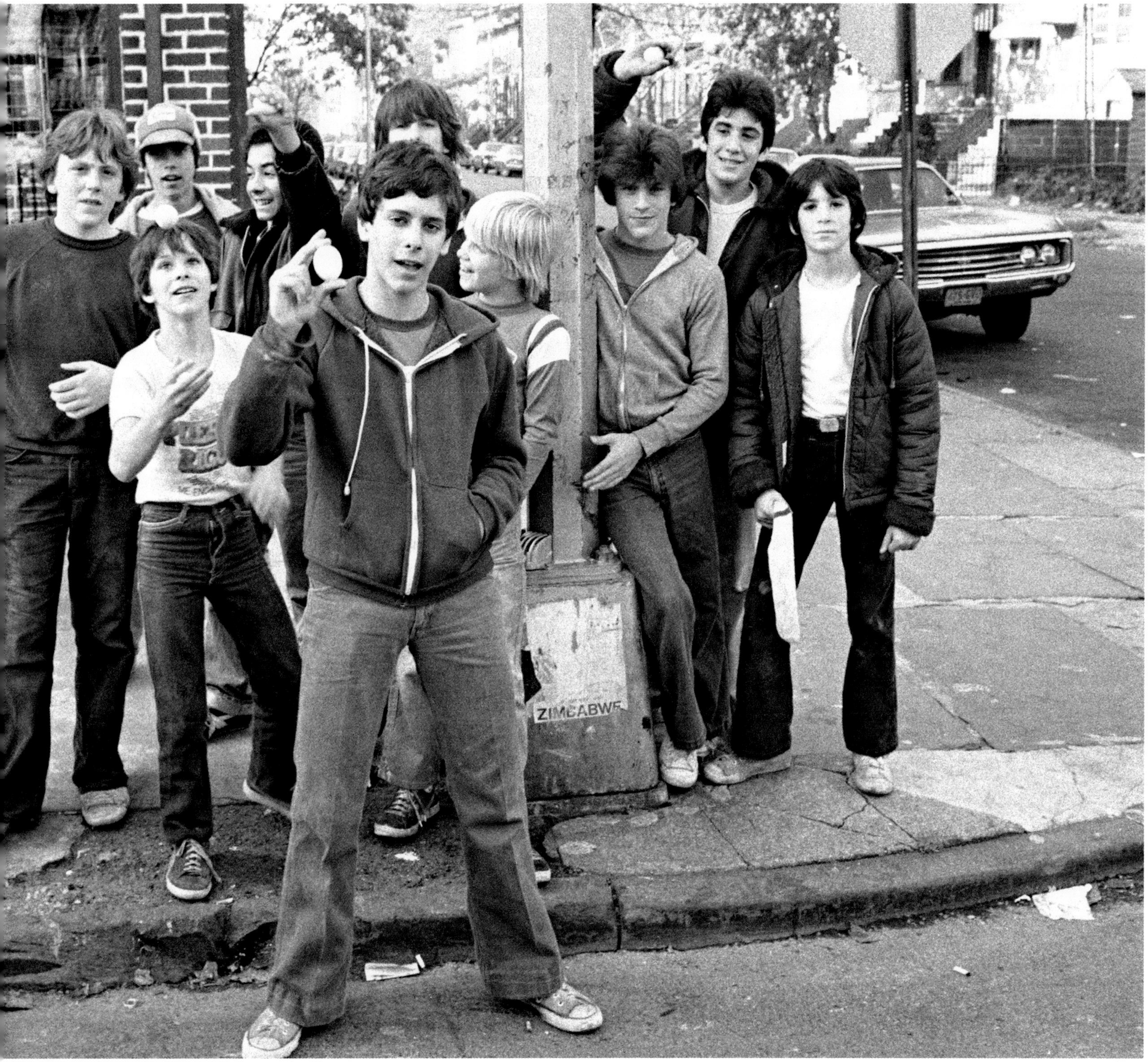

Boy holding an egg, with friends, 1979, Brooklyn.

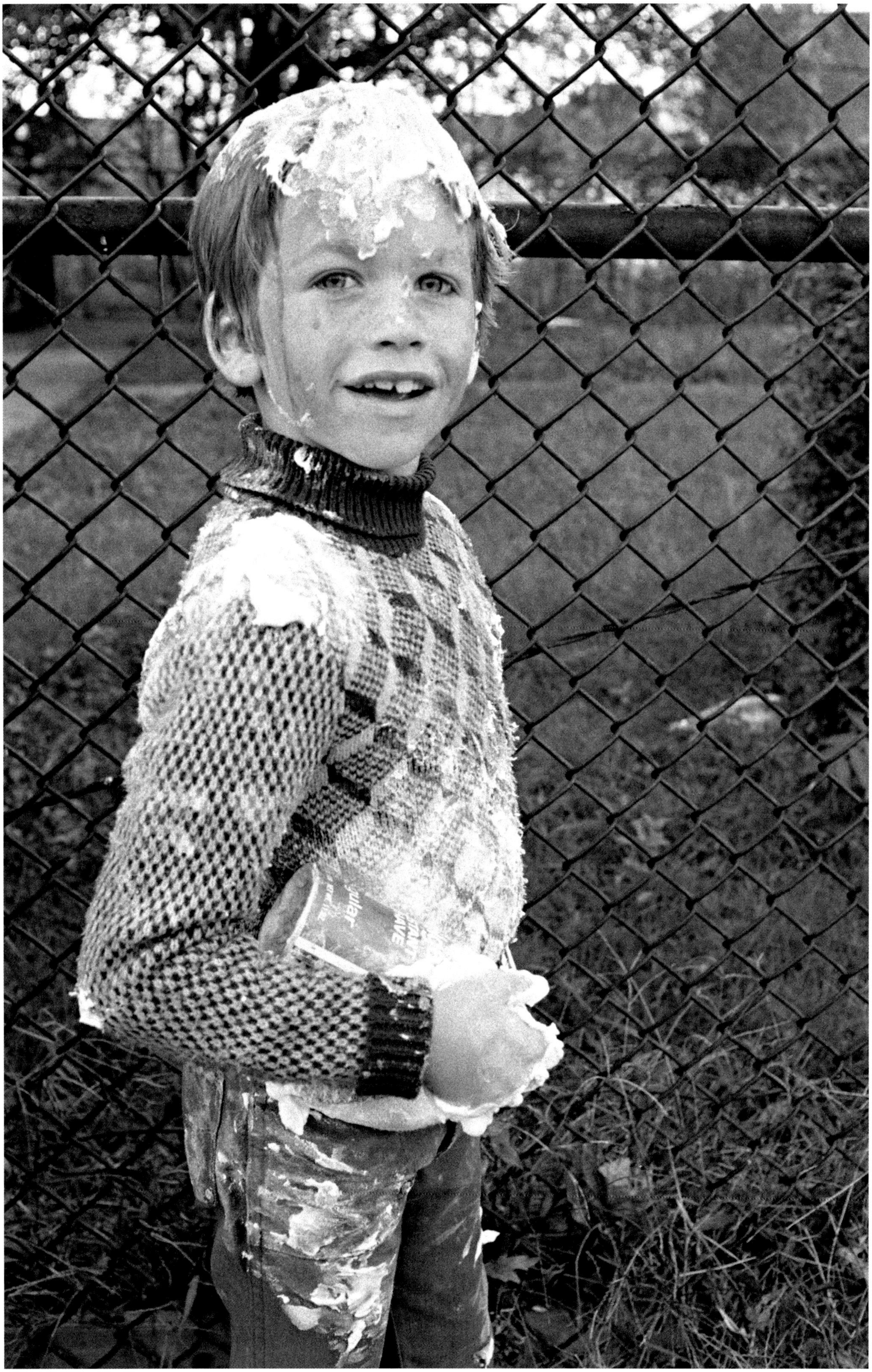

Happy boy
covered with
shaving cream,
1979, Brooklyn.

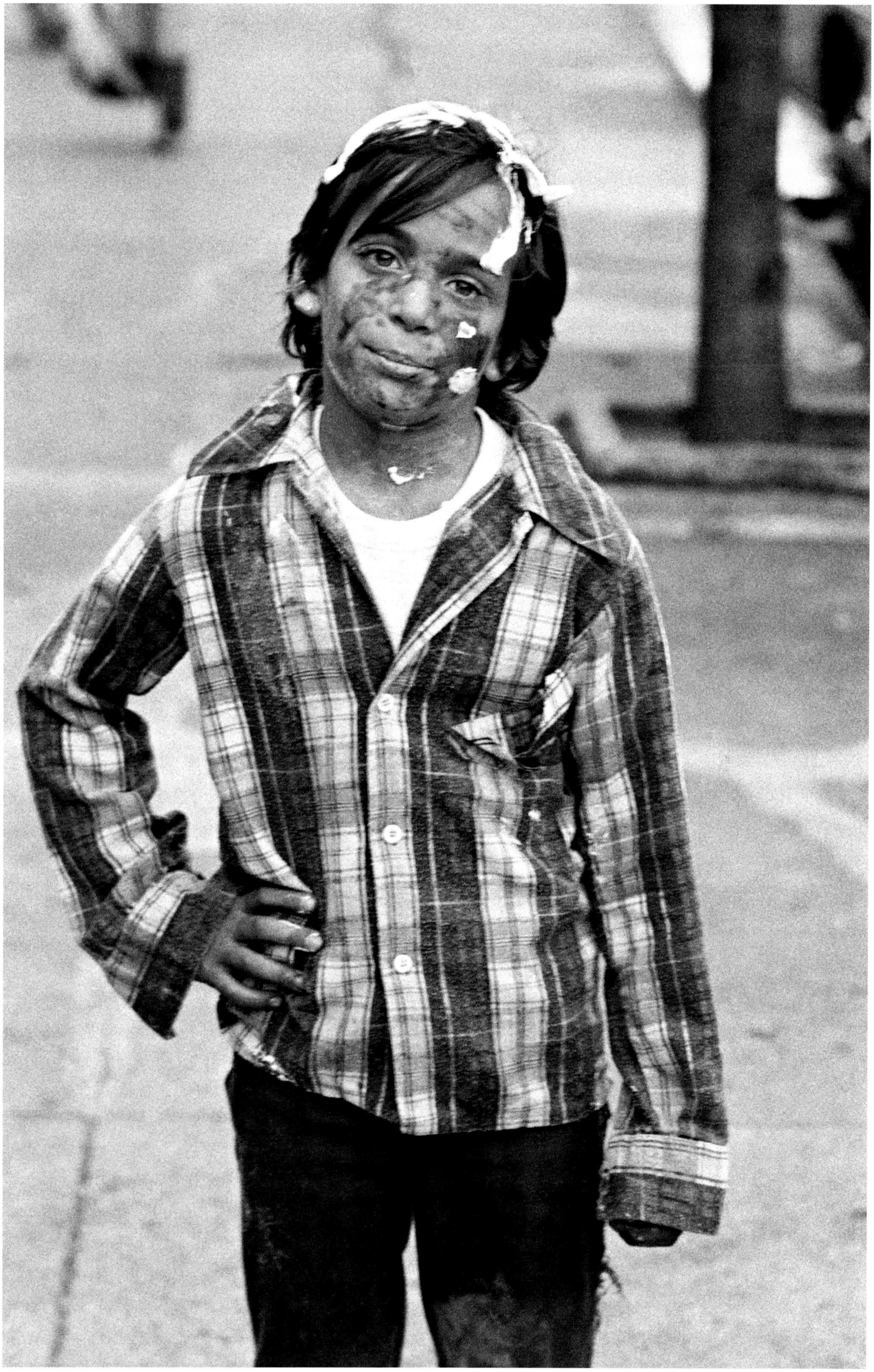

Exasperated boy covered with shaving cream, 1979, Brooklyn.

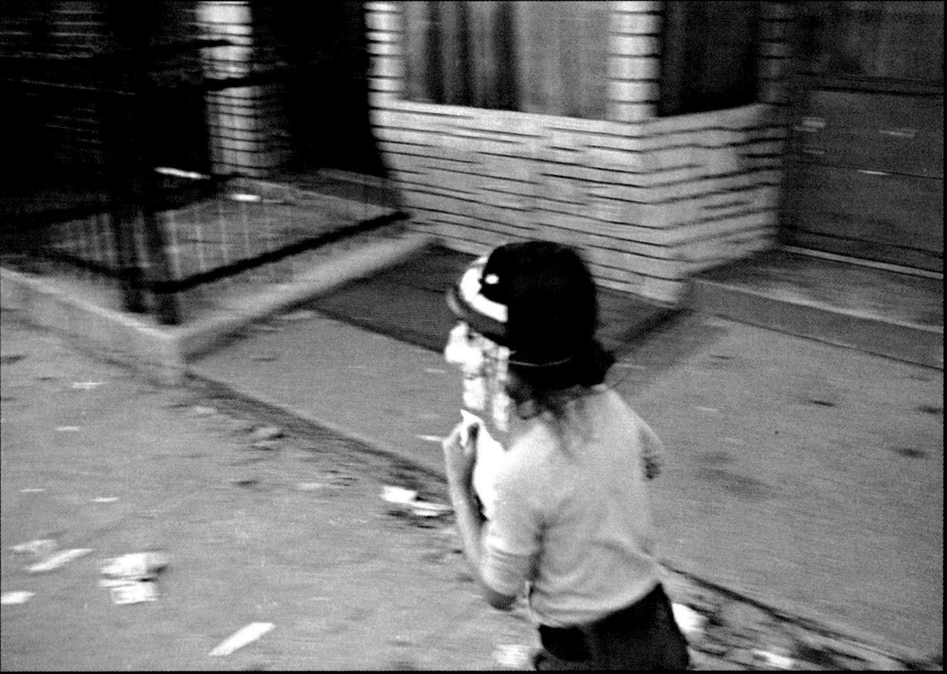

Witch on the run,
1976, Brooklyn.

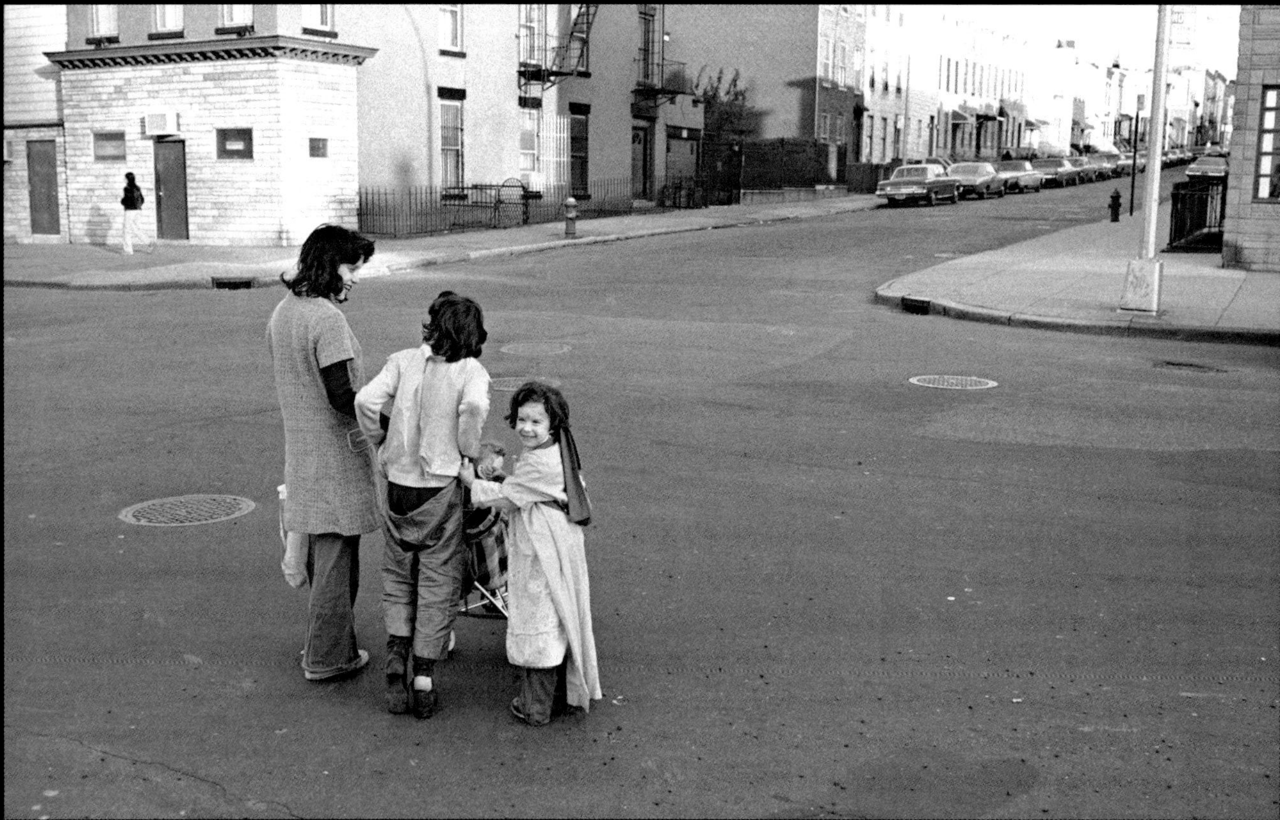

Crossing
6th Avenue,
1975, Brooklyn.

Overweight tramp, 1976, Brooklyn.

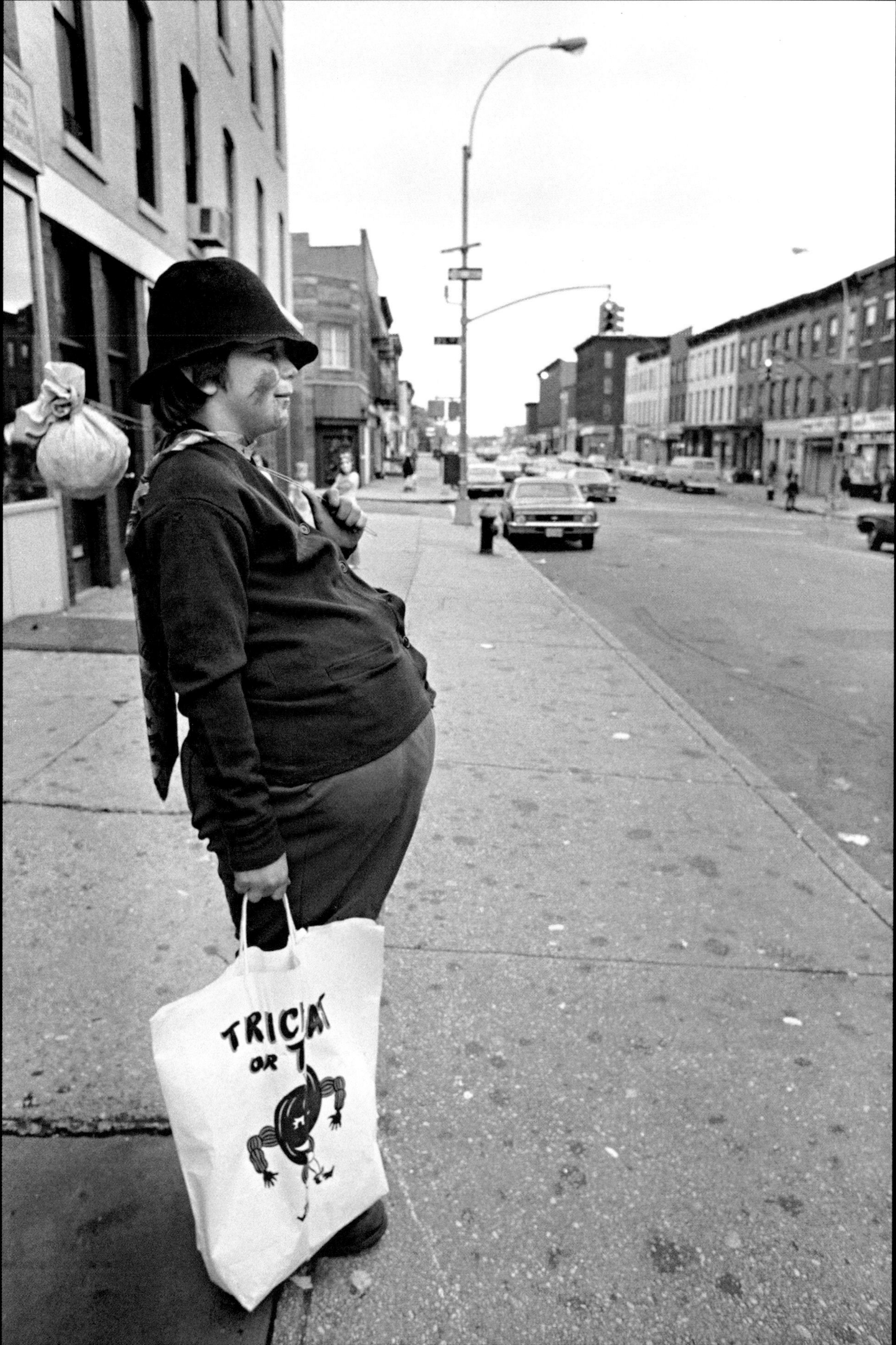

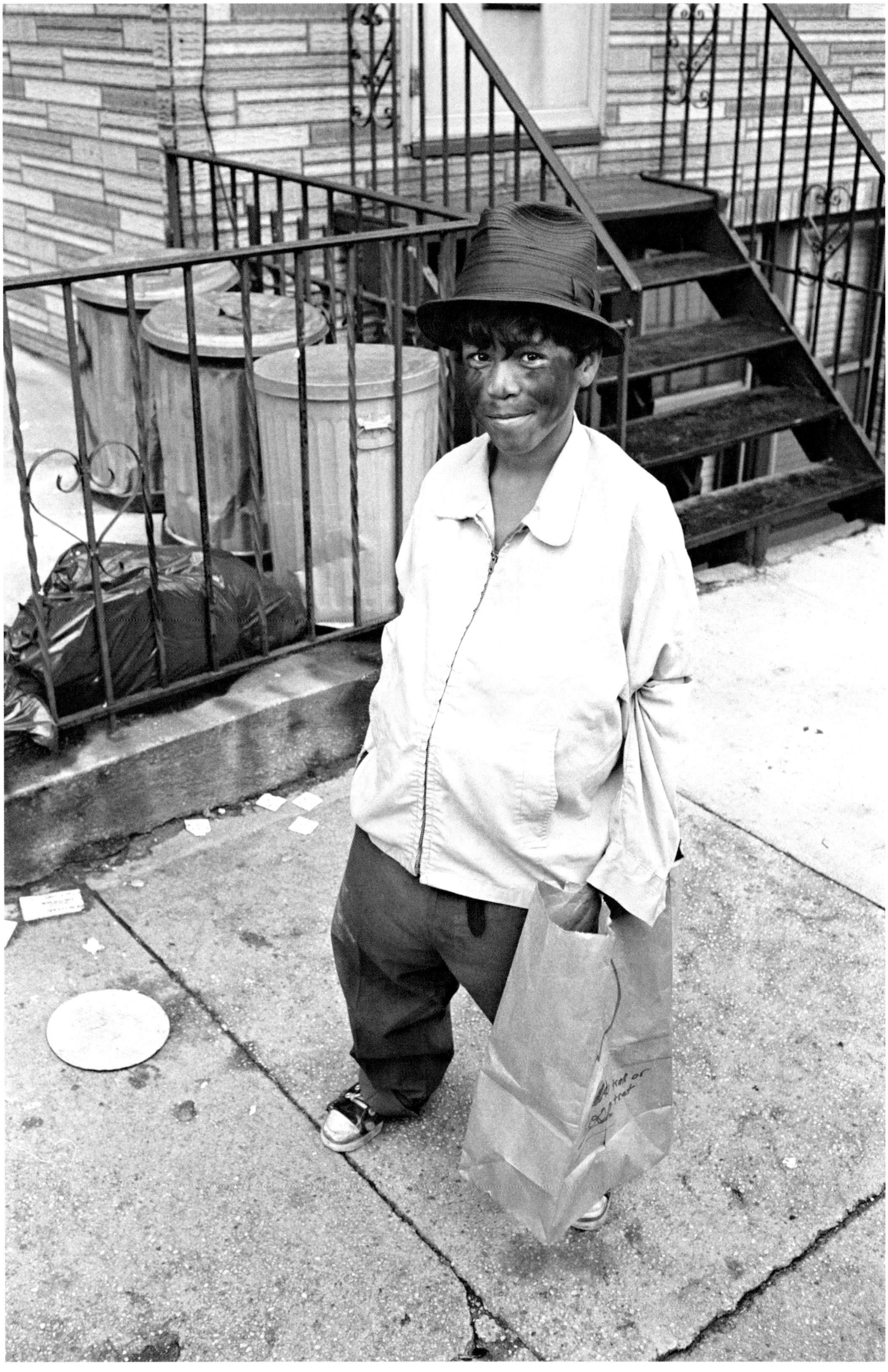

Tramp with a dirty face, 1976, Brooklyn.

Minimalist vampire and friend, 1980, Brooklyn.

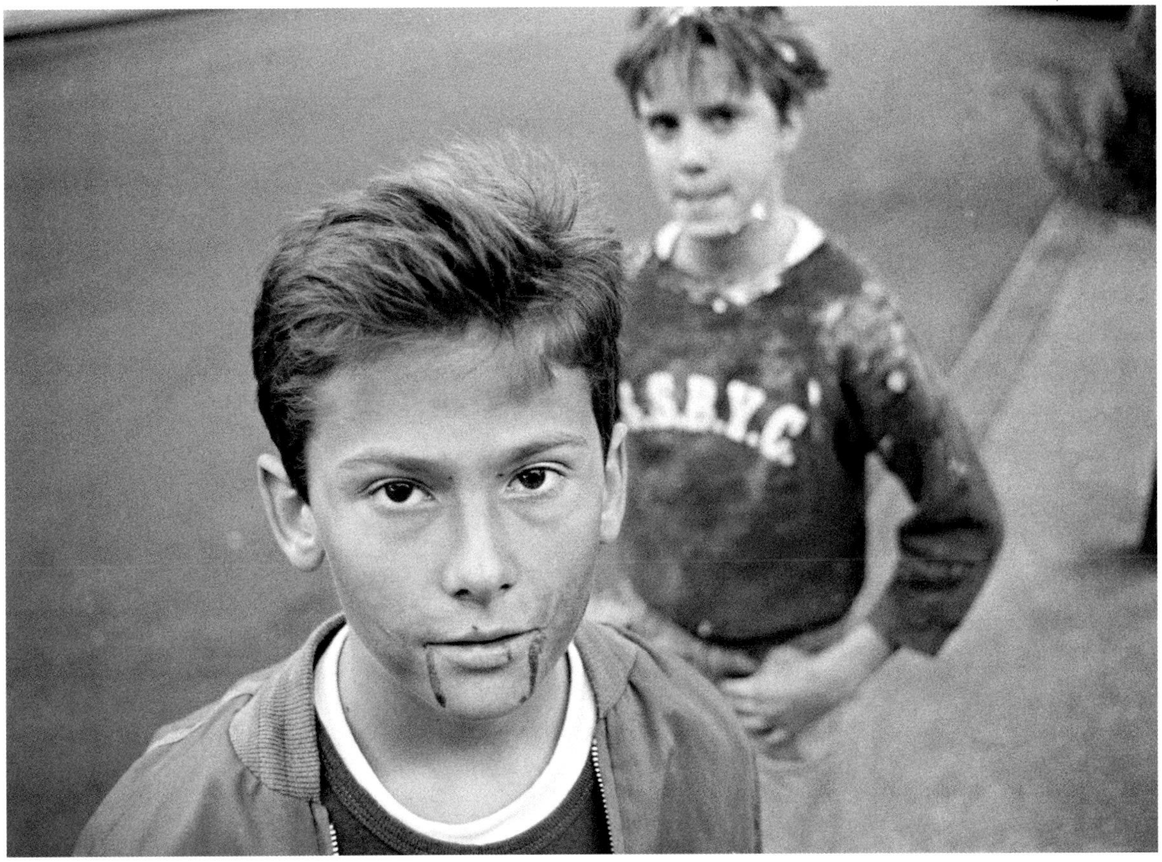

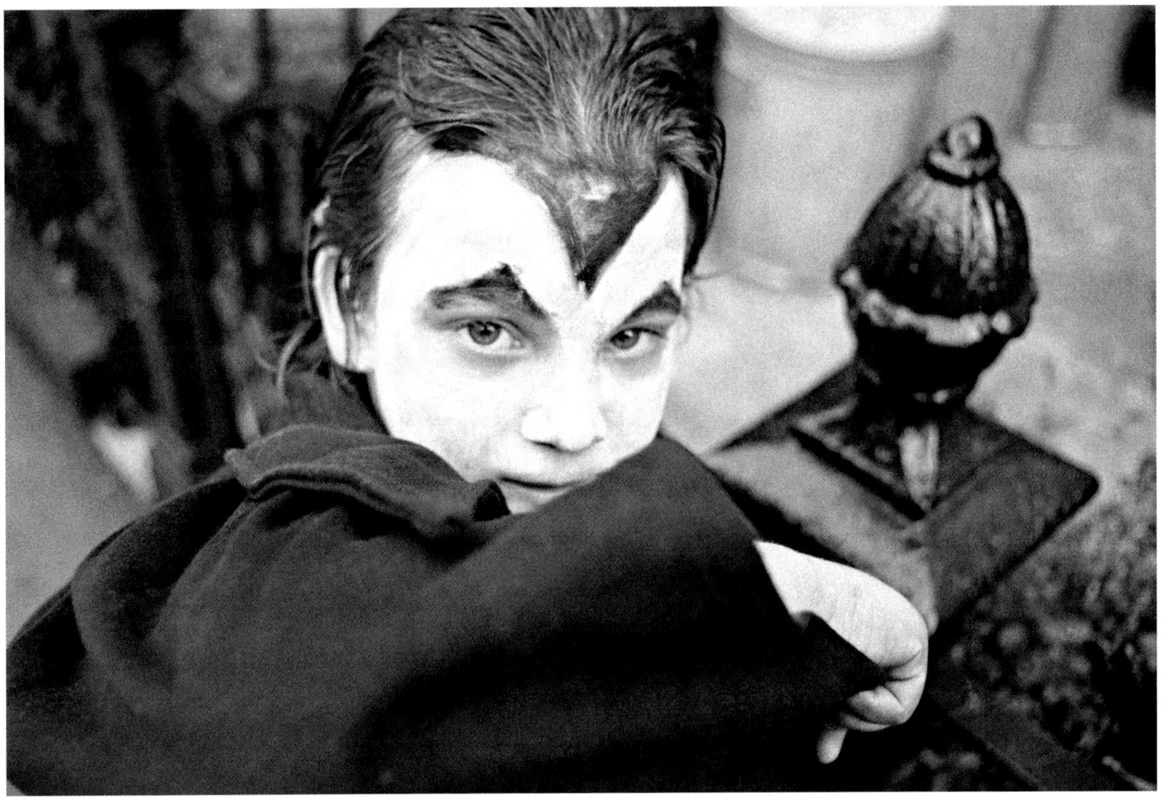

Classic caped vampire, 1980, Brooklyn.

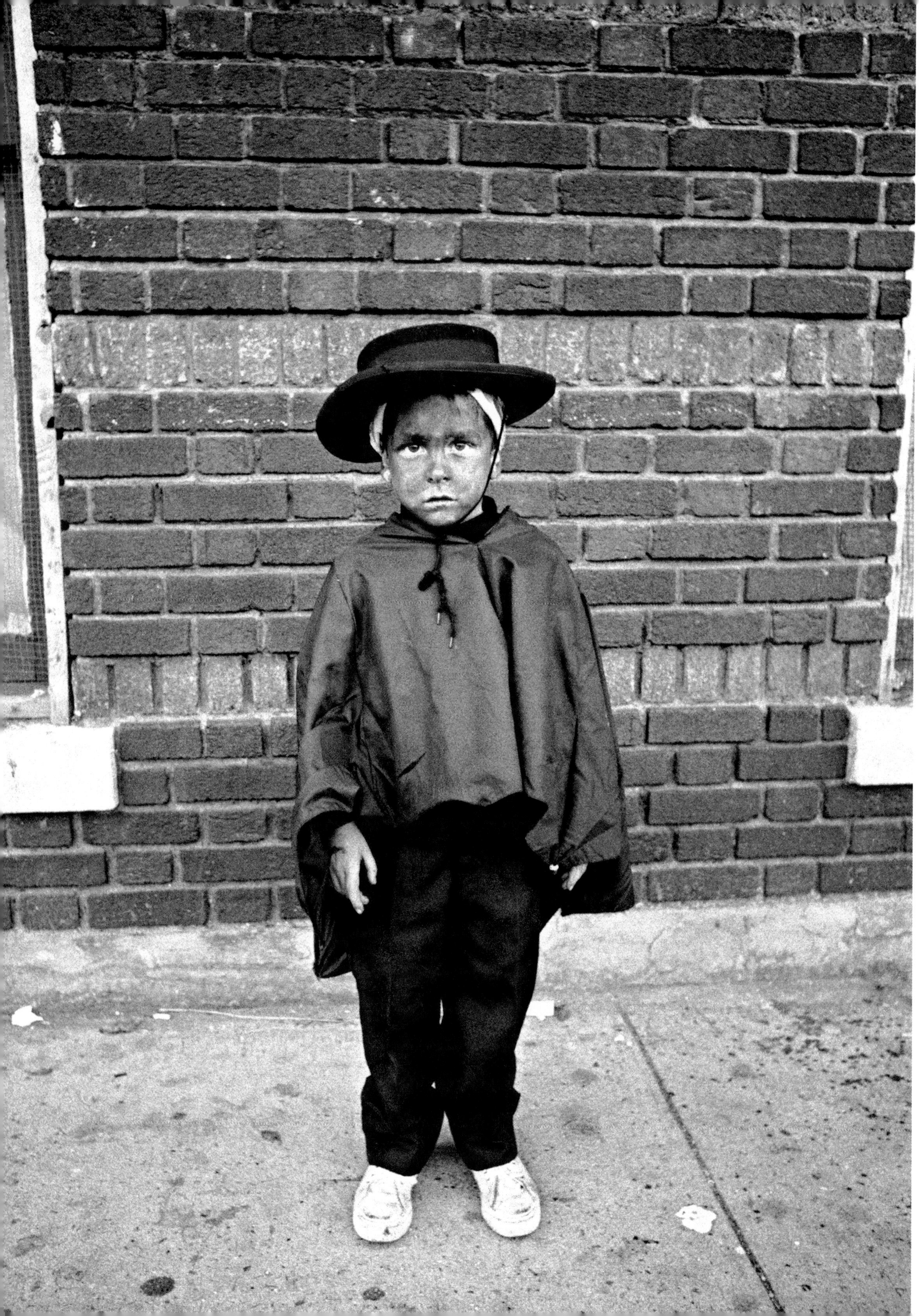

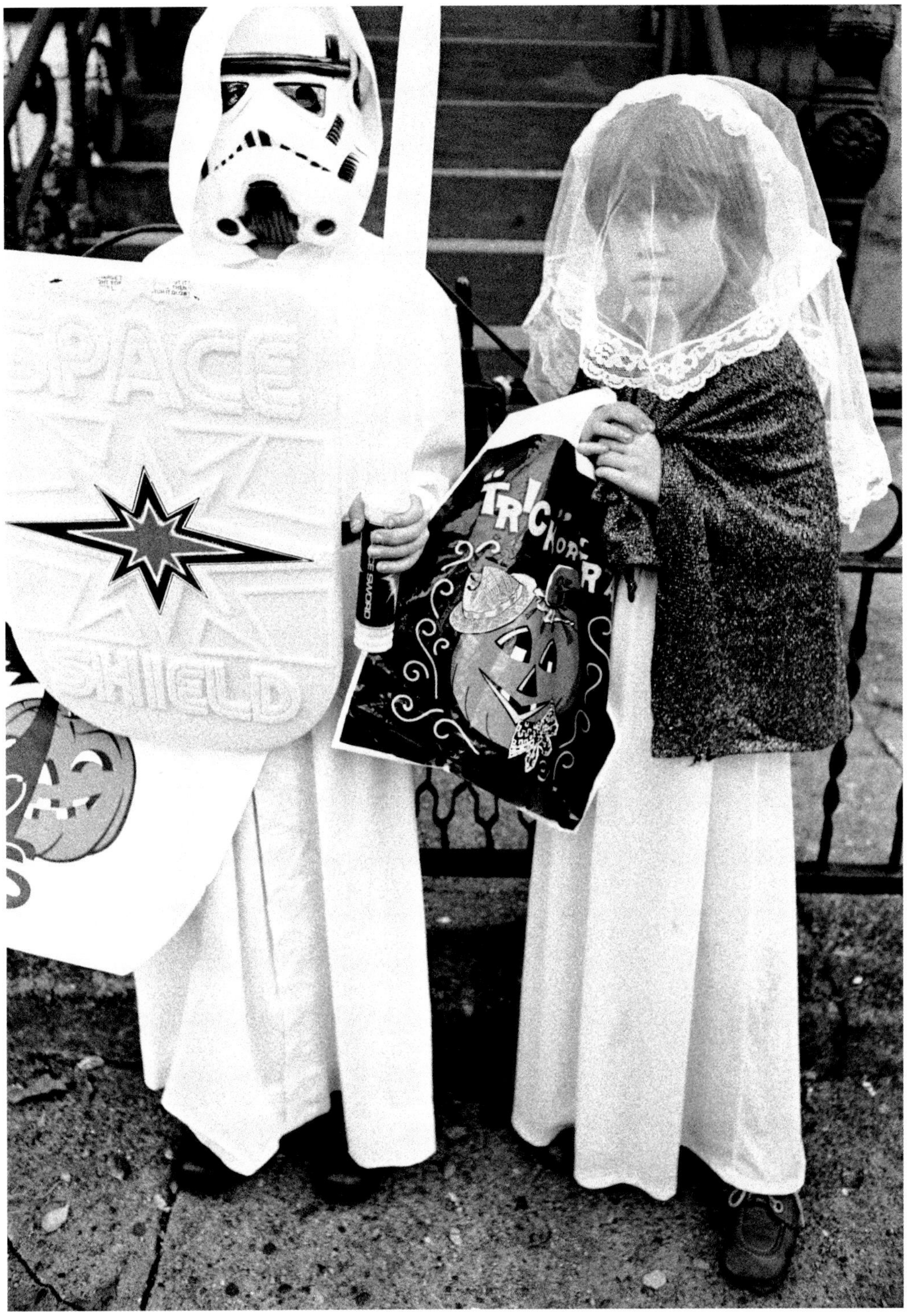

Above: Stormtrooper and bride, 1978, Brooklyn.

Opposite: Zorro, 1978, Brooklyn.

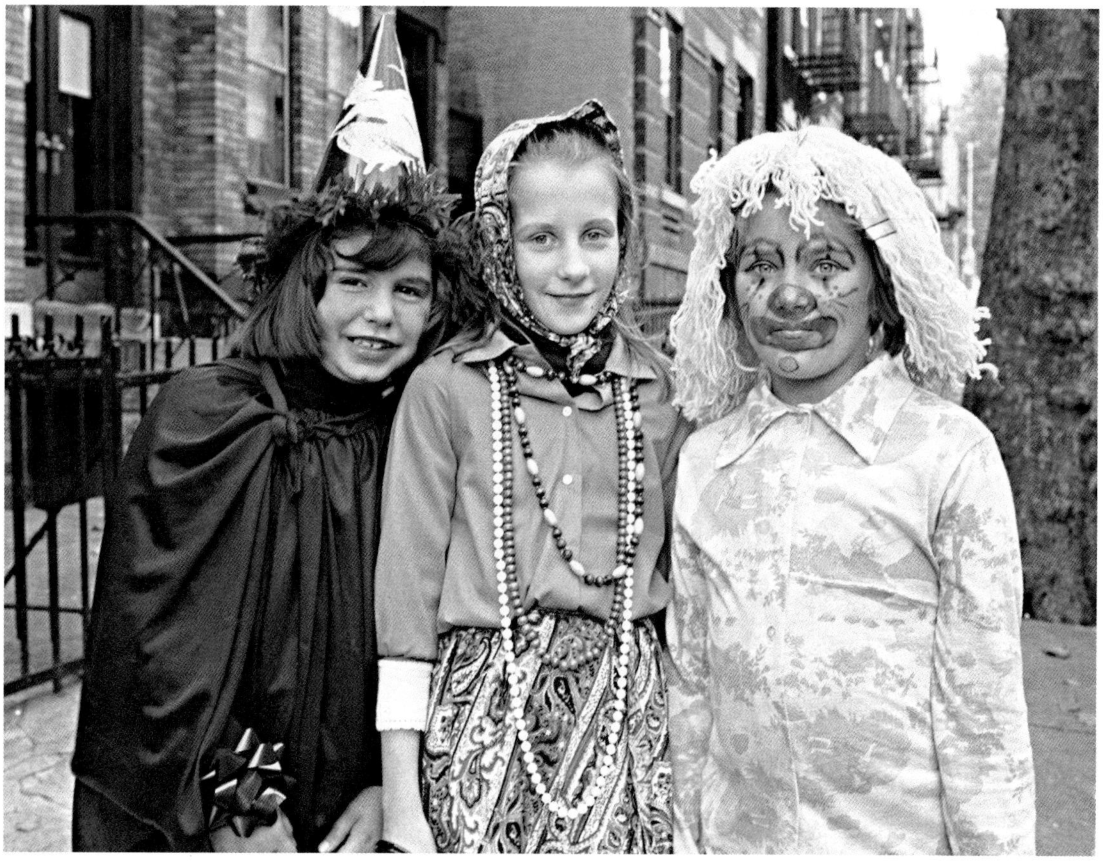

Three costumed girls, 1976, Brooklyn.

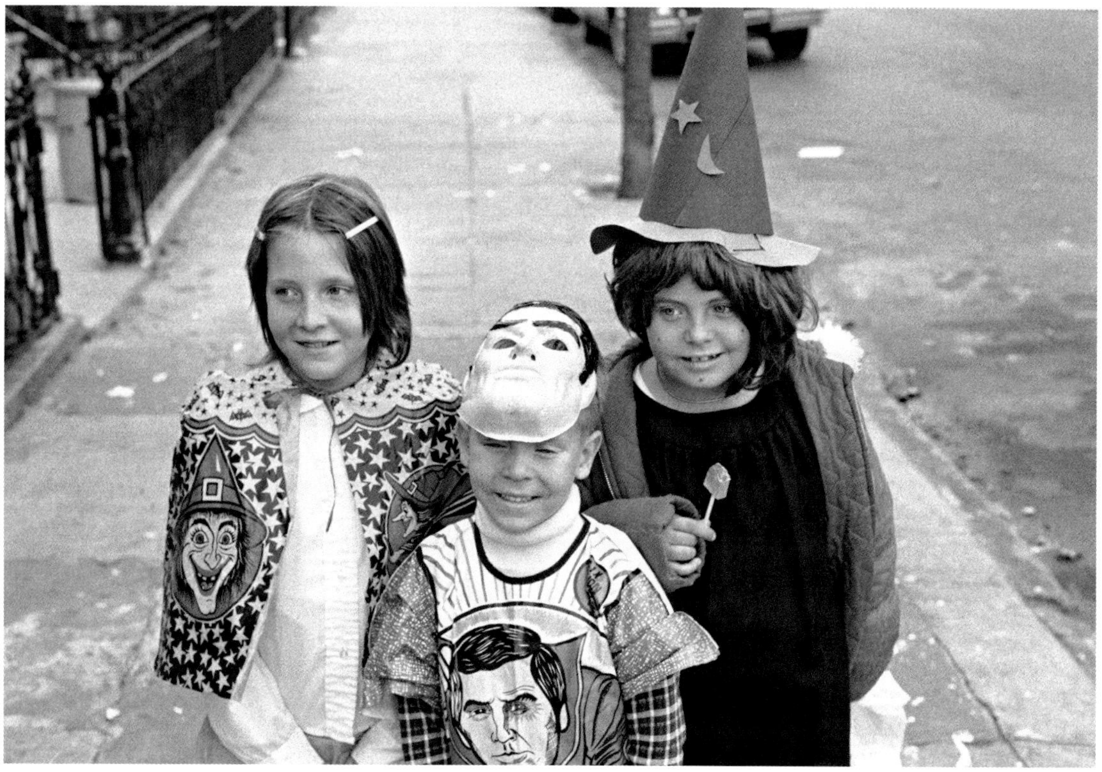

Two witches and the Six Million Dollar Man, 1978, Brooklyn.

Witch in a long black cape, 1976, Brooklyn.

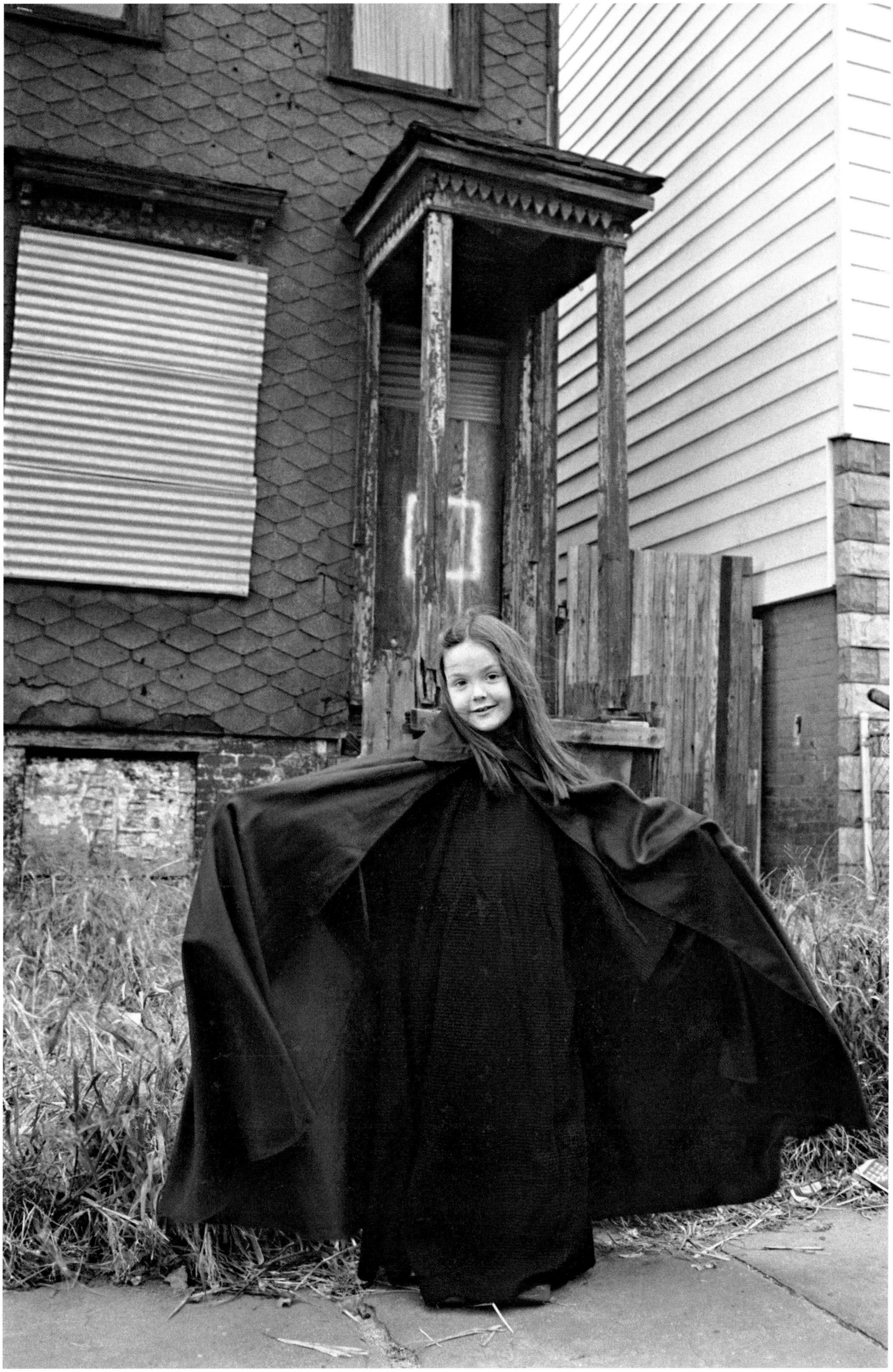

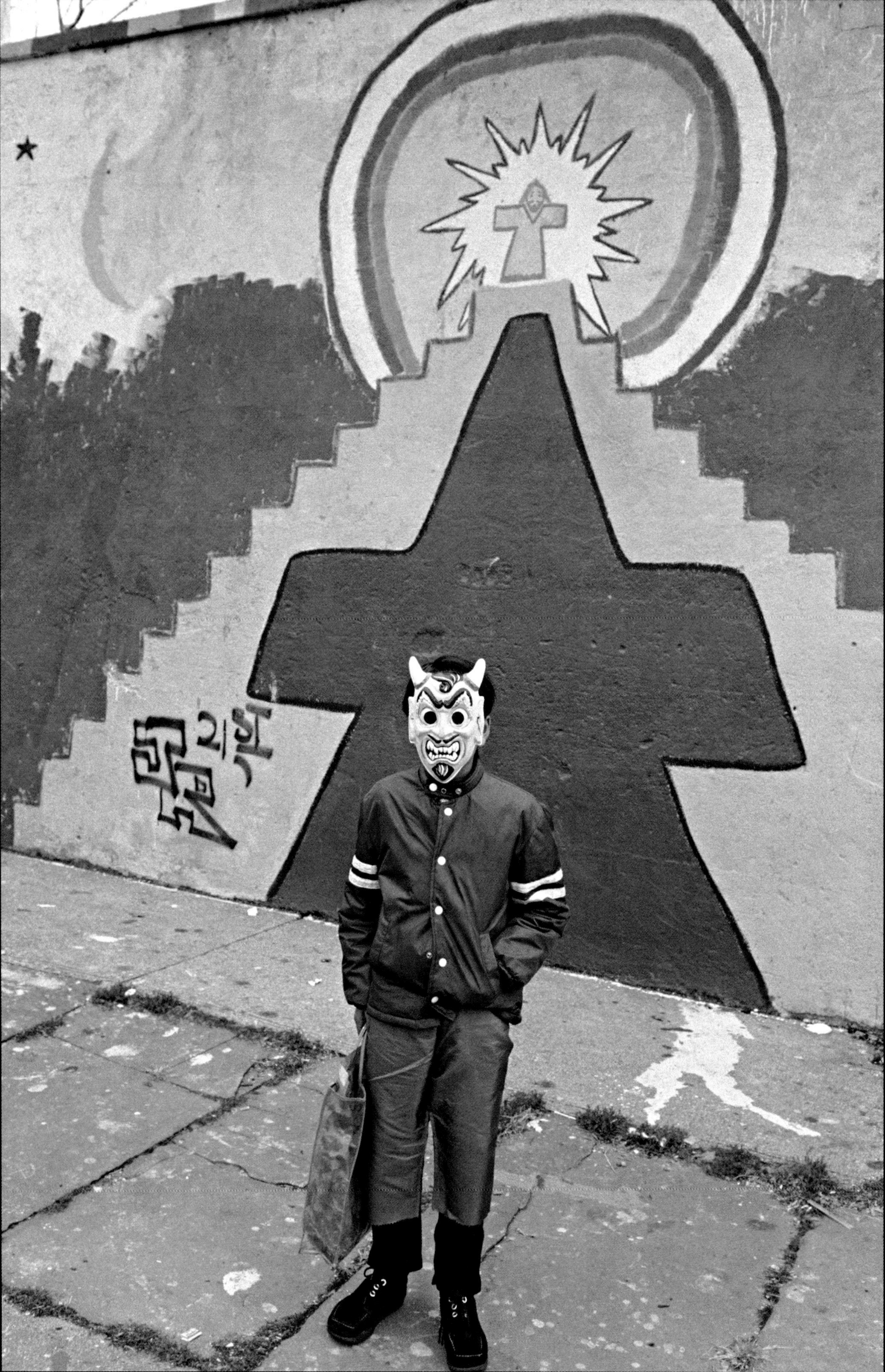

Boy in a devil mask, 1976, Brooklyn.

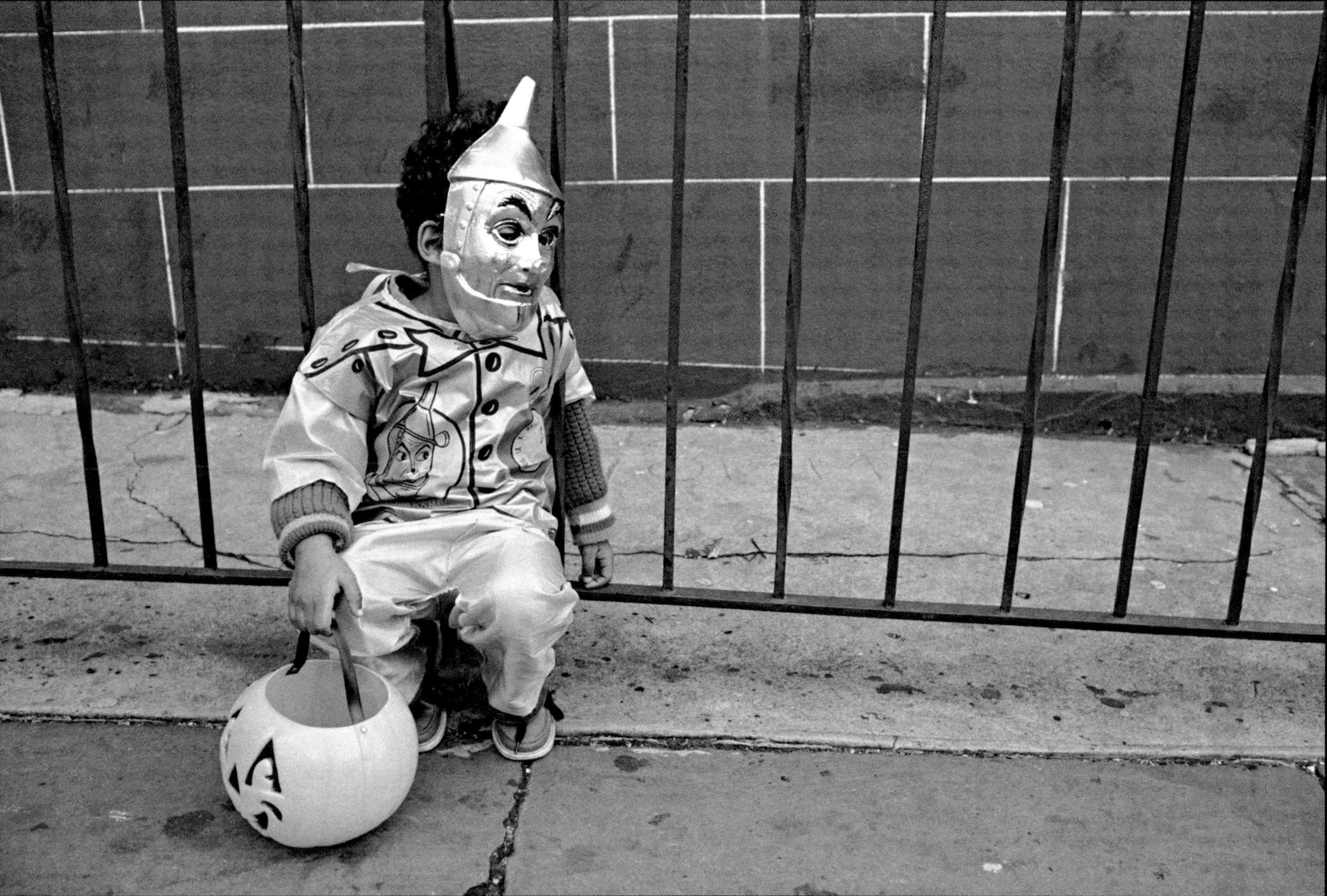

The Tin Man,
1976, Brooklyn.

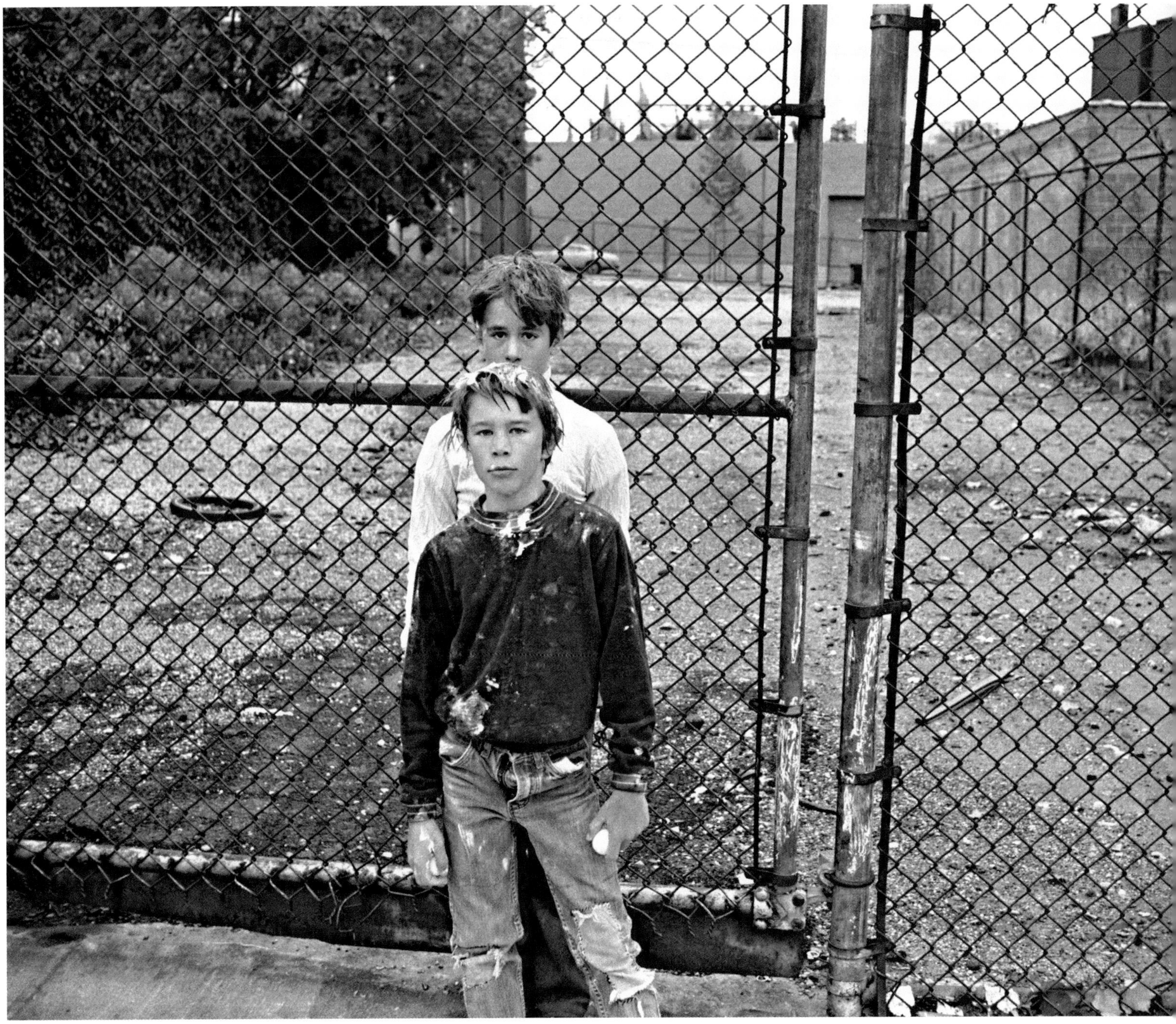

Shaving cream fighters
with eggs, 1976, Brooklyn.

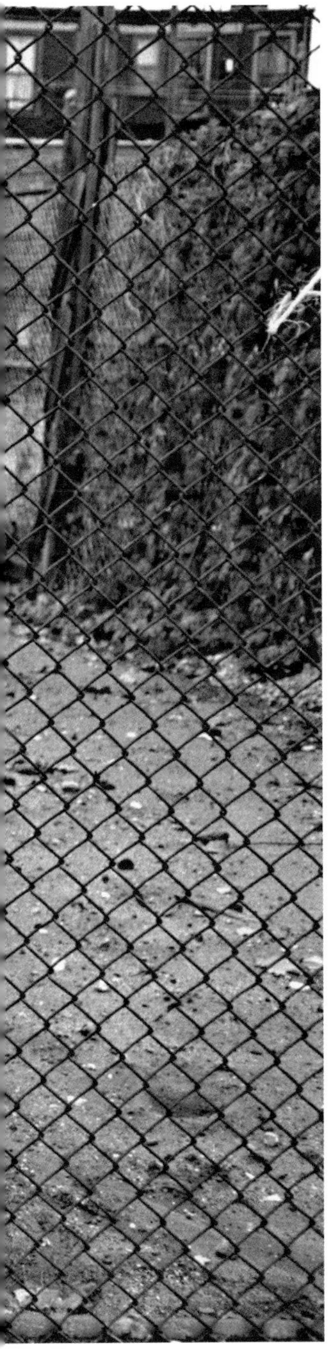

Girl with aluminum foil wings, 1977, Brooklyn.

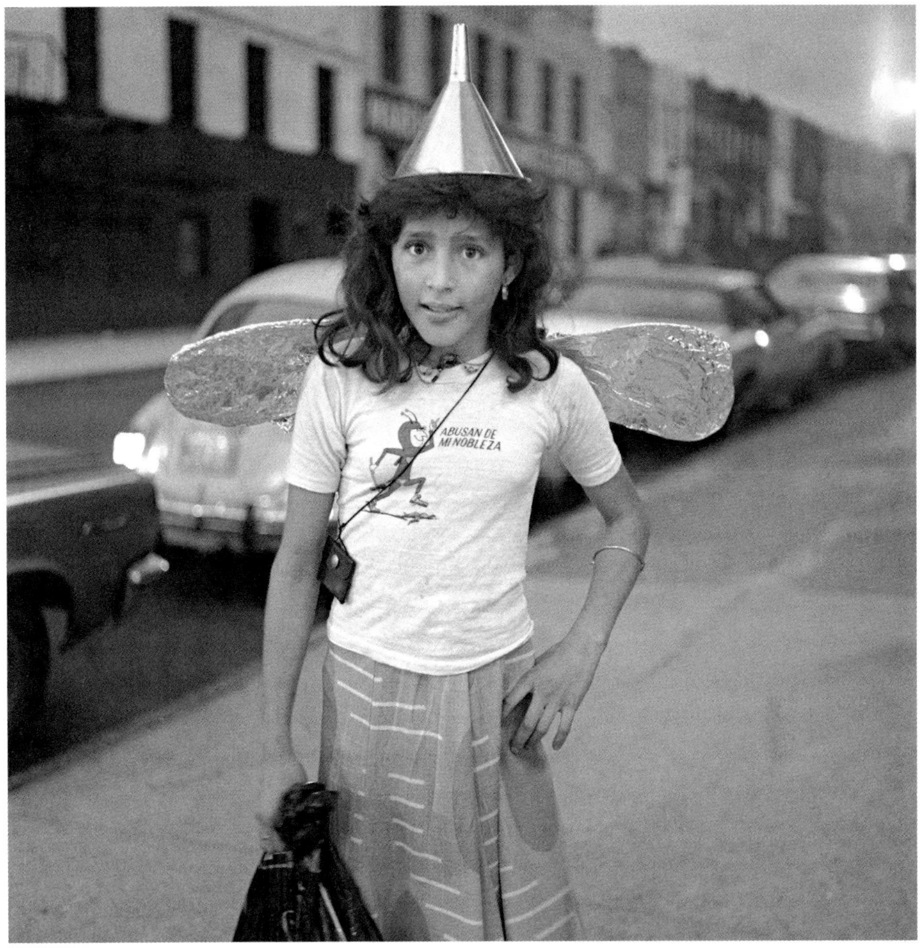

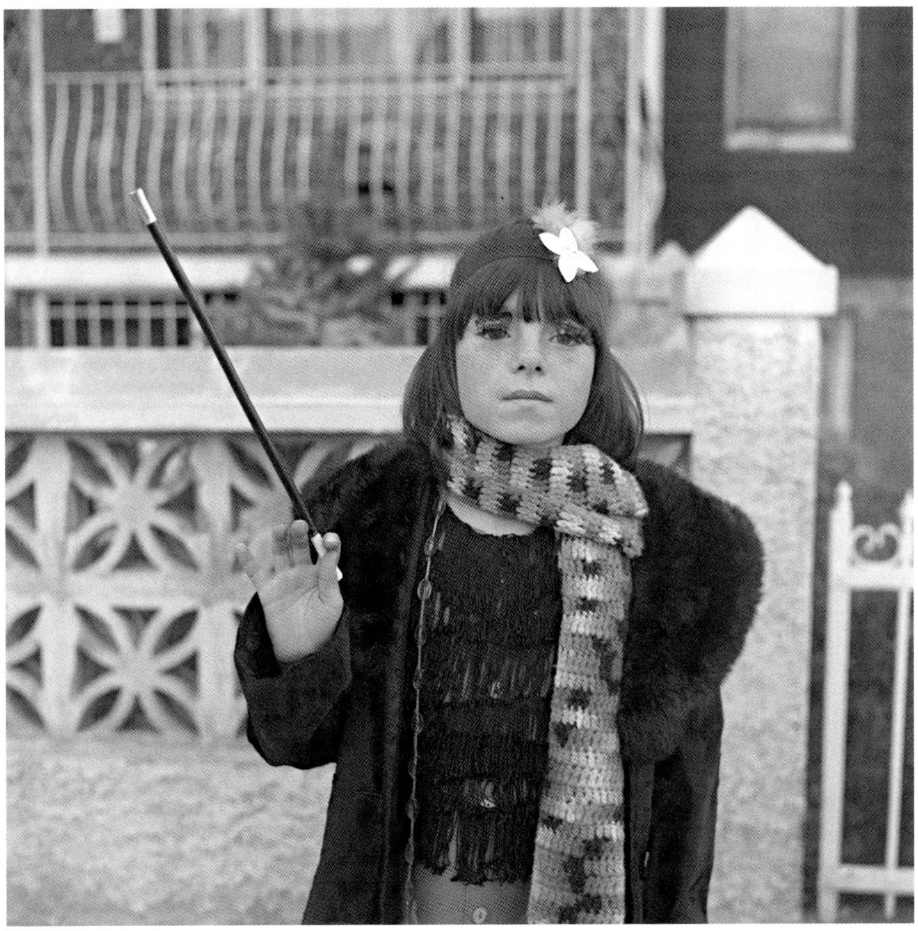

1920s flapper, 1977, Brooklyn.

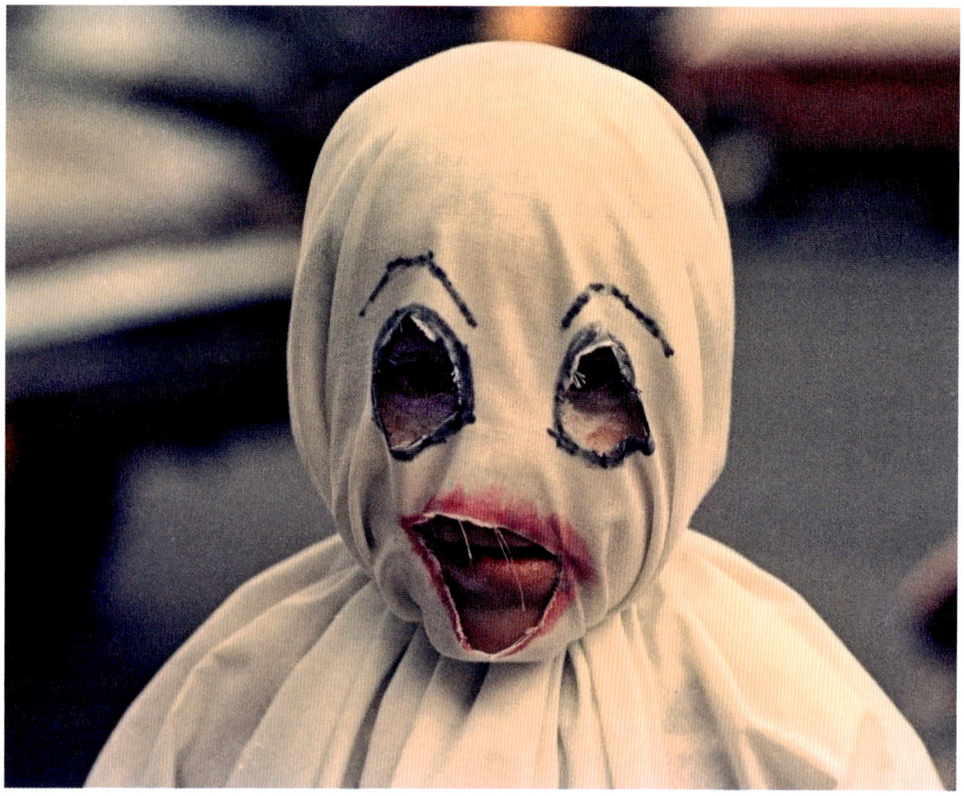

Ghost close-up,
1979, Brooklyn.

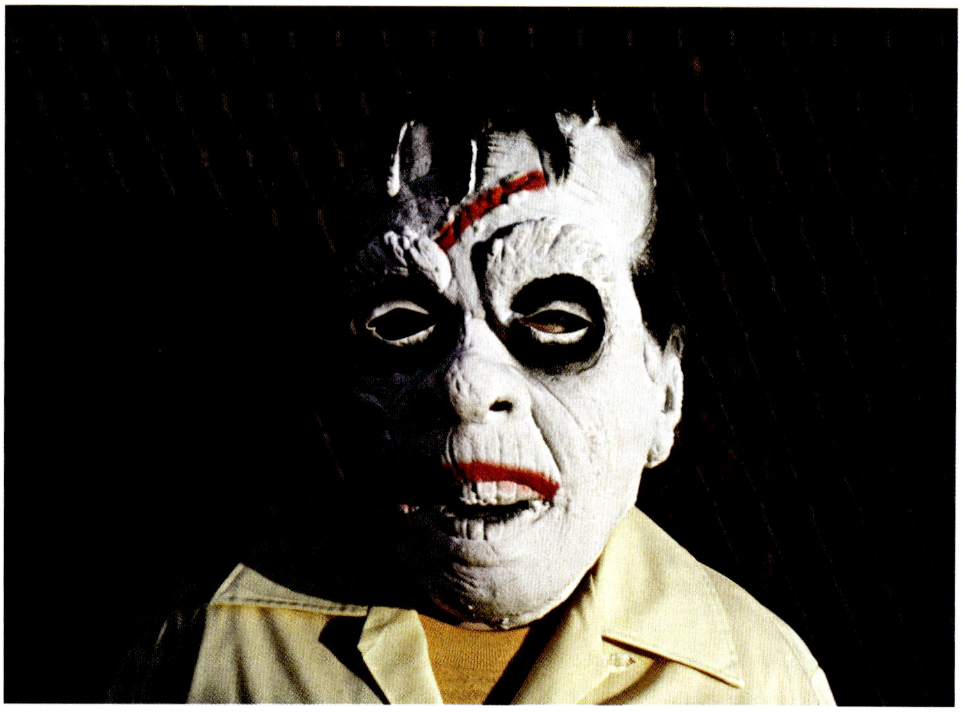

Frankenstein close-up,
1977, Brooklyn.

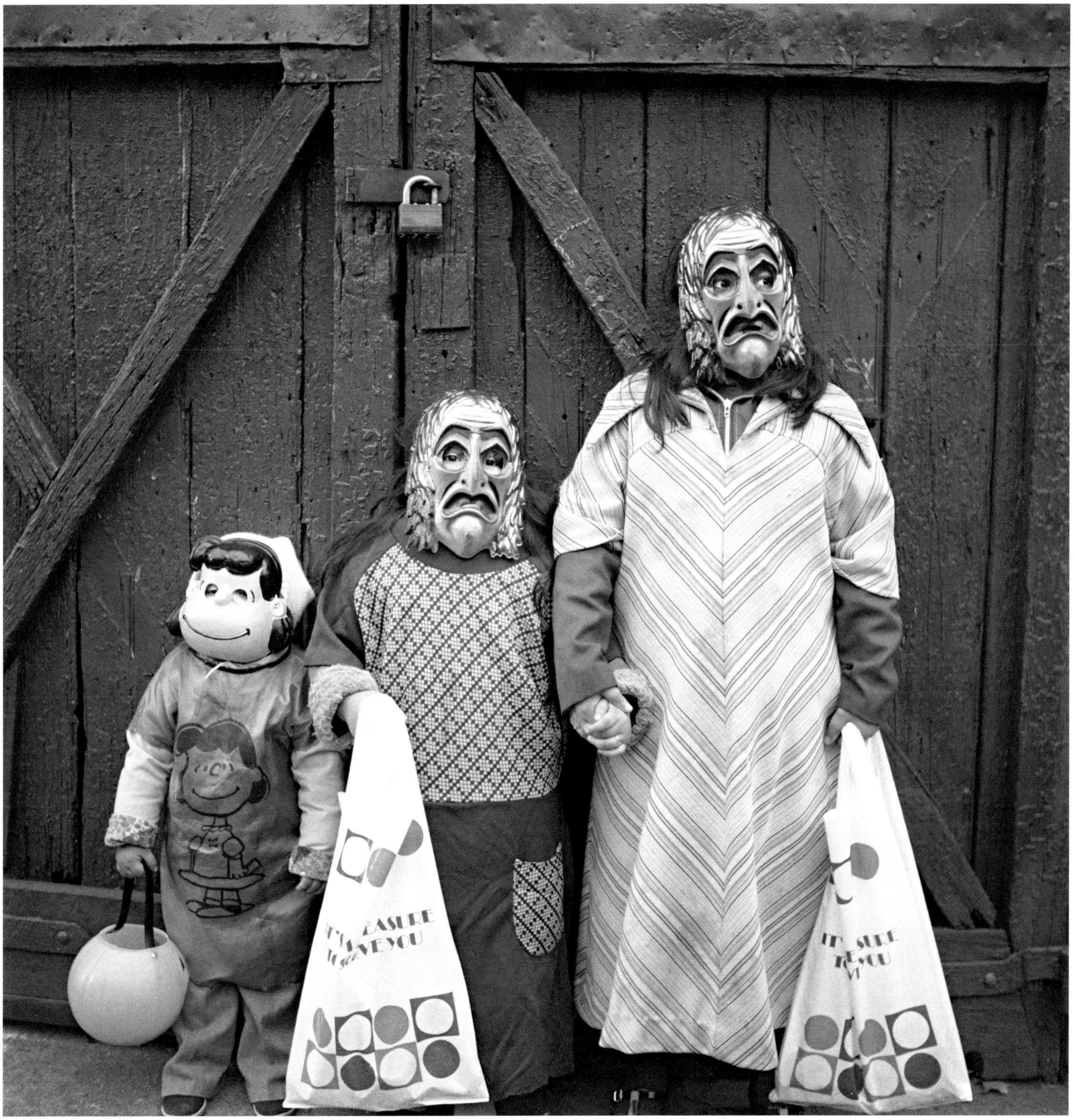

Lucy and two scary friends, 1977, Brooklyn.

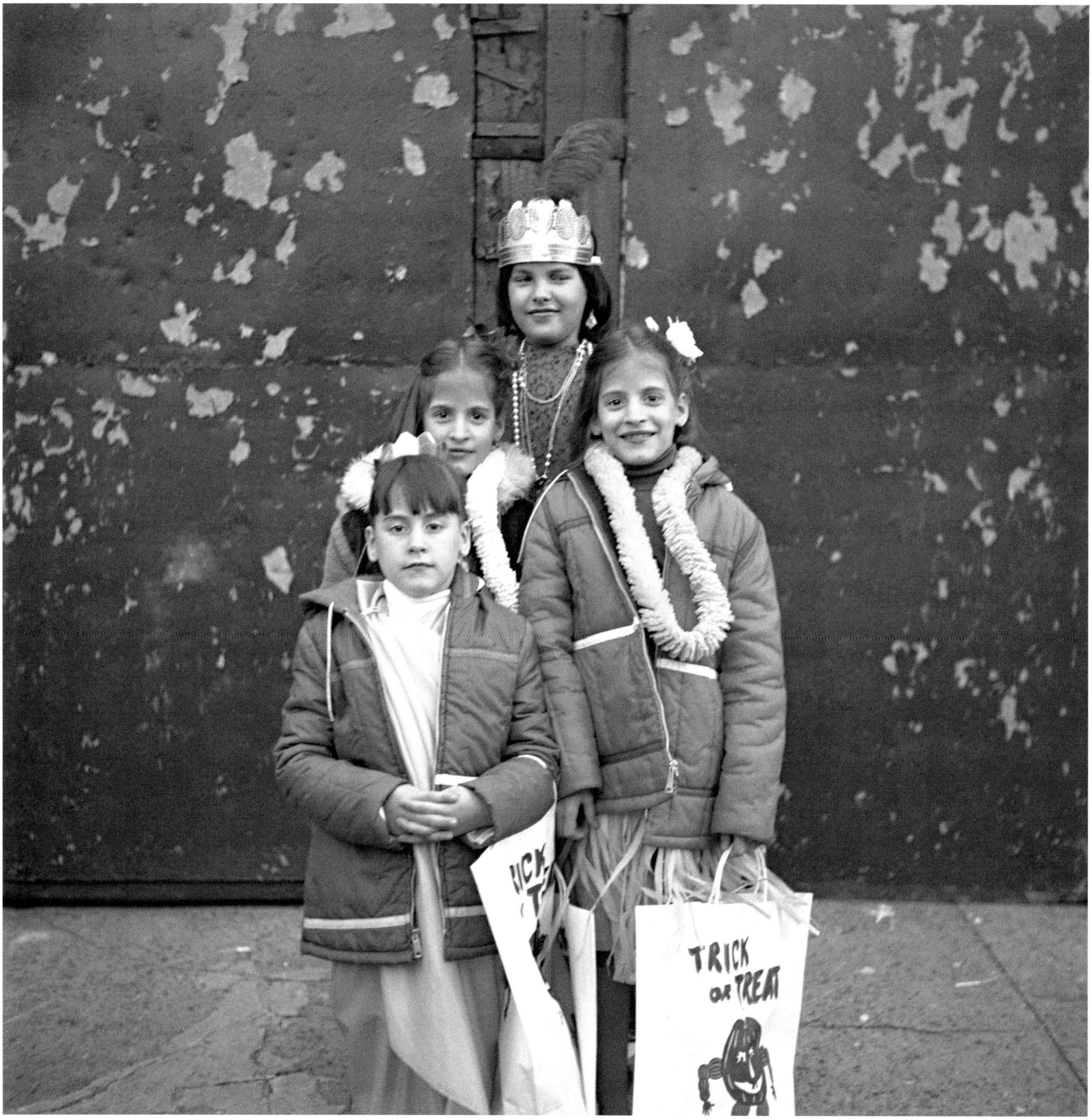

Four girls, two with
leis, 1977, Brooklyn.

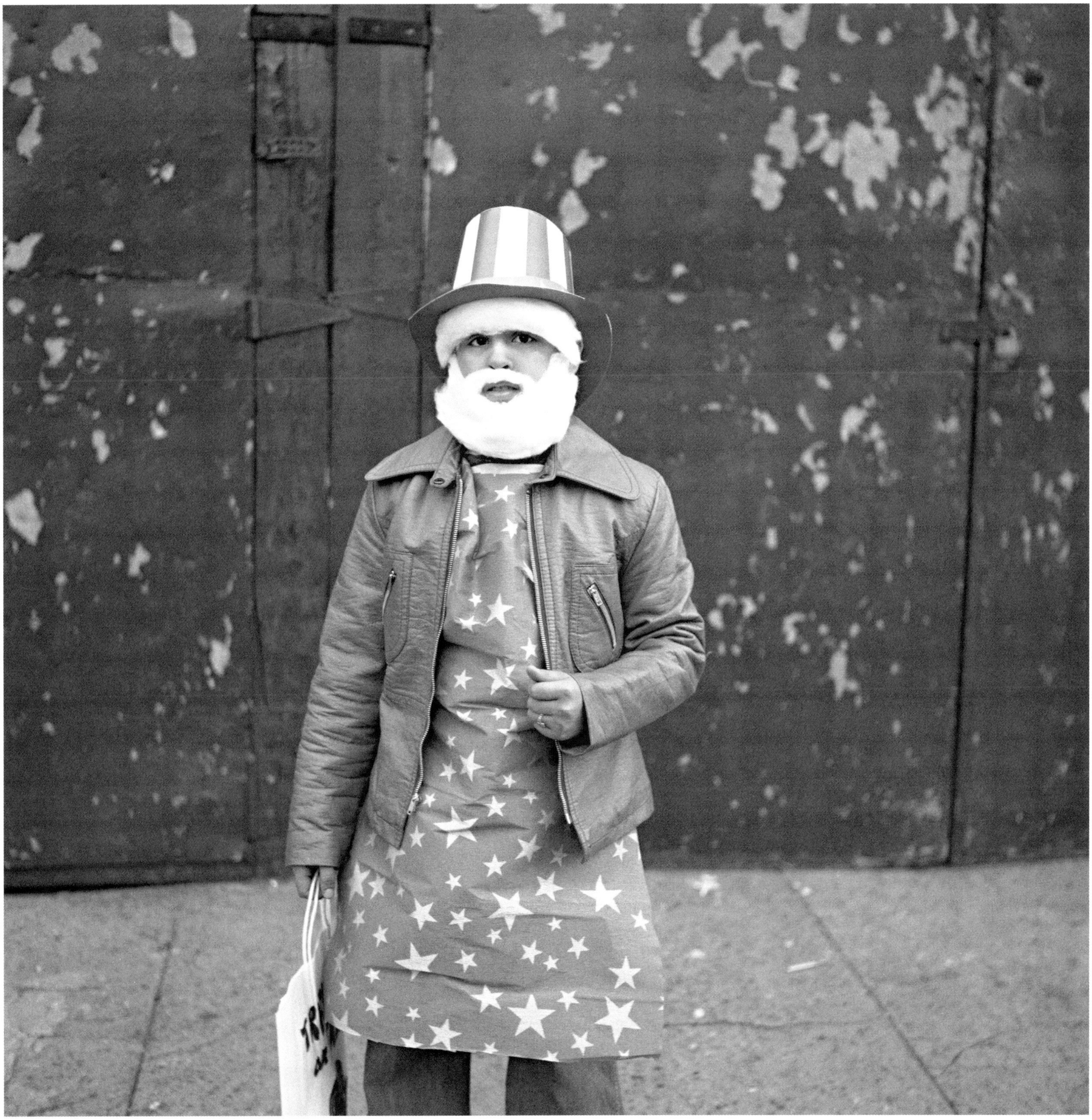

Uncle Sam, 1977, Brooklyn.

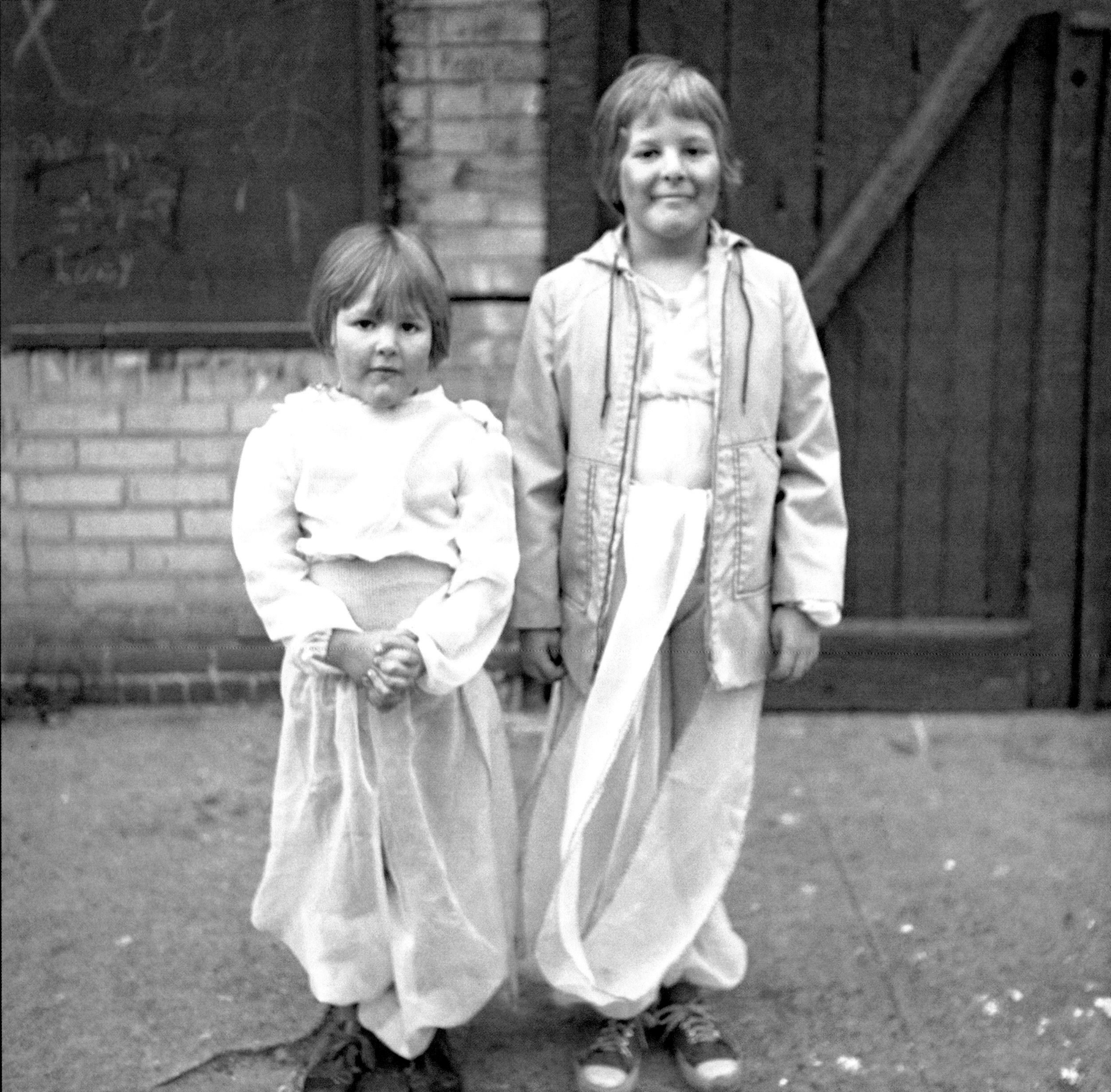

Two girls in long dresses,
1977, Brooklyn.

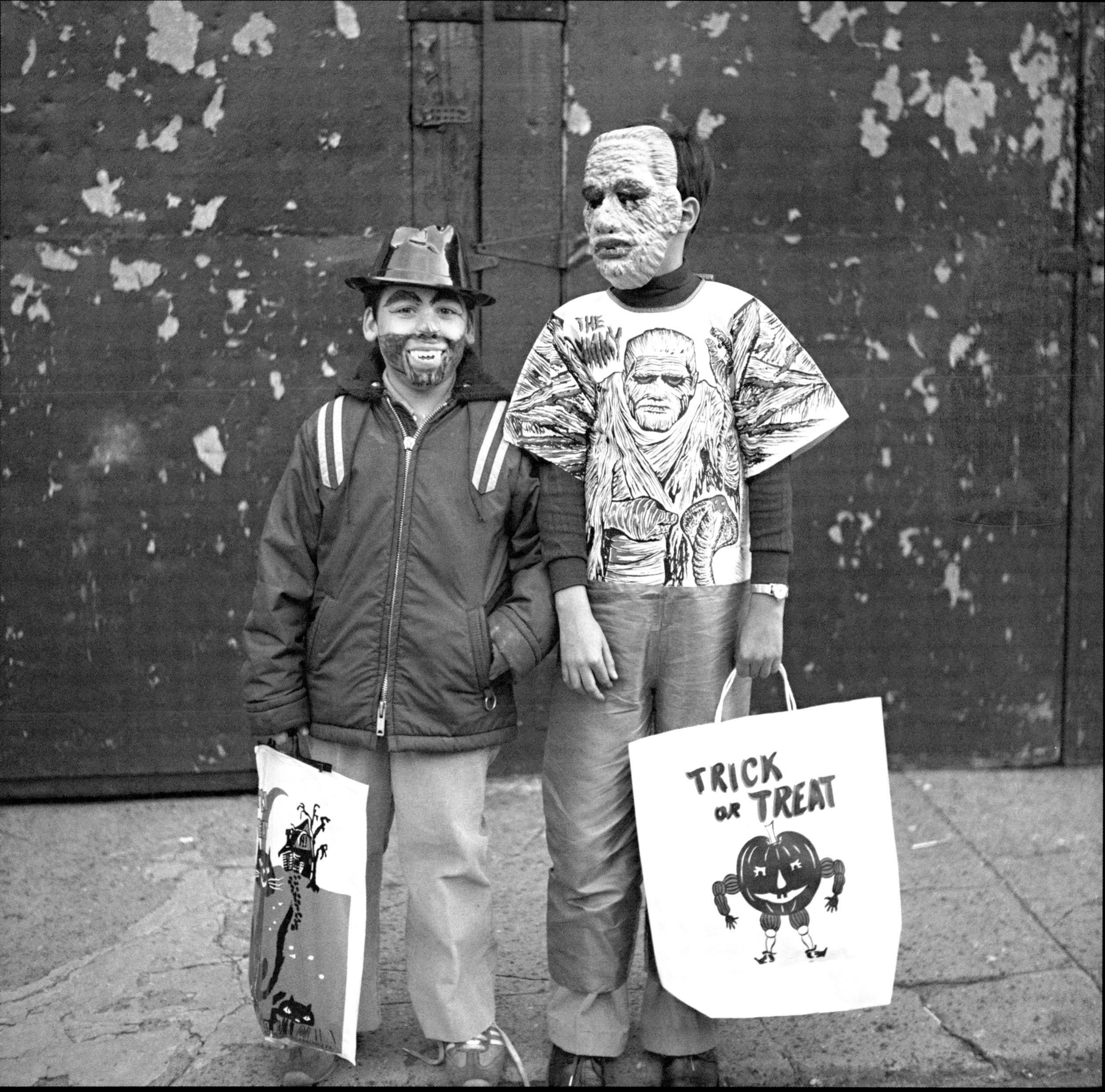

Vampire and the Mummy,
1977, Brooklyn.

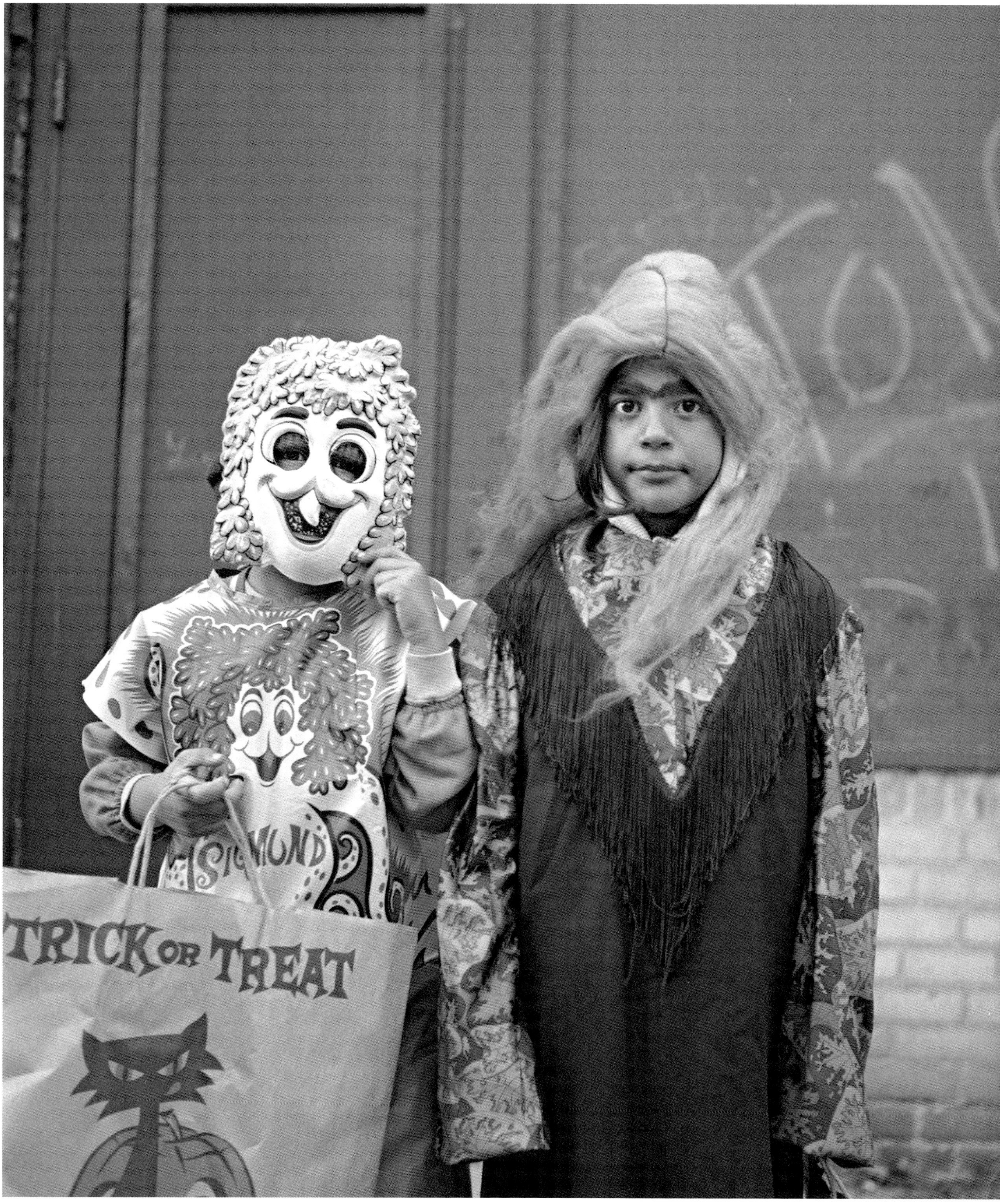
SIGMUND
TRICK OR TREAT

Two girls, one masked, one wigged, 1977, Brooklyn.

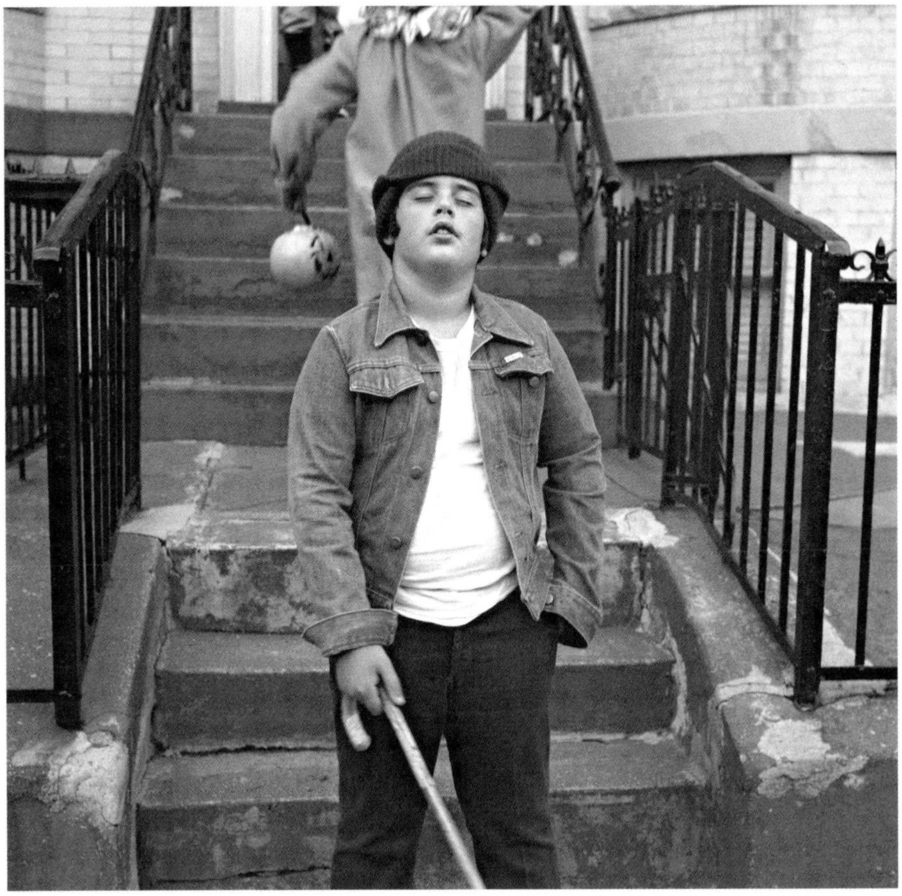

Boy with cane, 1977, Brooklyn.

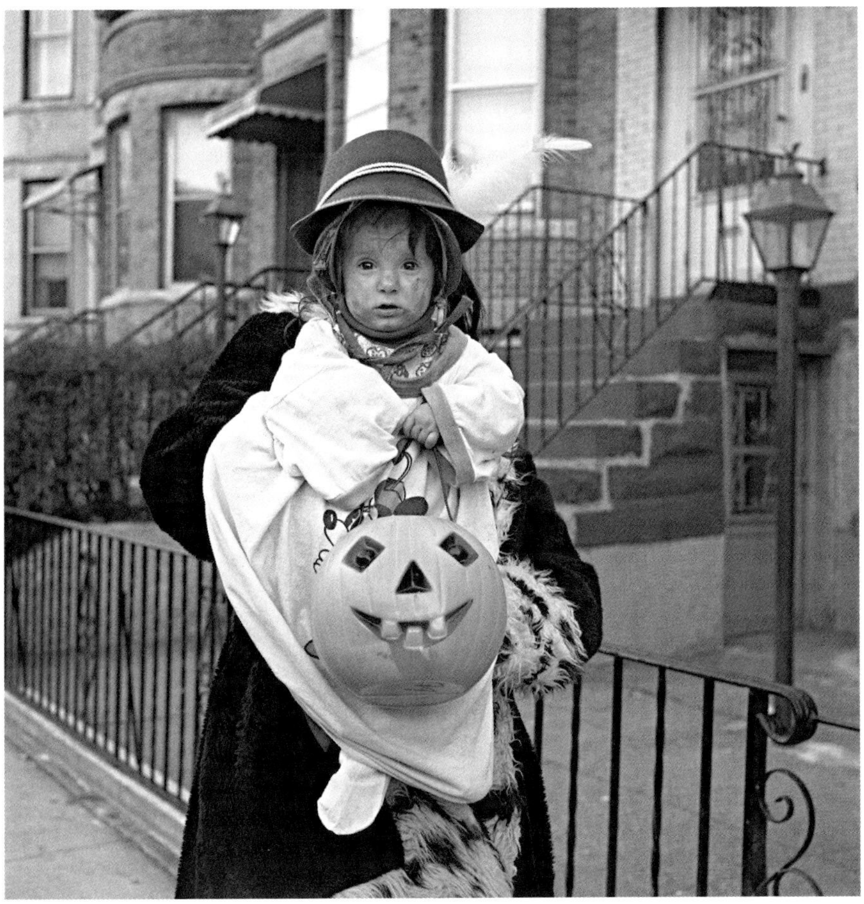

Optical illusion with pumpkin, 1977, Brooklyn.

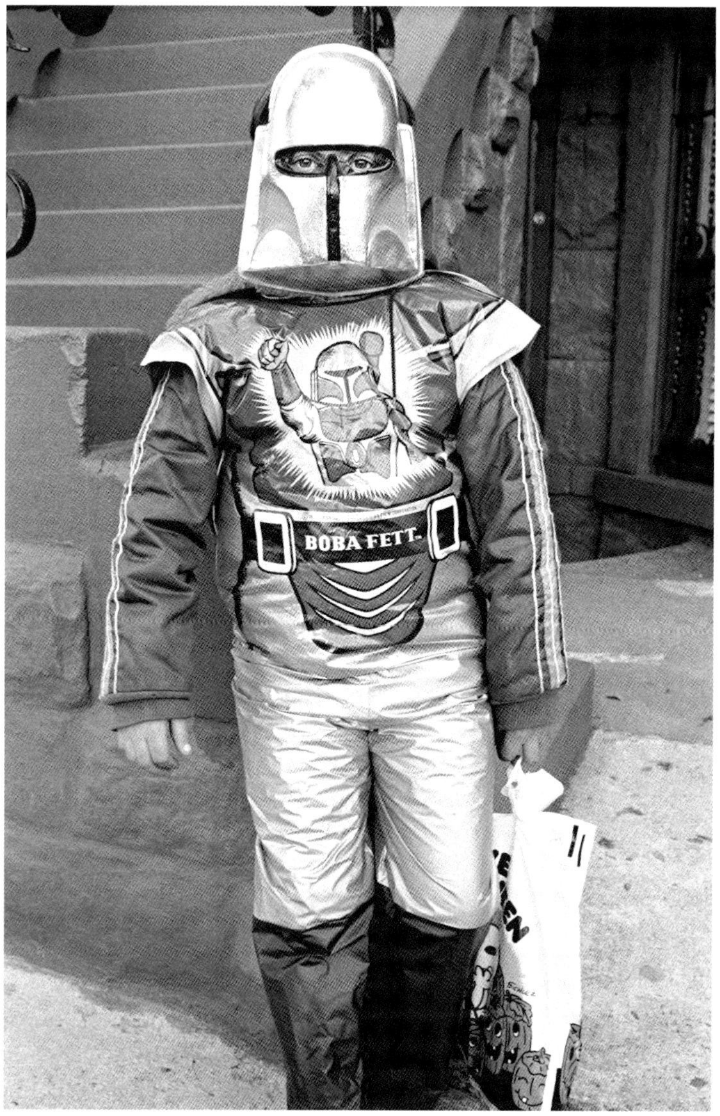

Boba Fett, 1980,
Brooklyn.

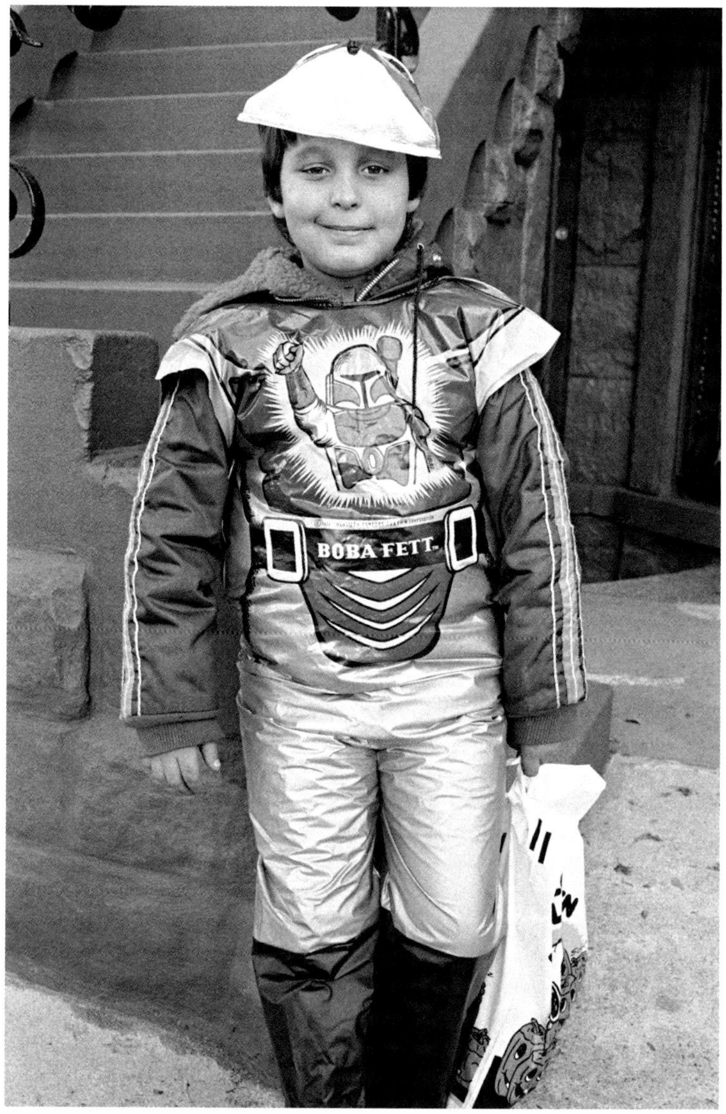

Boba Fett (unmasked),
1980, Brooklyn.

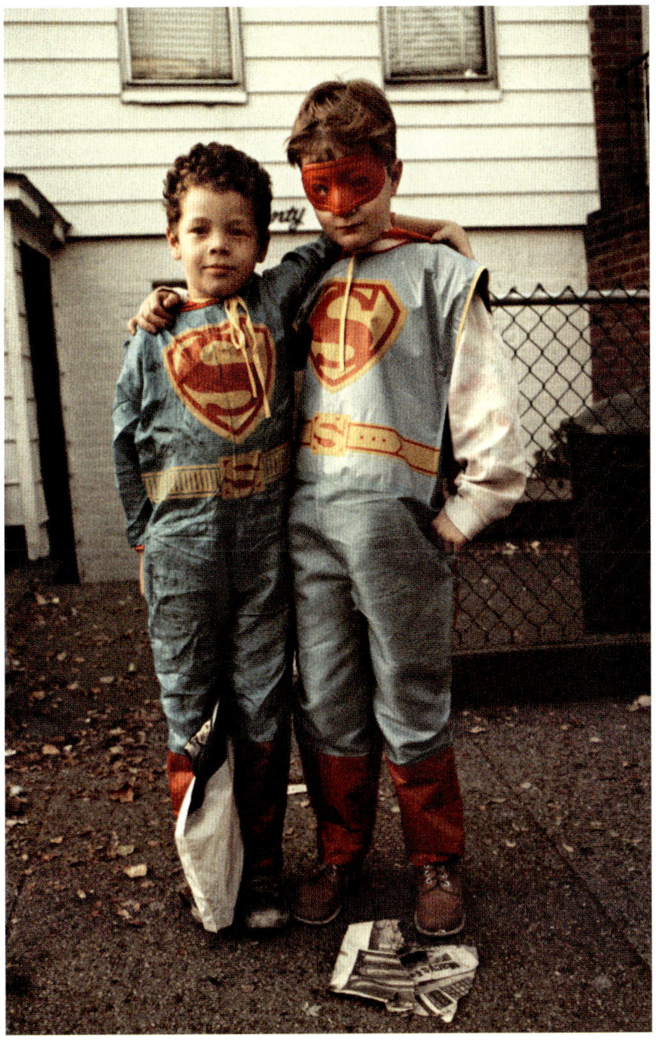

Two Supermen,
1975, Brooklyn.

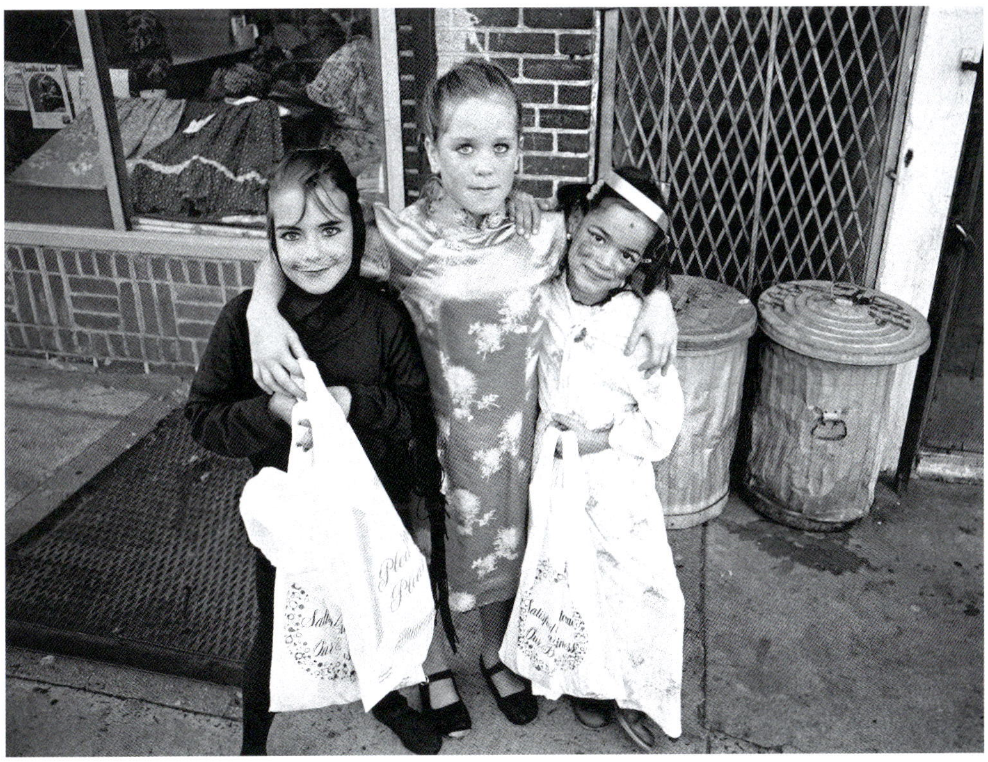

Three girls in costume,
1978, Brooklyn.

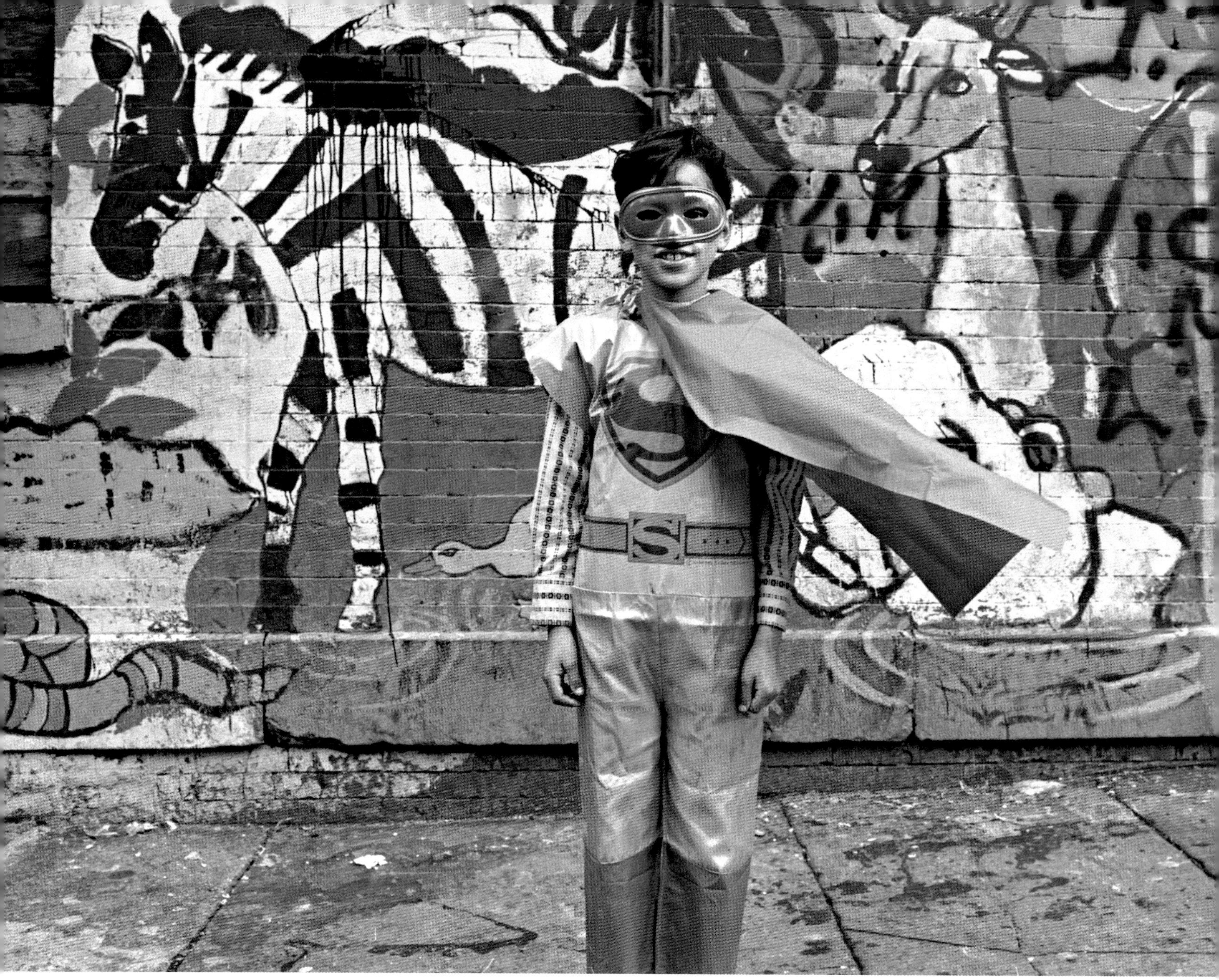

Superman with flowing
cape, 1976, Brooklyn.

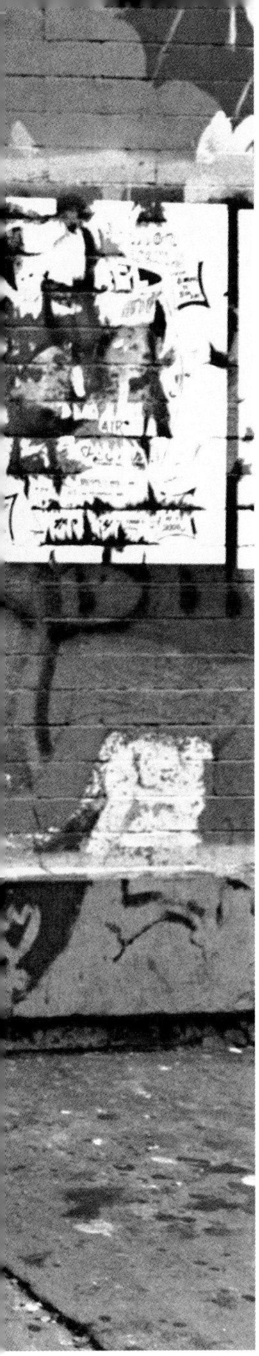

Vampire with pumpkin, 1980, Brooklyn.

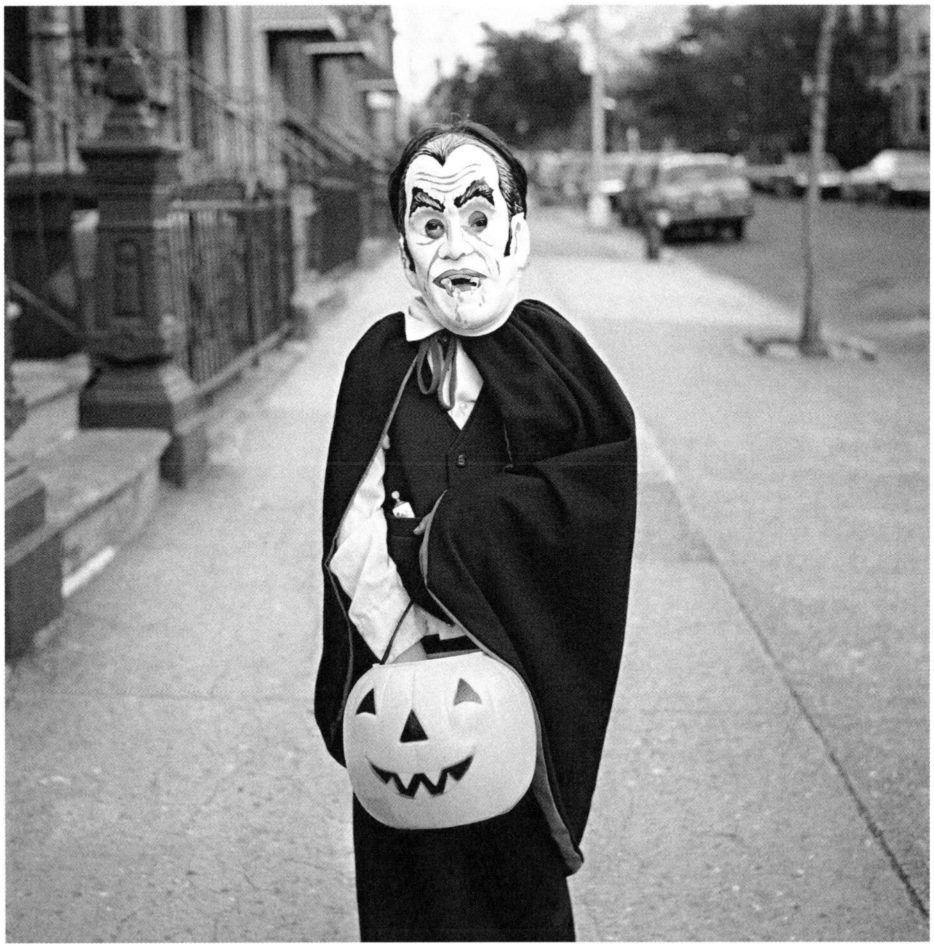

Cat with pumpkin, 1980, Brooklyn.

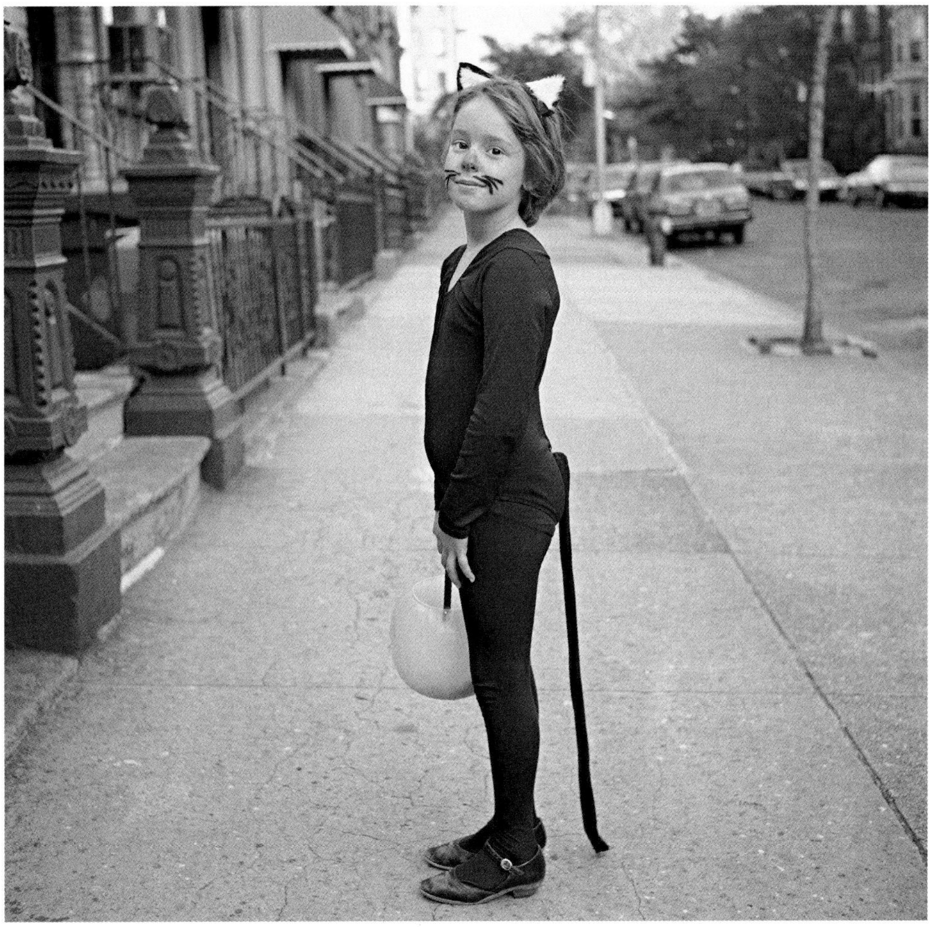

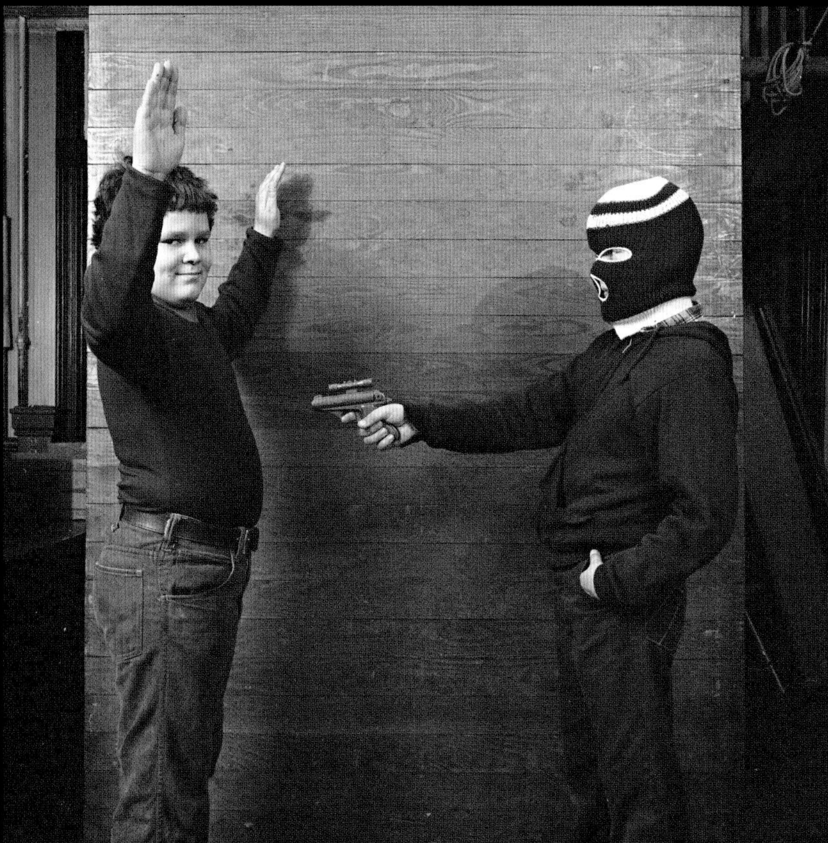

Robber and victim, 1980, Brooklyn.

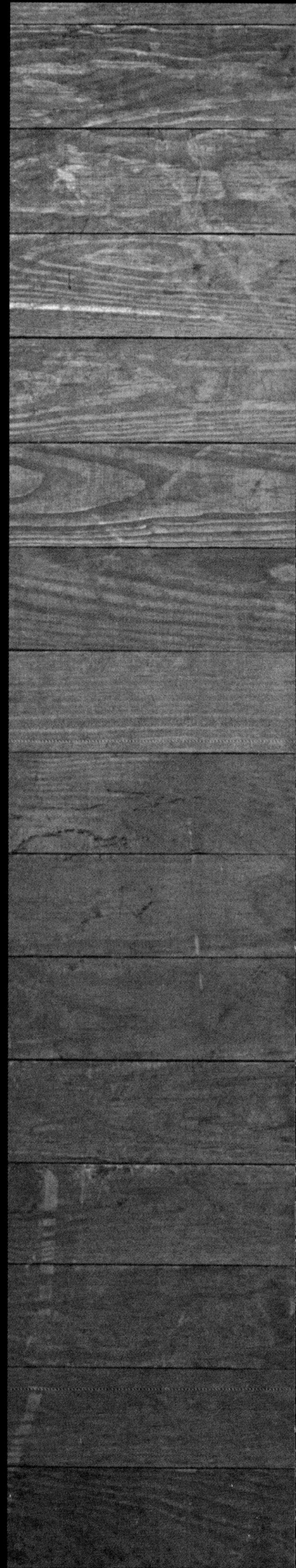

Mummy, 1980, Brooklyn.

But 1980 would include something new: my Aunt Angie called to tell me that her local Catholic church, St. John the Evangelist, in Brooklyn was hosting a Halloween party for parish children, and I would be welcome there. I had recently bought my first studio strobe outfit—a used Balcar power pack—with two lights and stands. I thought that this party would be a great opportunity to start using this equipment. The party was in the school auditorium. I found a wooden flat on the auditorium's stage and stood it straight up as a background. With crossed fingers, I plugged in the power pack and arranged the lights. Then, I took out my 120mm Yashica Mat-124 G Twin Lens Reflex camera and asked the costumed kids to come forward to be photographed.

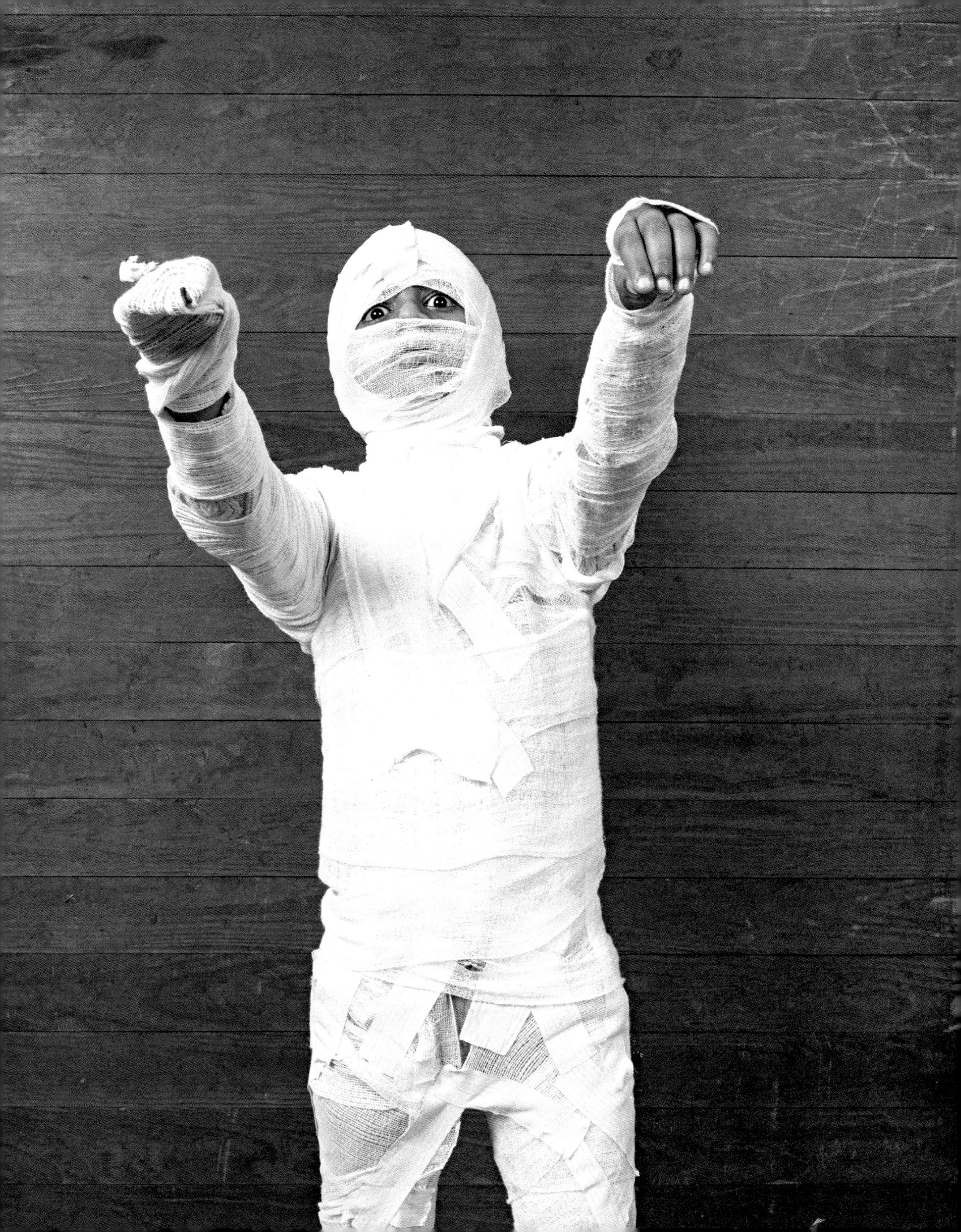

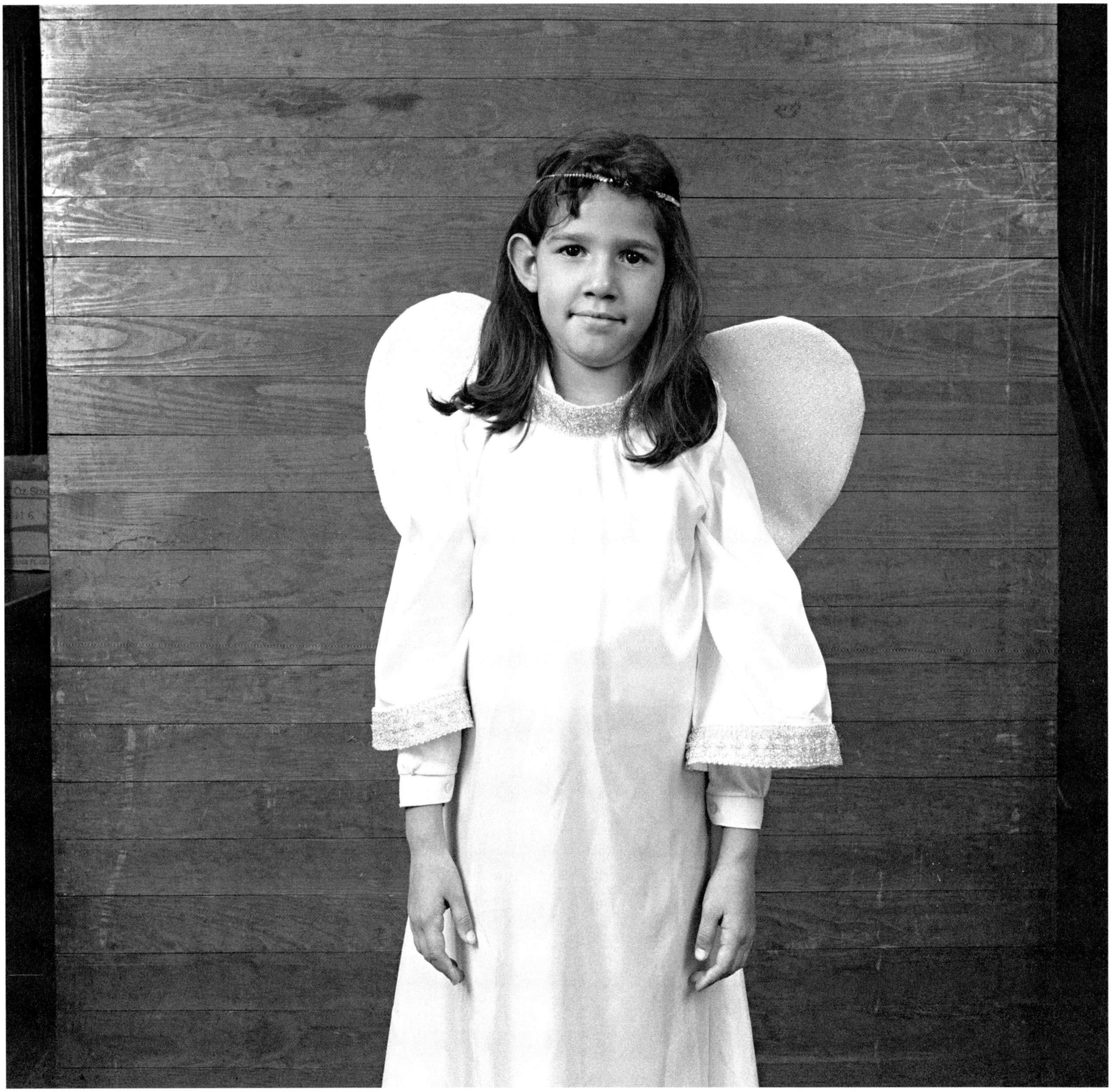

Angel, 1980, Brooklyn.

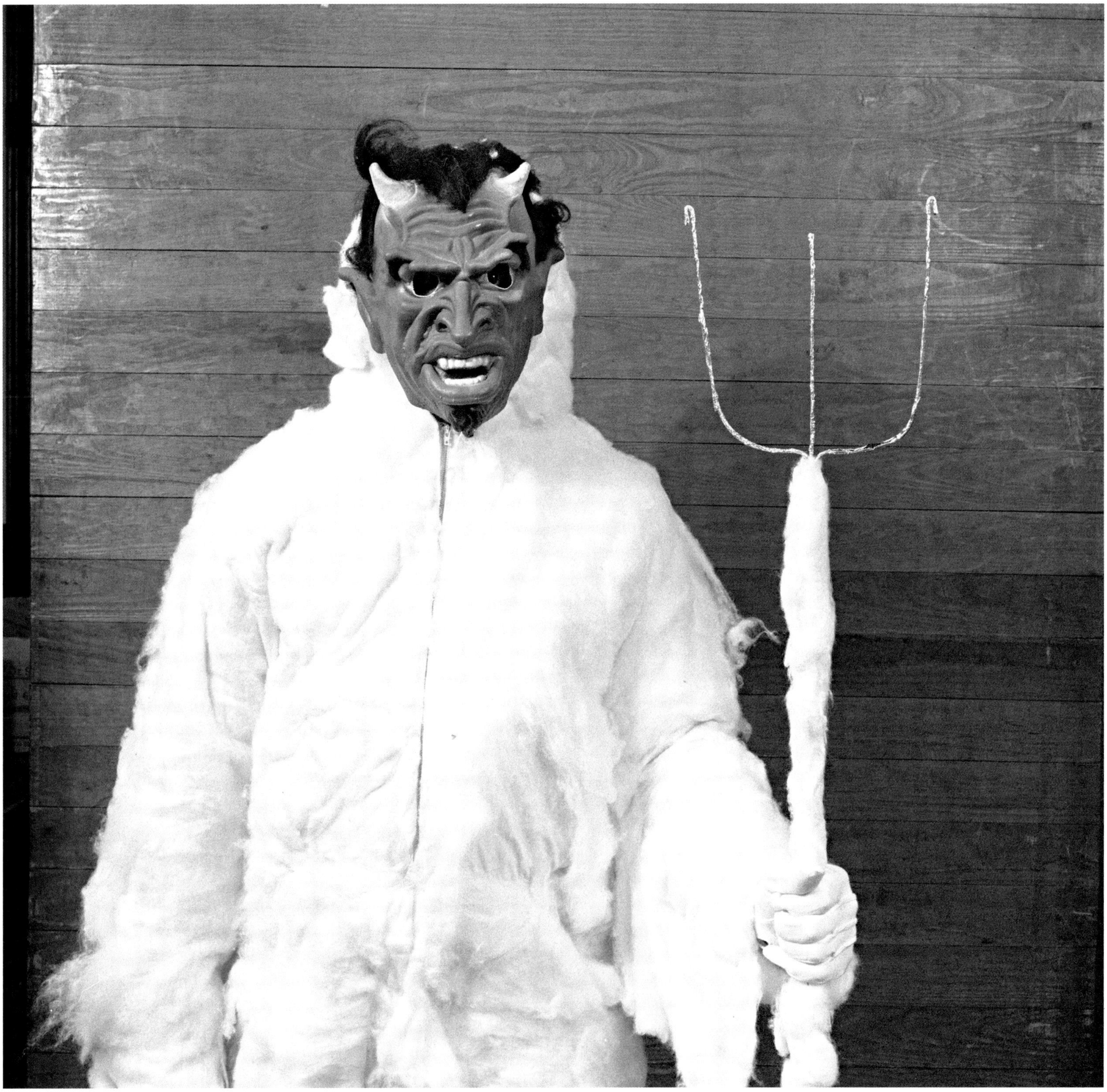

White devil, 1980, Brooklyn.

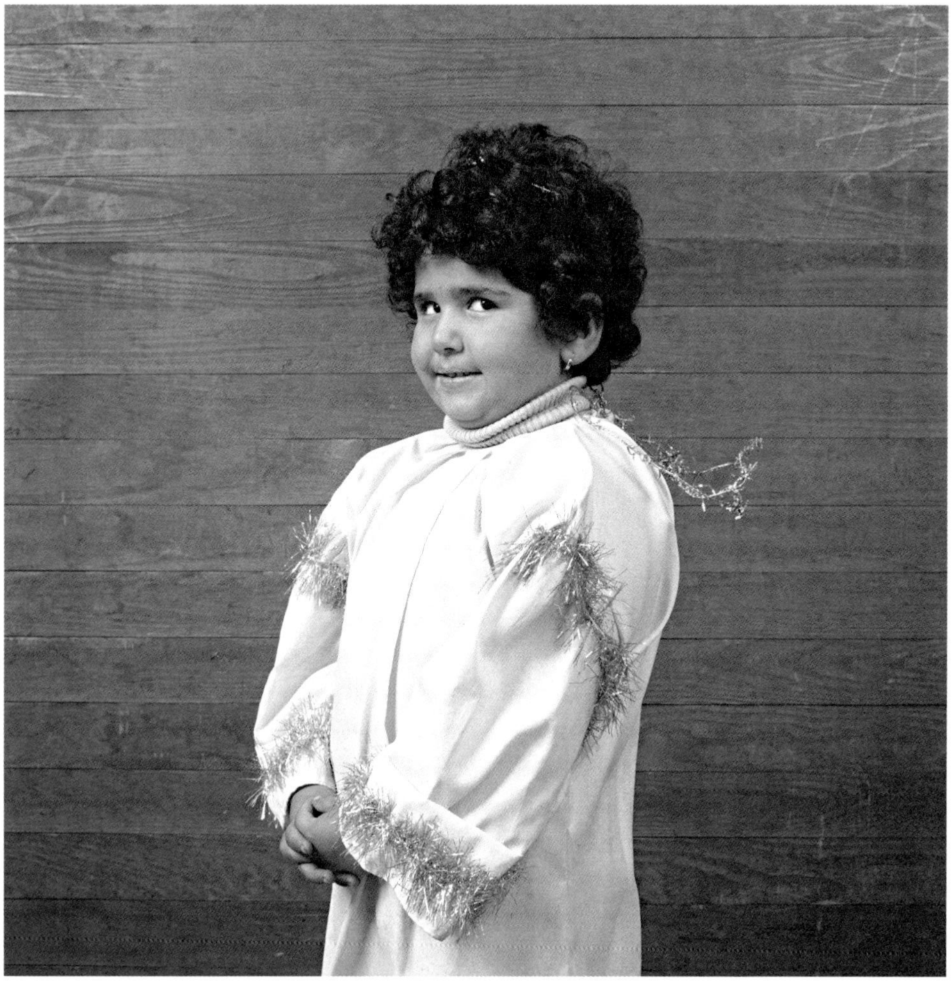

Angel with small wings, 1980, Brooklyn.

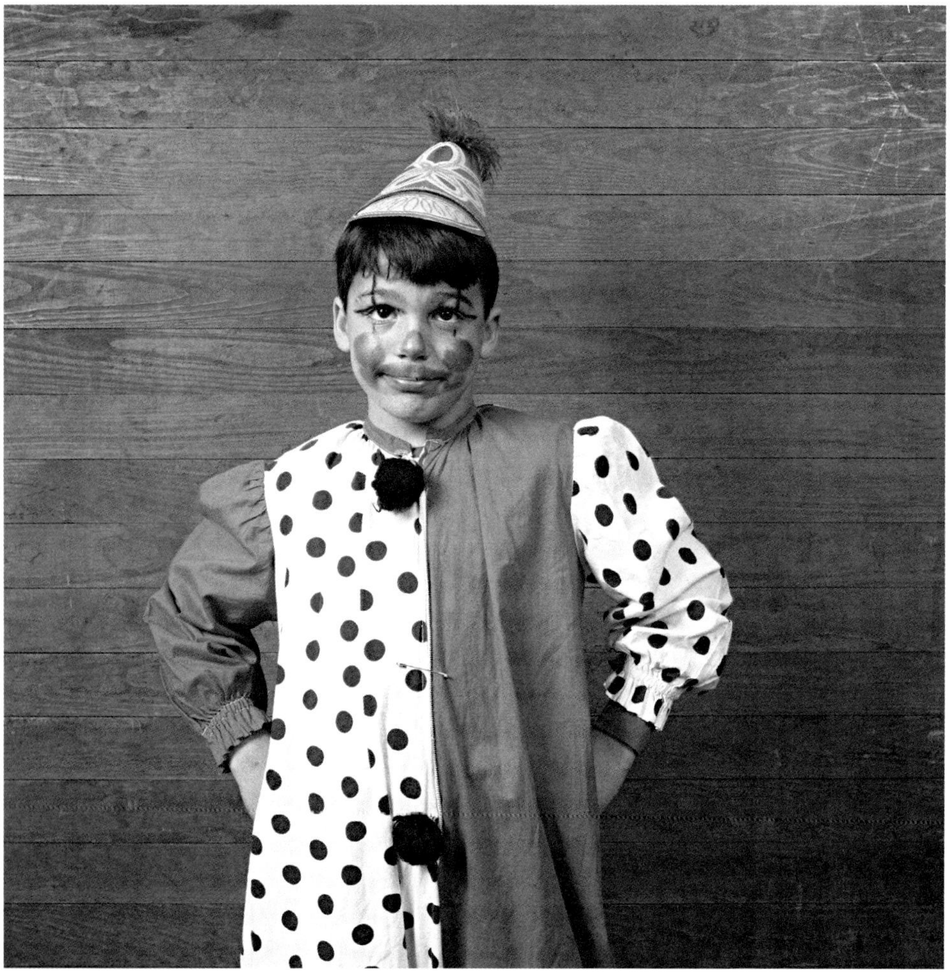

Clown, 1980, Brooklyn.

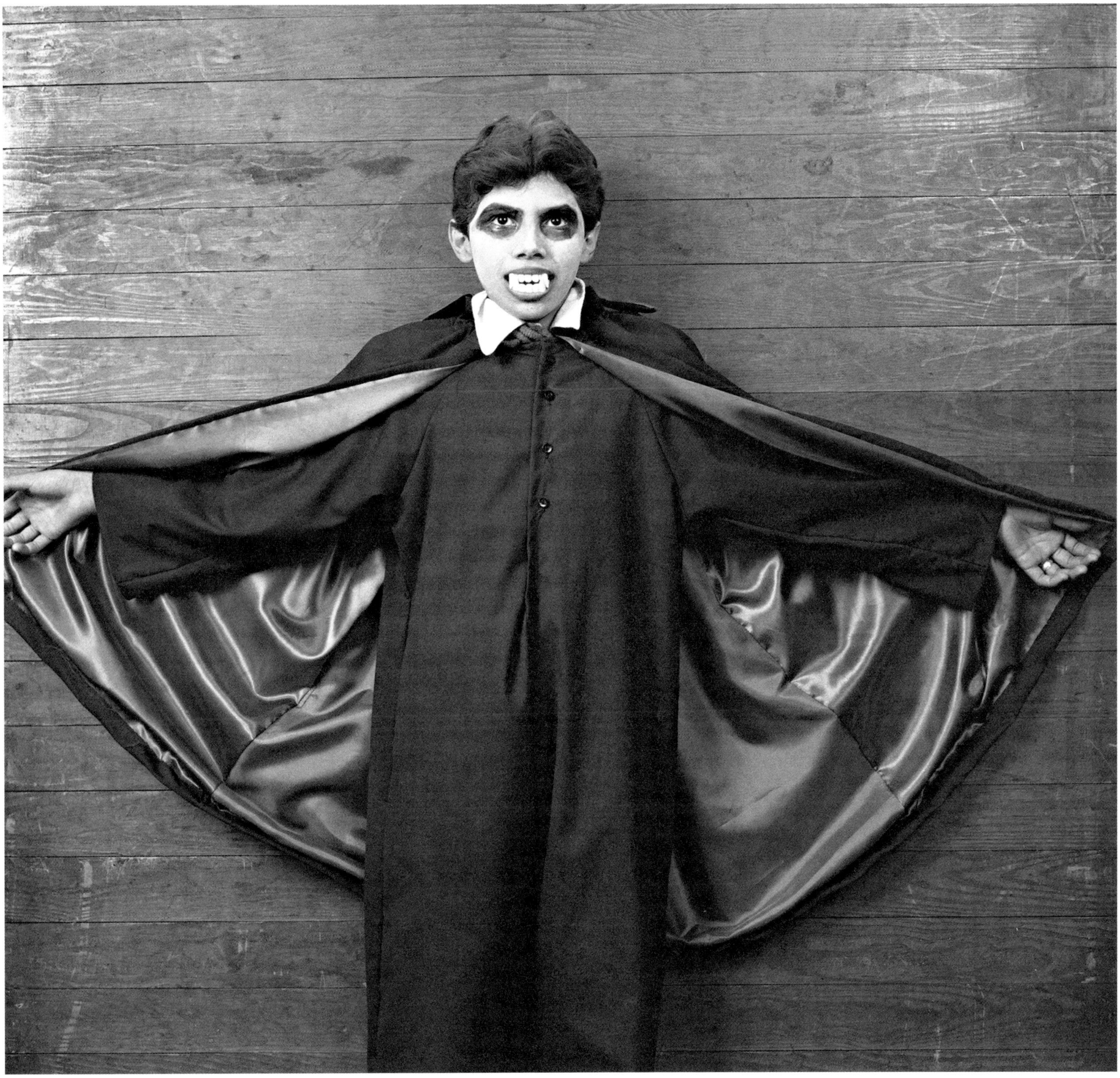

Vampire with spread cape, 1980, Brooklyn.

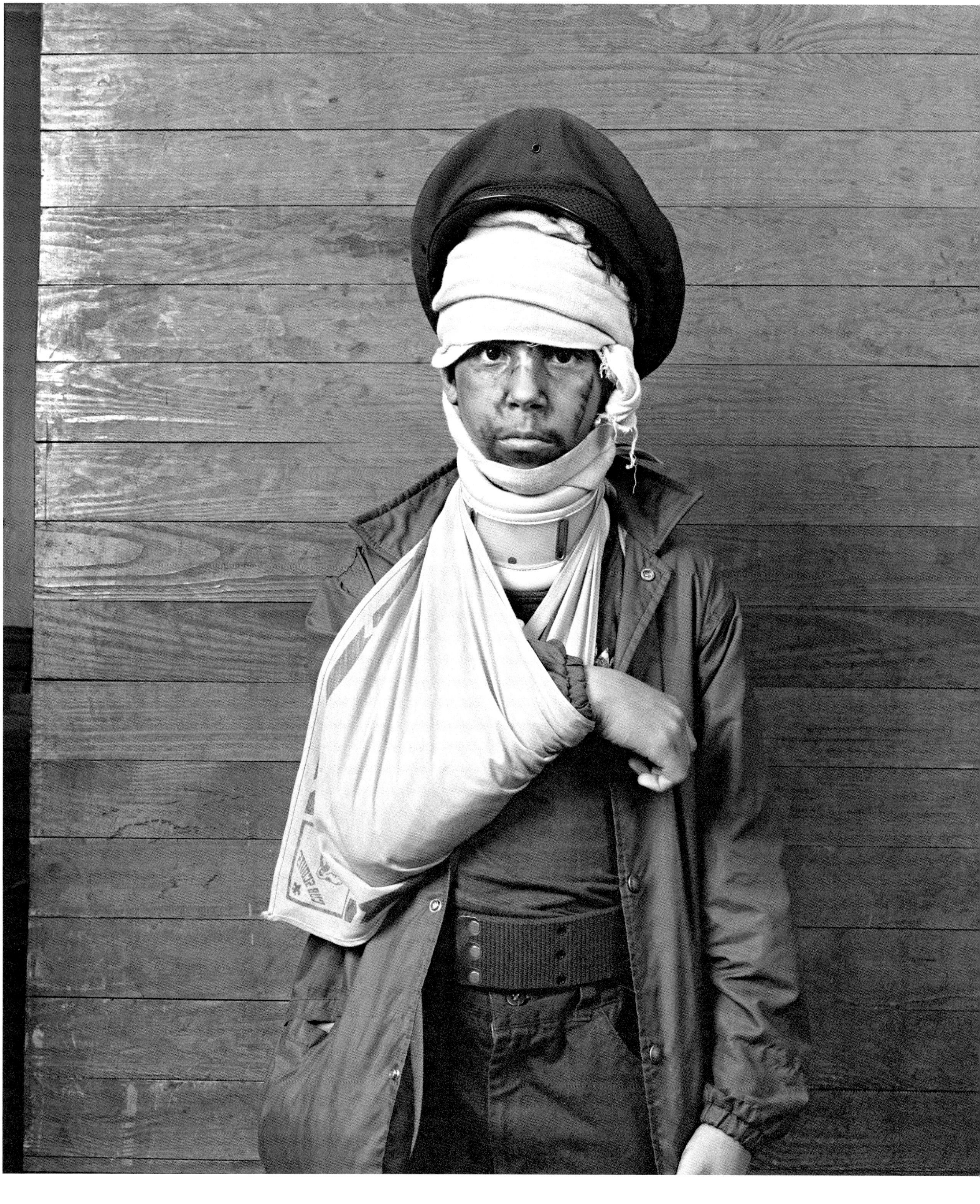

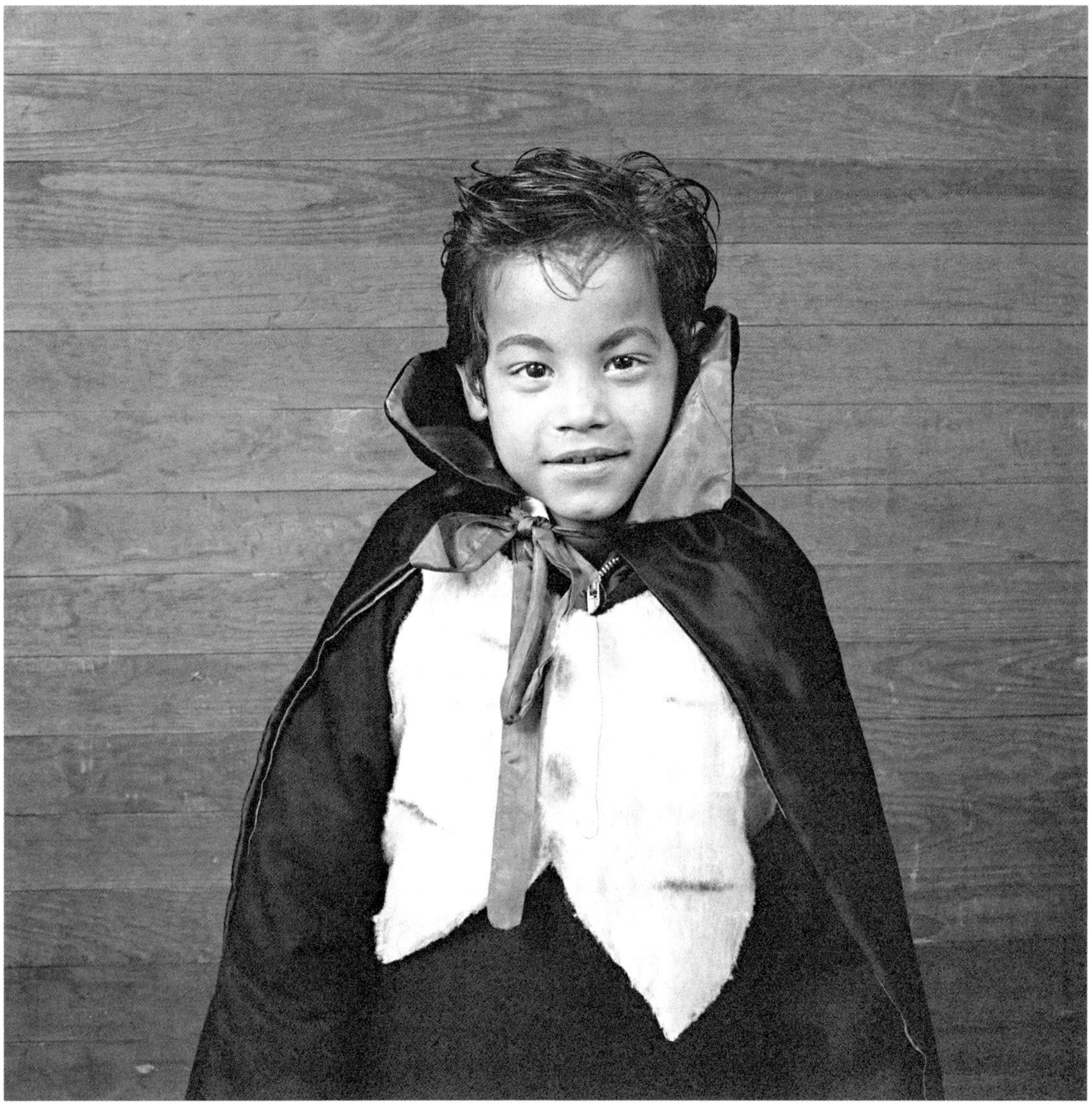

Well-dressed vampire,
1980, Brooklyn.

Wounded soldier,
1980, Brooklyn.

Small Batman at night,
1982, Brooklyn.

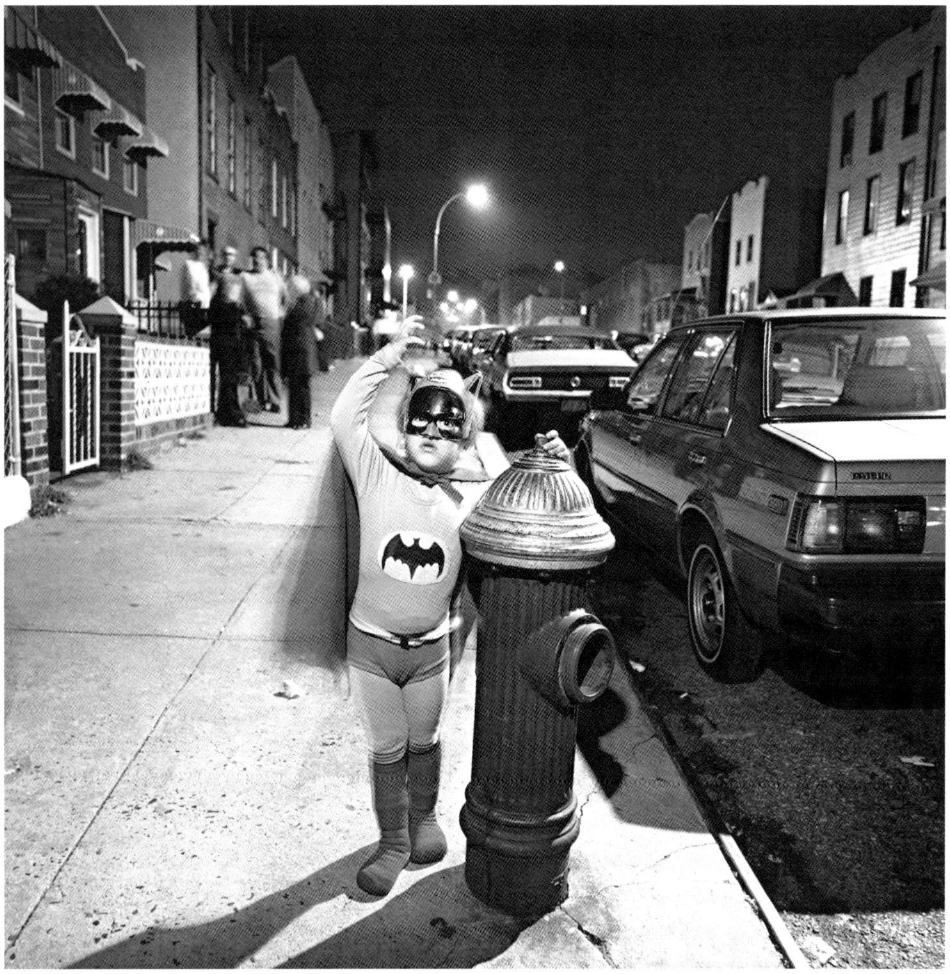

1982 was a great year for Halloween photography in Brooklyn. I photographed on the street at night . . .

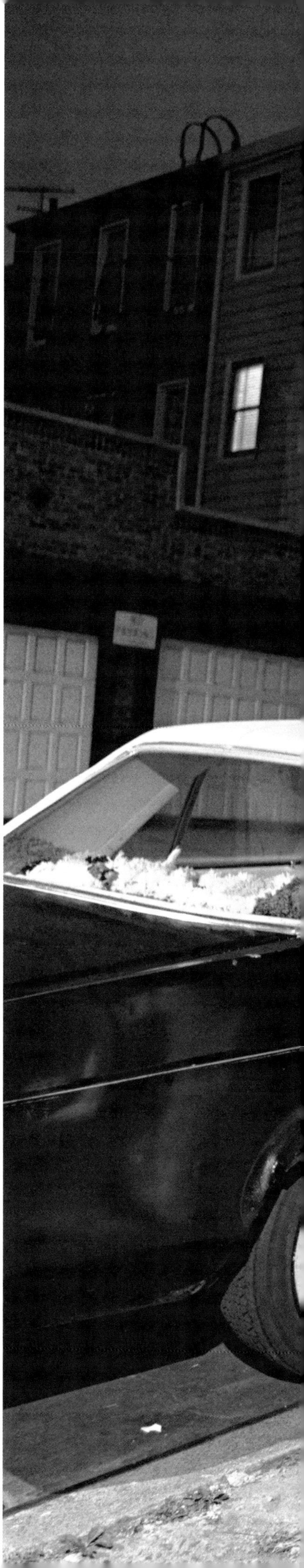

Ghost with skull mask at night, 1982, Brooklyn.

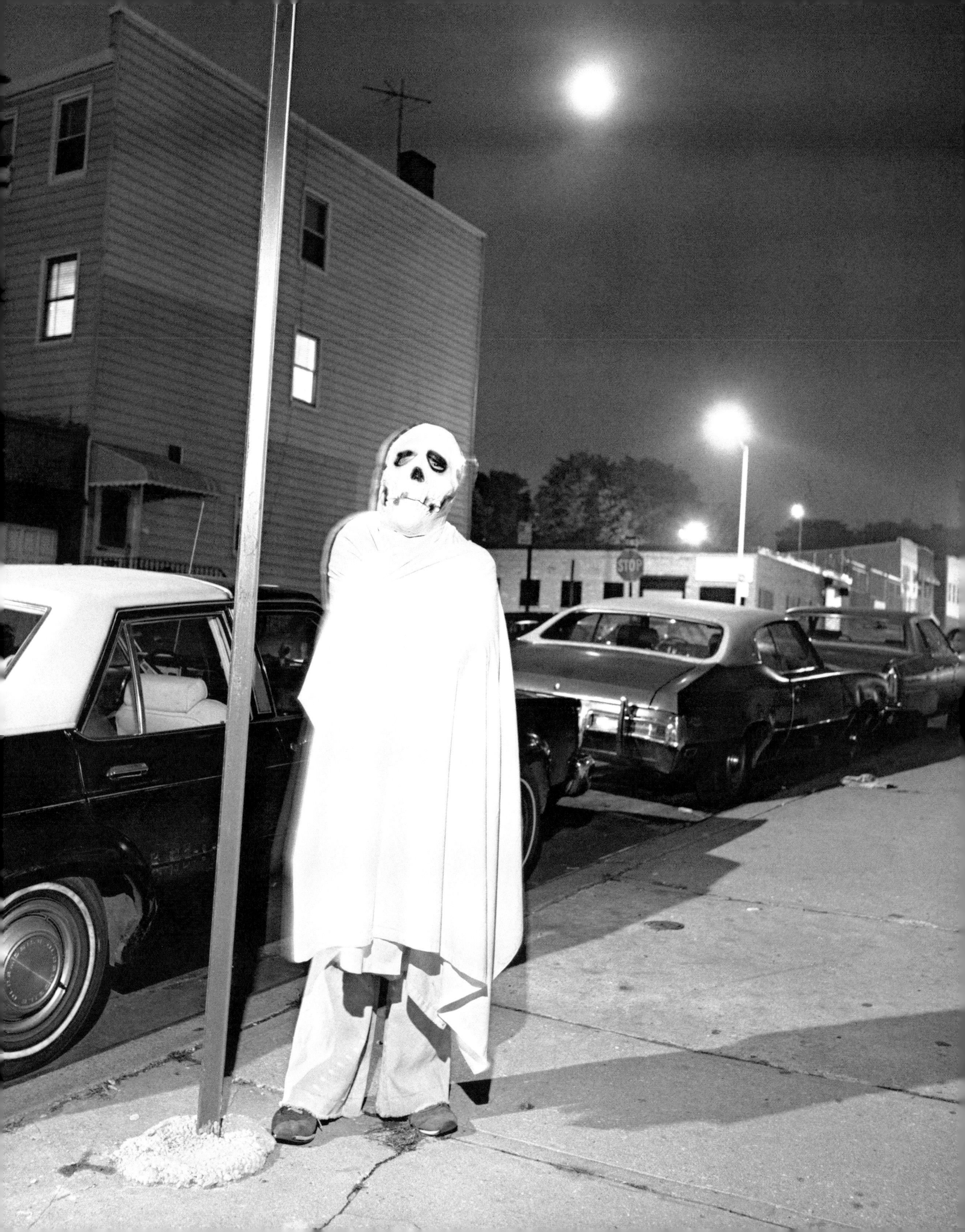
STOP

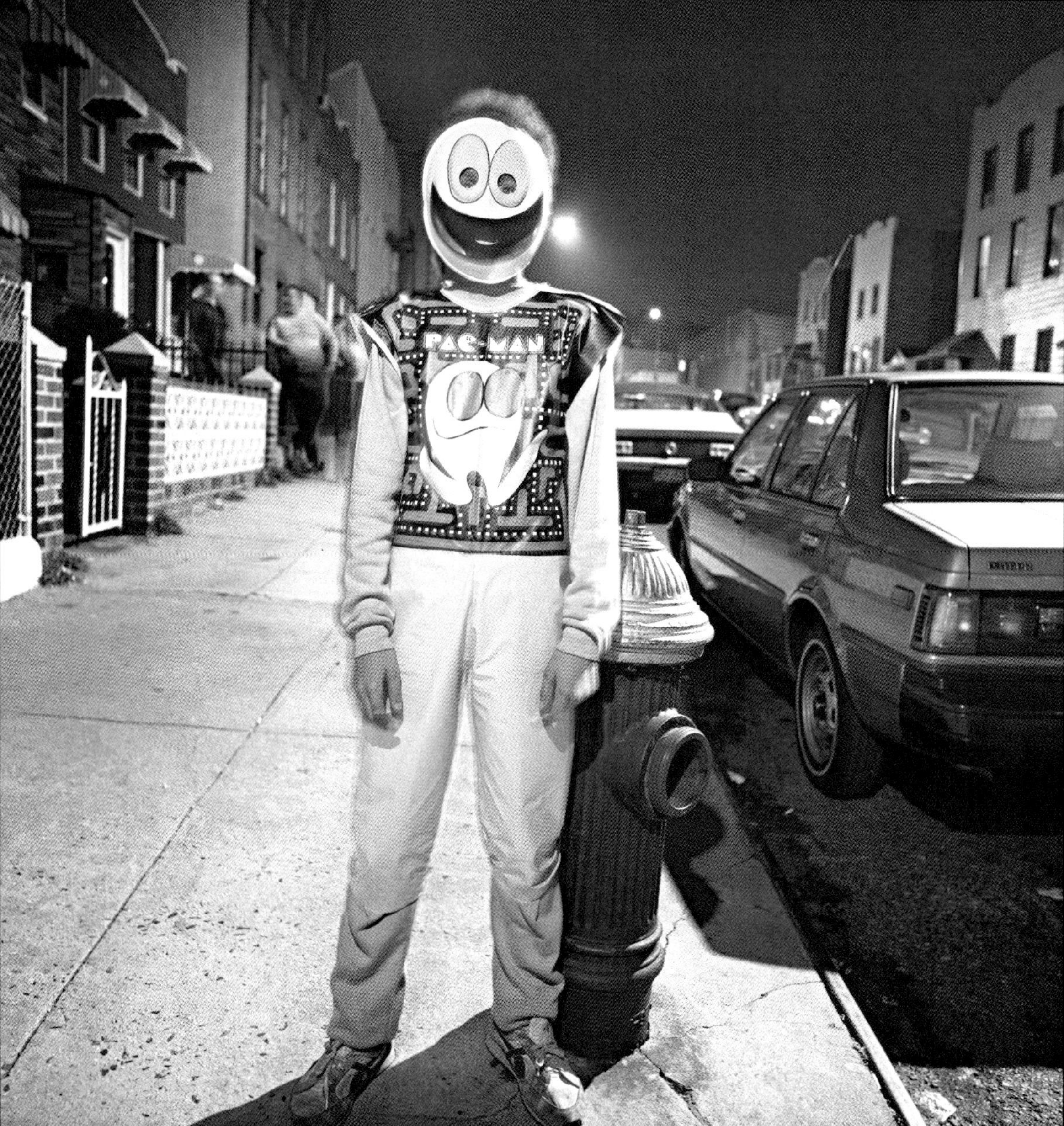

Pac-Man at night,
1982, Brooklyn.

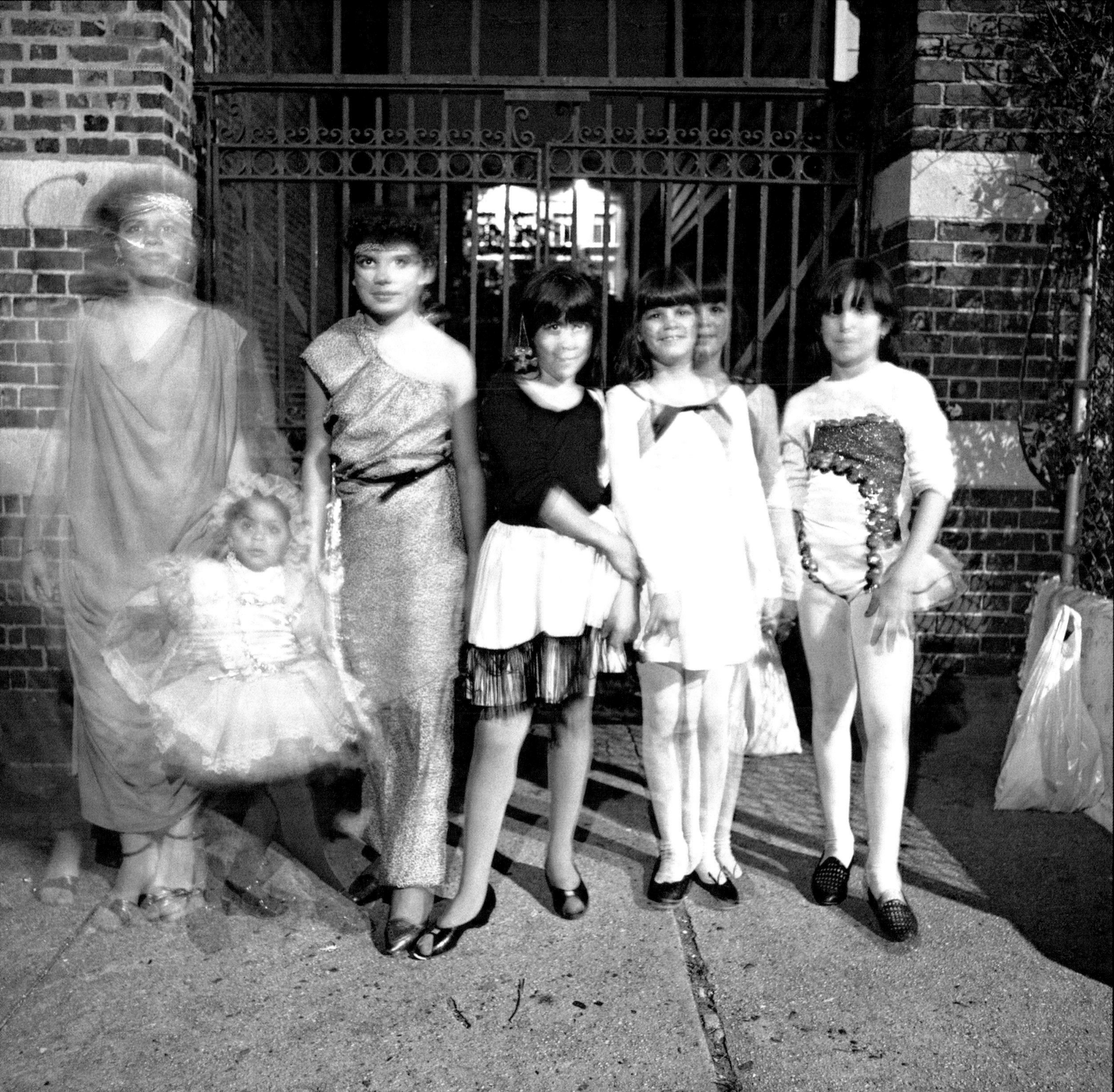

Six kids at night,
1982, Brooklyn.

. . . and at two parties. The first party was the Park Slope Food Coop's Halloween party on Saturday night. I asked my brother if he'd like to come with me to the Coop's party. He surprised me with his response: "Nah, too intellectual for me." So I went alone. However, my brother's take was correct. The first person I photographed was dressed as Walt Whitman, with long white hair, a beard, and a copy of *Leaves of Grass*. Later on, I encountered a partygoer wearing a long white shift and holding a wooden sword. When I asked who he was, the man responded snarkily, "I'm Hamlet's father."

I had a great time and shot several rolls of film using a new technique. I put my Hasselblad camera on a tripod, set the 50mm lens aperture to f/8, and made one-second exposures along with one "pop" of my handheld flash. When I processed the film, I really liked the combination of blur and stillness. Each photo was slightly different depending on how still the subject was during the exposure.

Walt Whitman,
1982, Brooklyn.

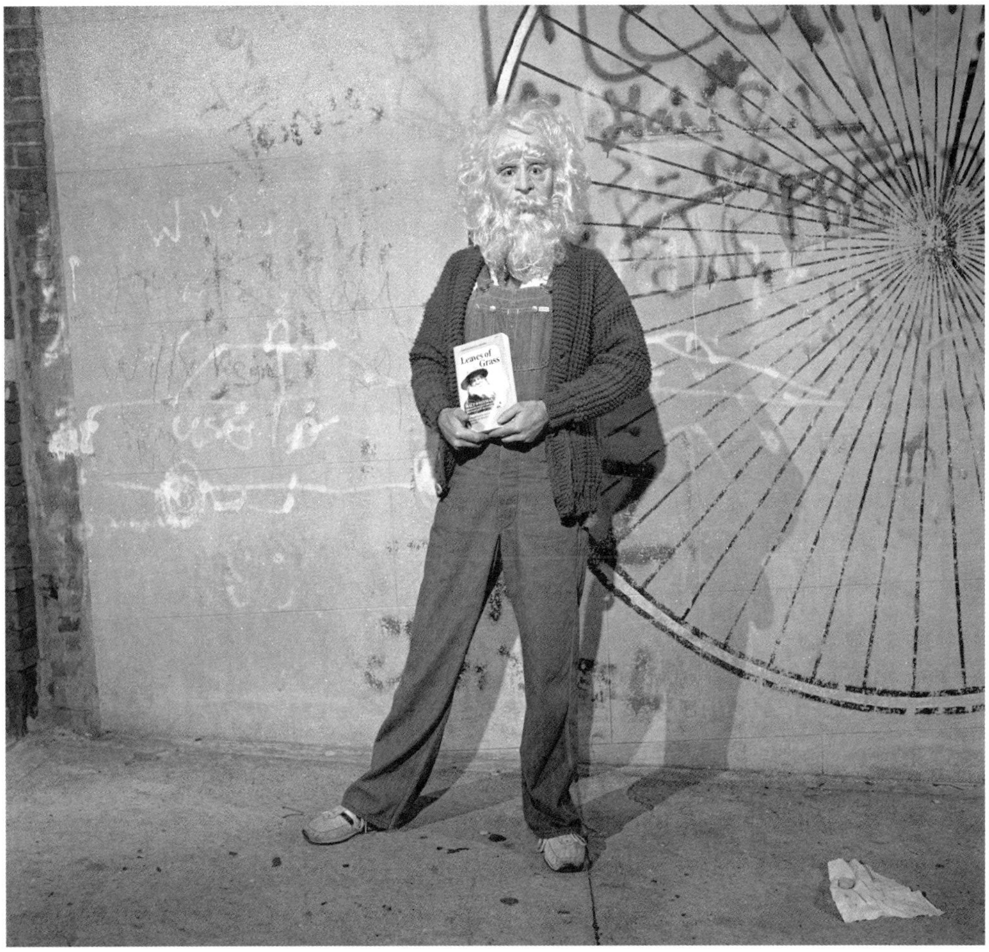

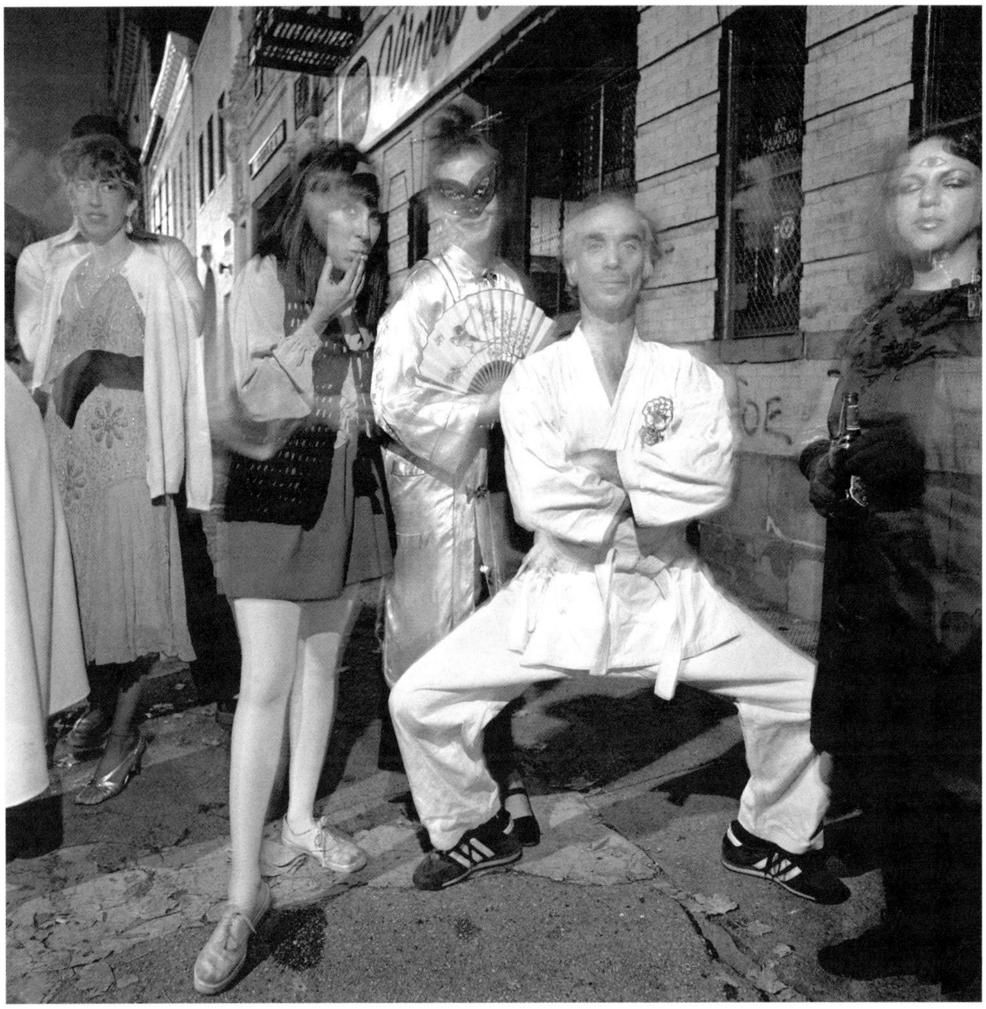

Group outside Coop,
1982, Brooklyn.

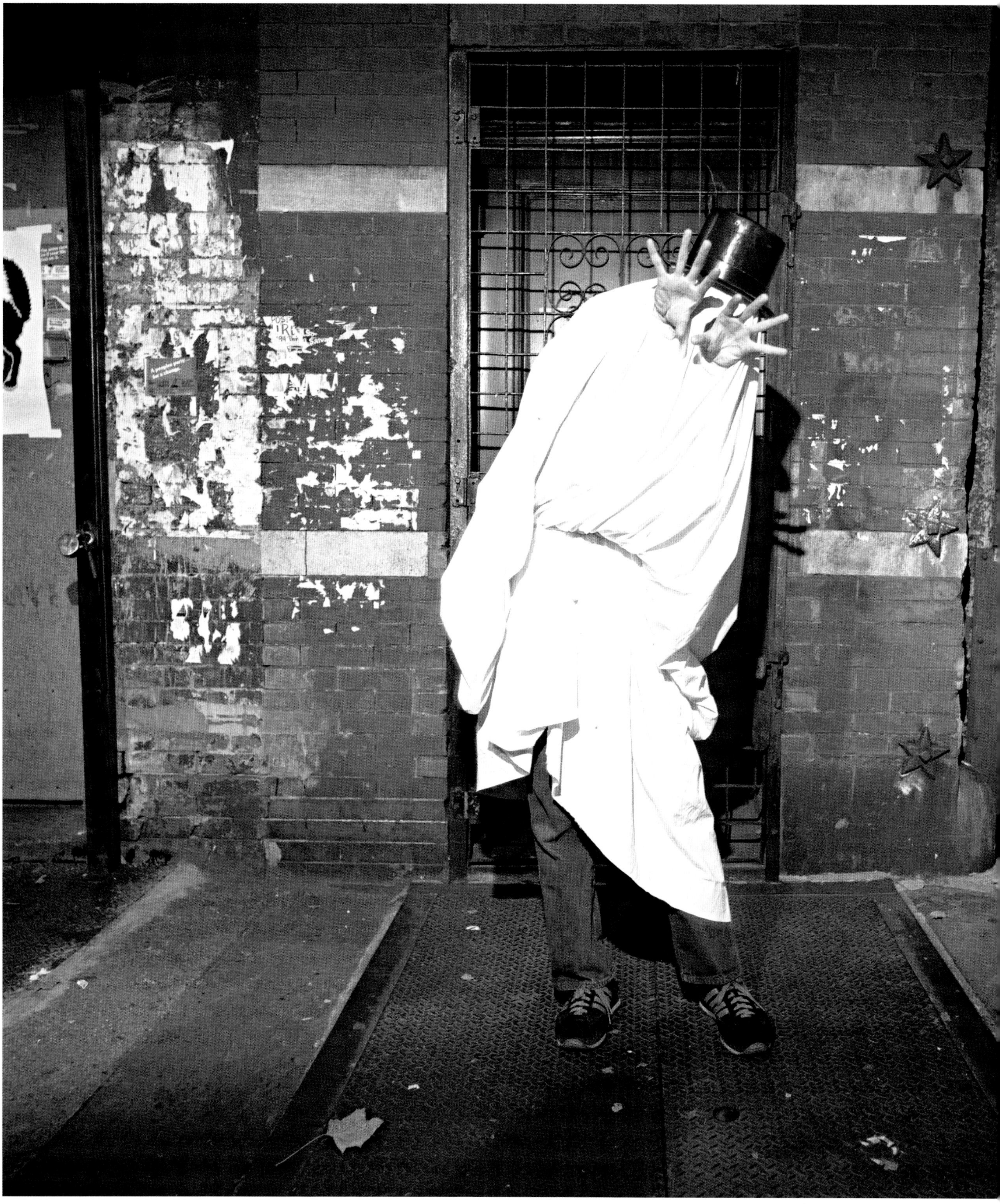

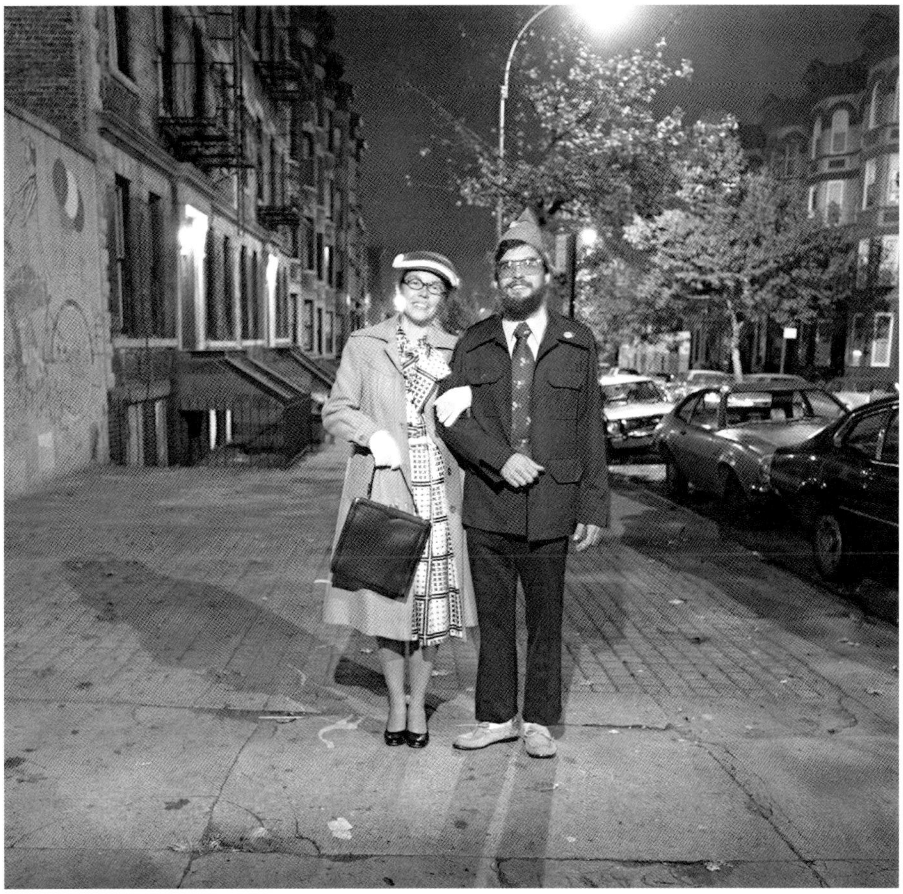

Mamie and Ike Eisenhower, 1982, Brooklyn.

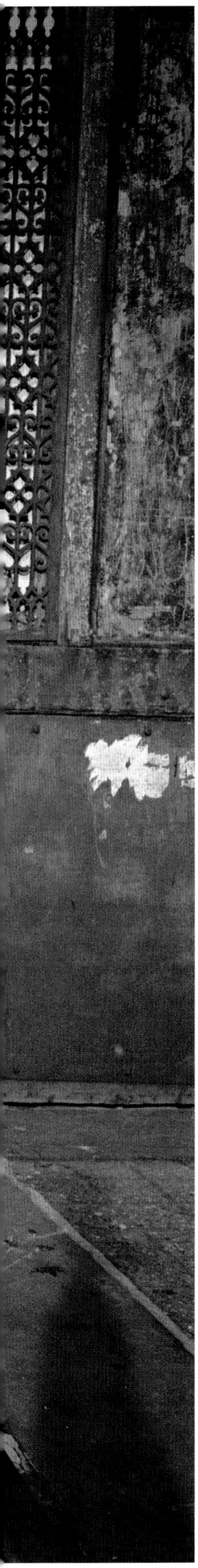

Figure with hands, 1982, Brooklyn.

Pirate and Wonder Woman, 1982, Brooklyn.

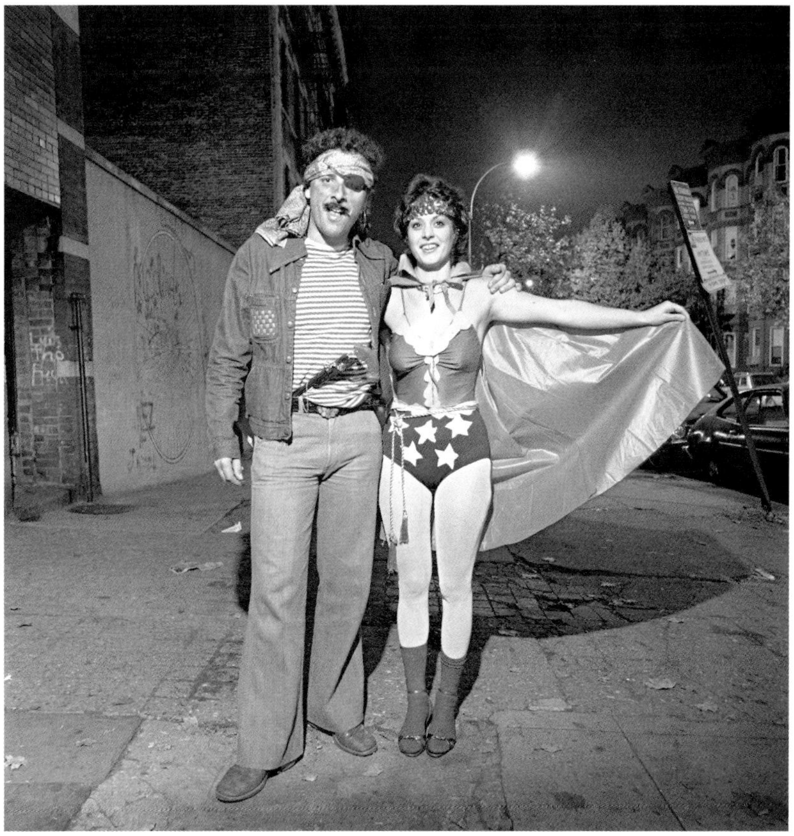

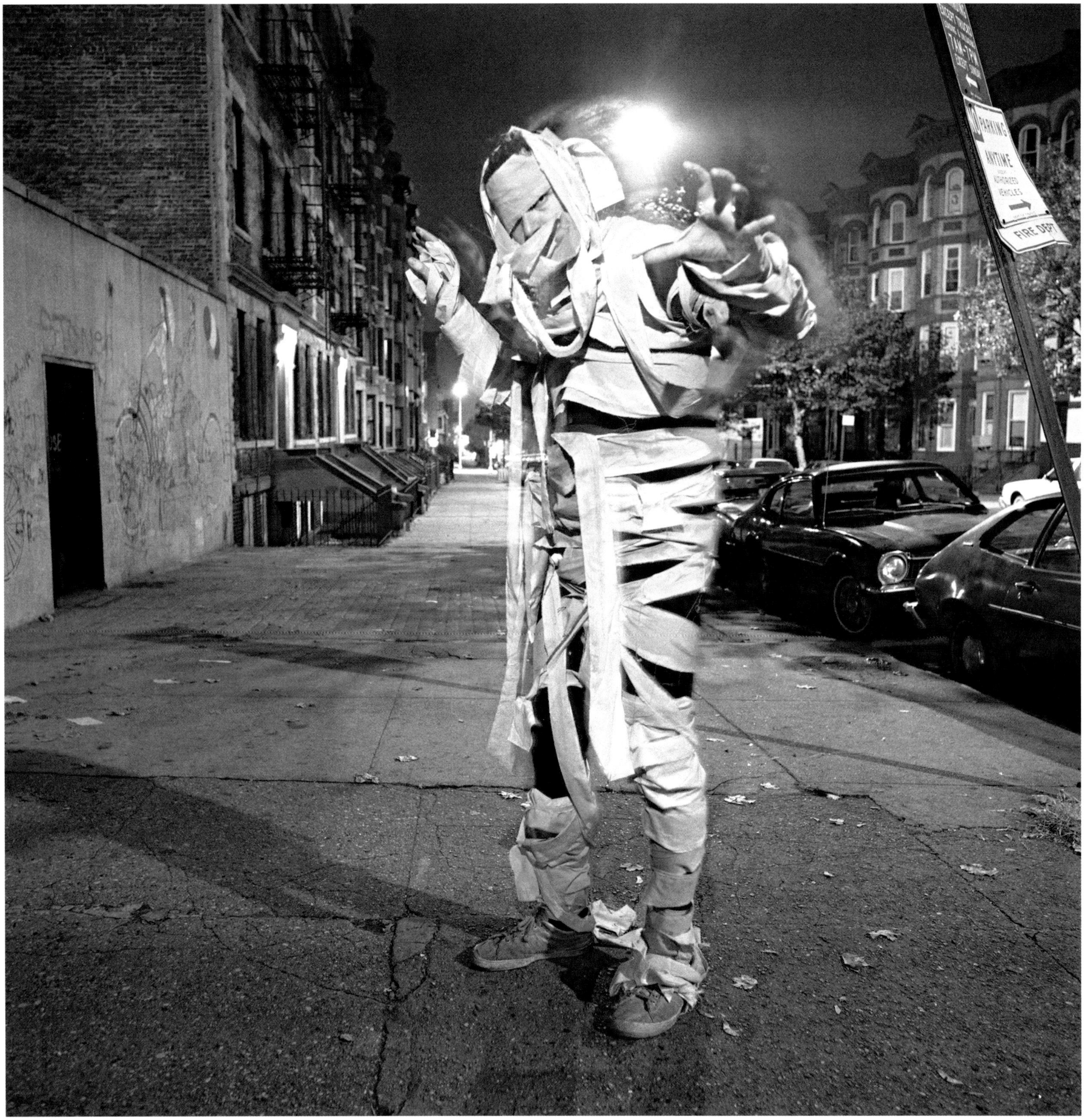

The Mummy, 1982, Brooklyn.

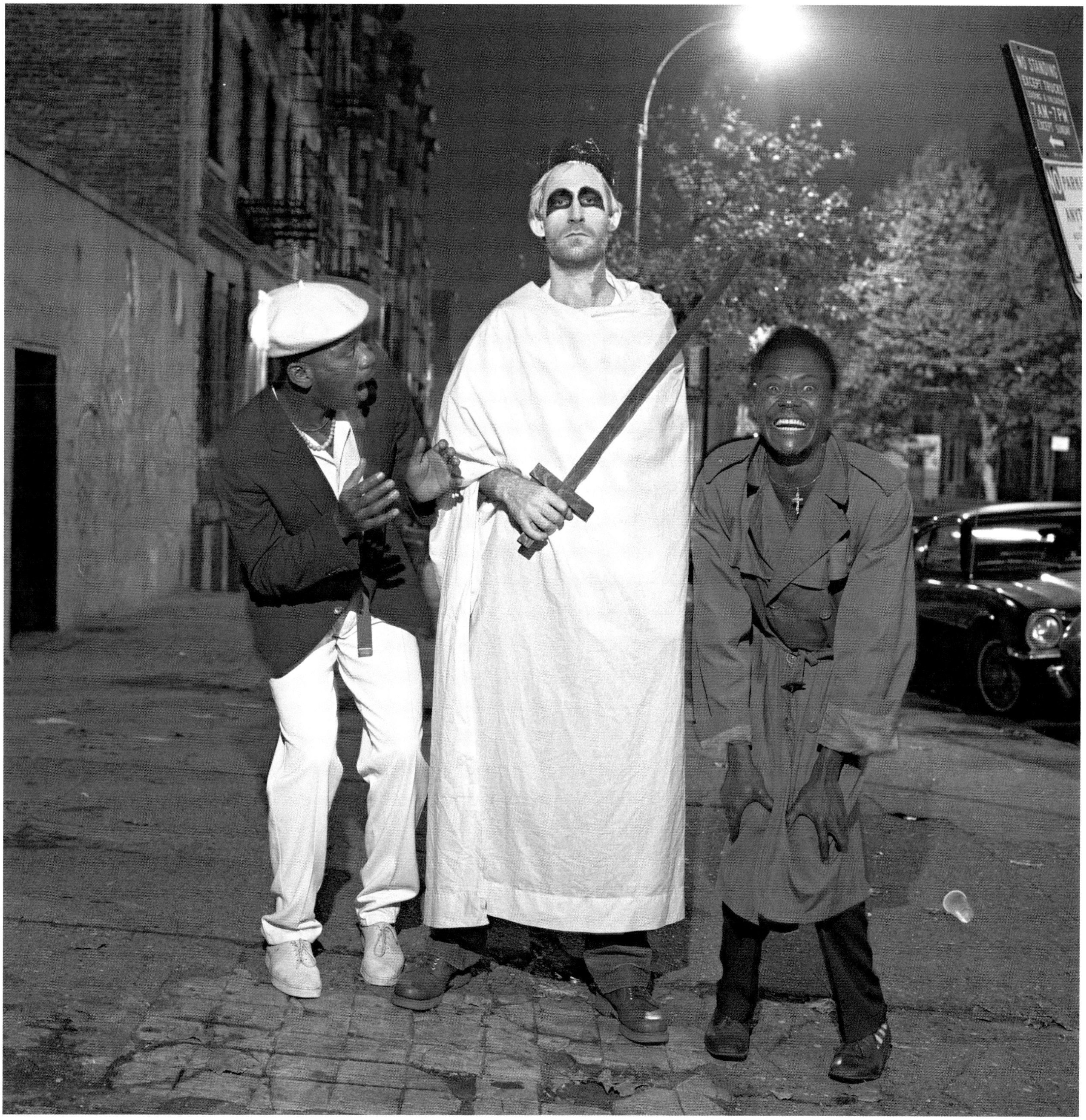

Hamlet's father and
passersby, 1982, Brooklyn.

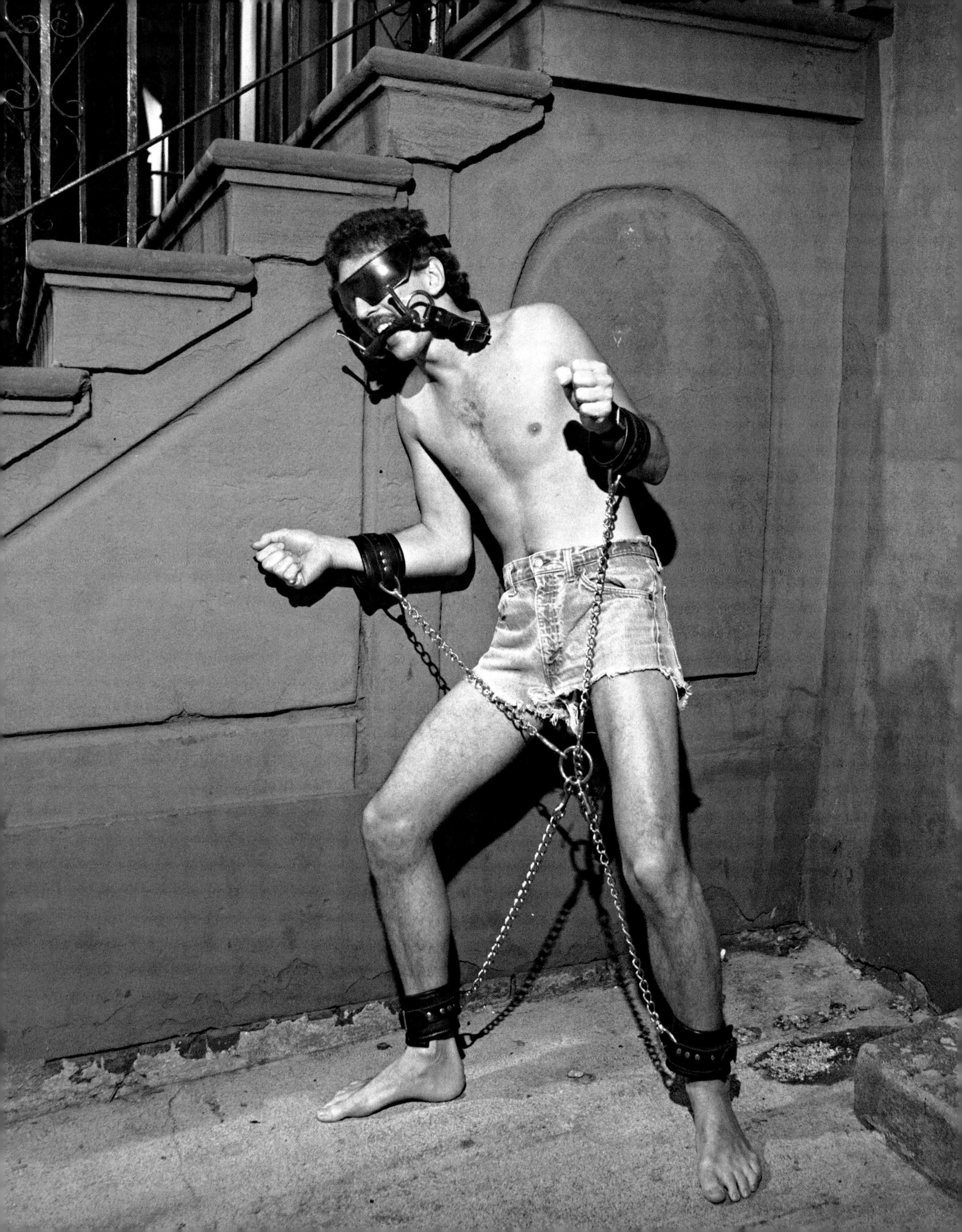

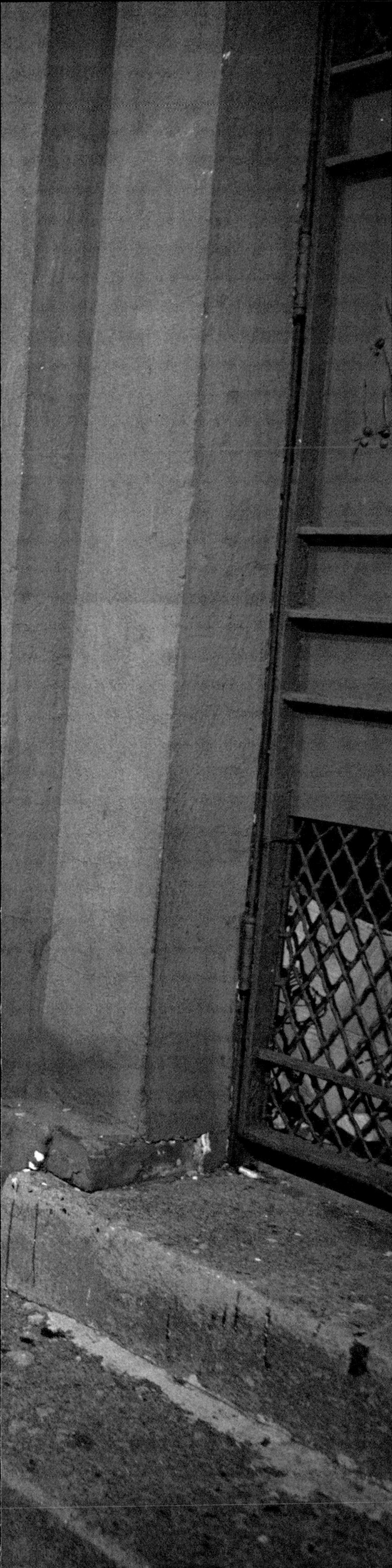

The second party took place the following night, at the SHIRTS house, the home base of my brother Robert's band. At the time, I lived on the top floor of this three-story home that included the band's rehearsal studio. I used the same technique to photograph this party as I had the night before.

Howie in chains,
1982, Brooklyn.

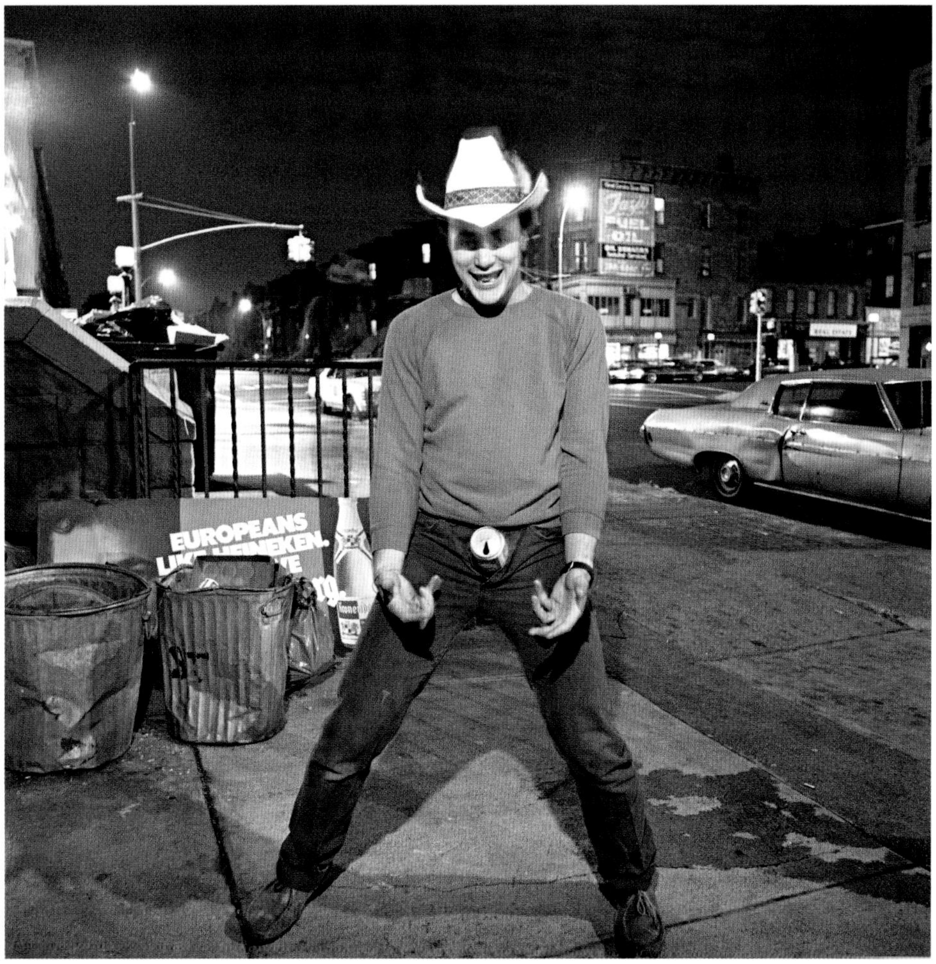

Larry with a beer can,
1982, Brooklyn.

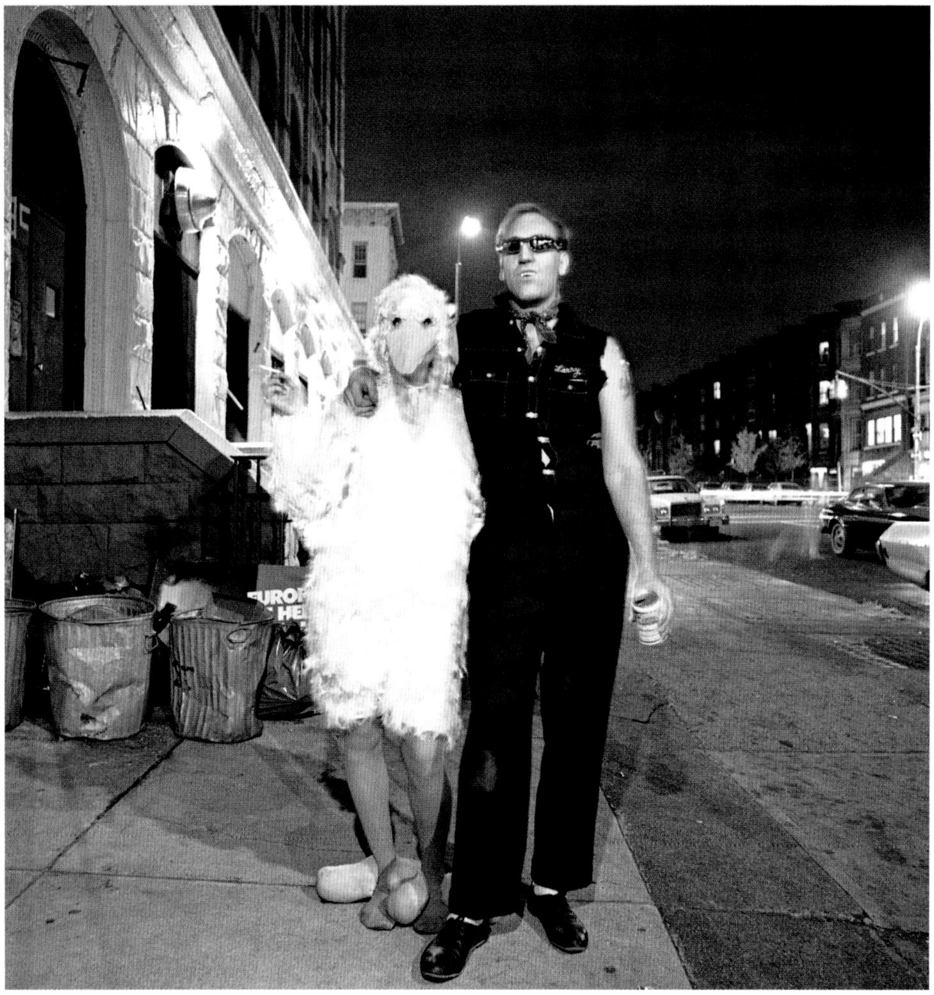

Big Bird and vampire,
1982, Brooklyn.

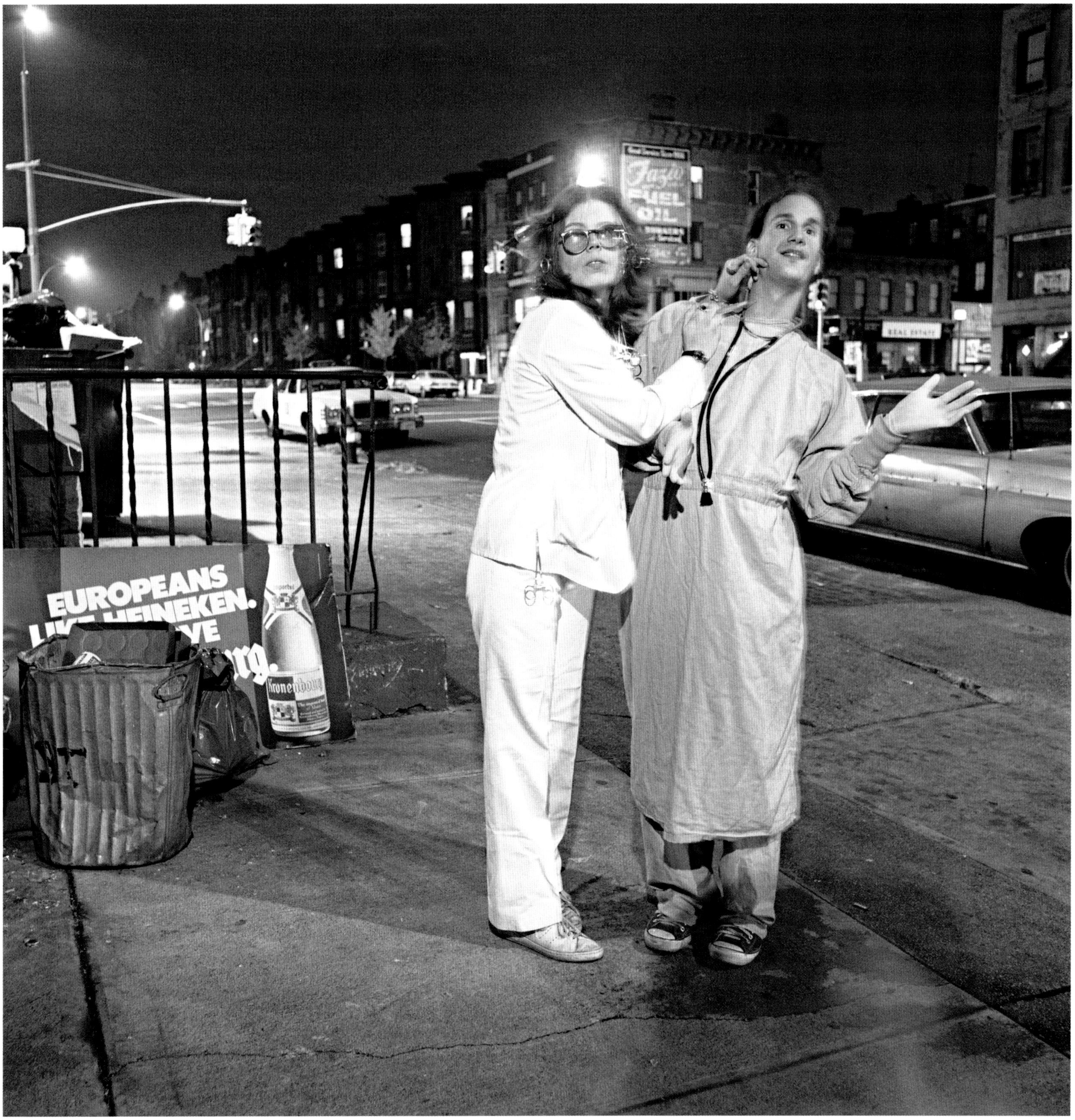

Two nurses, 1982, Brooklyn.

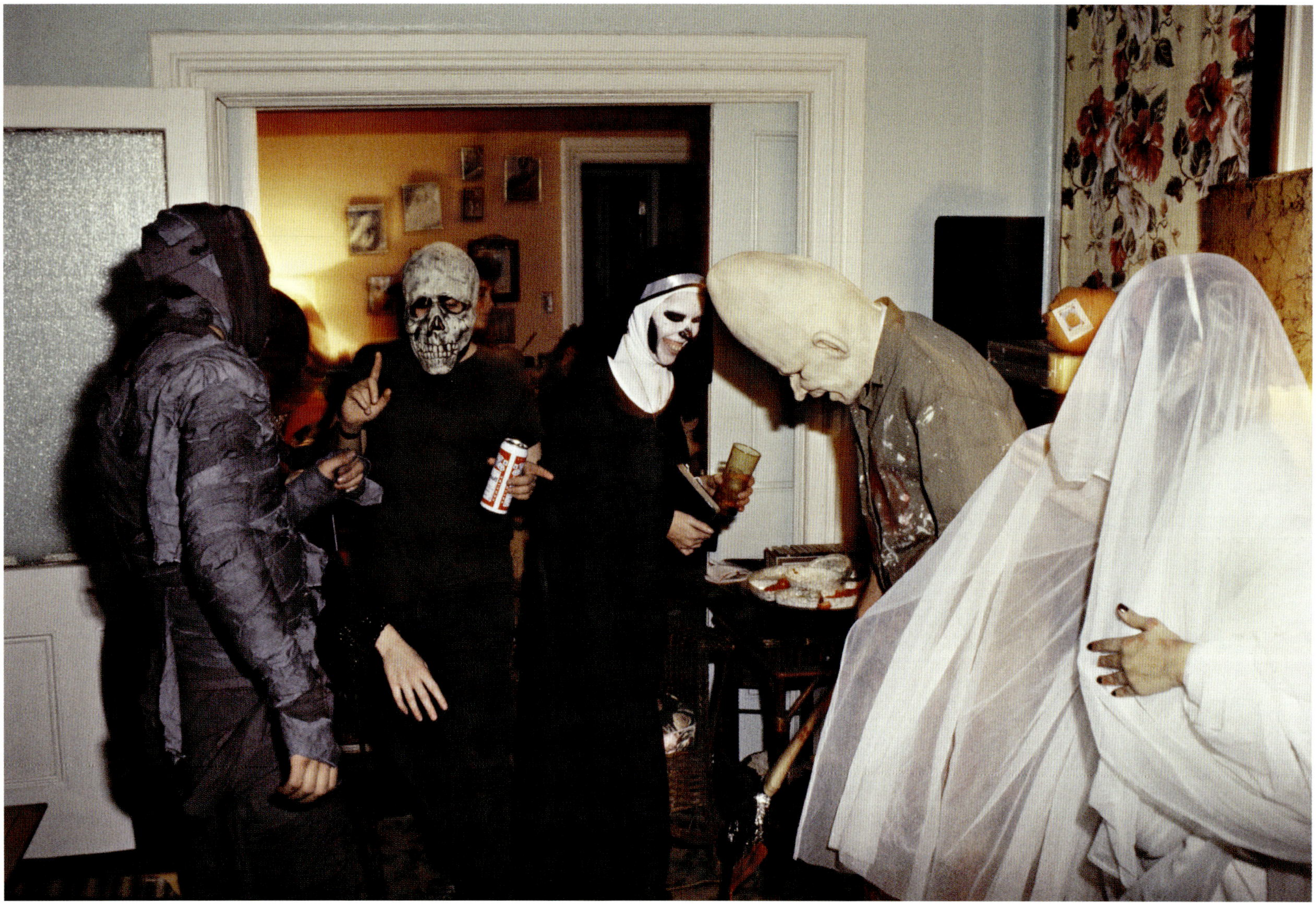

Nun and Conehead
dancing, 1987, Brooklyn.

I also used a flash when photographing at night in bars and at parties.

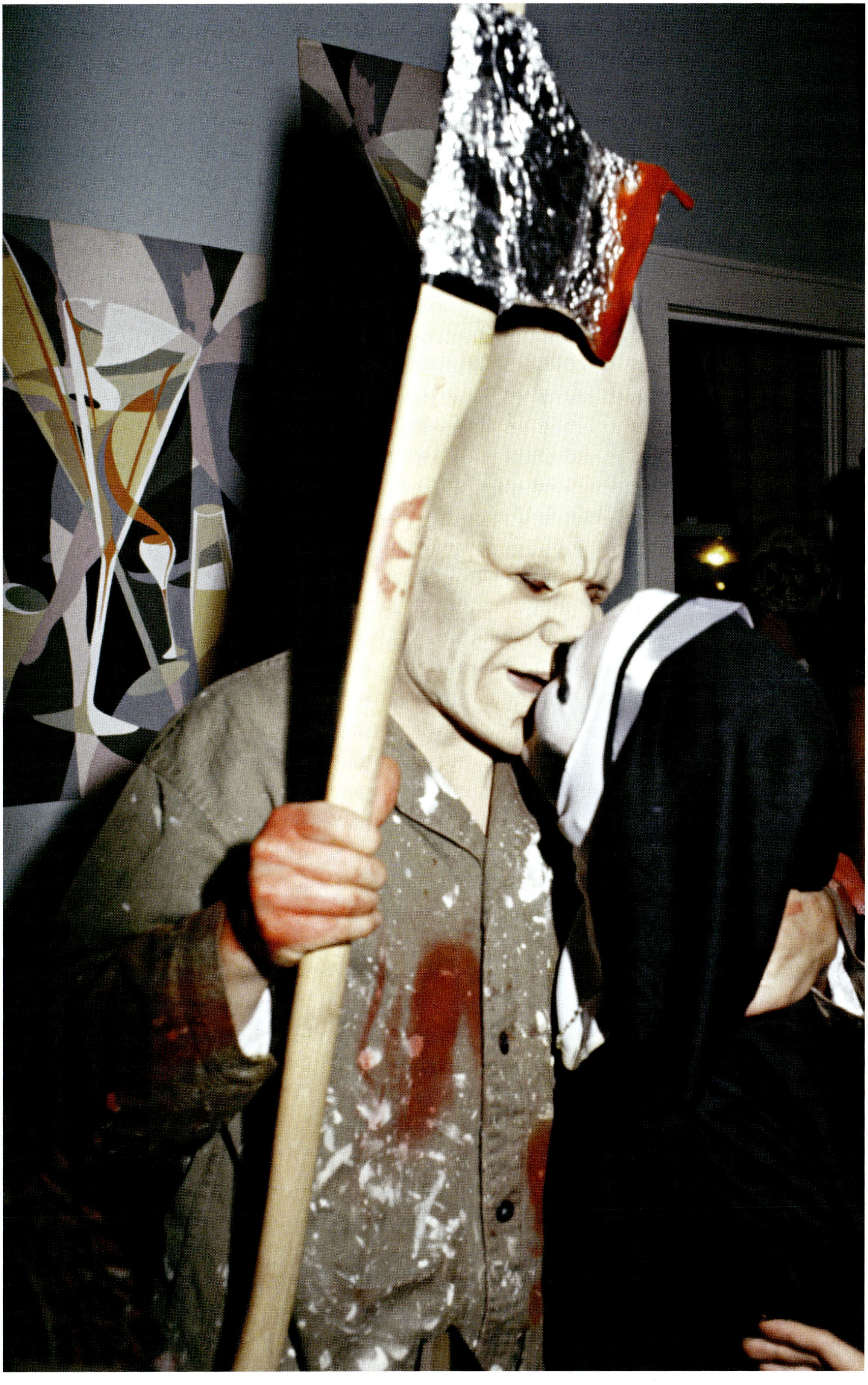

Kissing Conehead
with axe, 1987,
Brooklyn.

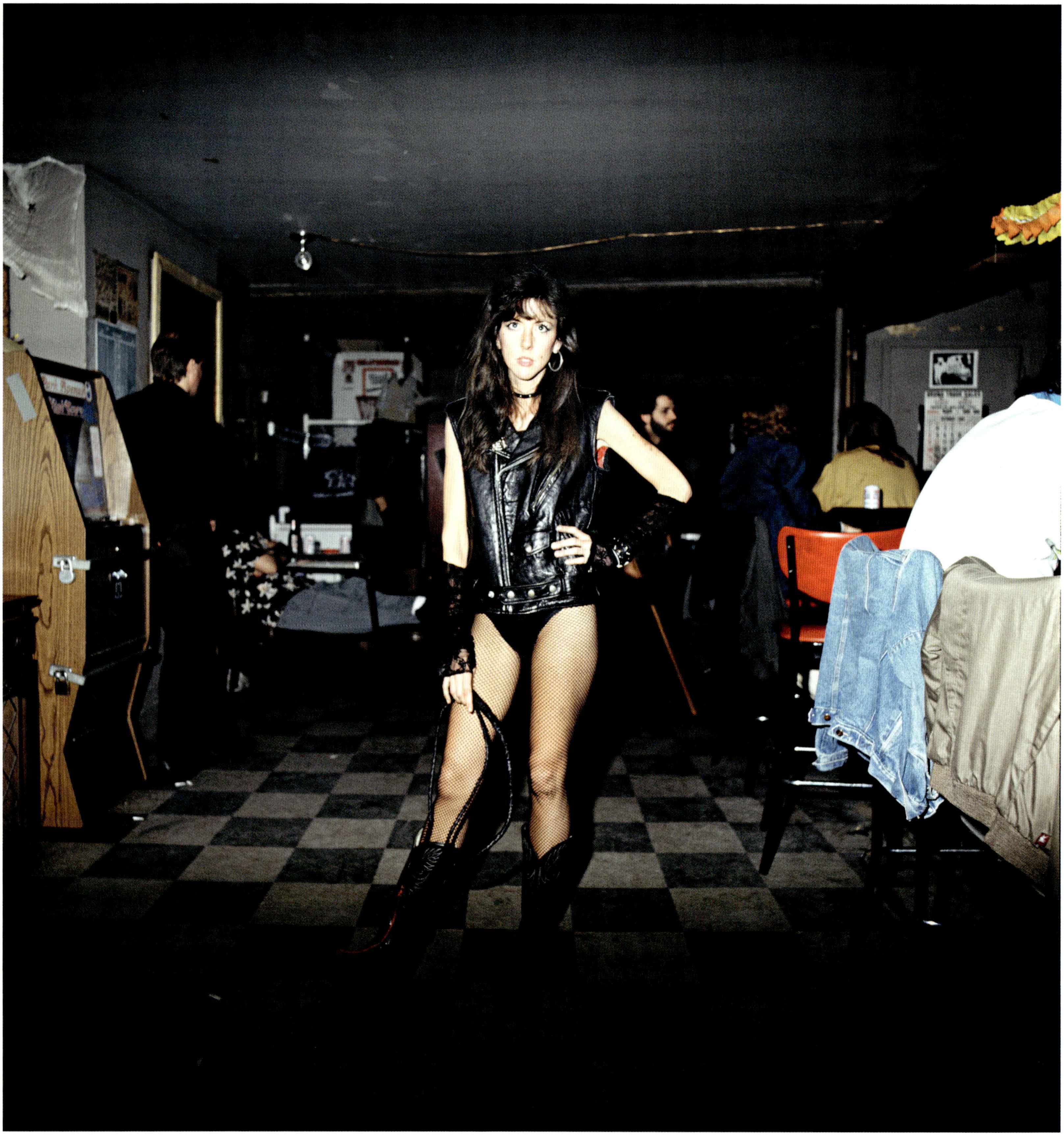

Dominatrix at
Lauterbach's' bar,
1987, Brooklyn.

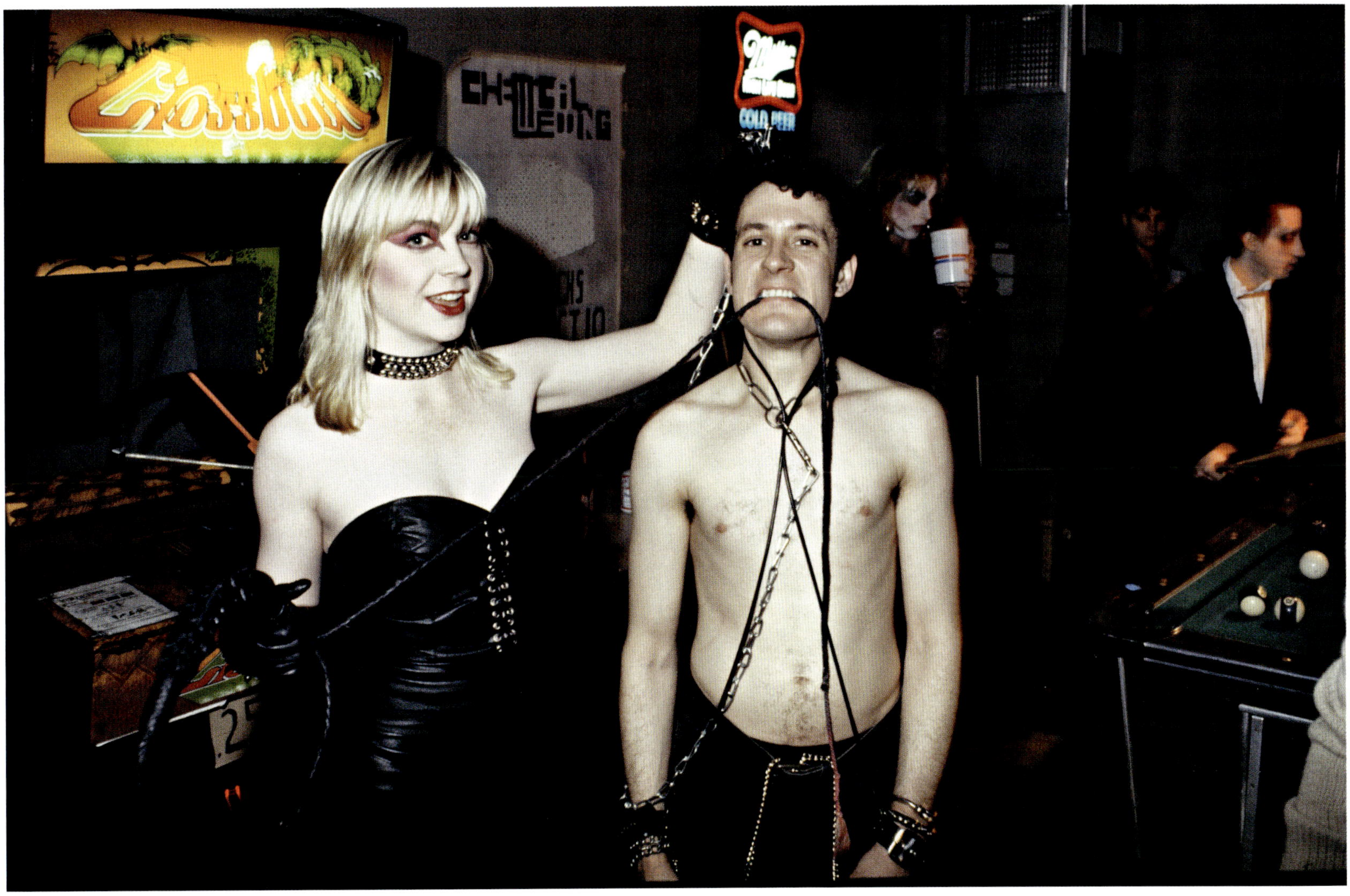

S&M couple at
Lauterbach's bar,
1987, Brooklyn.

After a Break, in Brooklyn and Queens

2020s

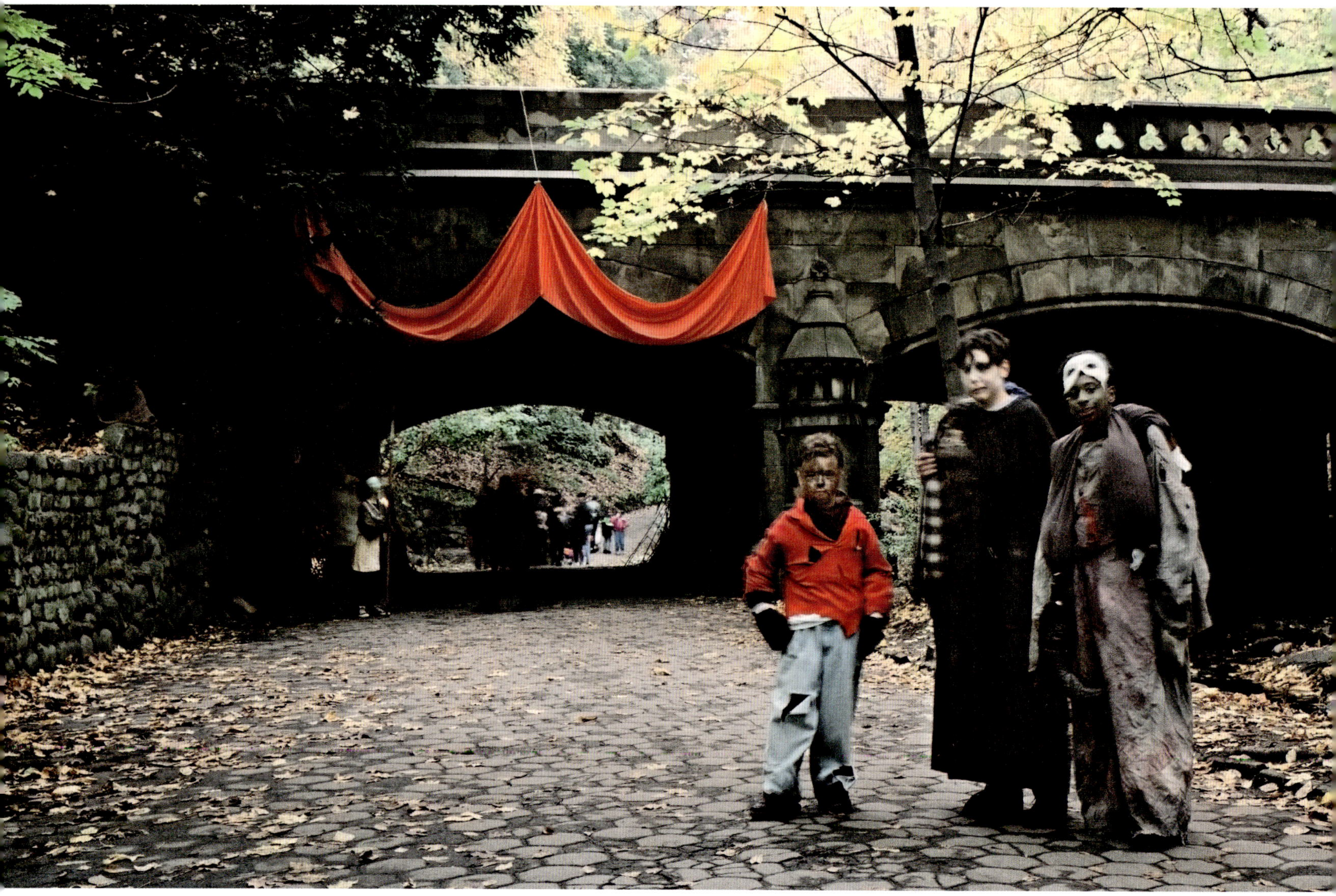

By 1983, I was having a hard time earning money as a photographer. I was doing more carpentry work to support myself. I went from shooting about 150 rolls of film per year to 10. Until I started working on this book, I was unaware that I did not photograph again on Halloween until 1992, when I shot one roll of film with my nephew in Prospect Park

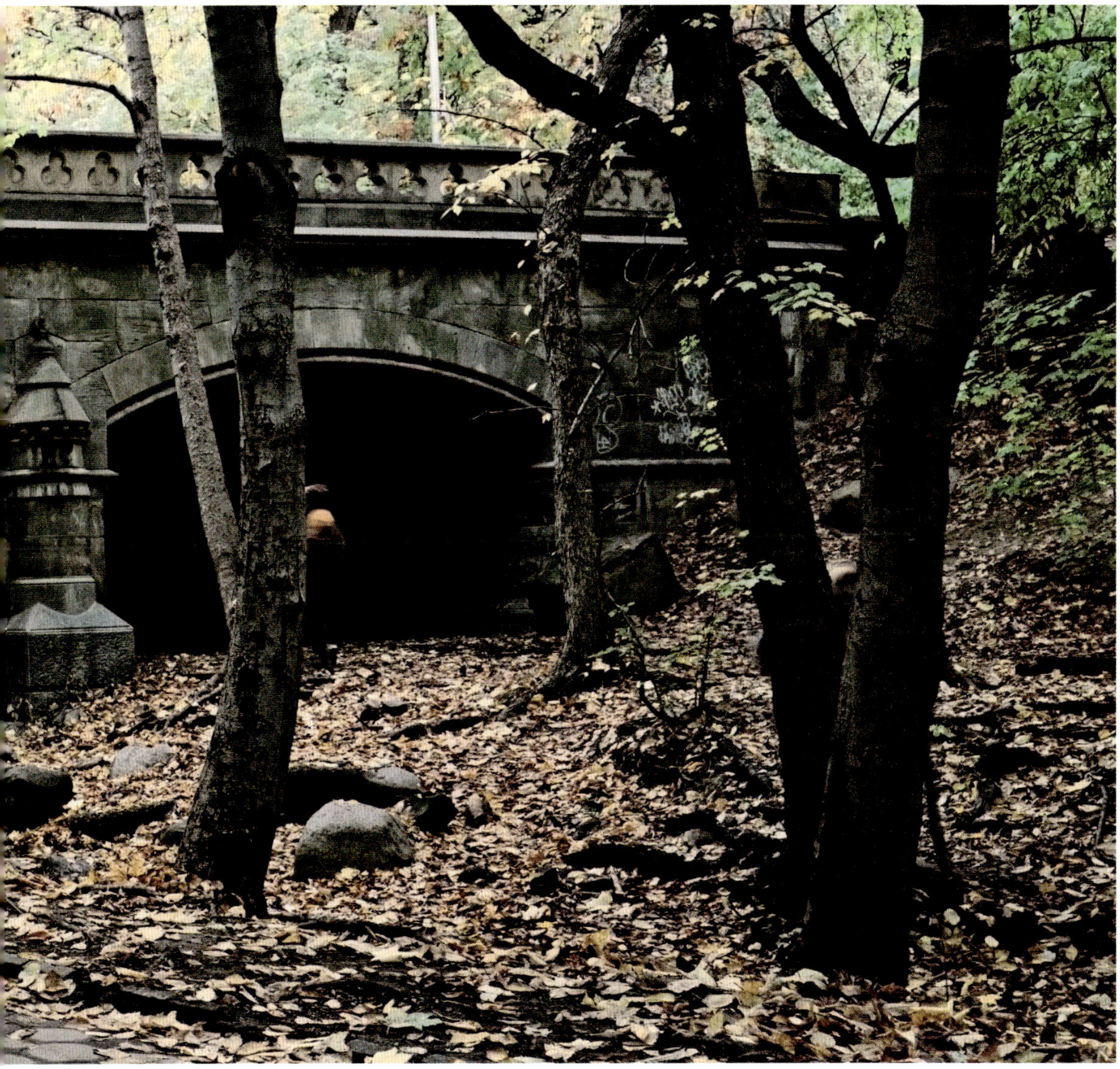

Michael in Prospect Park, 1992, Brooklyn.

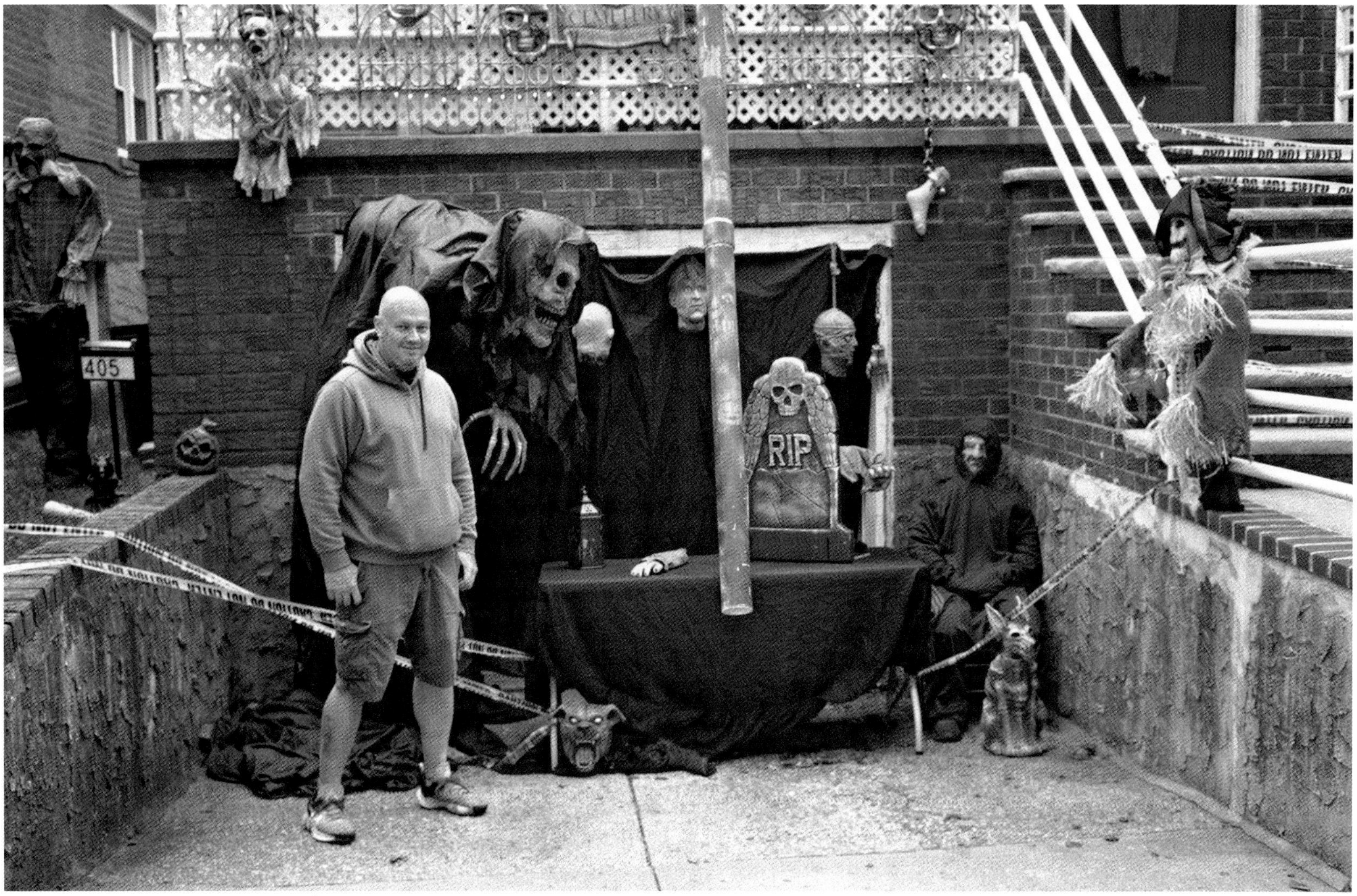

Man and haunted garage, 2023, Queens.

After I got married in 1991, I moved from Brooklyn to Rockaway, Queens, and began to photograph on Halloween in both boroughs. I started going to "haunted houses," parties, and unusual places I read about.

"Welcome to
all spirits . . . ,"
1995, Brooklyn.

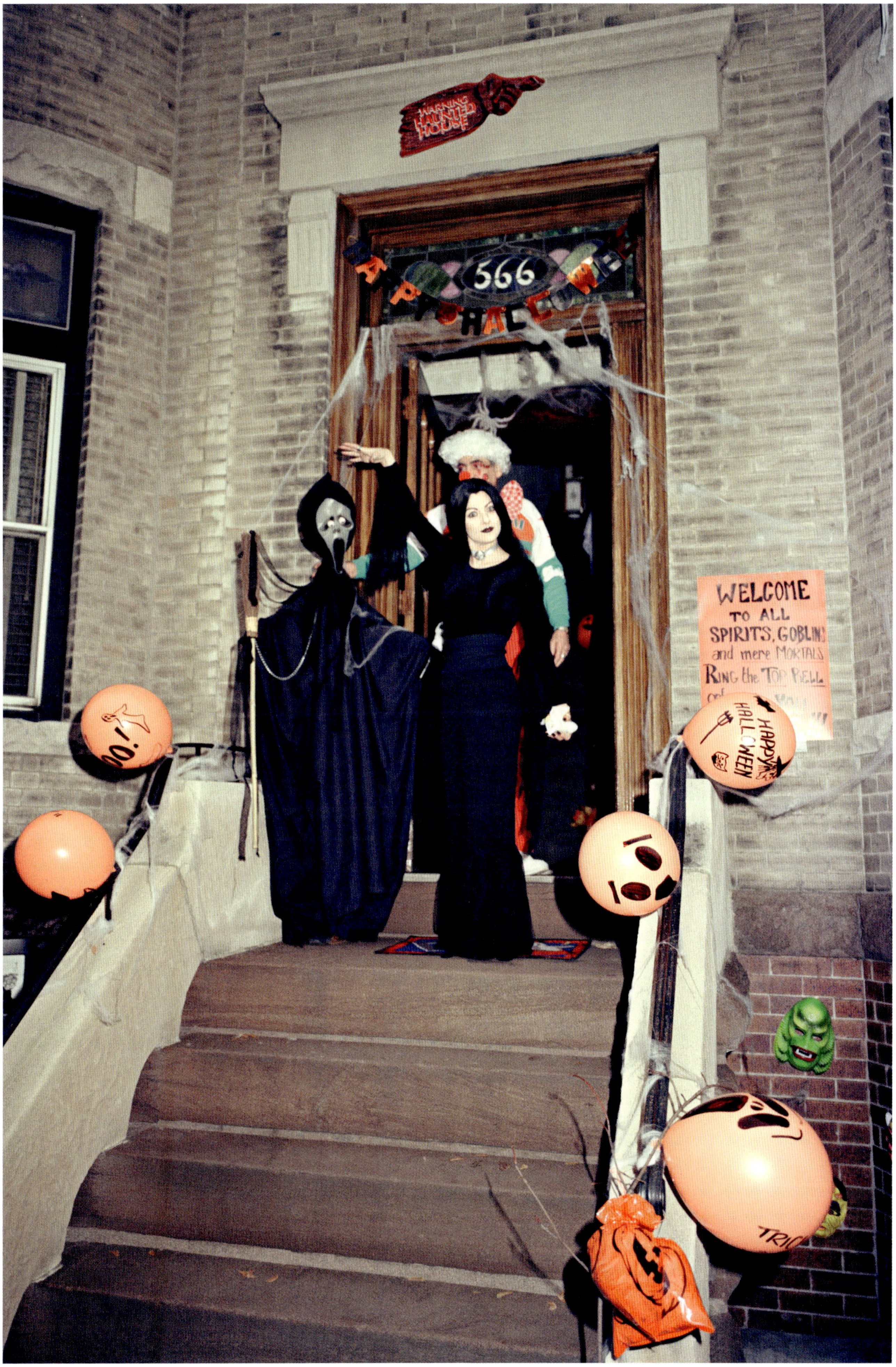

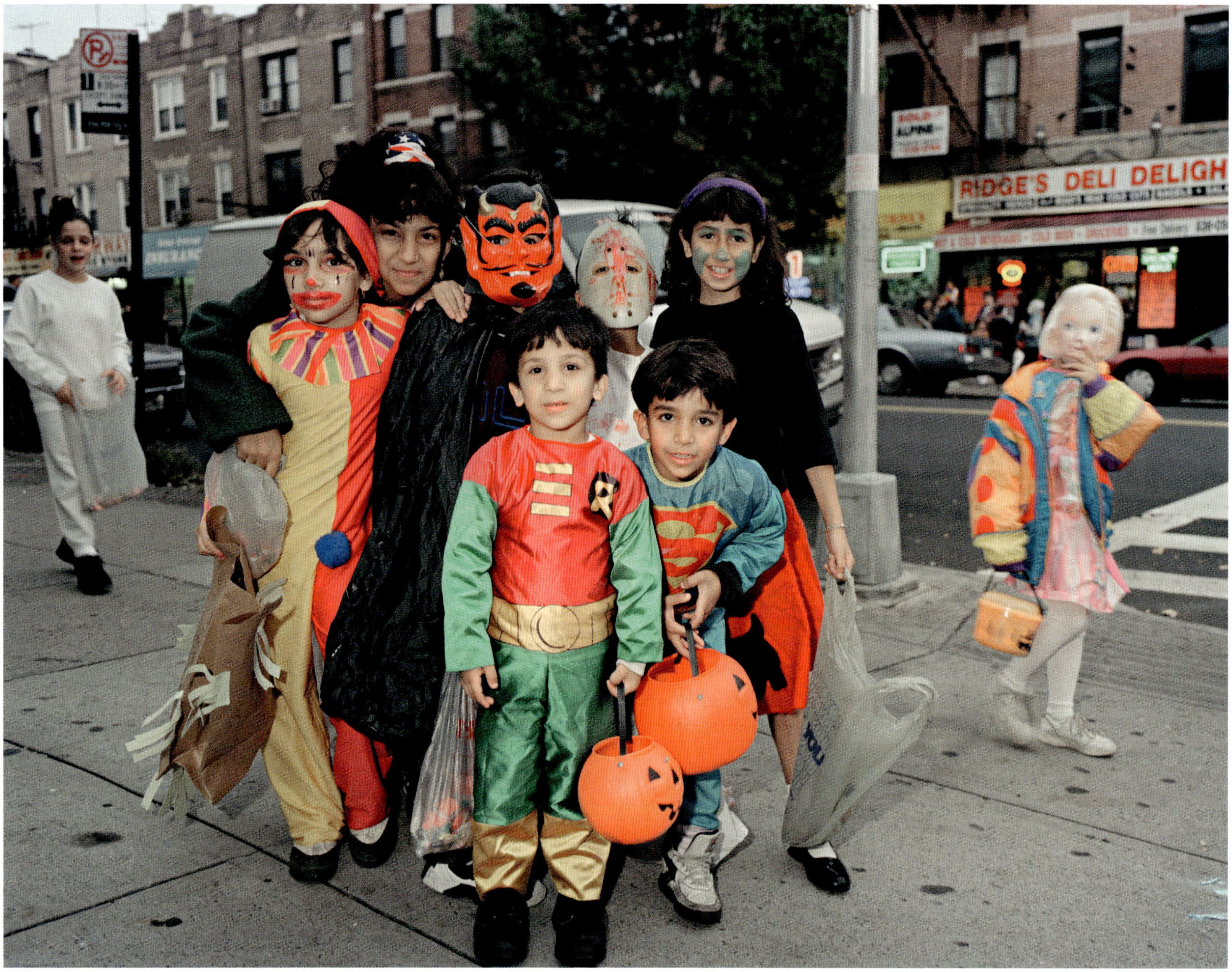

Costumed kids on 5th Avenue, 1995, Brooklyn.

With my finances in better shape, I went back to photographing seriously on Halloween in 1994 and 1995, splitting my time between South Brooklyn and Rockaway. (With very few exceptions, I have photographed on every Halloween since 1994.)

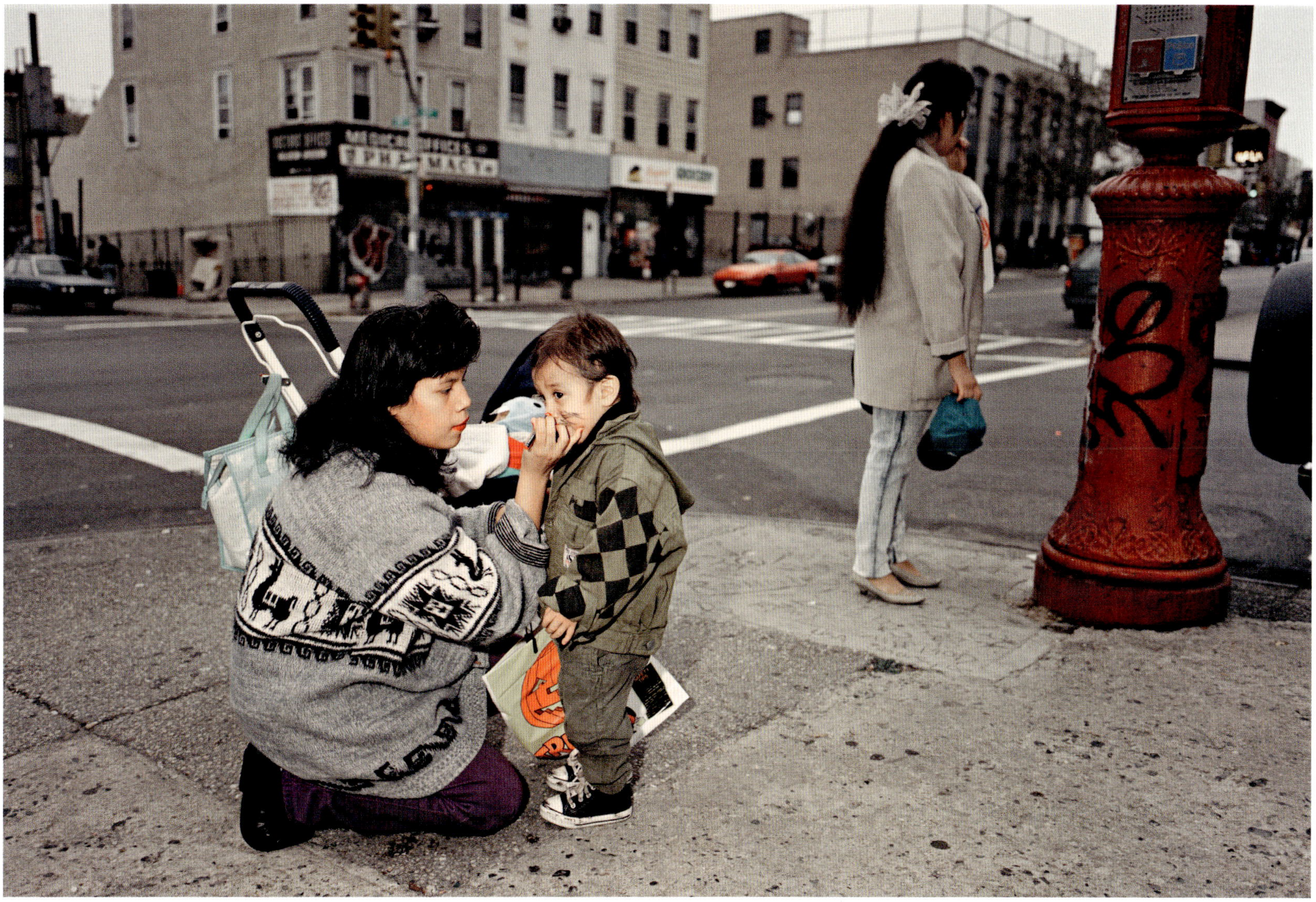

Woman applying cat makeup, 1994, Brooklyn.

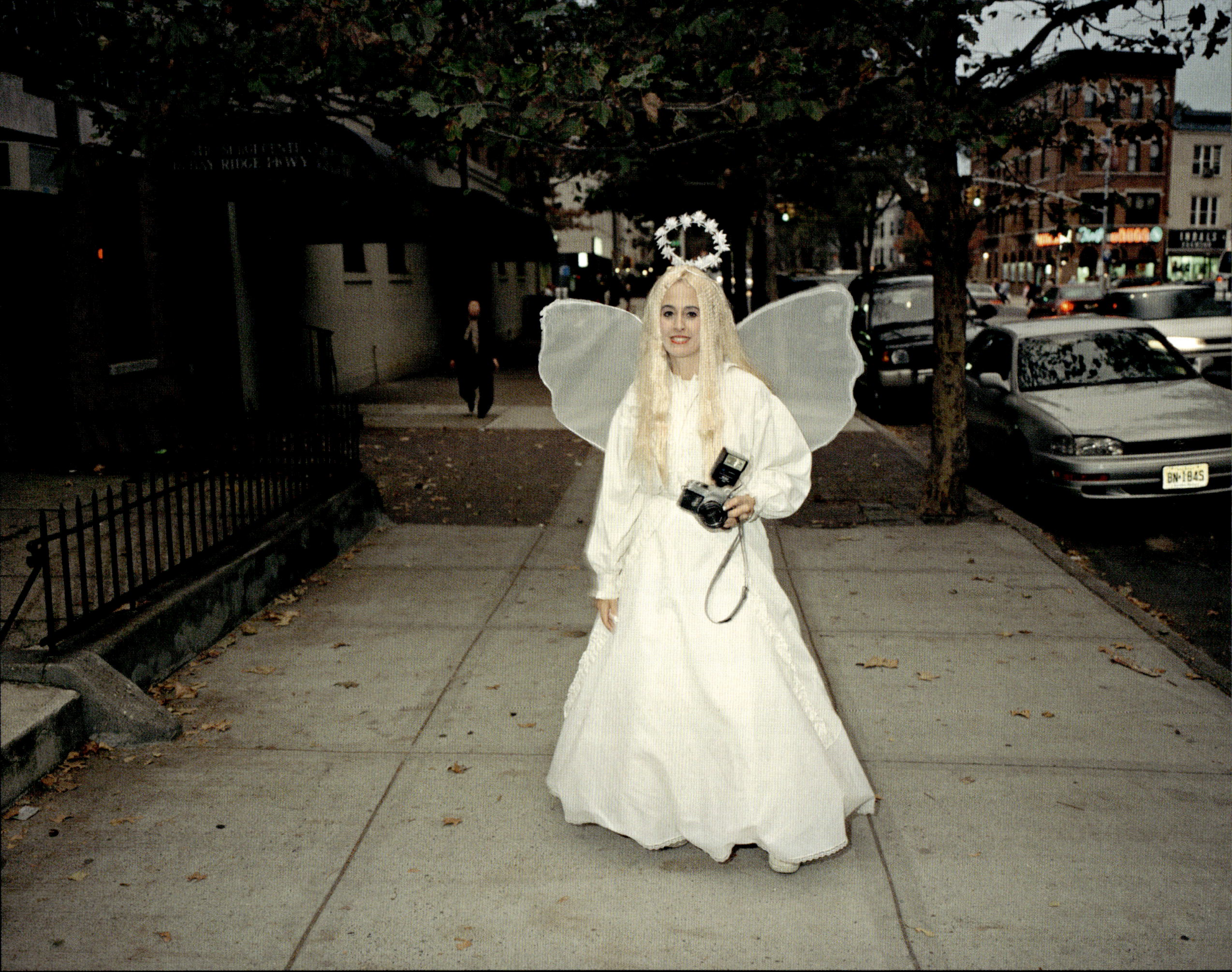

Angel with camera,
1995, Brooklyn.

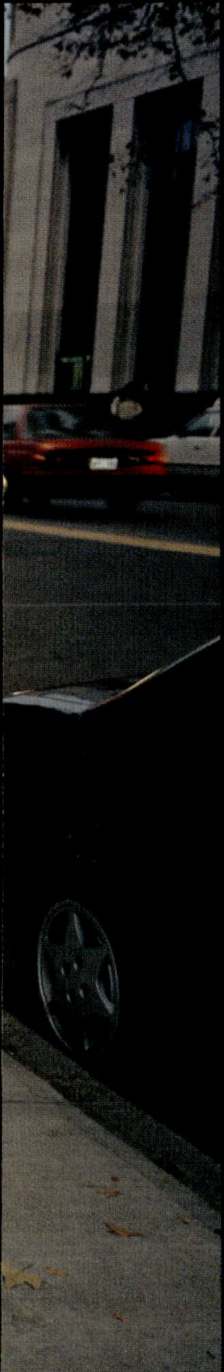

Batman and angel, 1994, Brooklyn.

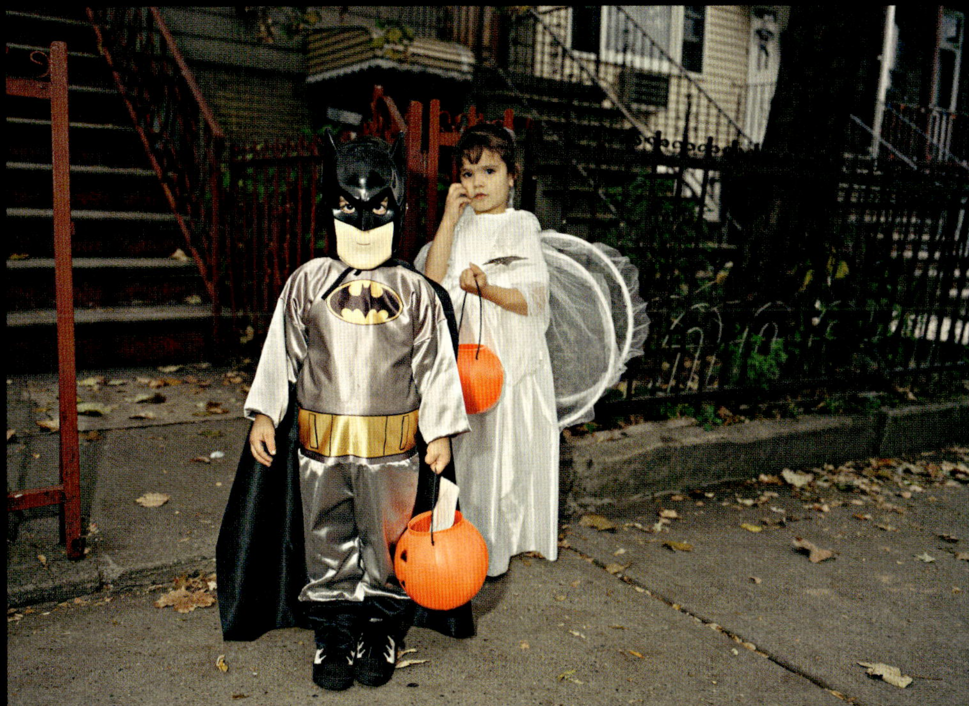

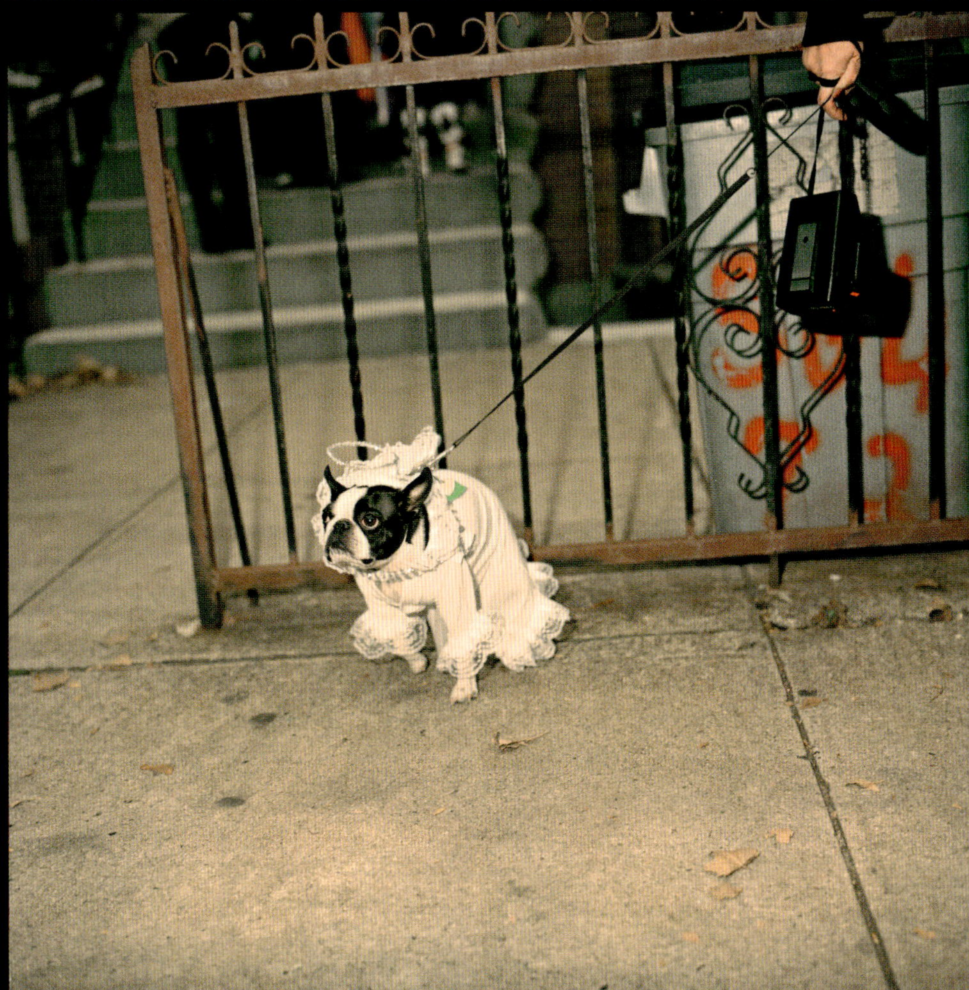

Small dog in angel costume, 1995, Brooklyn.

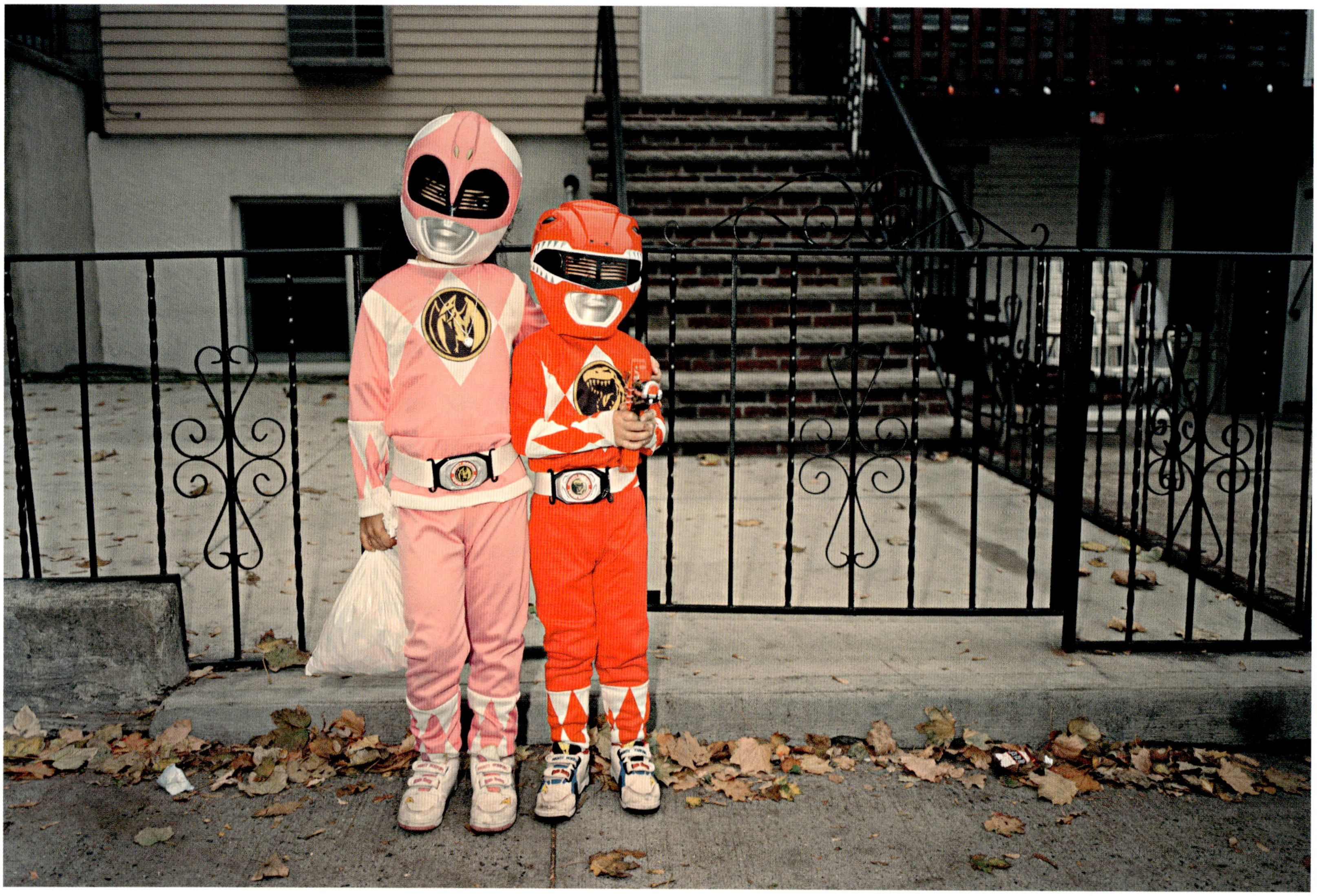

Above: Power Ranger kids and leaves, 1994, Brooklyn.

Opposite: Boy/Girl, 1995, Brooklyn.

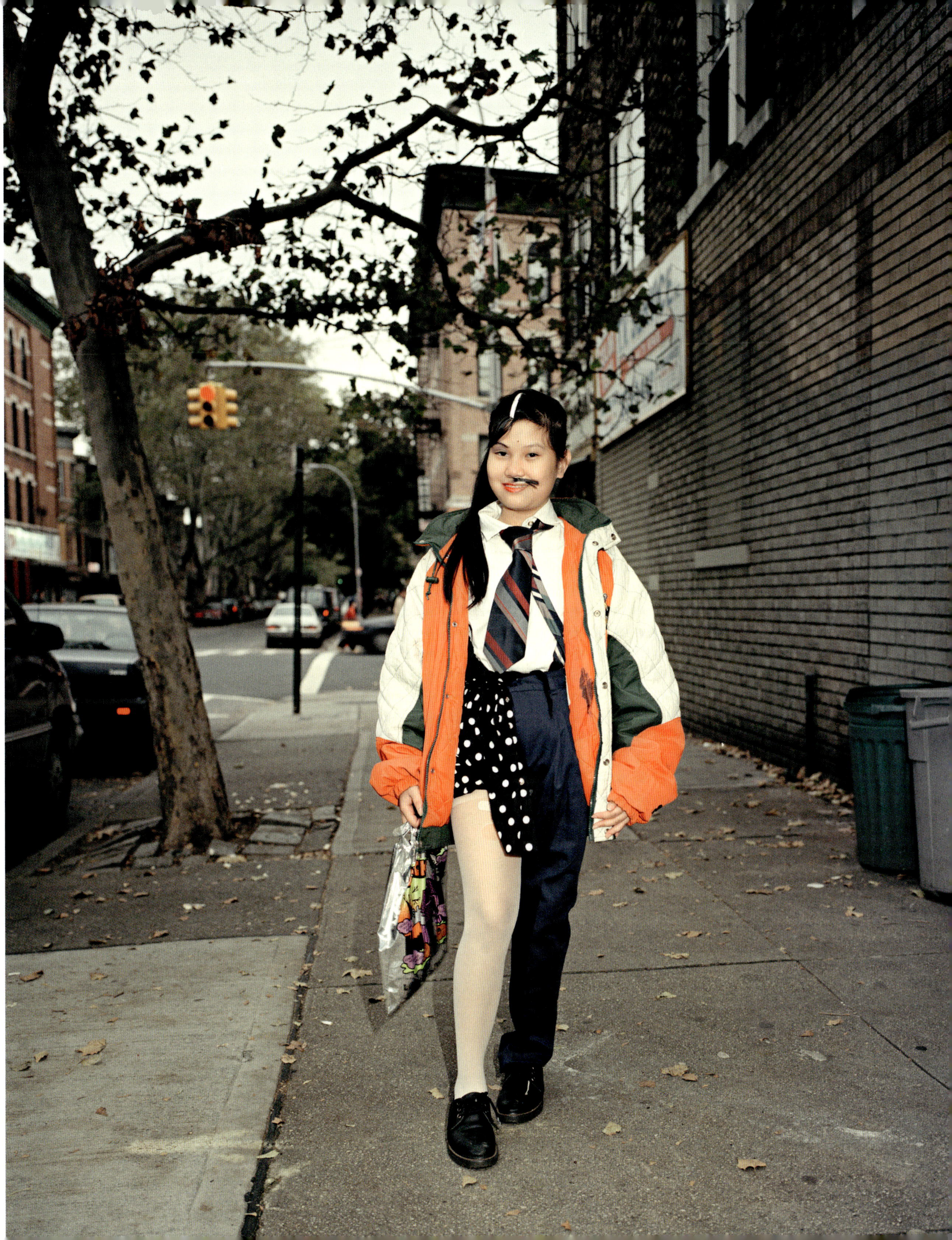

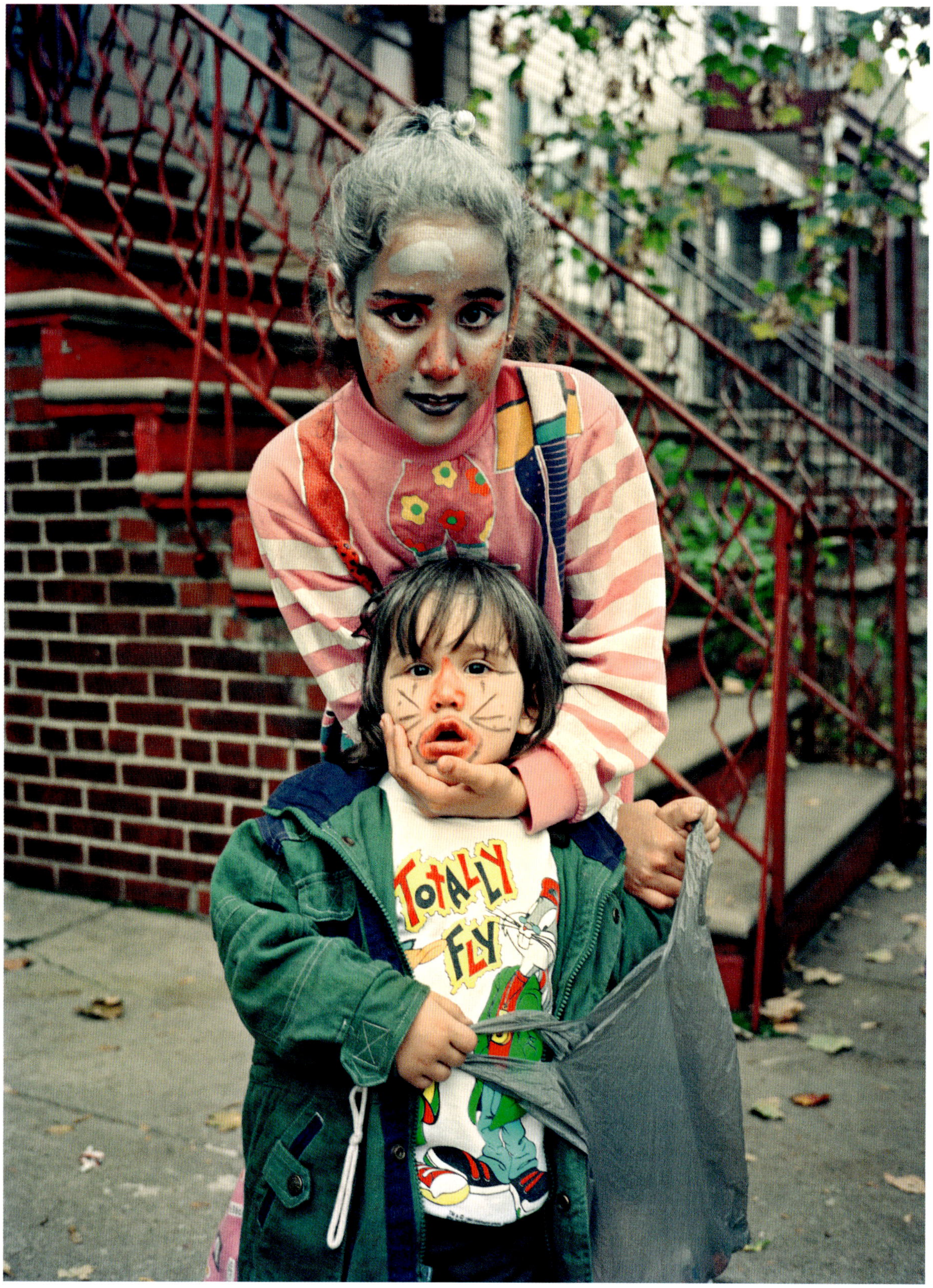

“Totally fly” kids,
1994, Brooklyn.

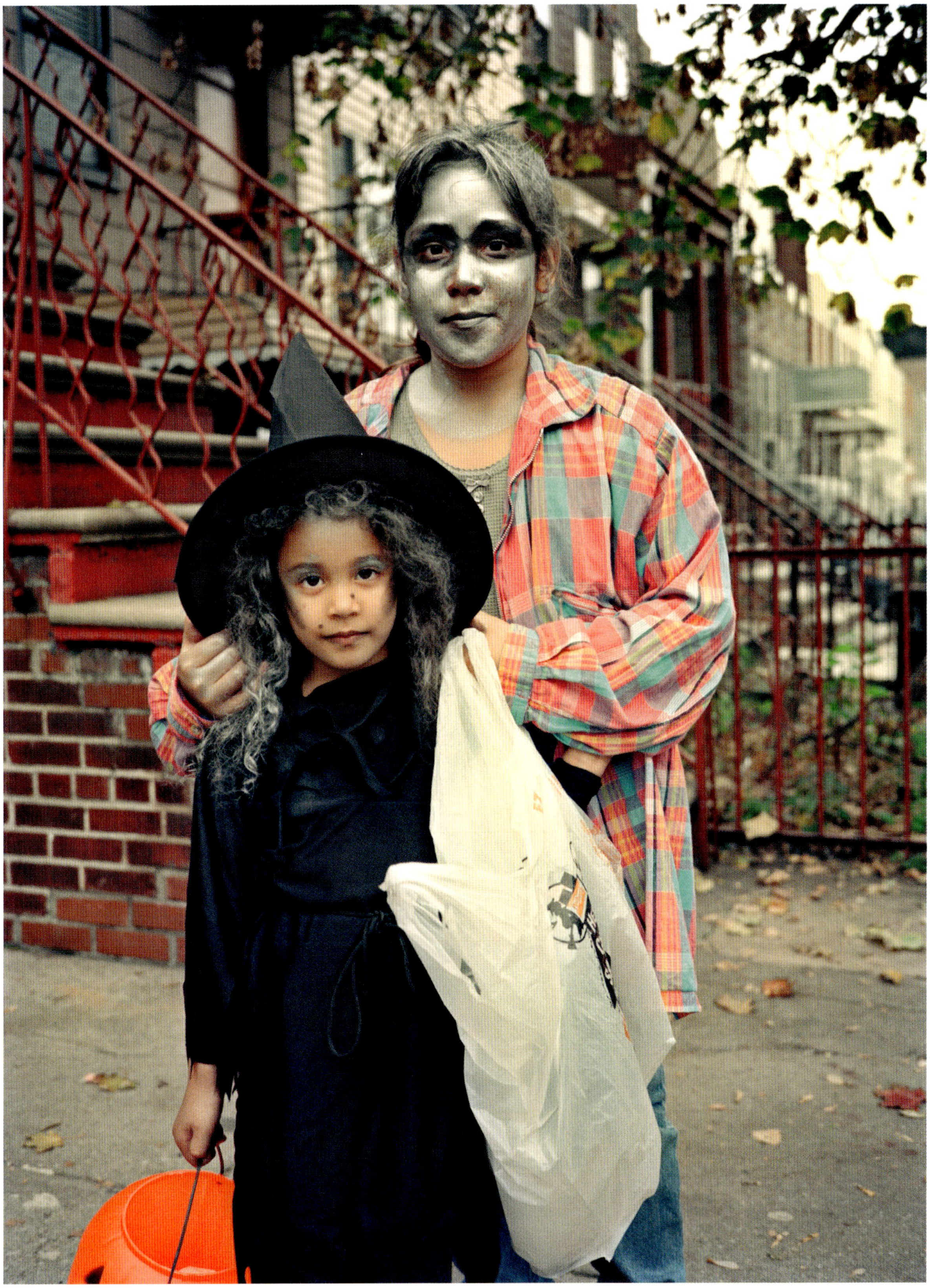

Silver face and witch,
1994, Brooklyn.

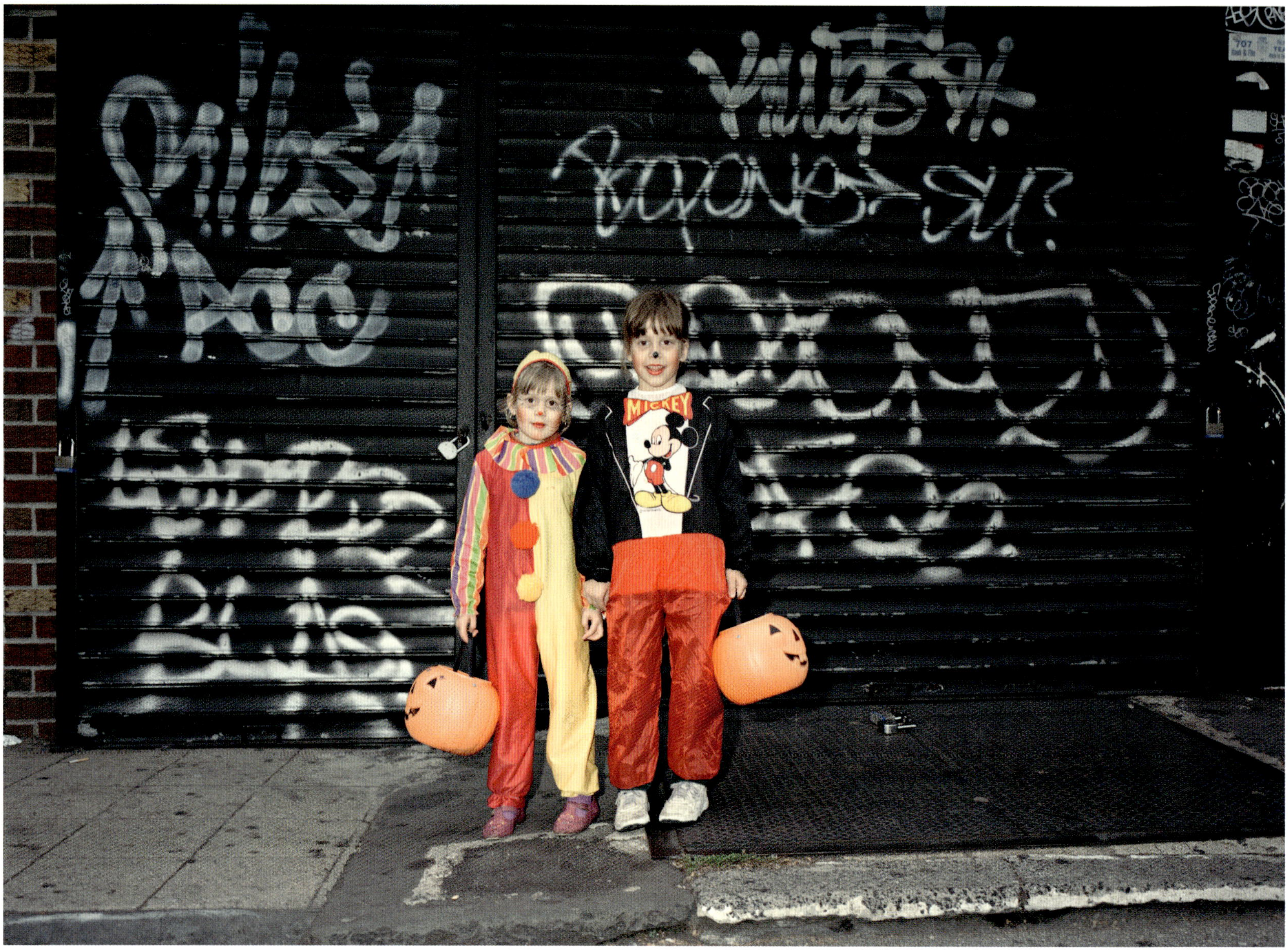

Clown and Mickey
Mouse, 1994, Brooklyn.

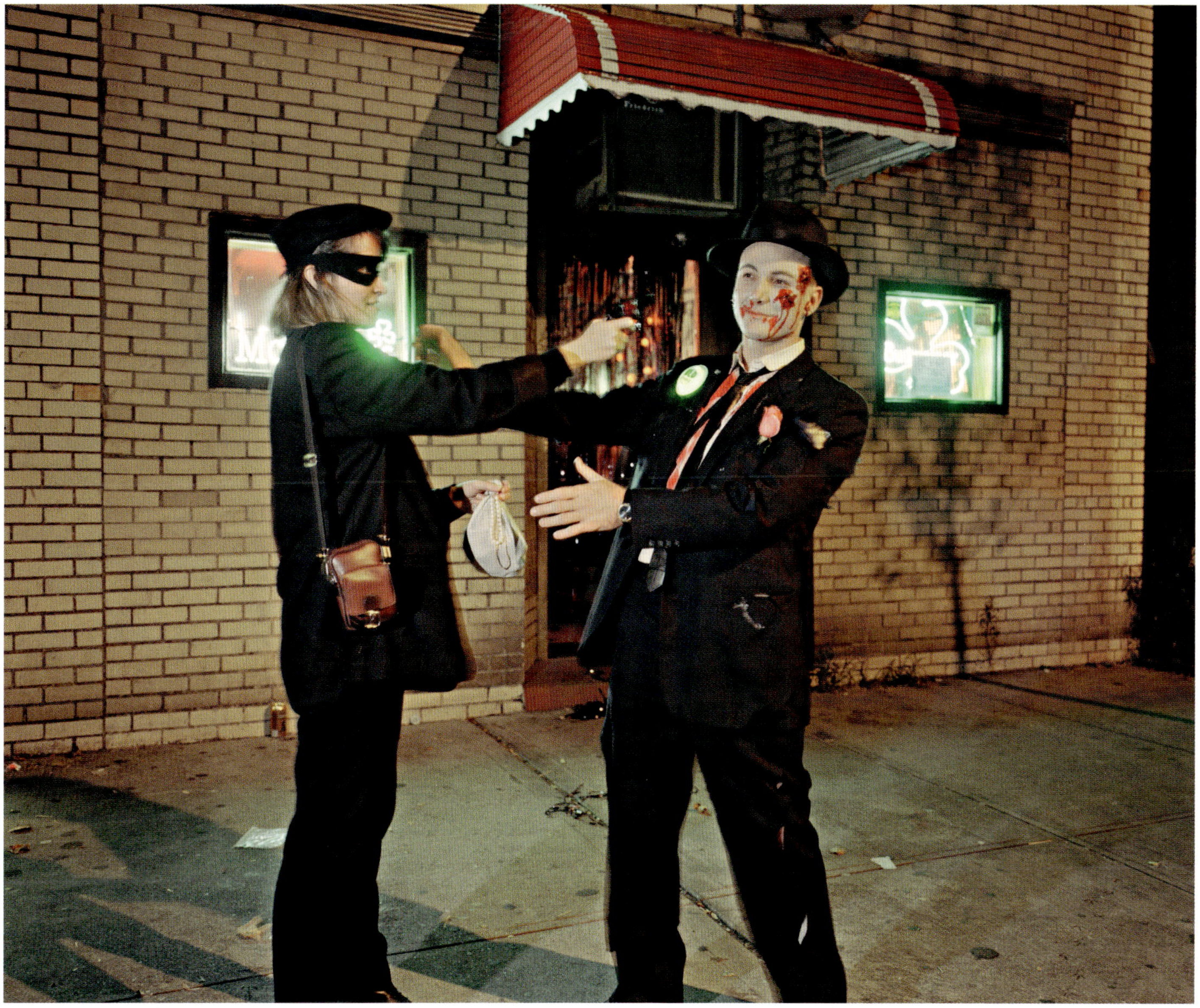

Mugger and victim,
1995, Queens.

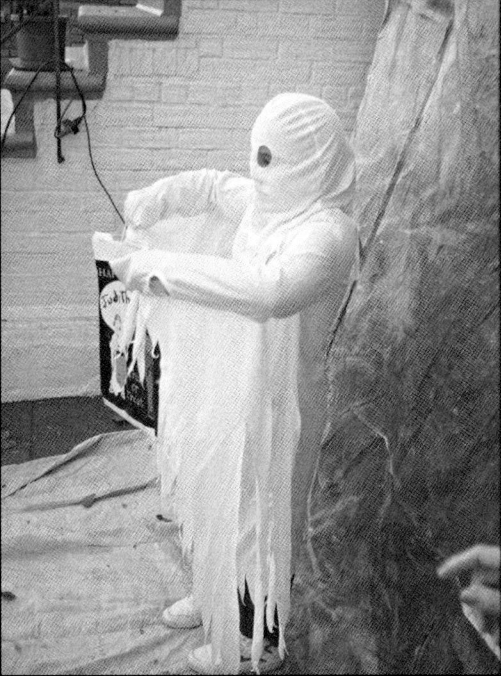

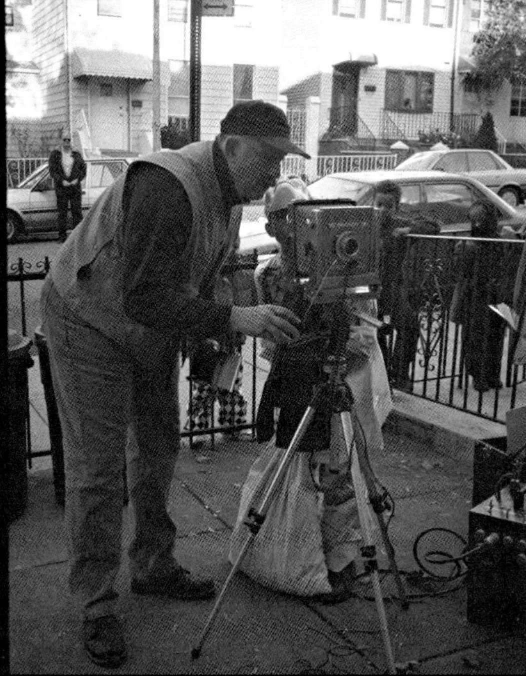

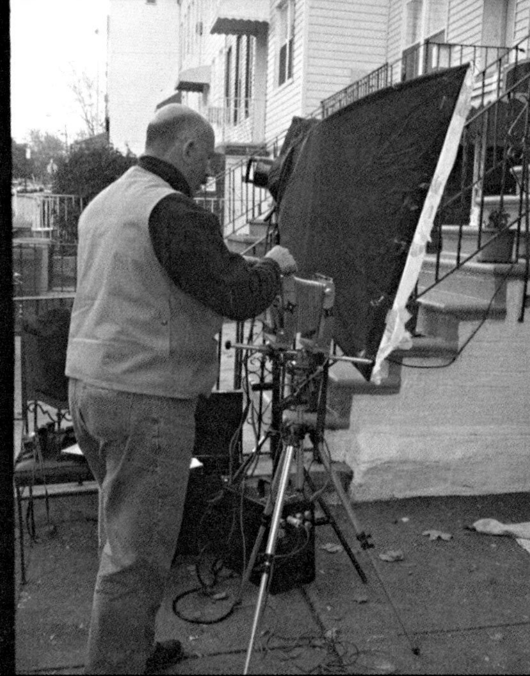

When I reviewed my 1994 and 1995 photos, I realized that I had made many of the best images near the house of my generous-with-treats Aunts Angelina and Anna on 18th Street in Brooklyn. So, in 1996, I decided to create a mini "studio" in front of their home. I hung a paint-spattered tarp from her second-story porch as a background and used a power pack and soft box to light my costumed subjects. I loaded my 4x5 camera with Polaroid Type 55 positive-negative film, which enabled me to give each subject

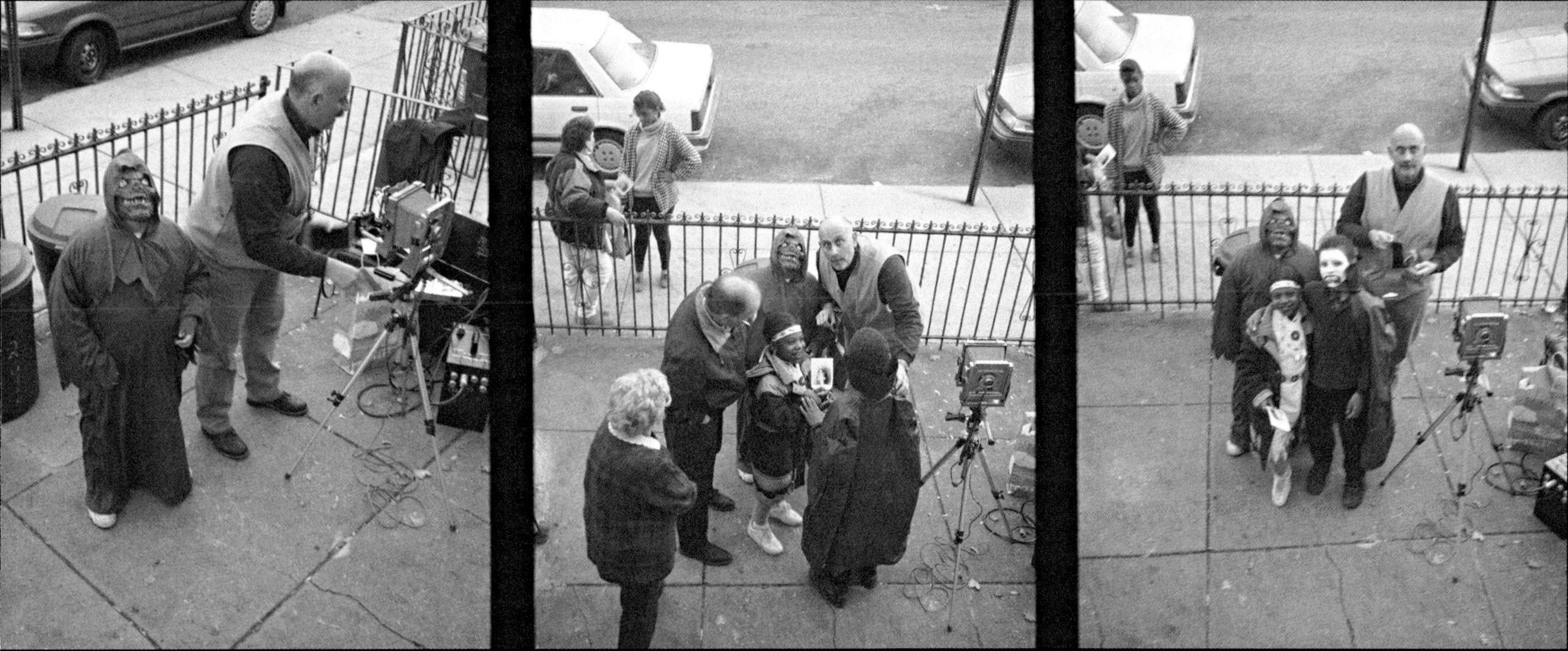

Larry photographing
sequence, 1996, Brooklyn.

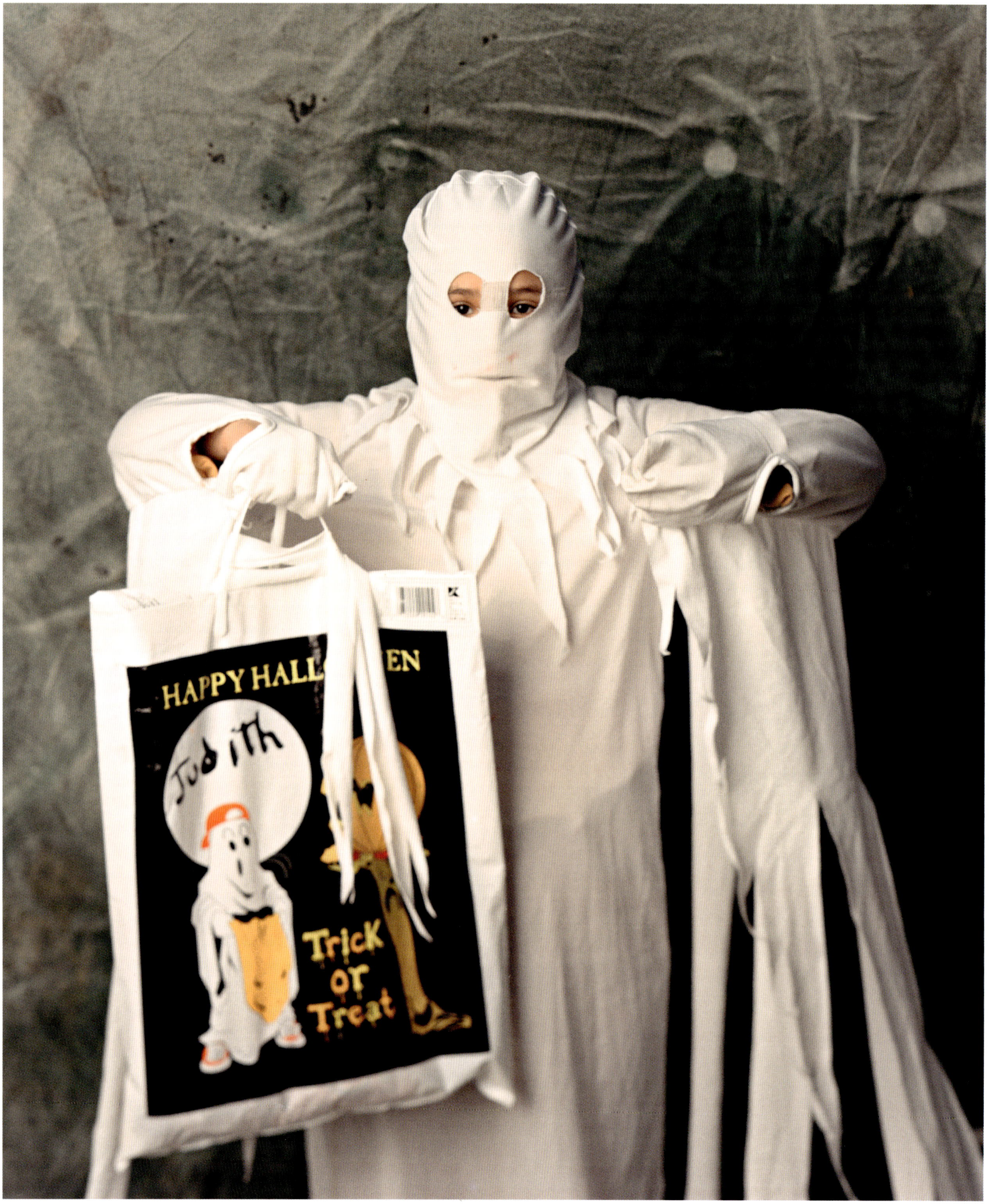
Judith
Trick or Treat

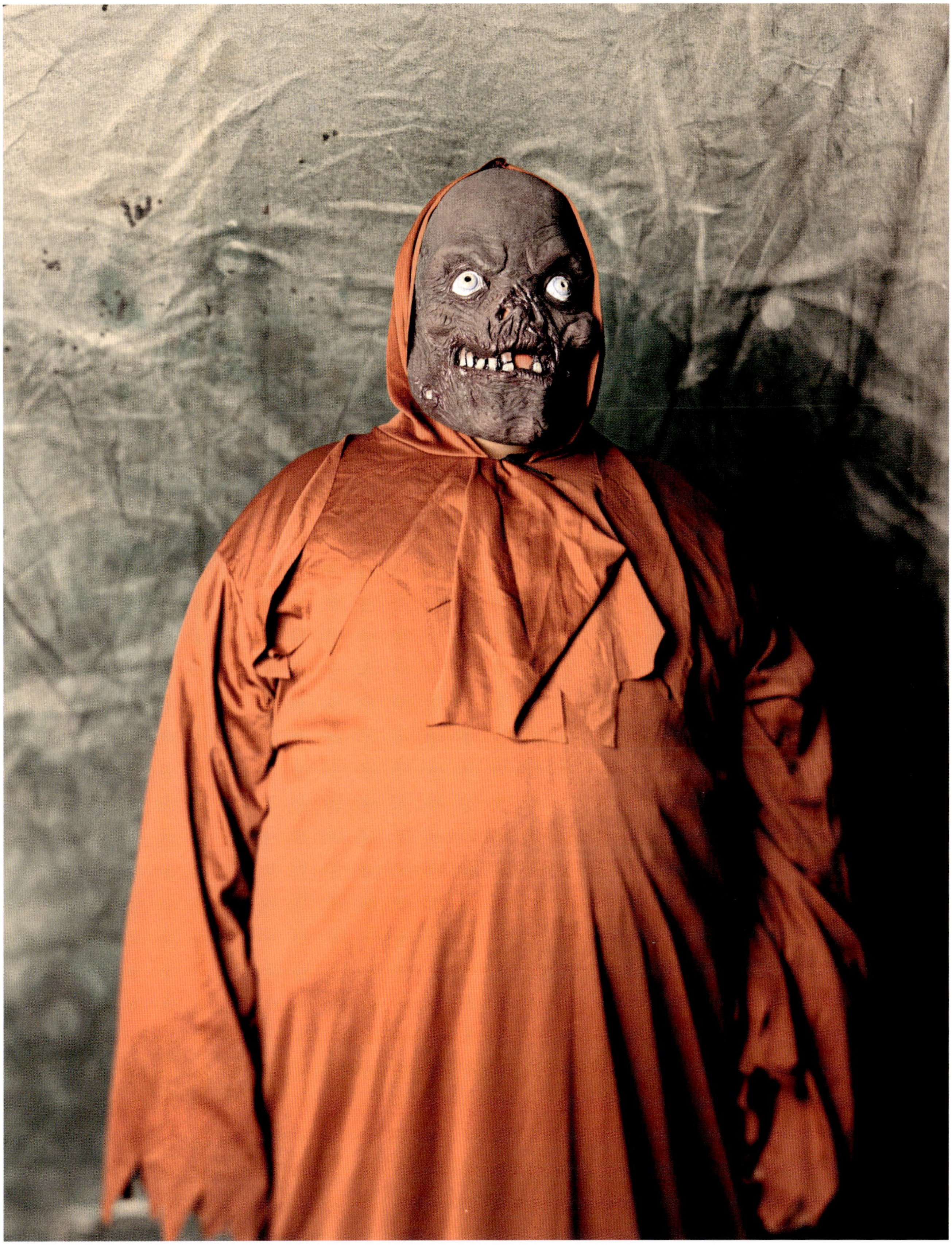

Above: Monster,
1996, Brooklyn.

Opposite: Ghost with
bag, 1996, Brooklyn.

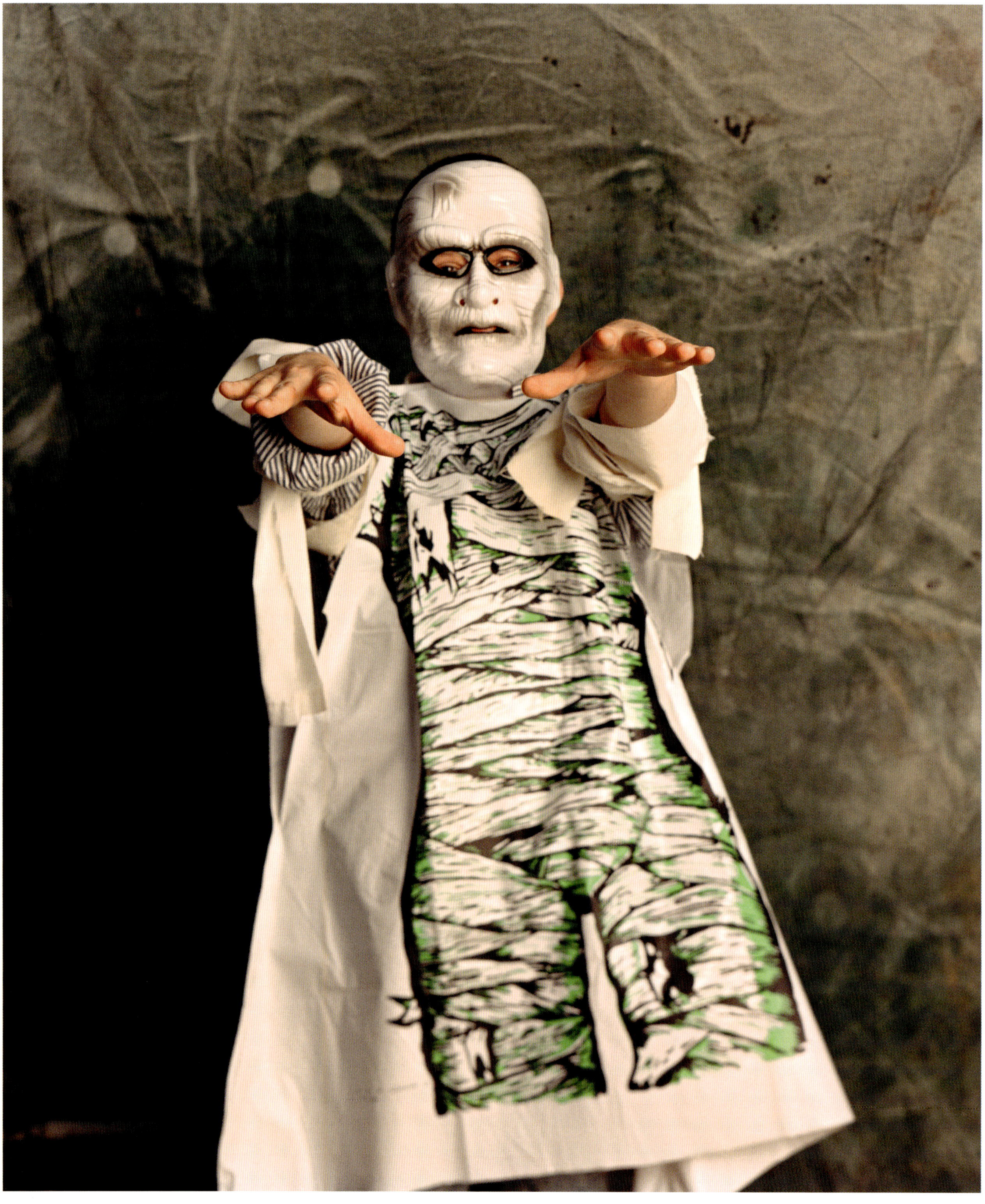

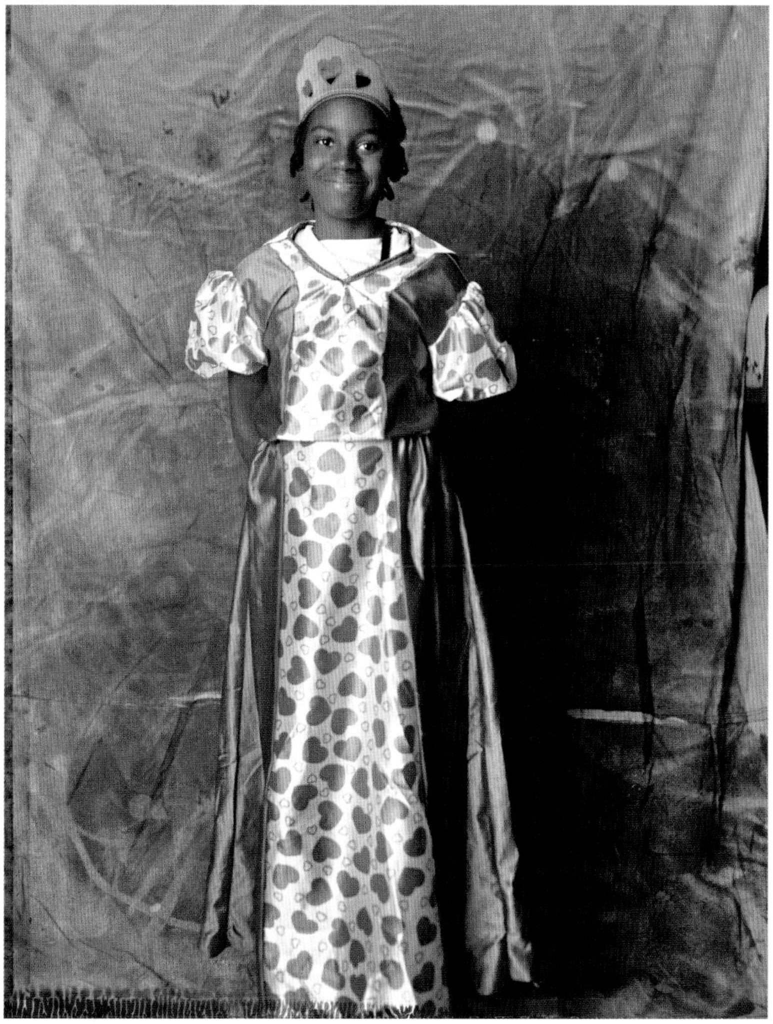

Above: Princess,
1996, Brooklyn.

Opposite: Mummy,
1996, Brooklyn.

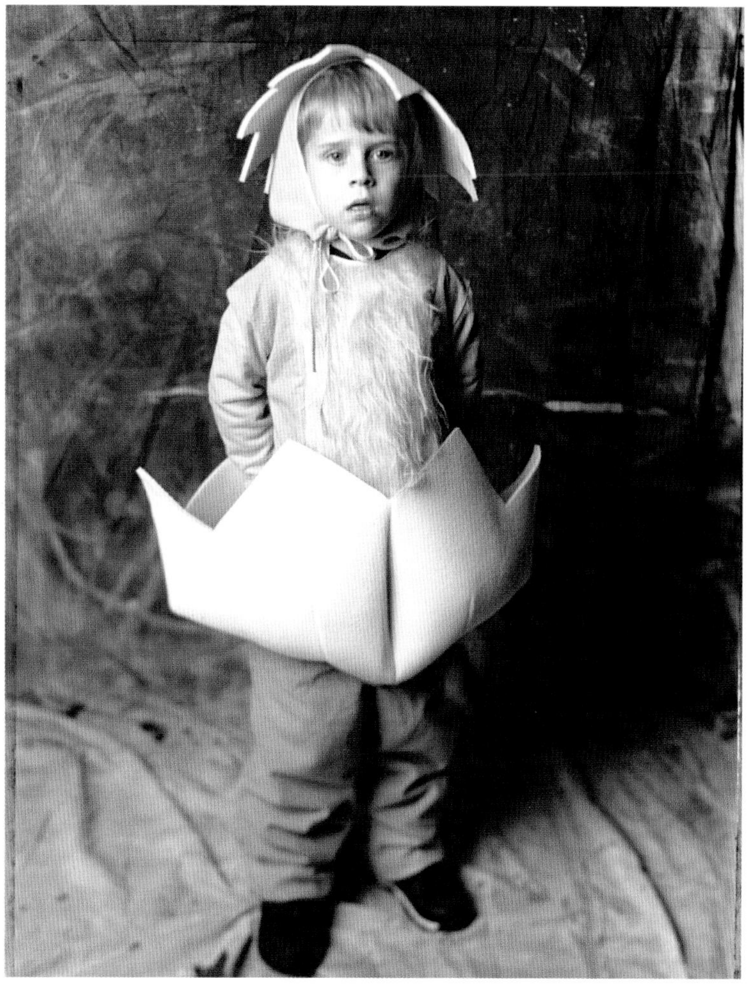

Eggshell boy, Brooklyn.

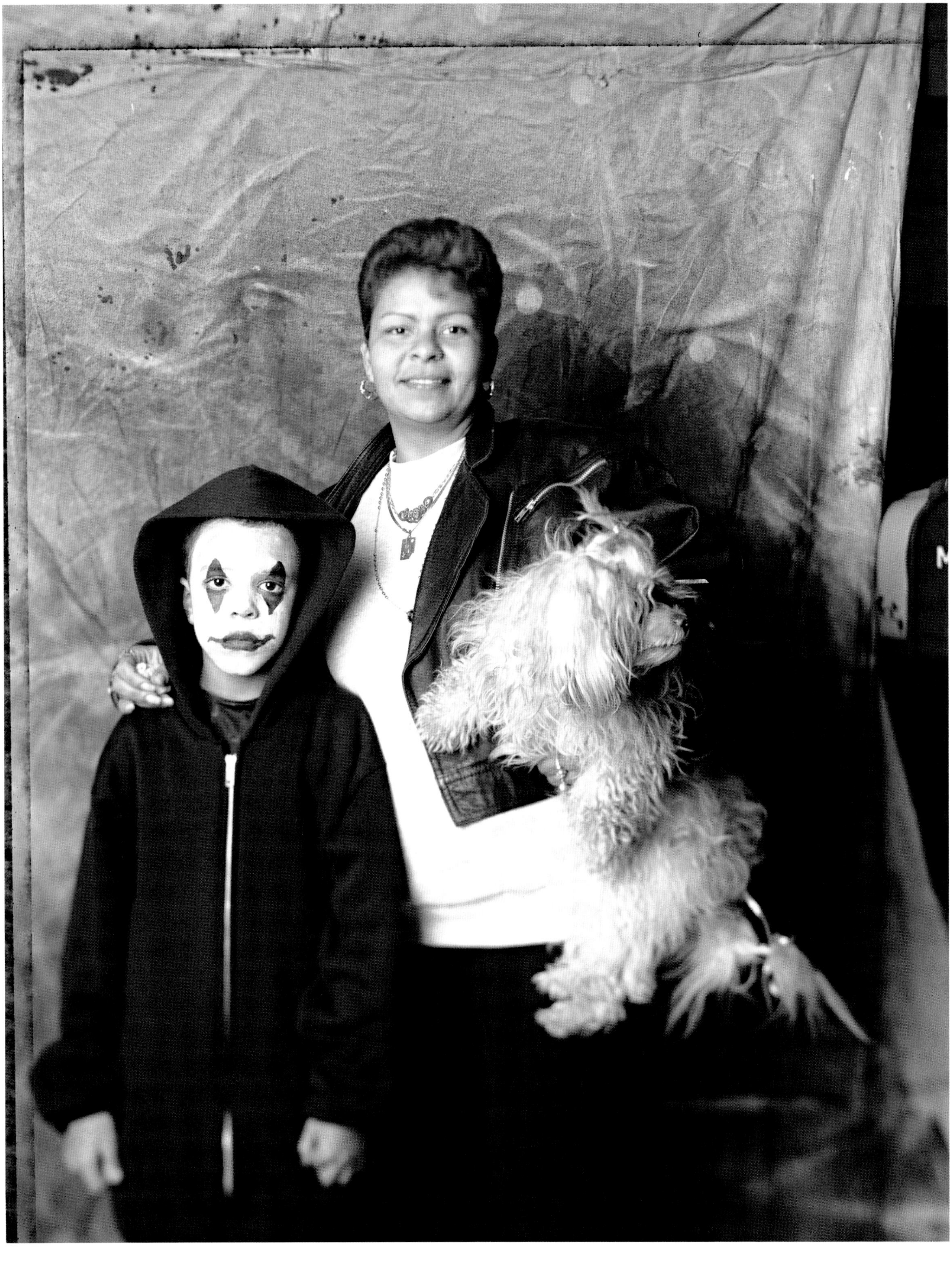

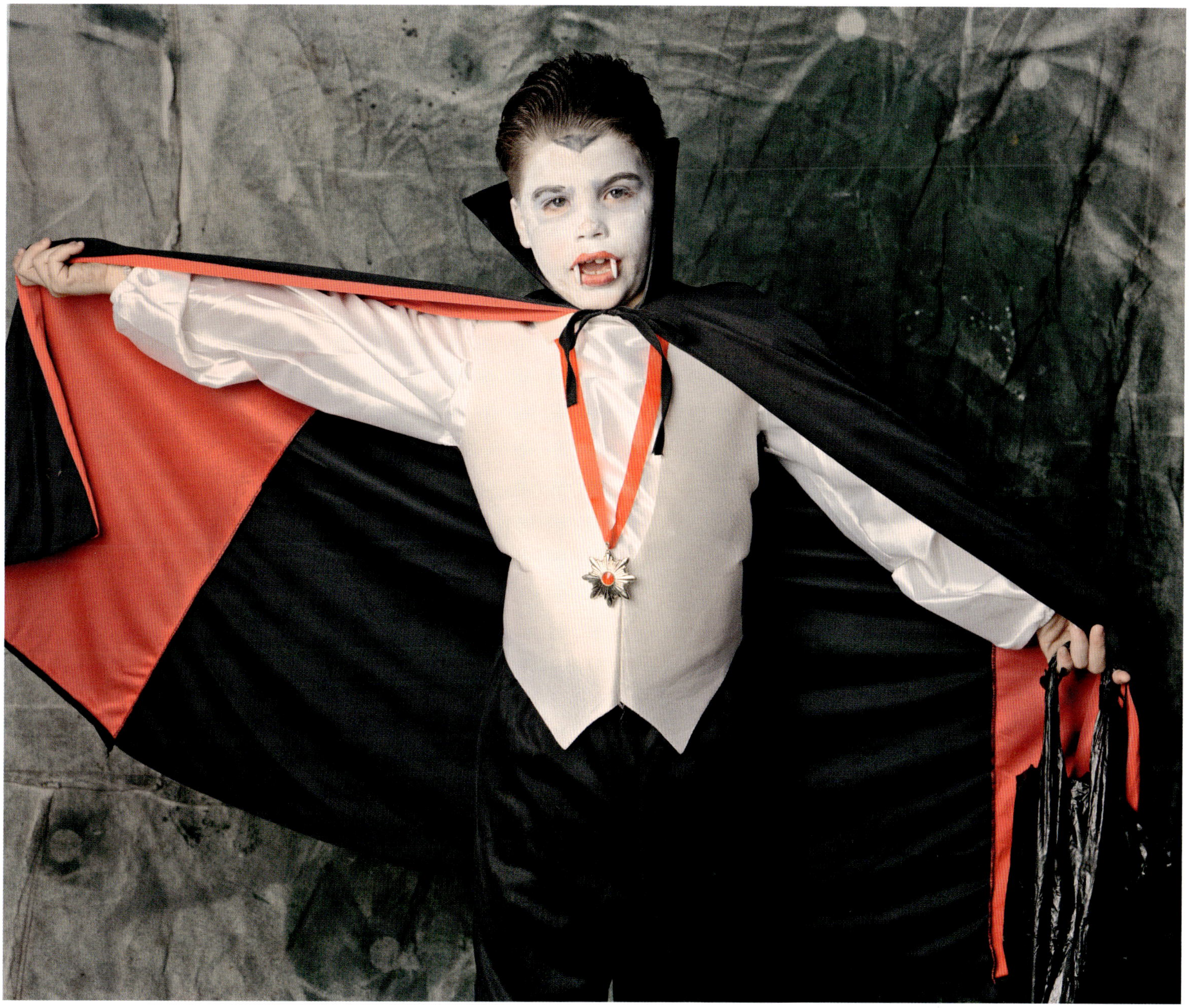

Above: Dracula with red cape, 1996, Brooklyn.

Opposite: Clown family and dog, 1996, Brooklyn.

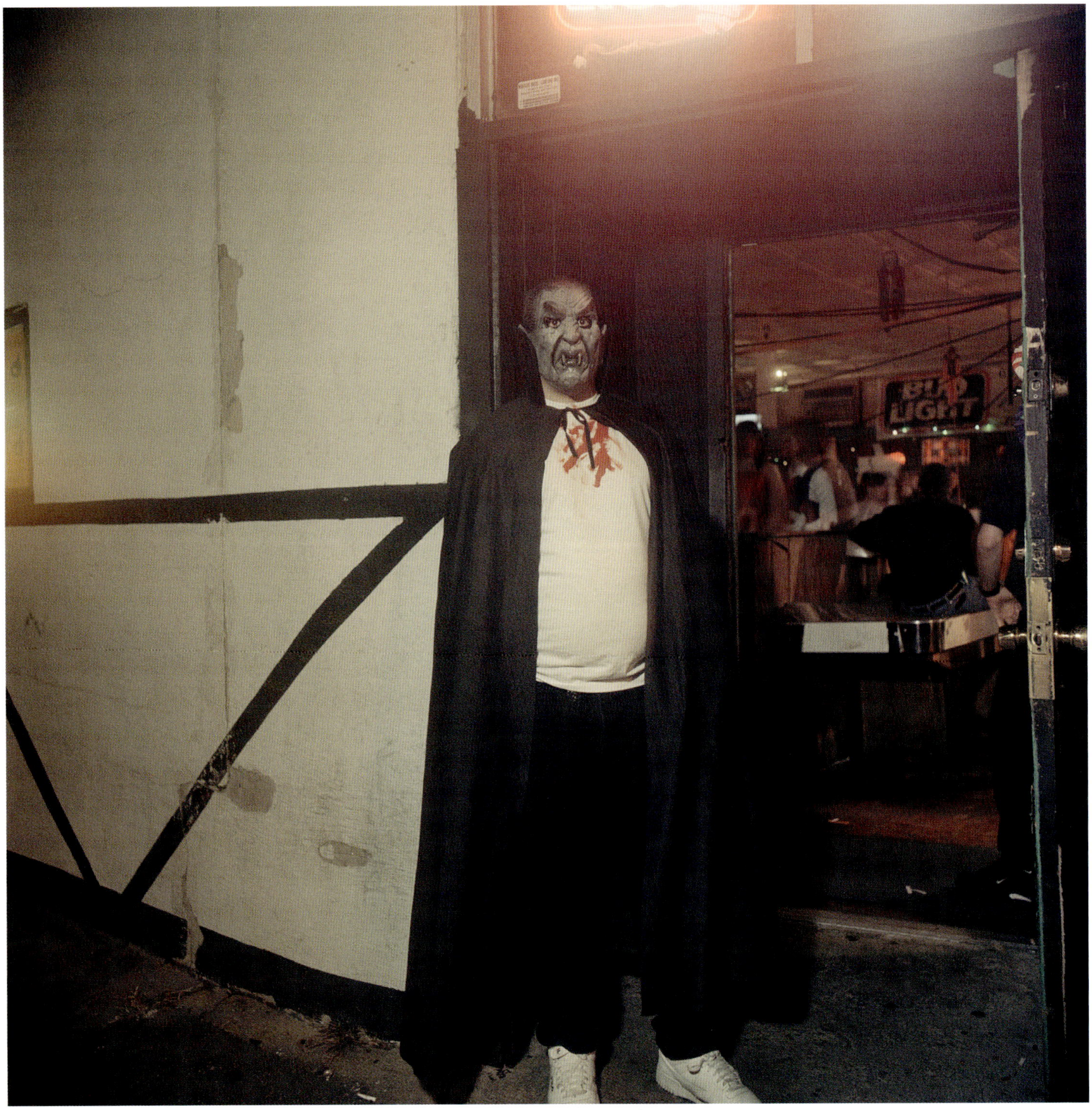

Vampire at O's Pub,
1996, Queens.

In 1996, I also photographed at O's Pub, a local bar in Rockaway, and was pleased with the results.

Madonna, 1996, Queens.

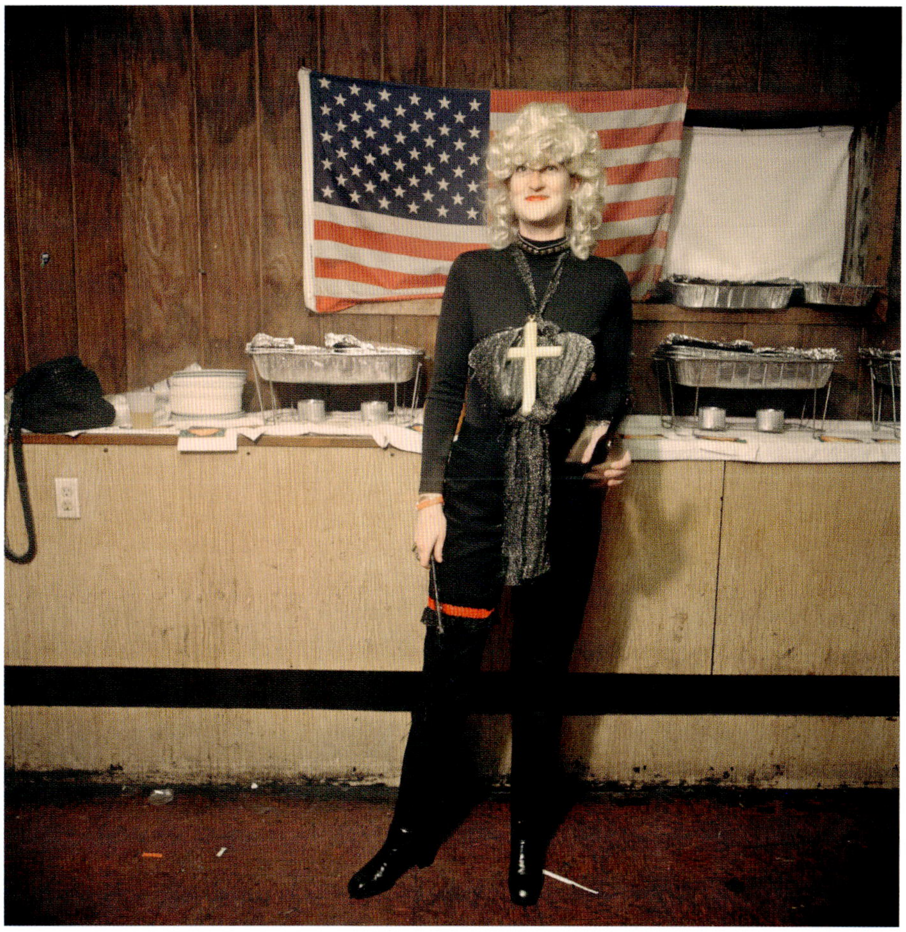

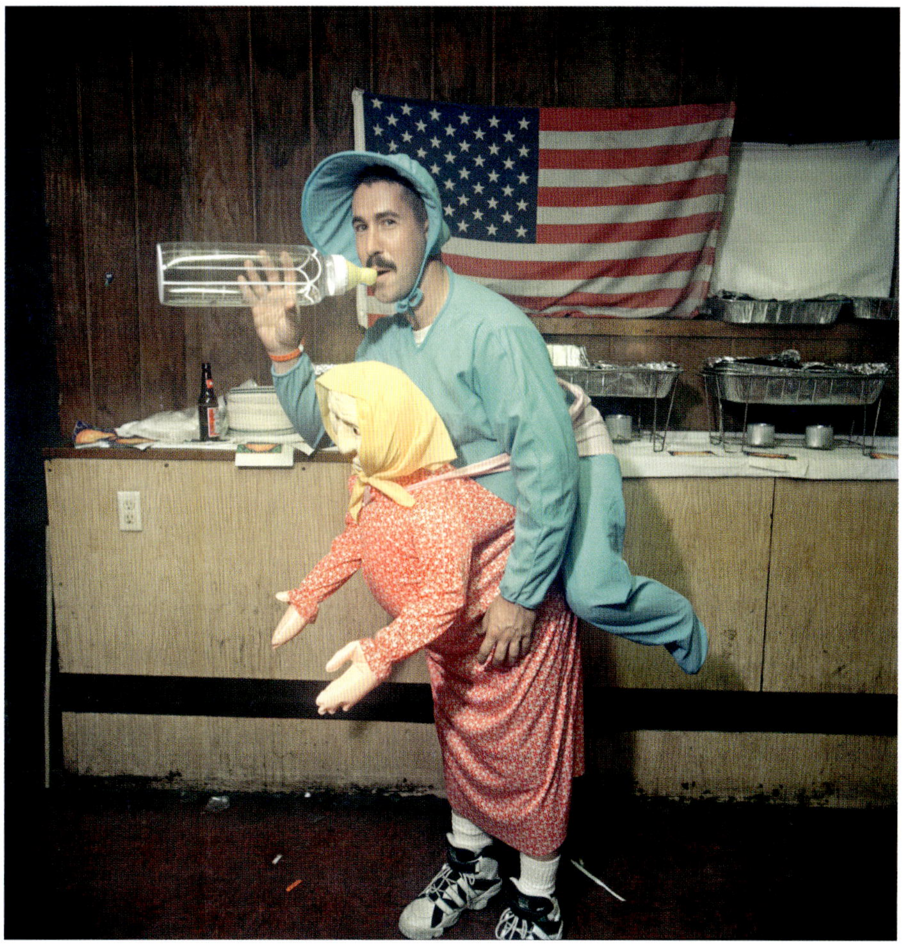

Old man/baby, 1996, Queens.

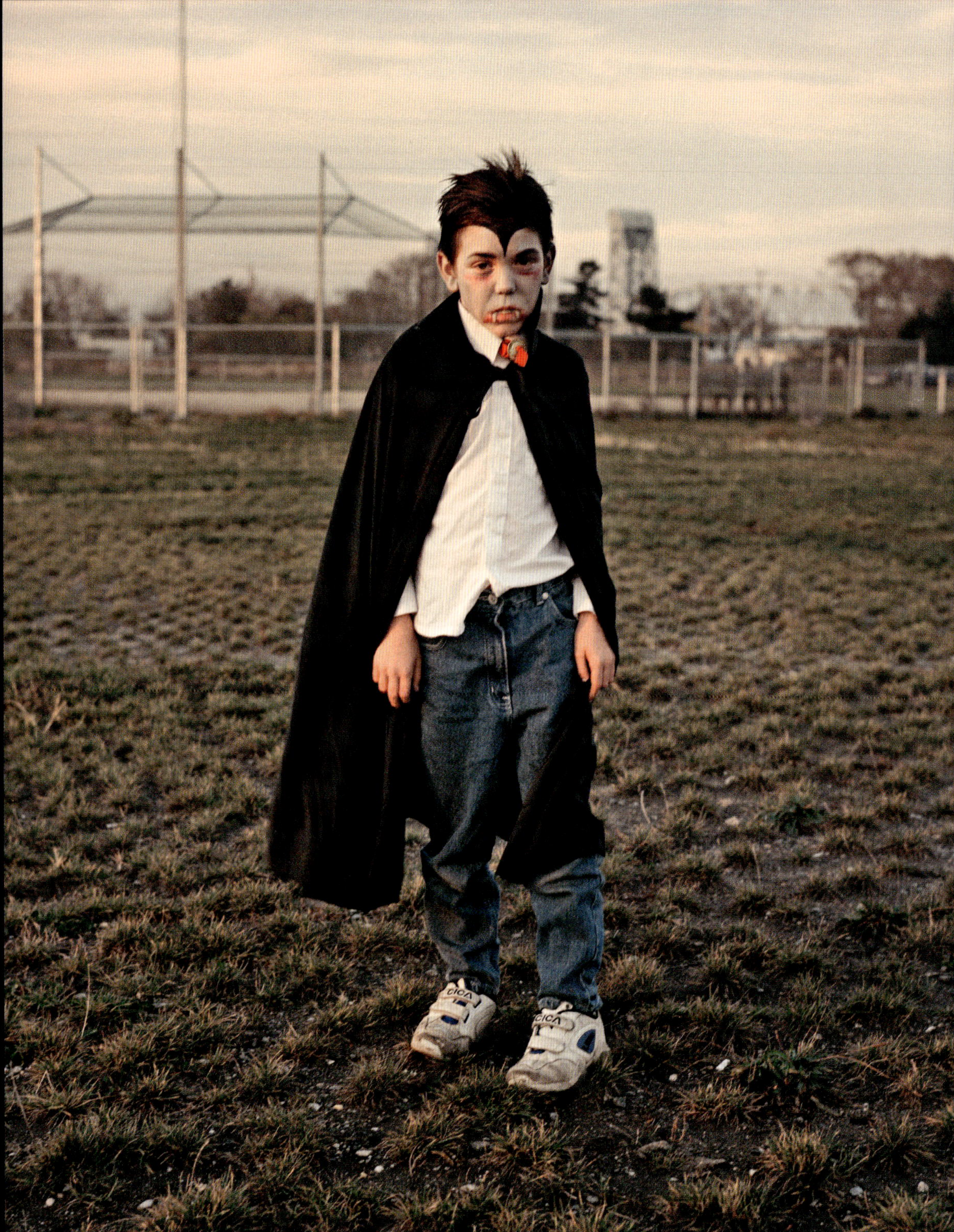

Vampire with long cape, 1997, Queens

From 1997 until 2024, I stayed closer to home and mostly photographed in Rockaway, at Fort Tilden . . .

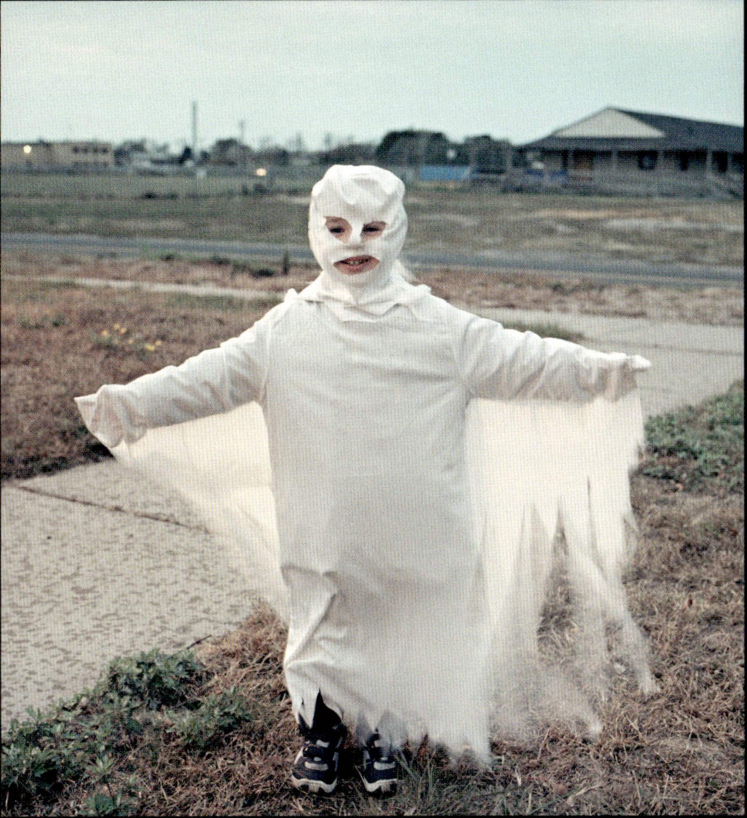

Ghost in the wind,
2001, Queens.

Ghost (fogged negative),
1997, Queens.

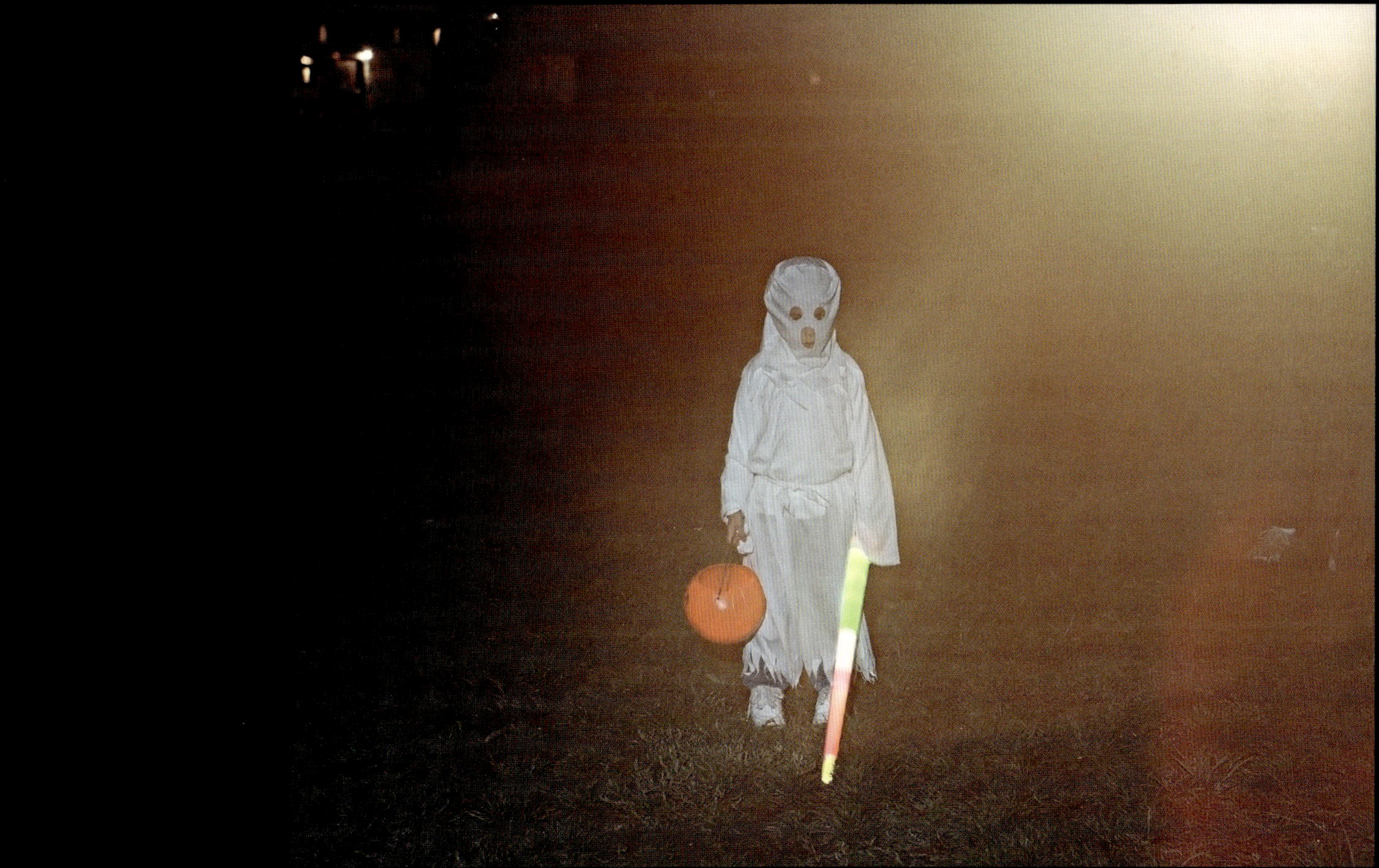

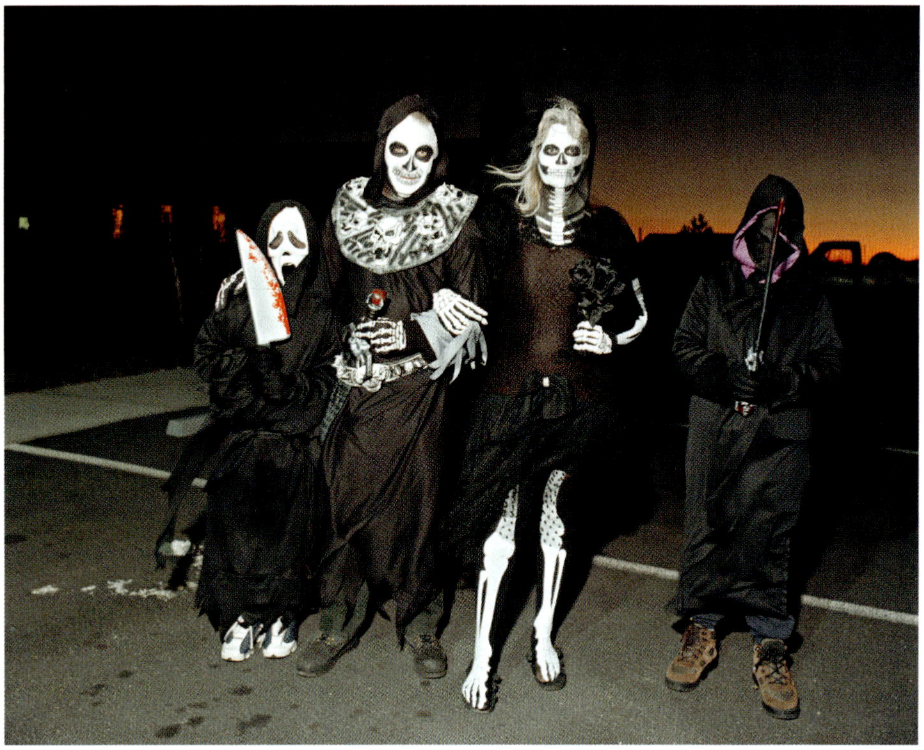

Scary foursome, 1998, Queens.

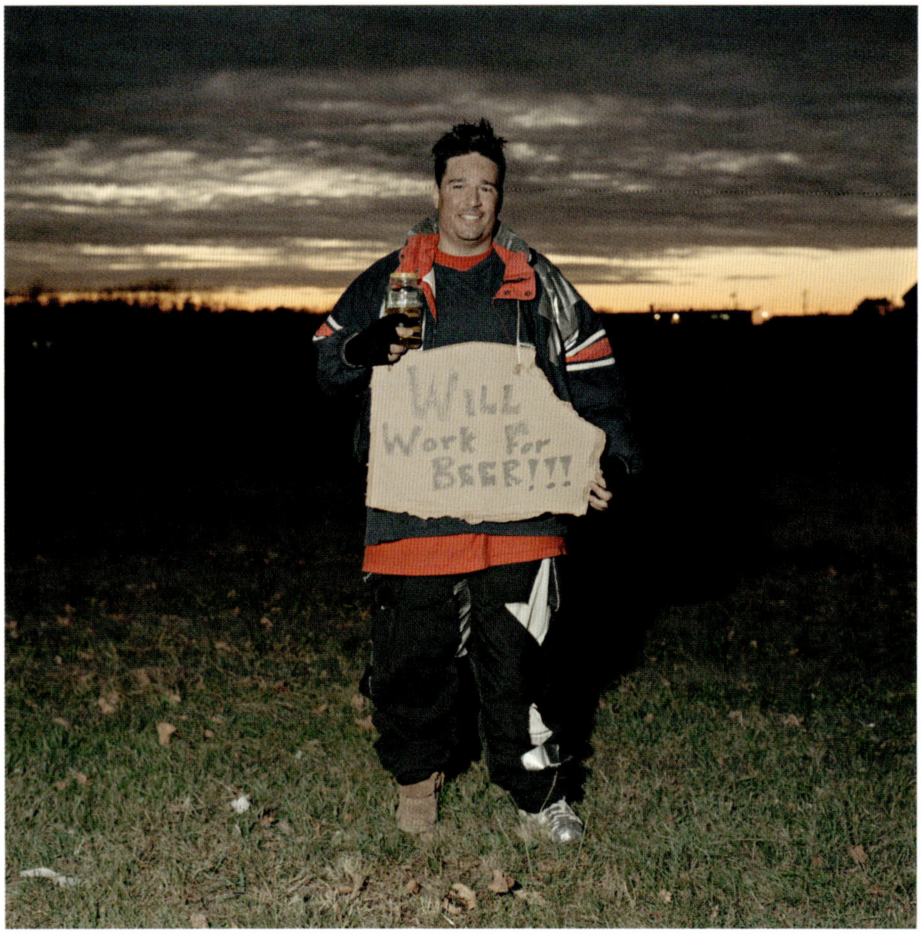

"Will work for beer!!!" 2000, Queens.

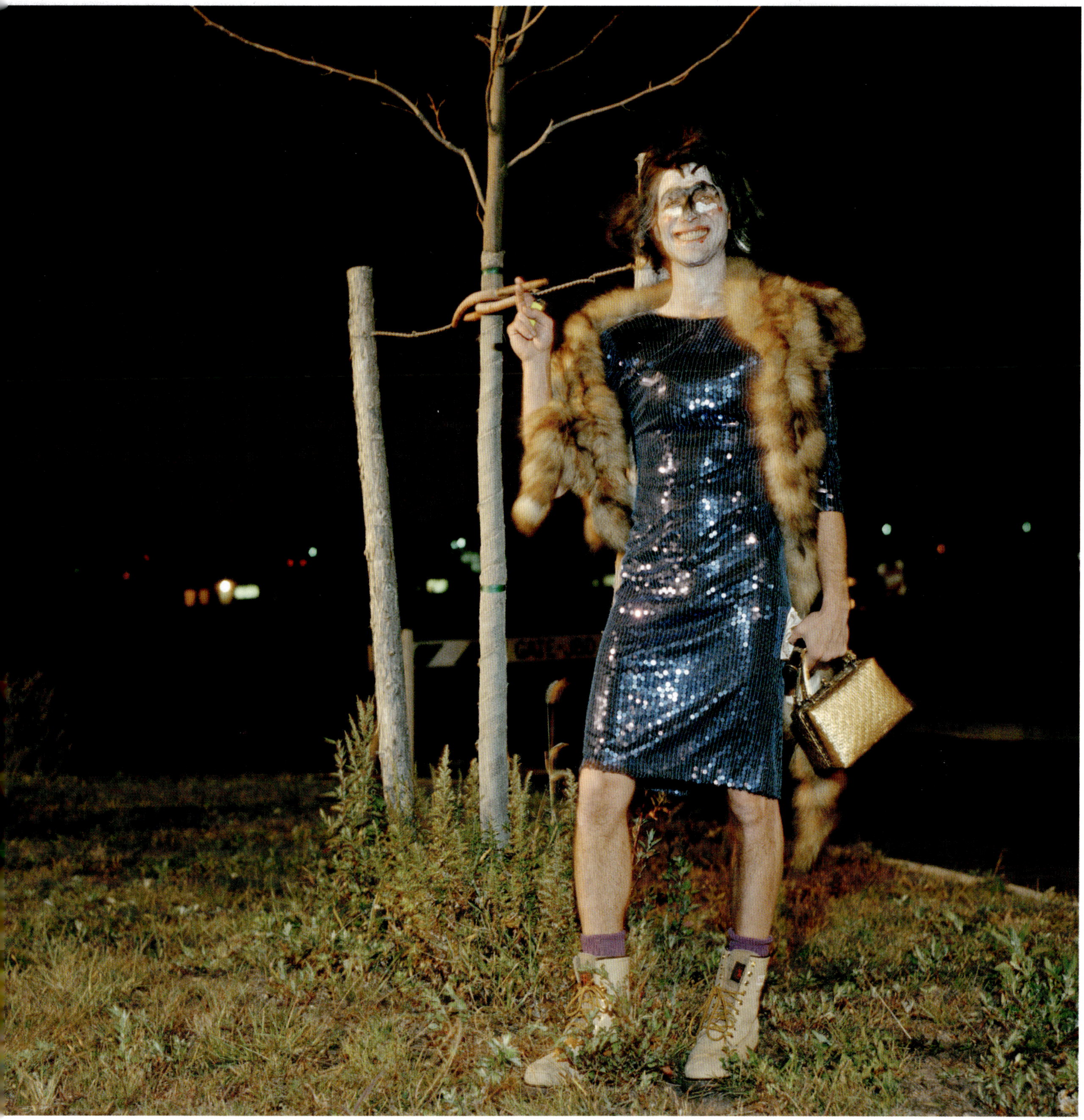

Man in drag,
1997, Queens.

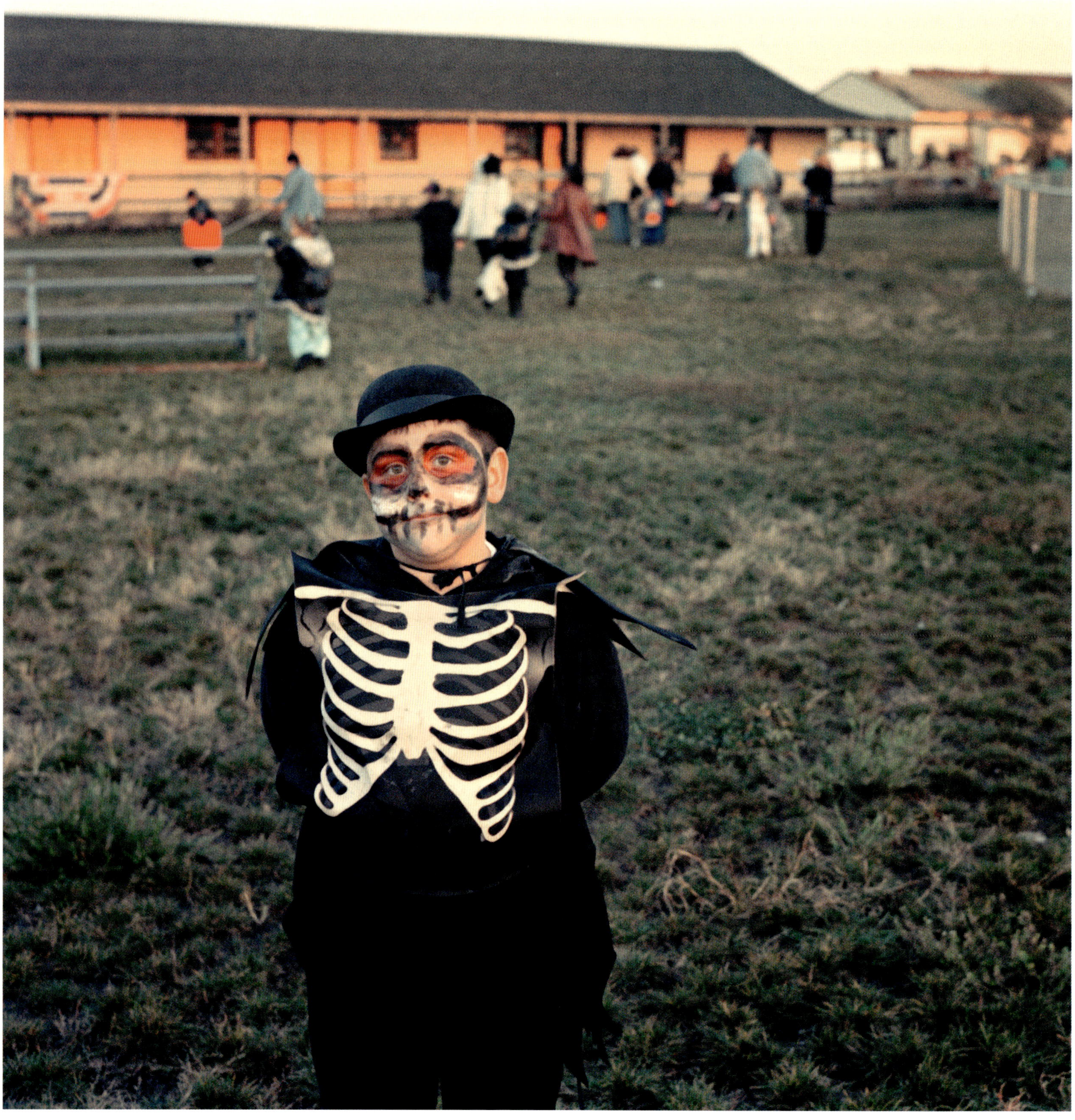

Boy with skeleton
shirt, 1997, Queens.

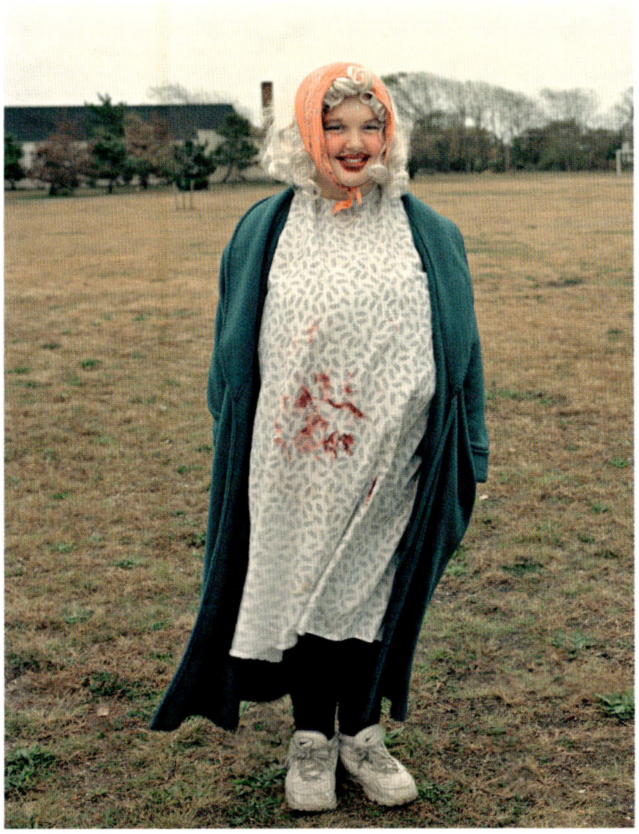

Old girl, 2001, Queens.

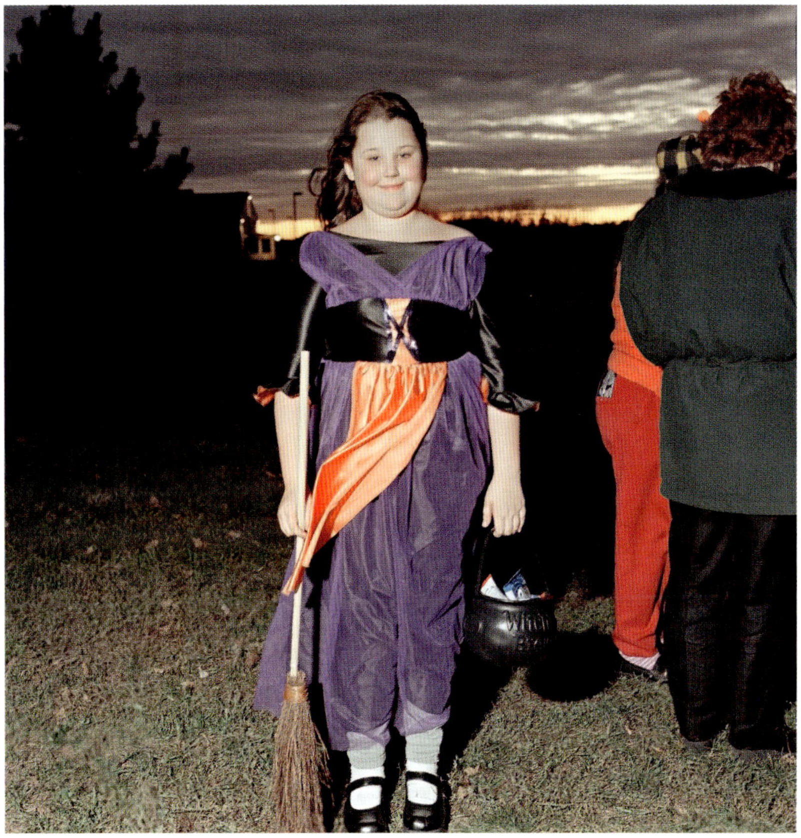

Young witch, 2000, Queens.

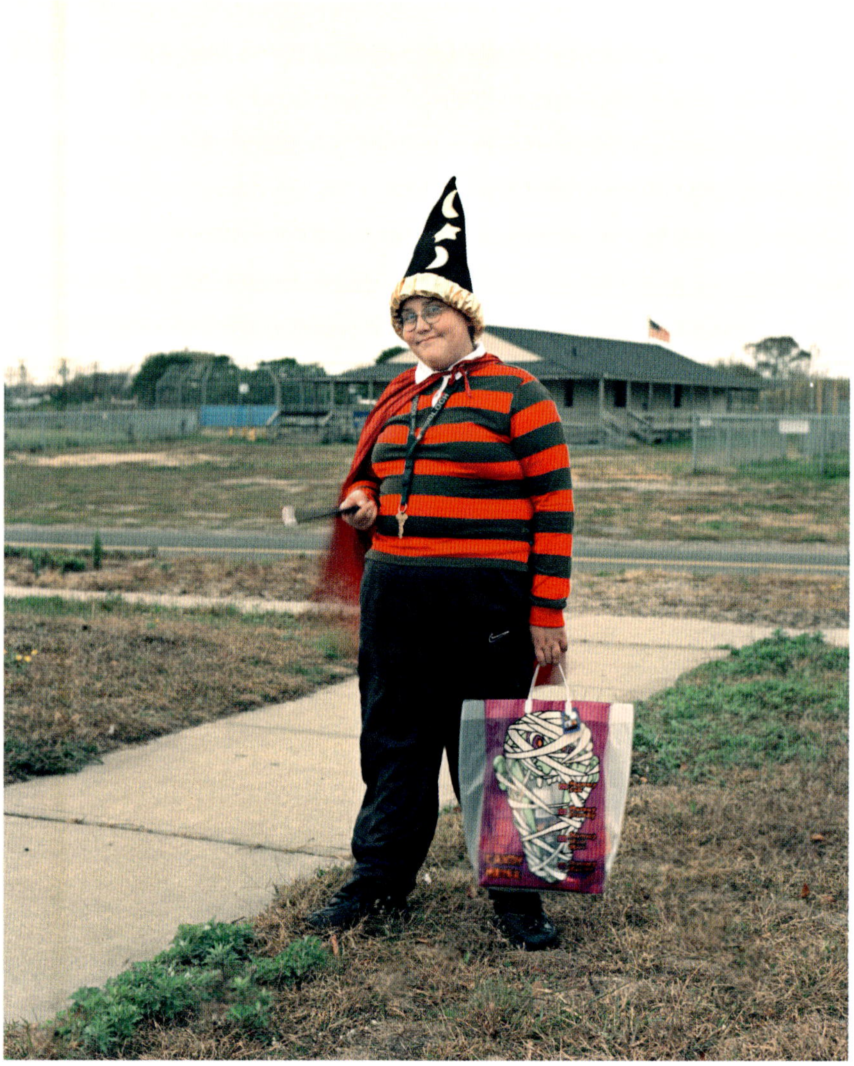

Wizard, 2001, Queens.

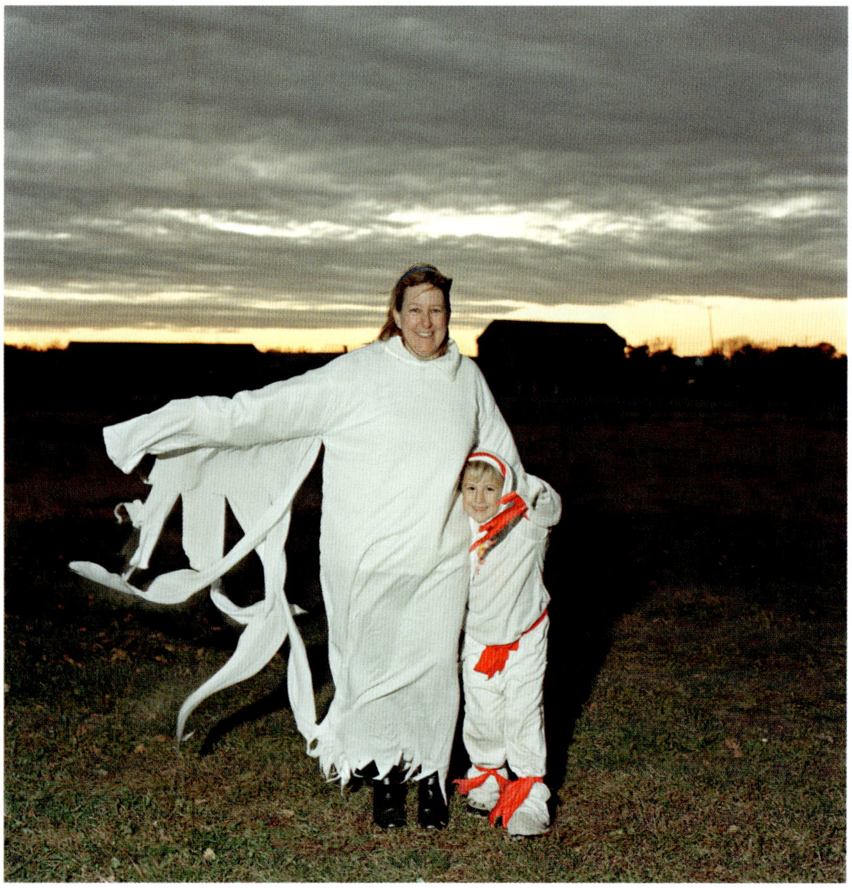

Mom and girl ghosts,
2000, Queens.

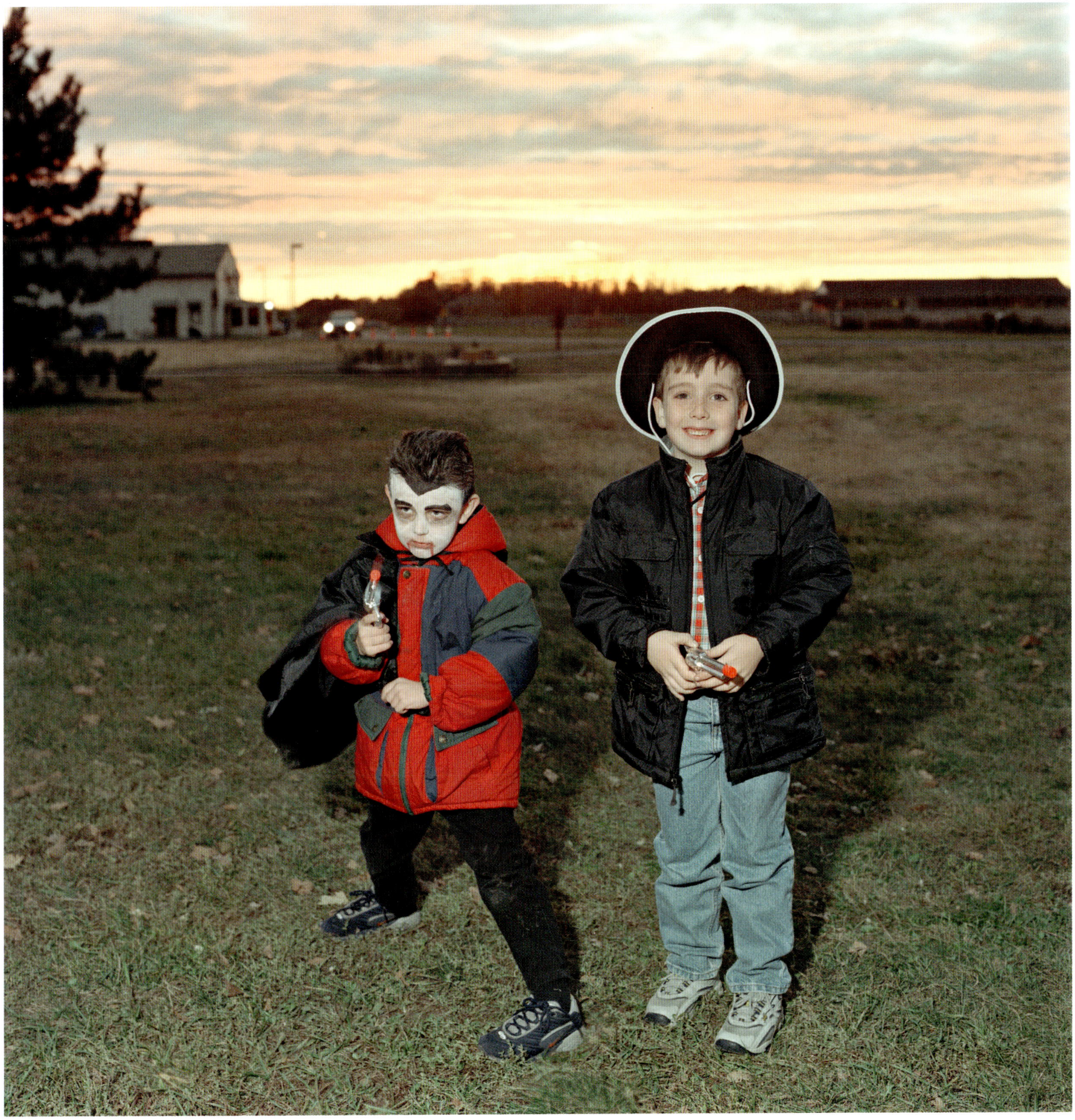

Cowboy and vampire,
2000, Queens.

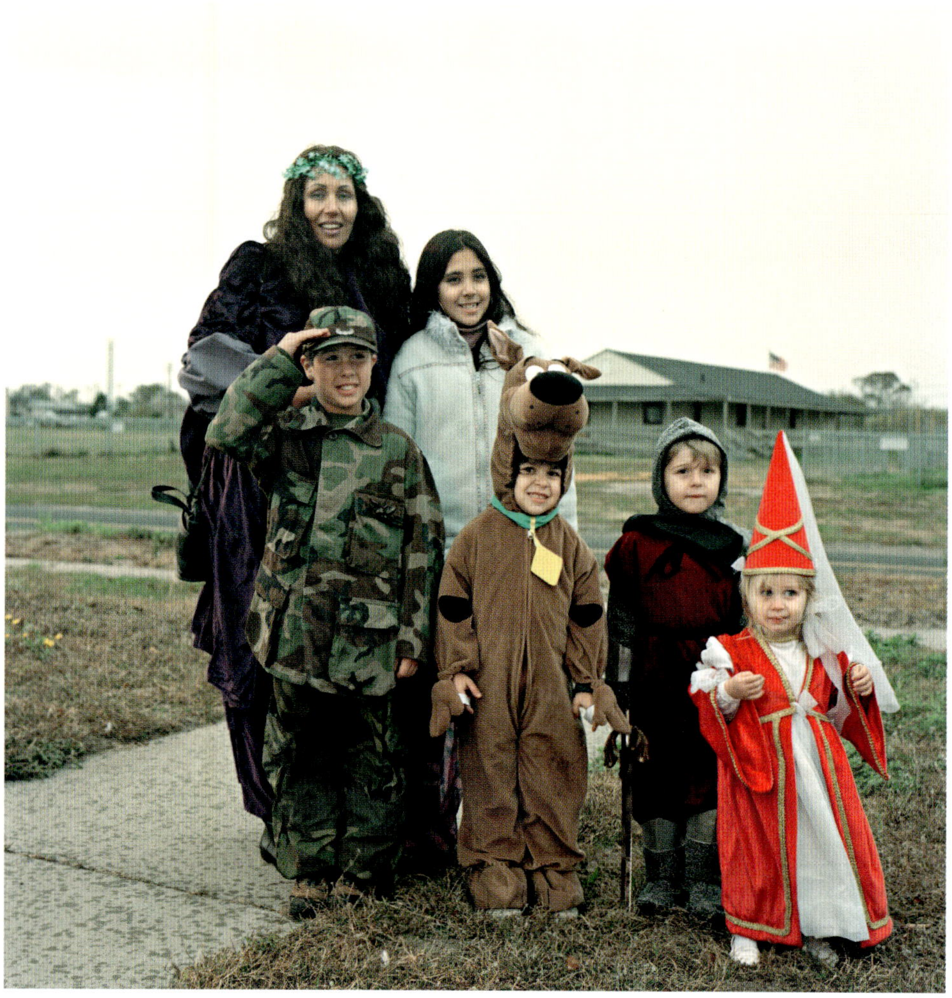

Soldier and family,
2001, Queens.

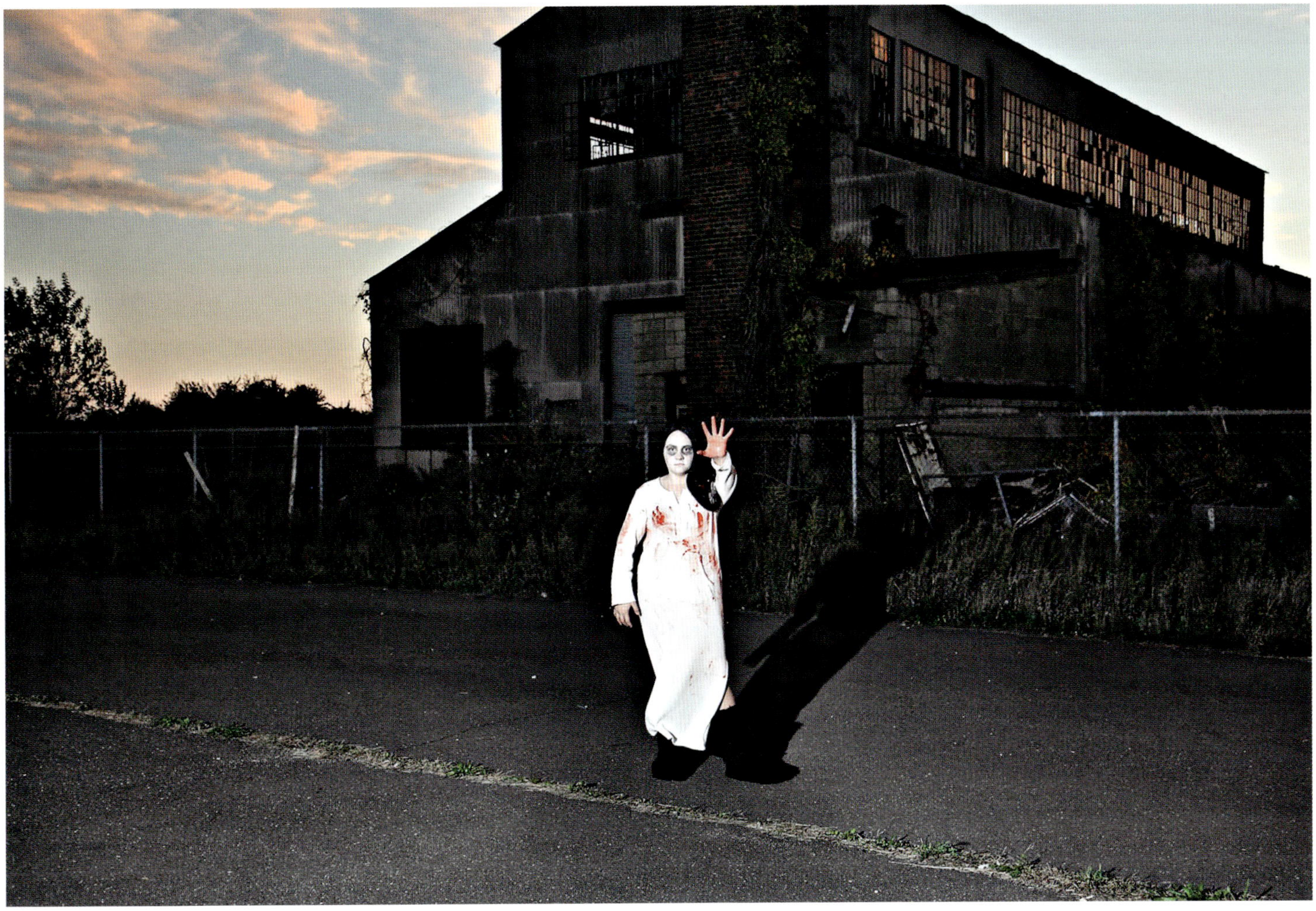

Bloody ghost,
2007, Queens.

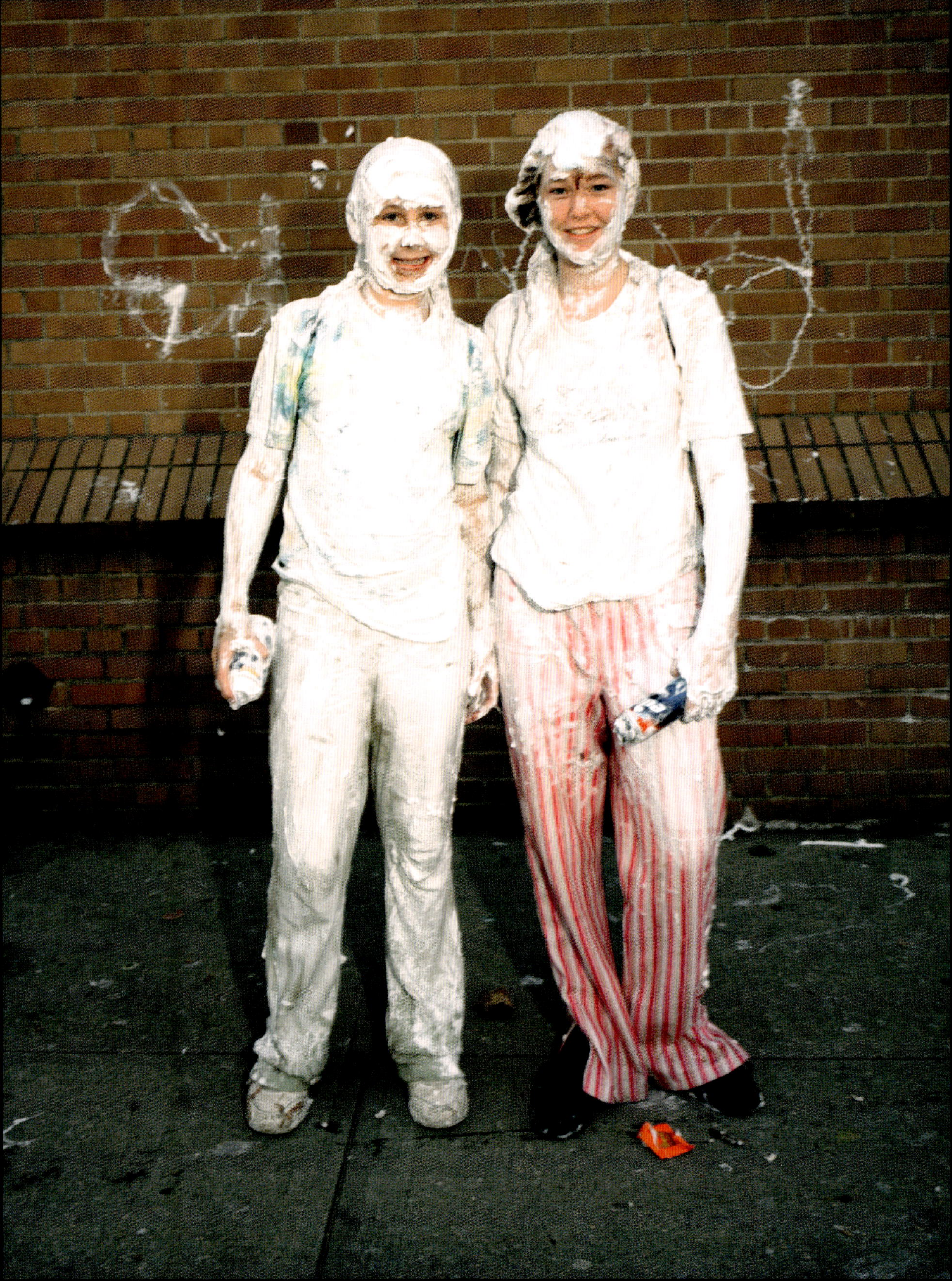

Shaving cream girls, 2005, Queens.

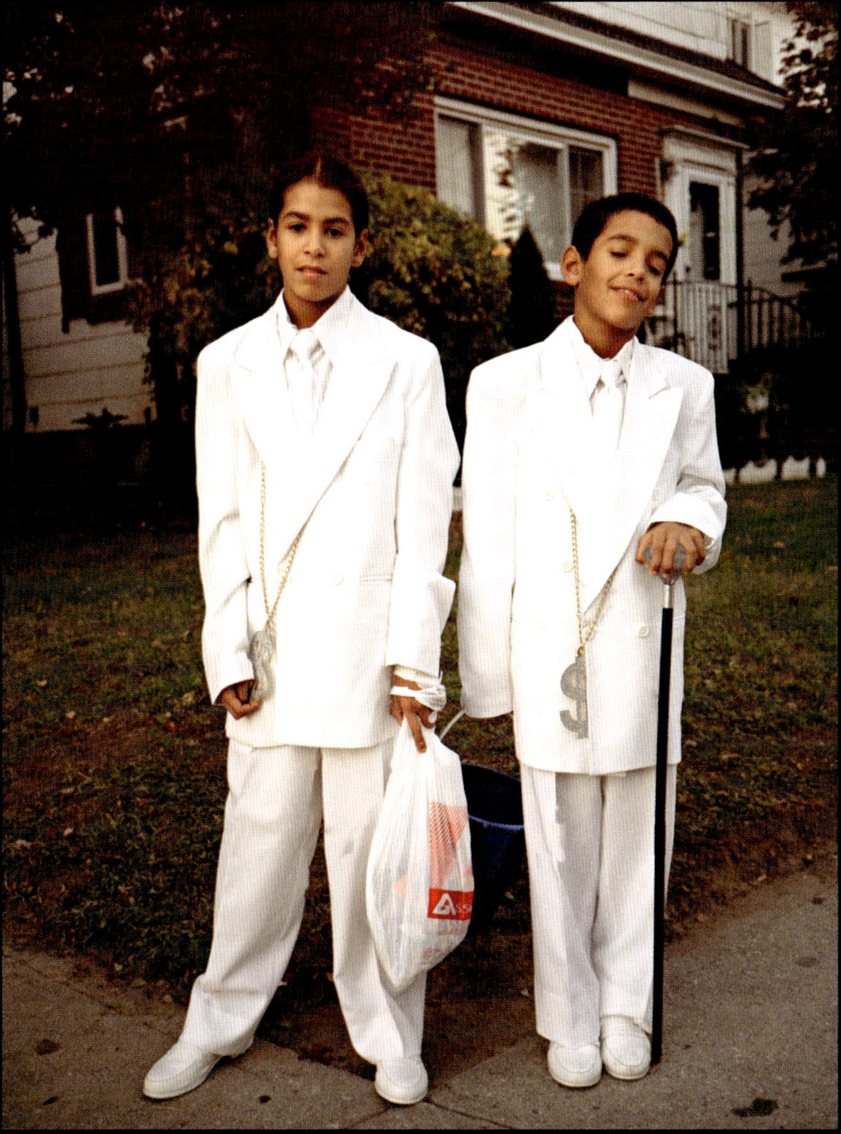

Rockaway dudes, 2005, Queens.

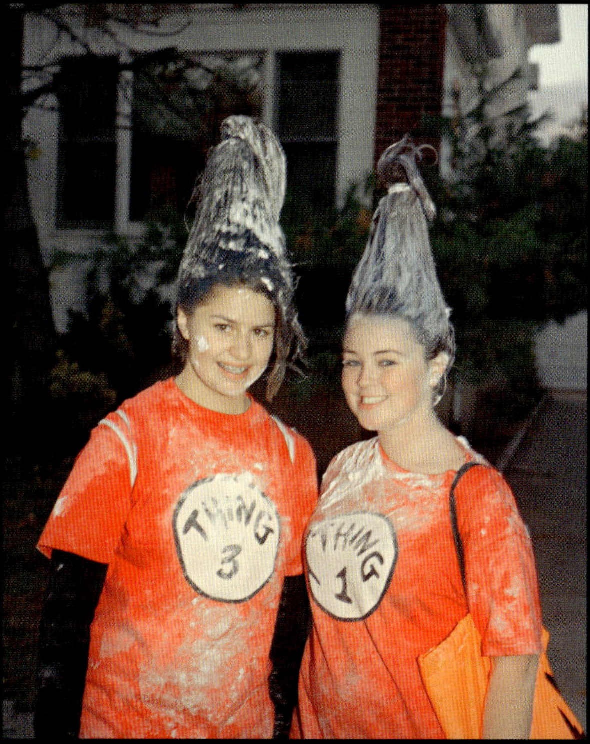

Two Things, 2010, Queens.

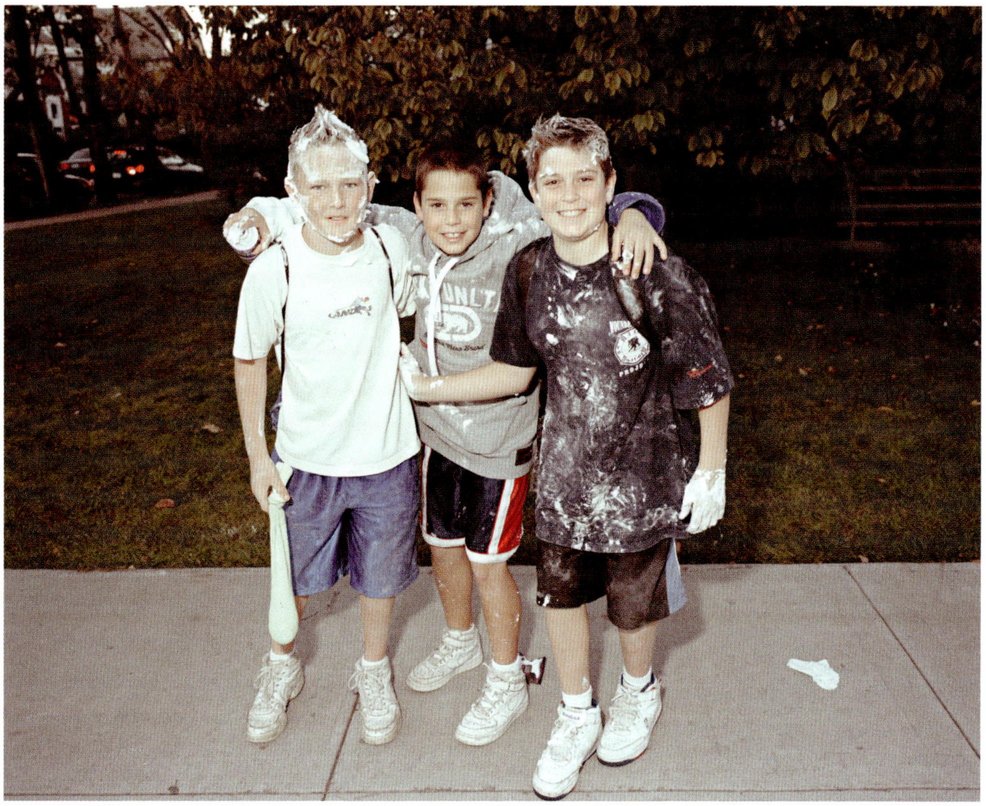

Left: Shaving cream boys with chalk sock, 2005, Queens.

Opposite: Witch and angel, 2006, Queens.

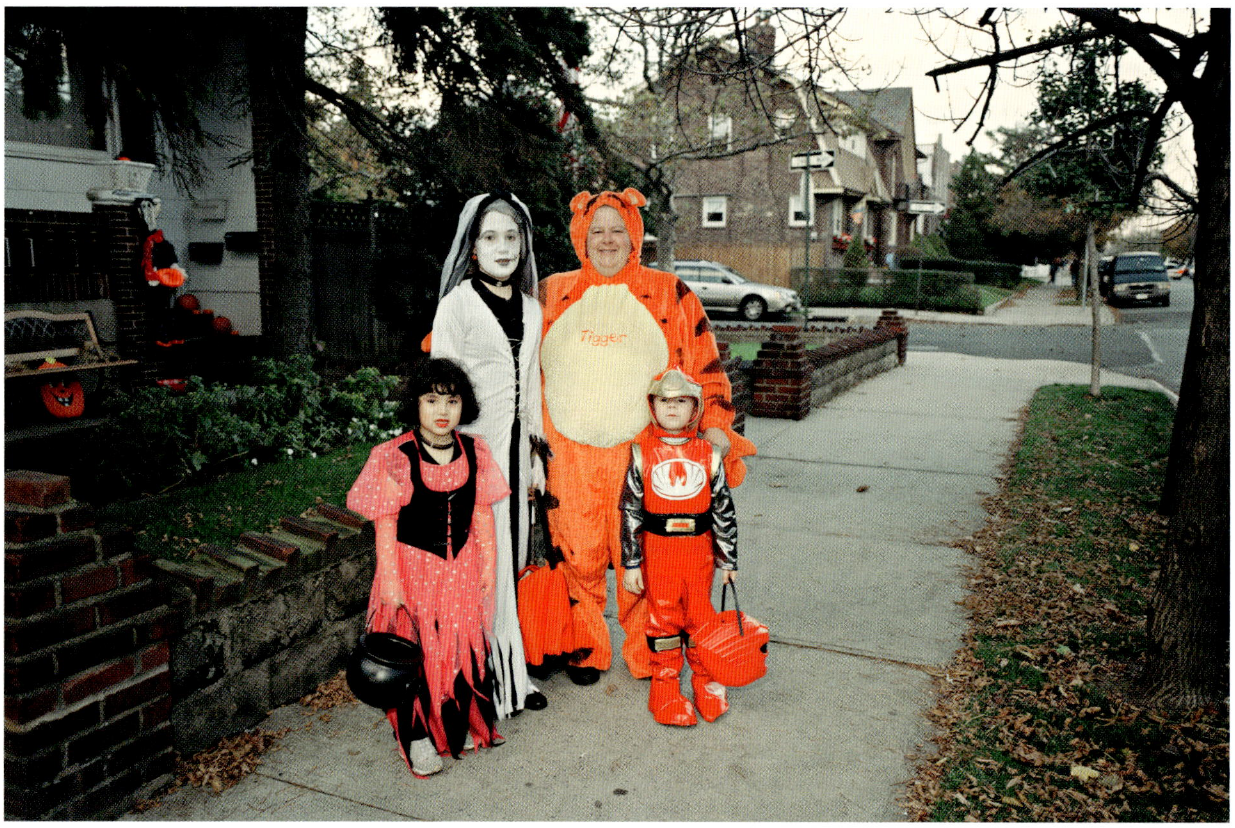

Tigger family, 2005, Queens.

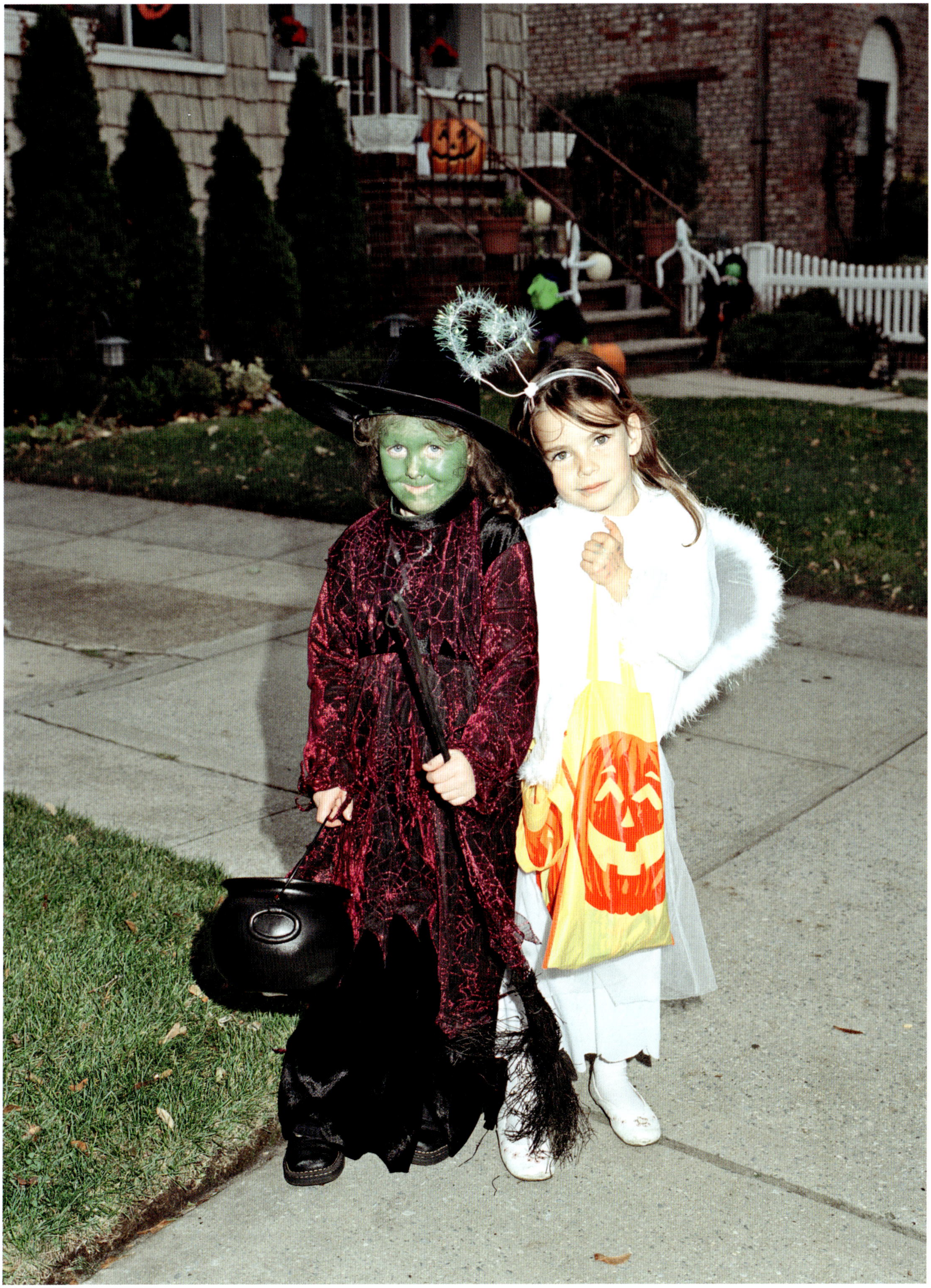

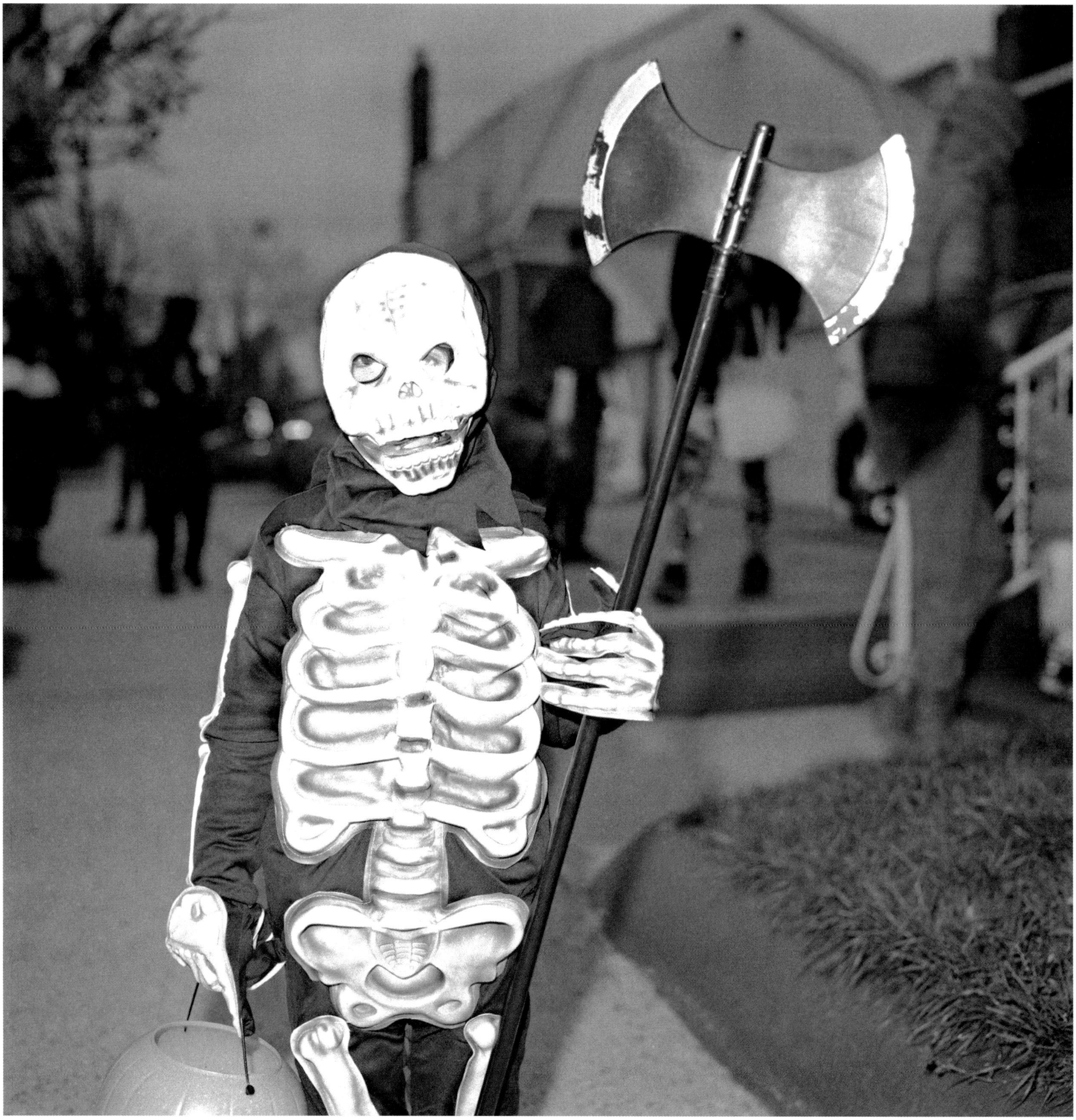

Skeleton with axe,
2021, Queens.

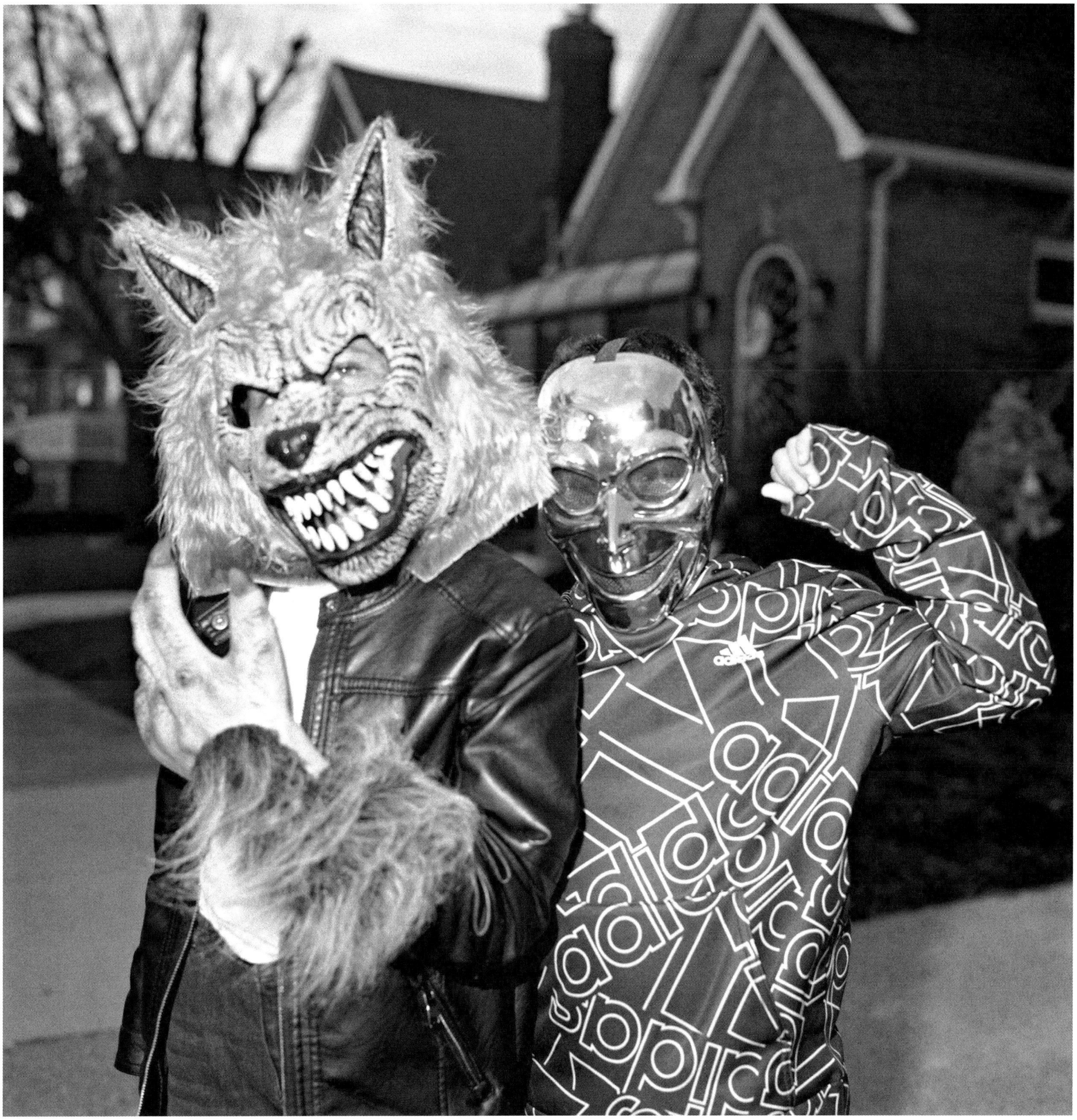

Wolf and Adidas
warrior, 2021, Queens.

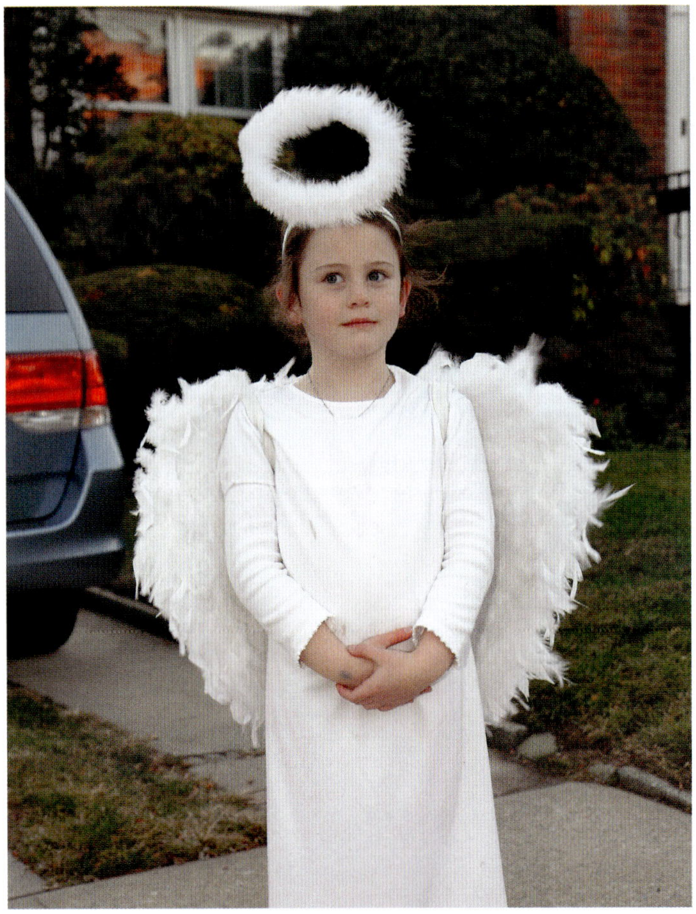

Angel, 2008, Queens.

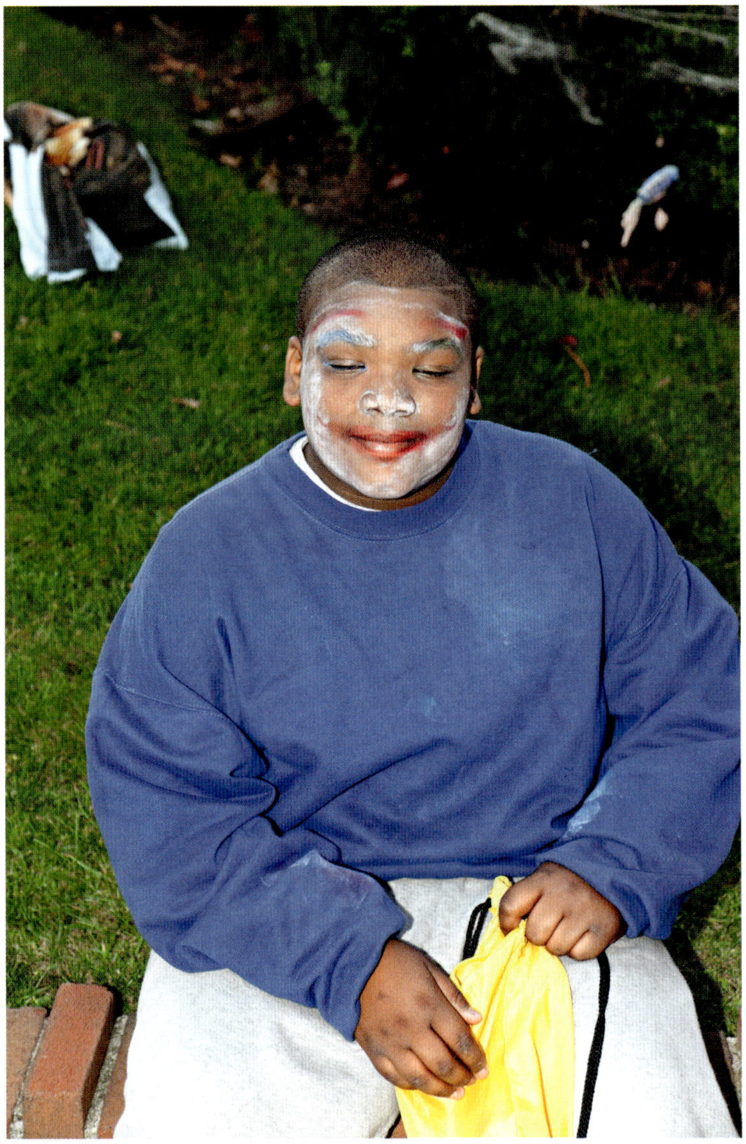

Happy trick-or-treater, 2008, Queens.

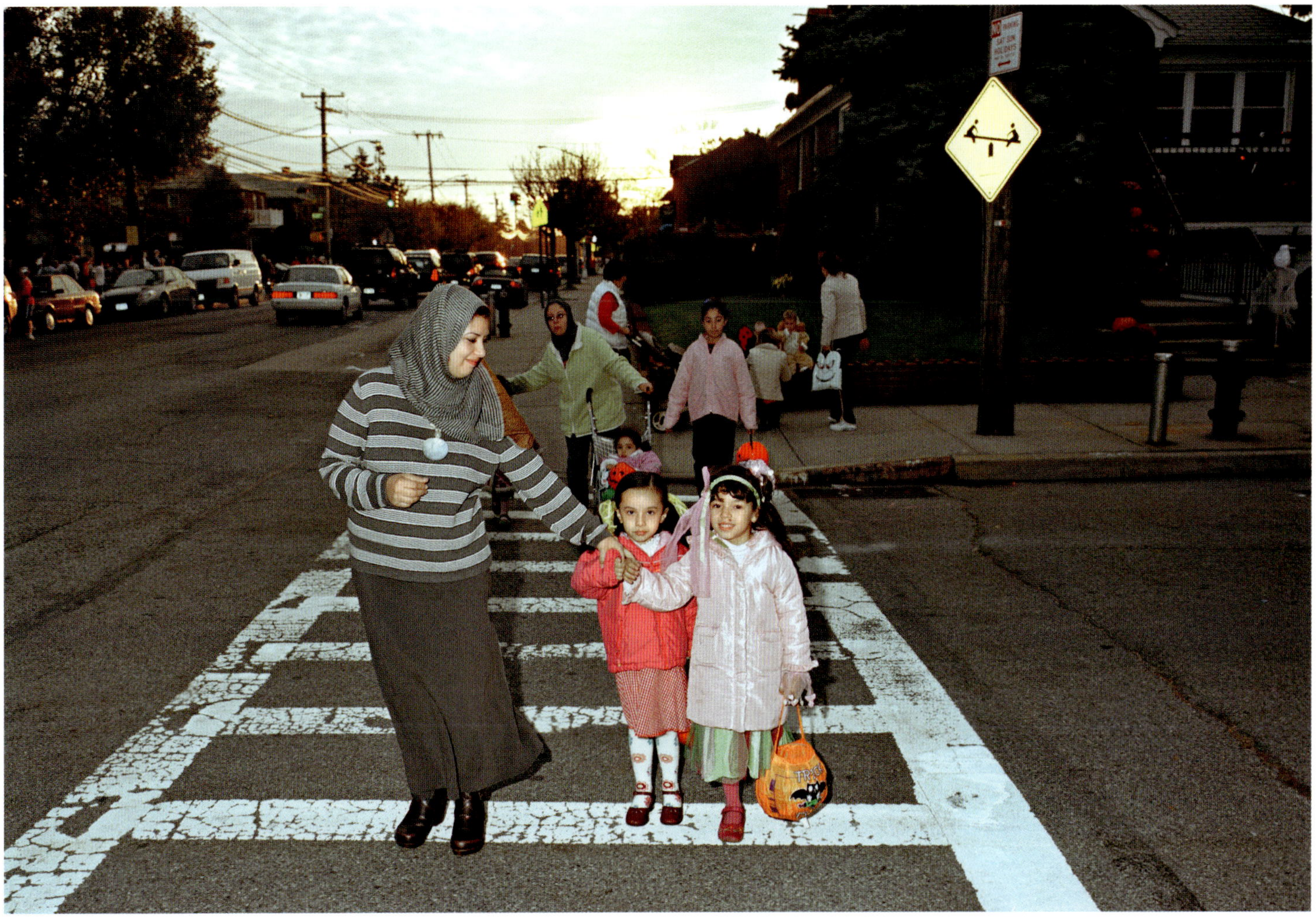

Family crossing street, 2006, Queens.

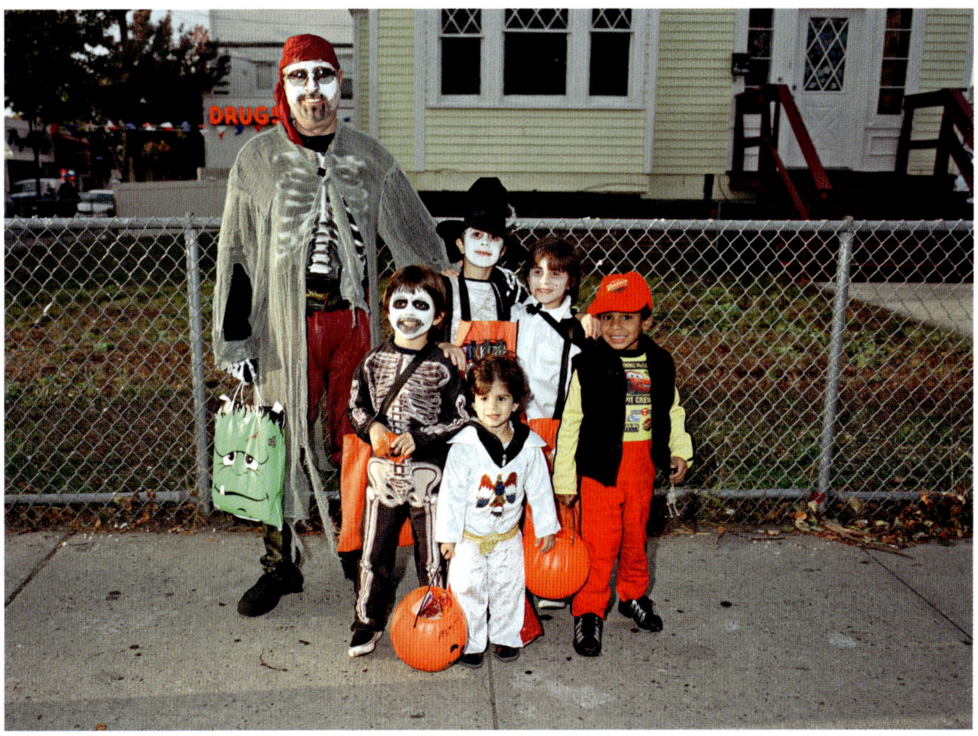

Costumed family, 2006, Queens.

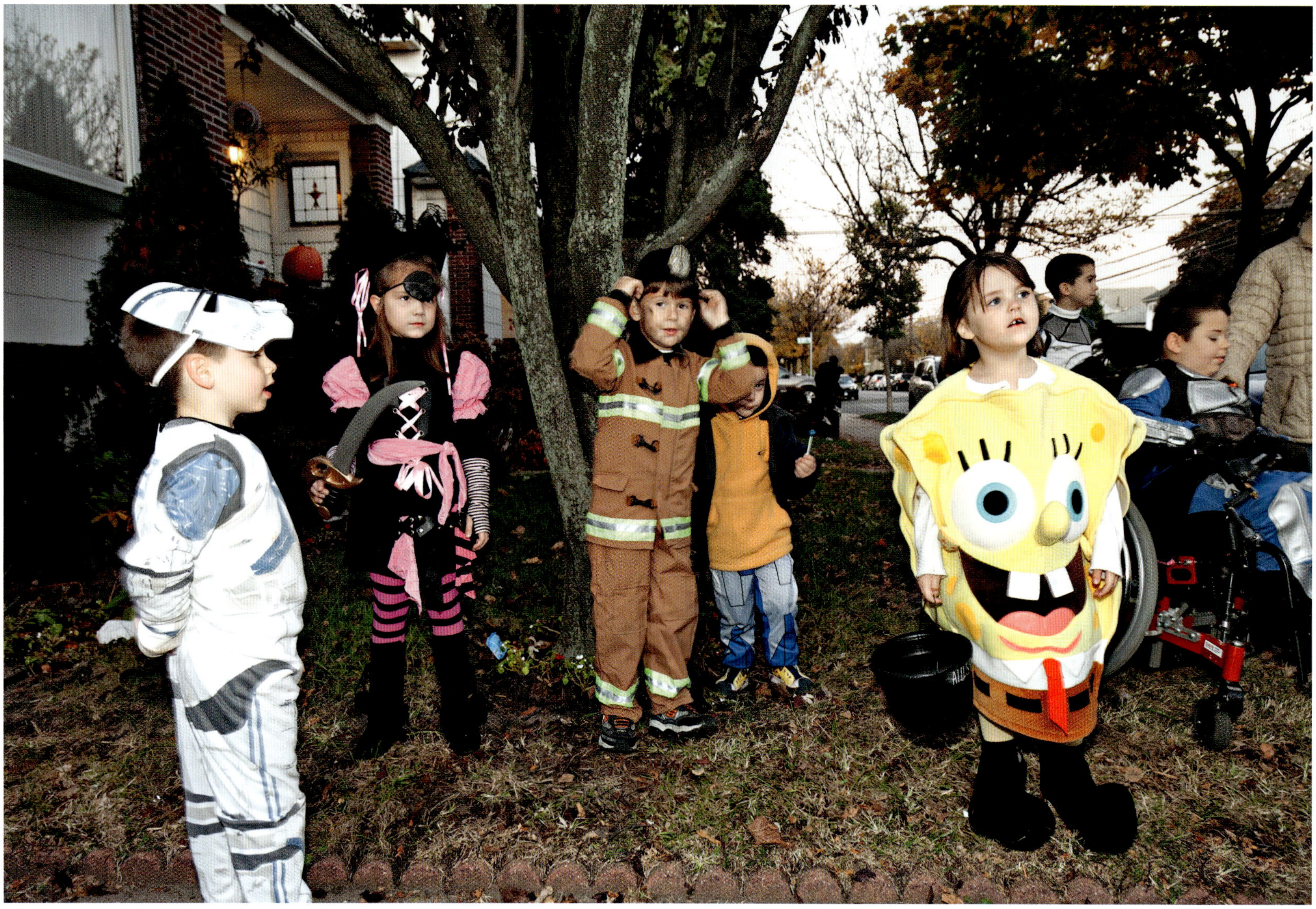

Kids under a tree,
2008, Queens.

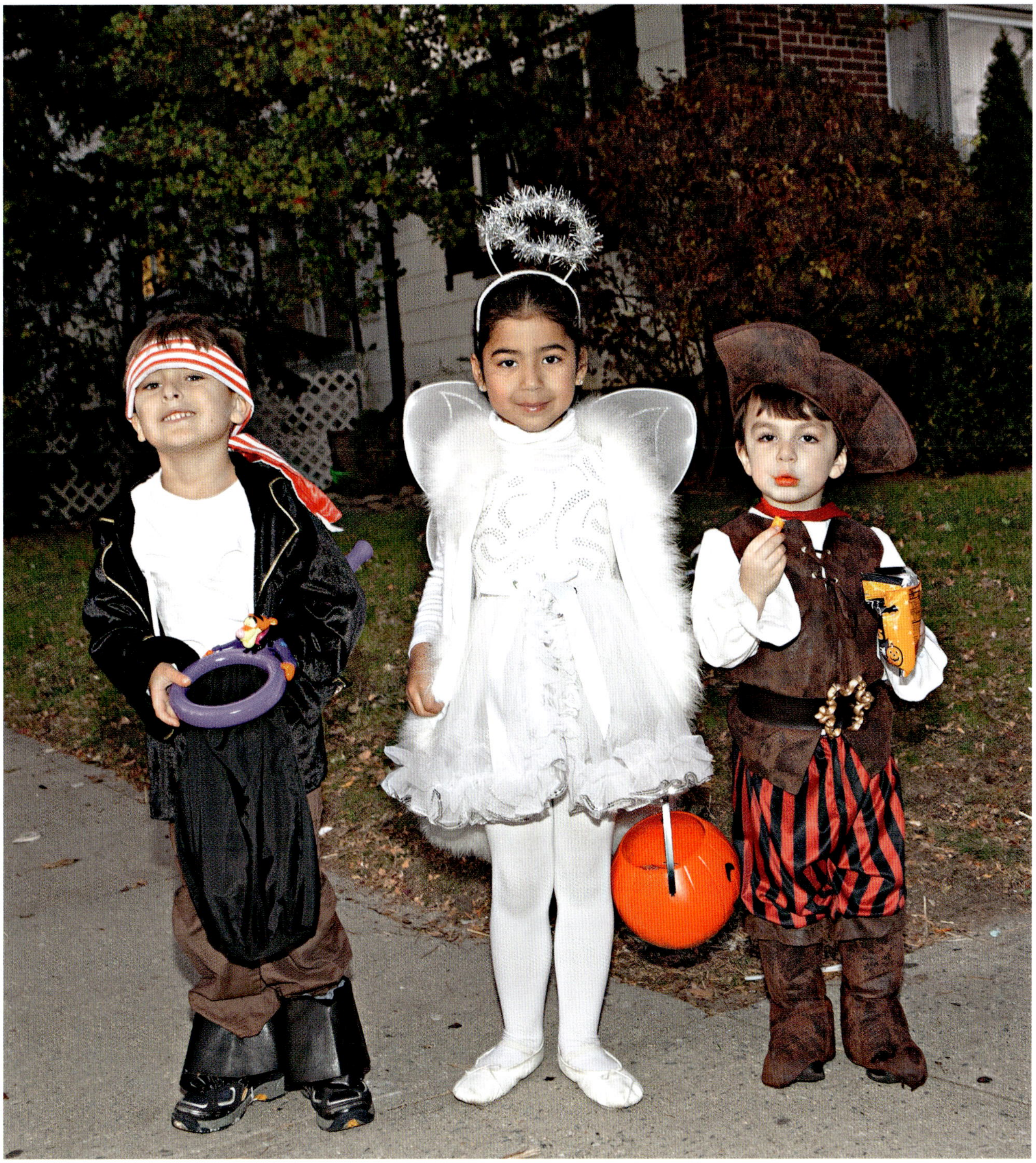

Angel and two boys,
2008, Queens.

Monster and Batman, 2016, Queens.

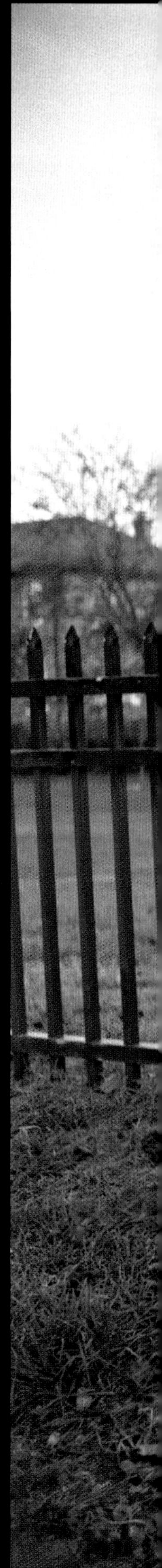

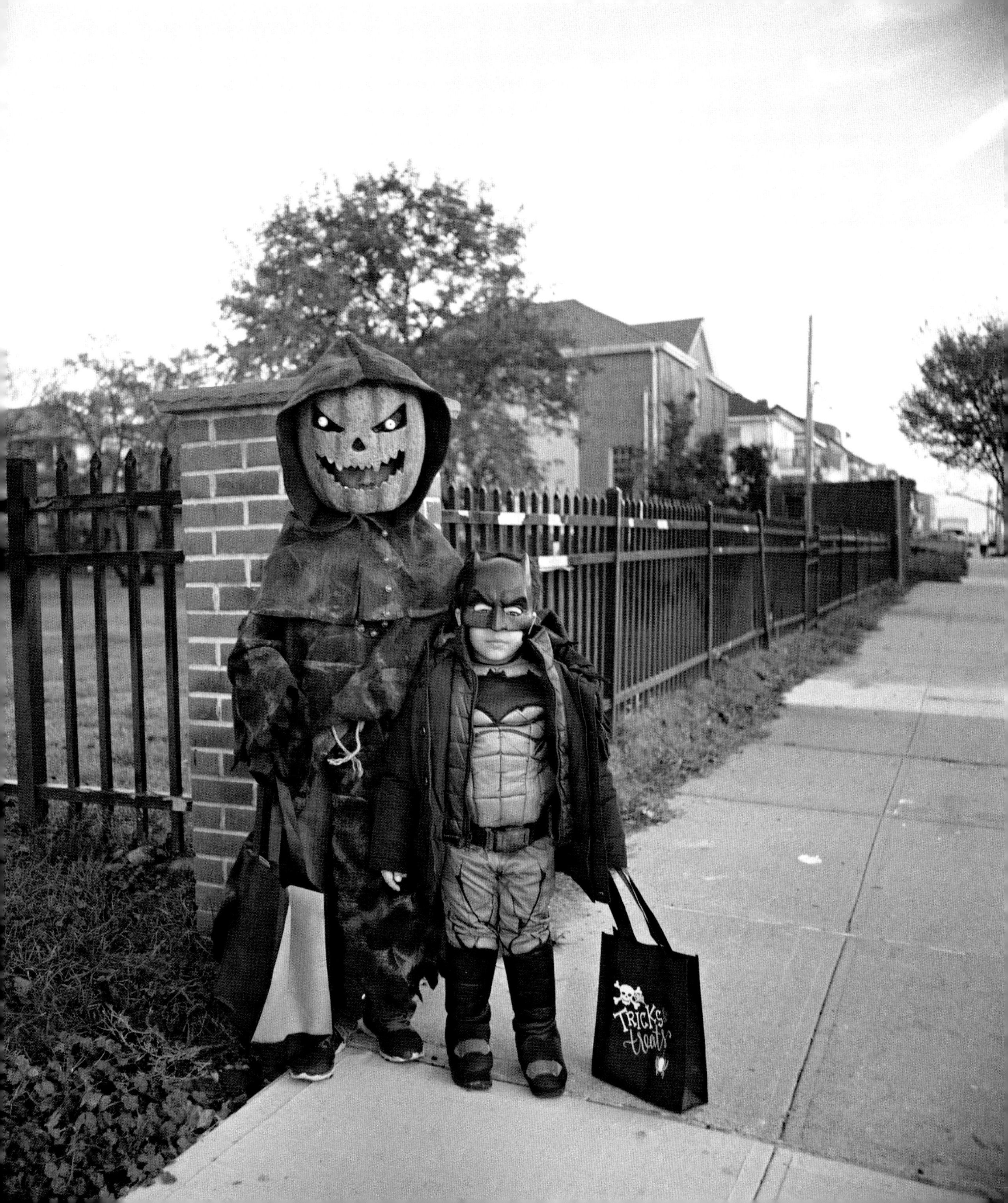
TRICKS
treats

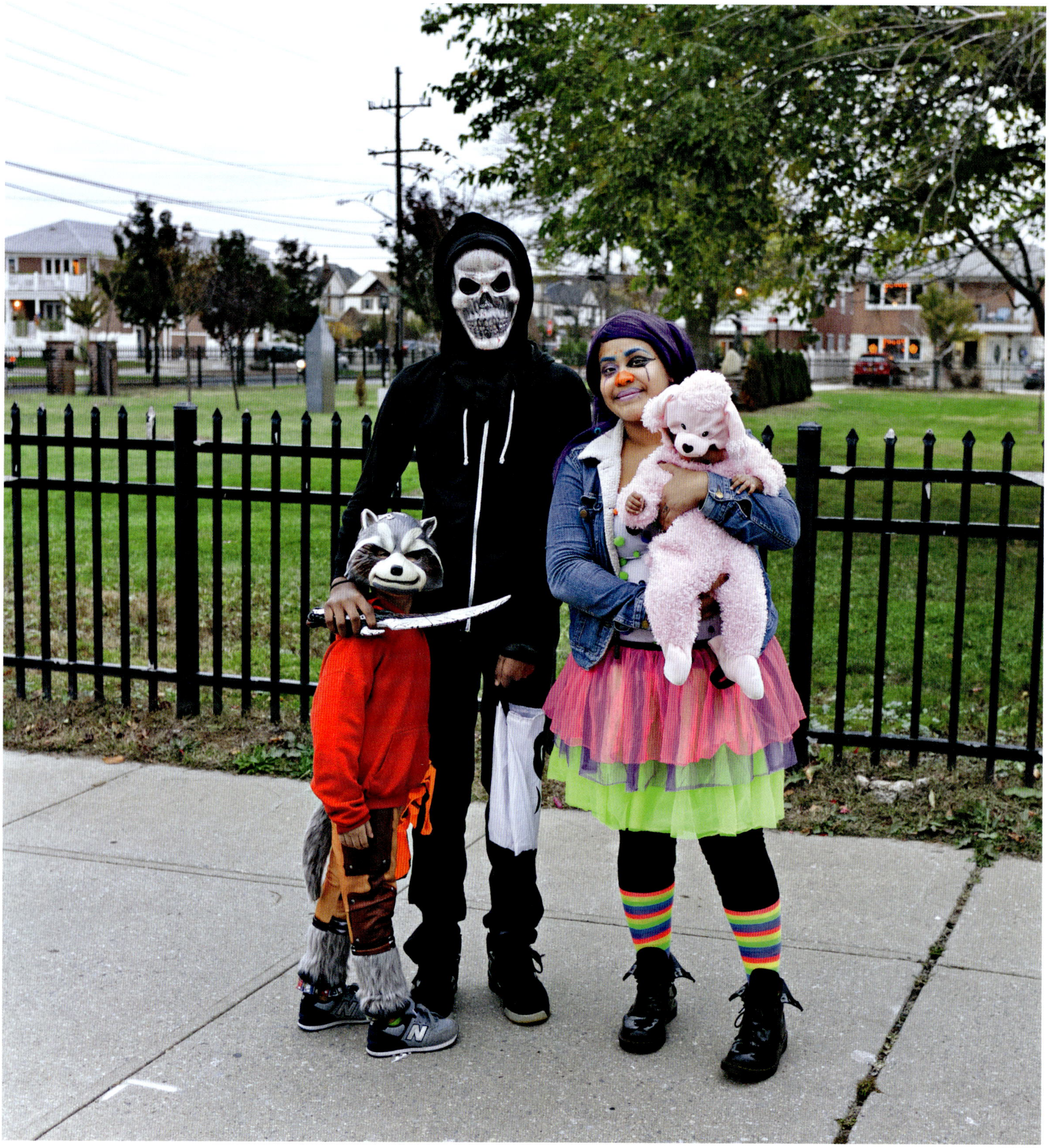

Scary/sweet family,
2015, Queens.

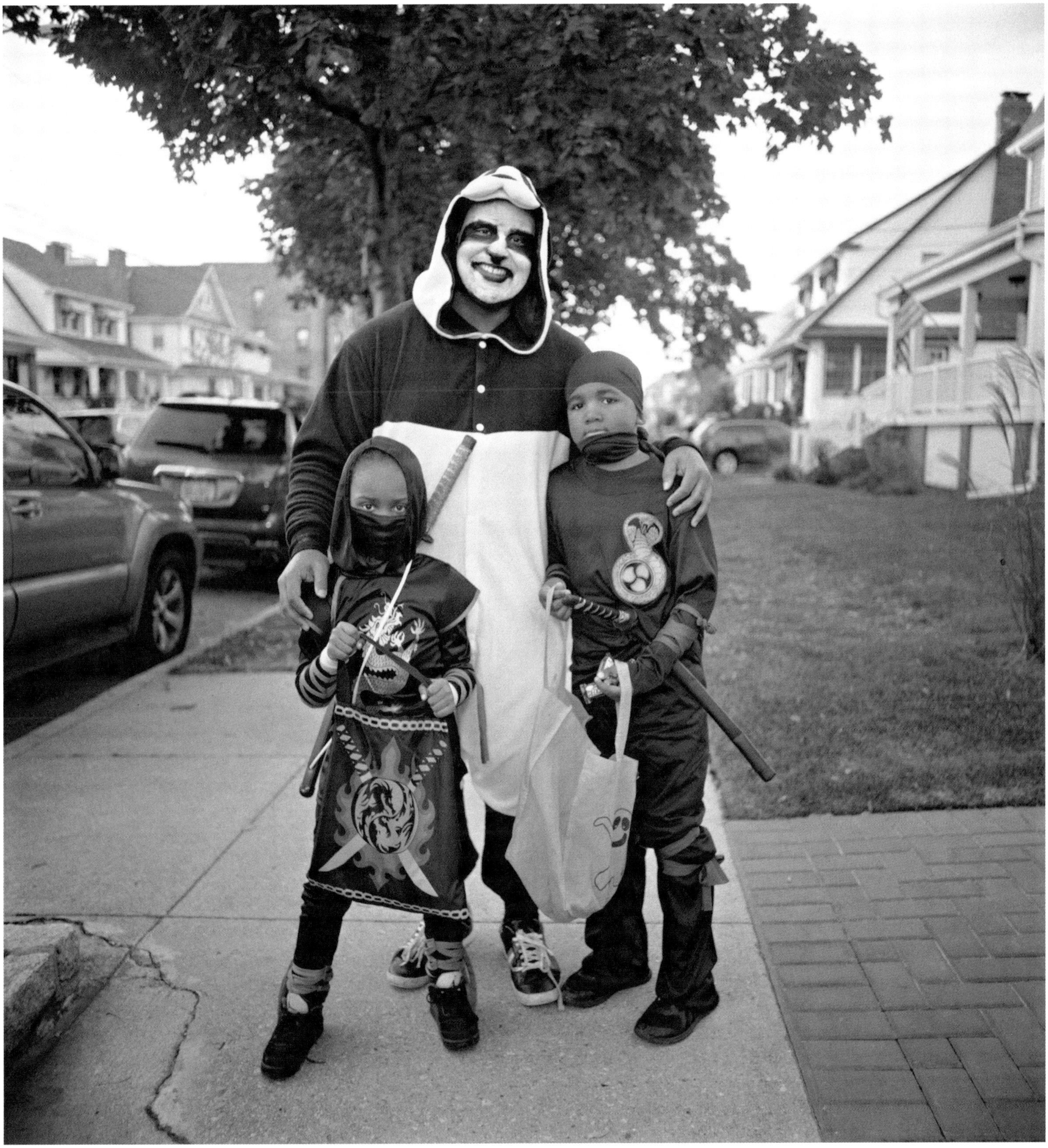

Ninja family, 2016, Queens.

Costumed family,
2018, Queens.

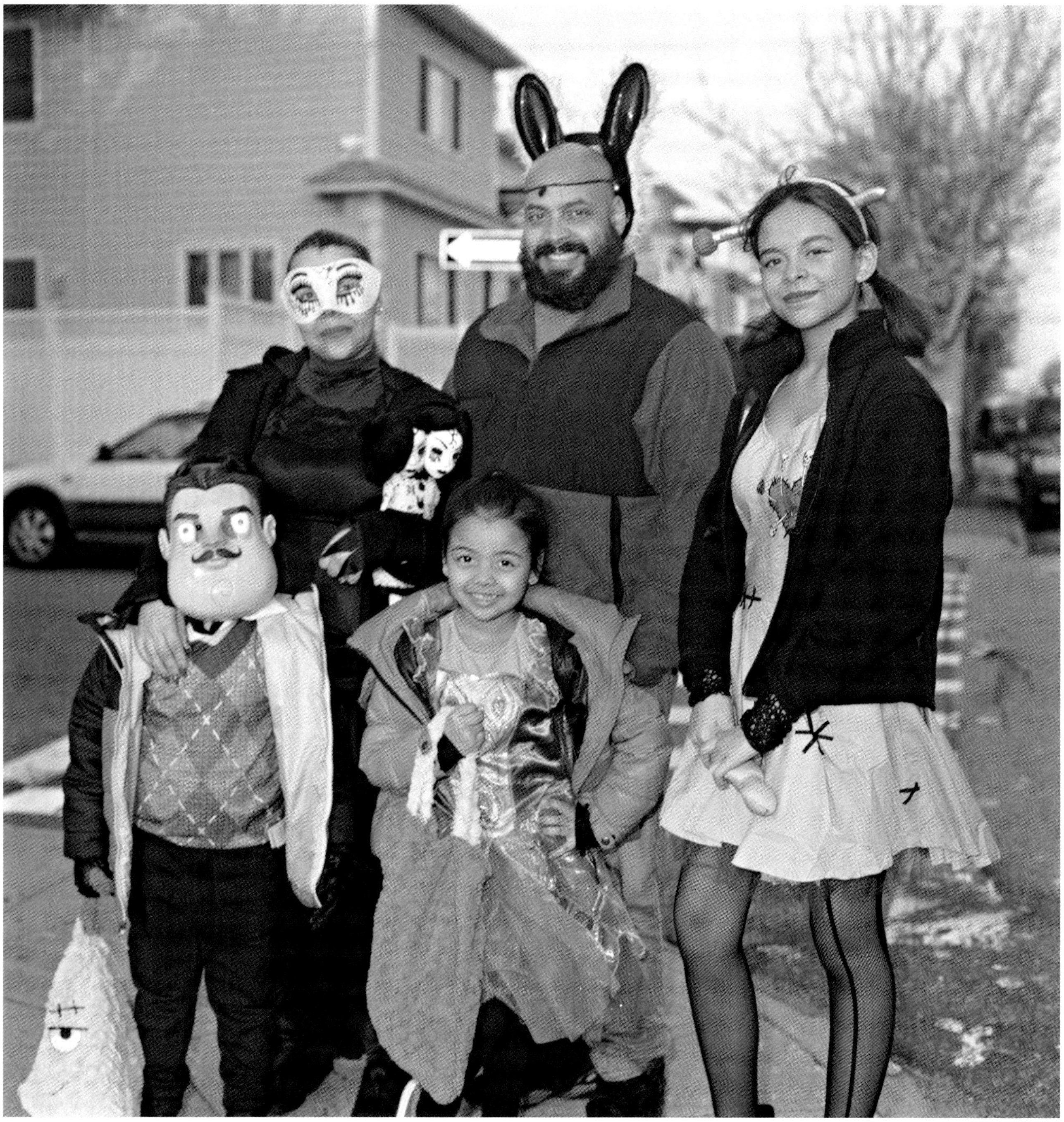

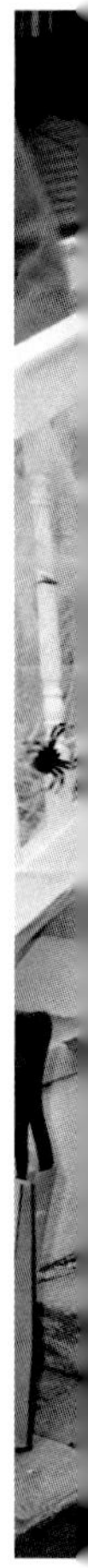

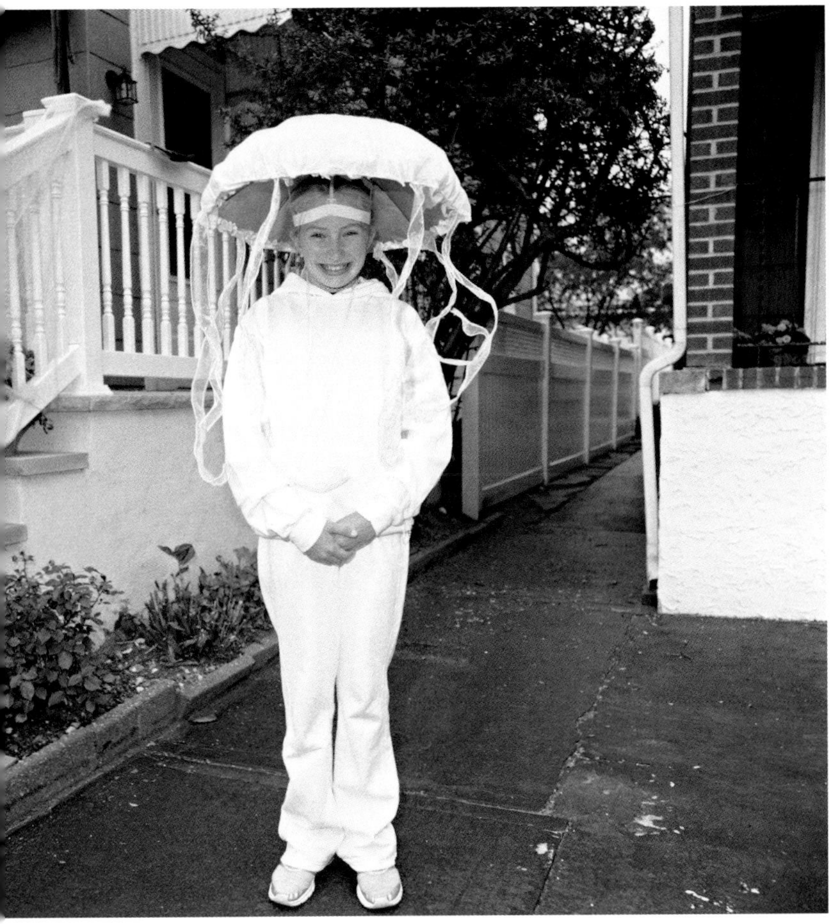

Squid girl, 2014, Queens.

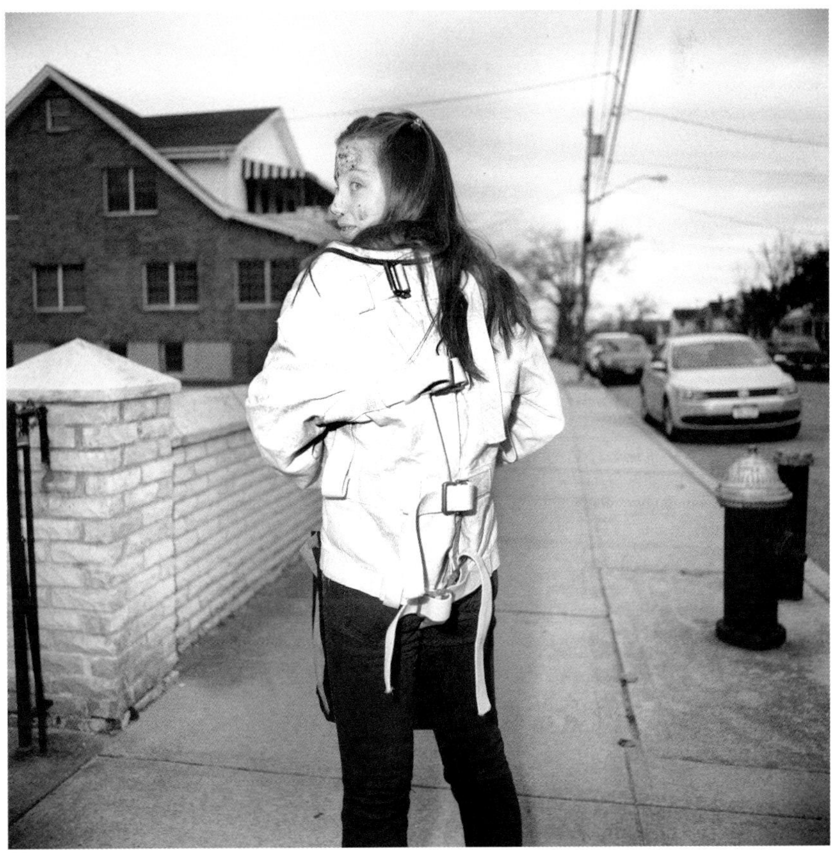

Girl in real straitjacket, 2014, Queens.

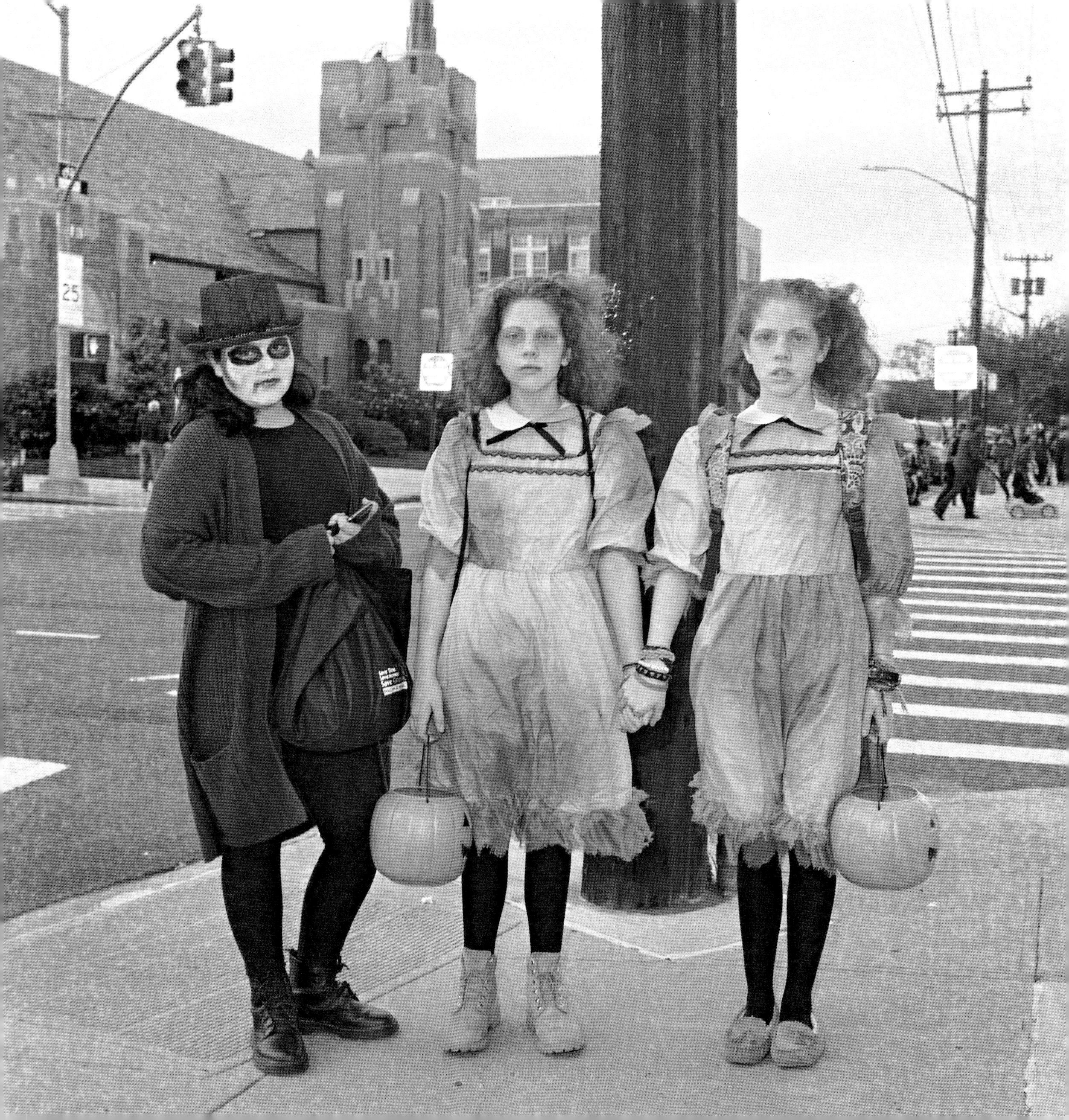
25

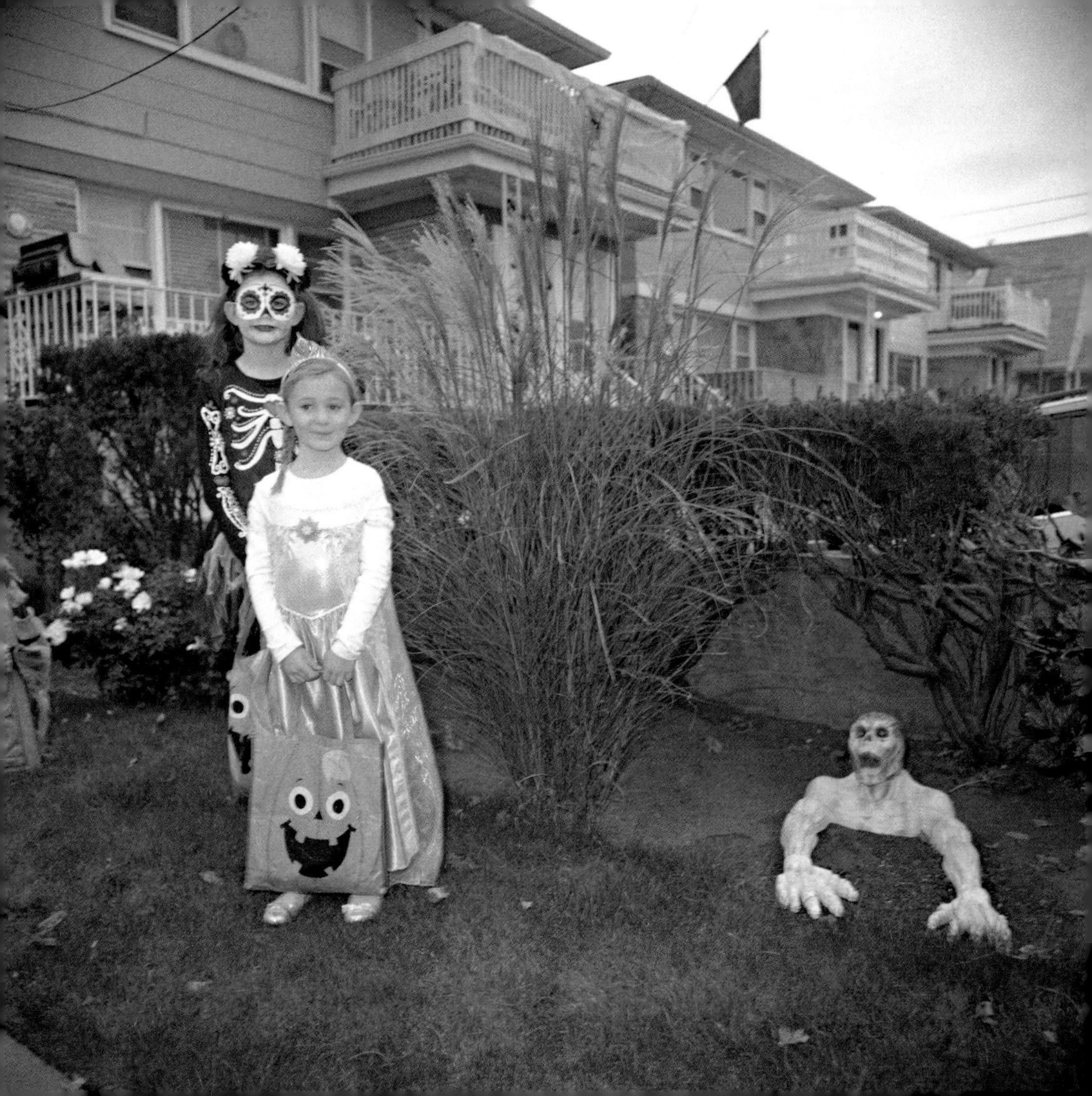

Robotics and kids,
2018, Queens.

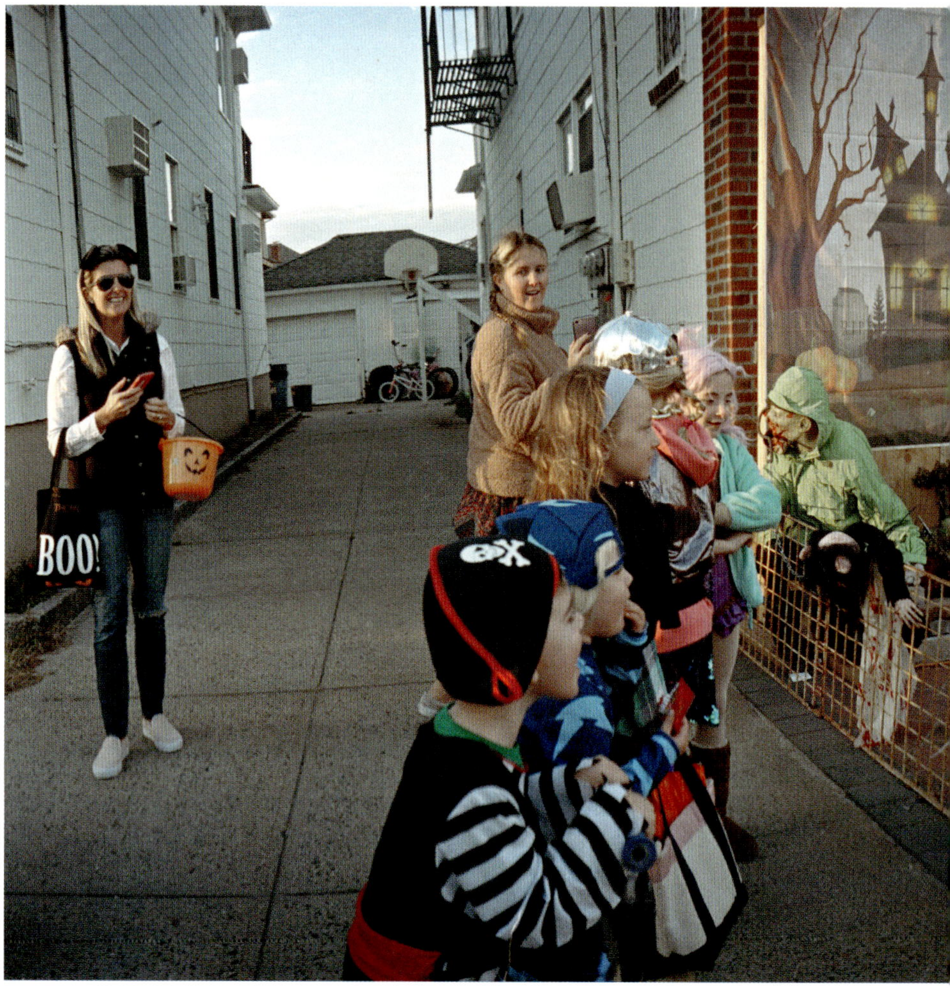

Haunted house,
2003, Queens.

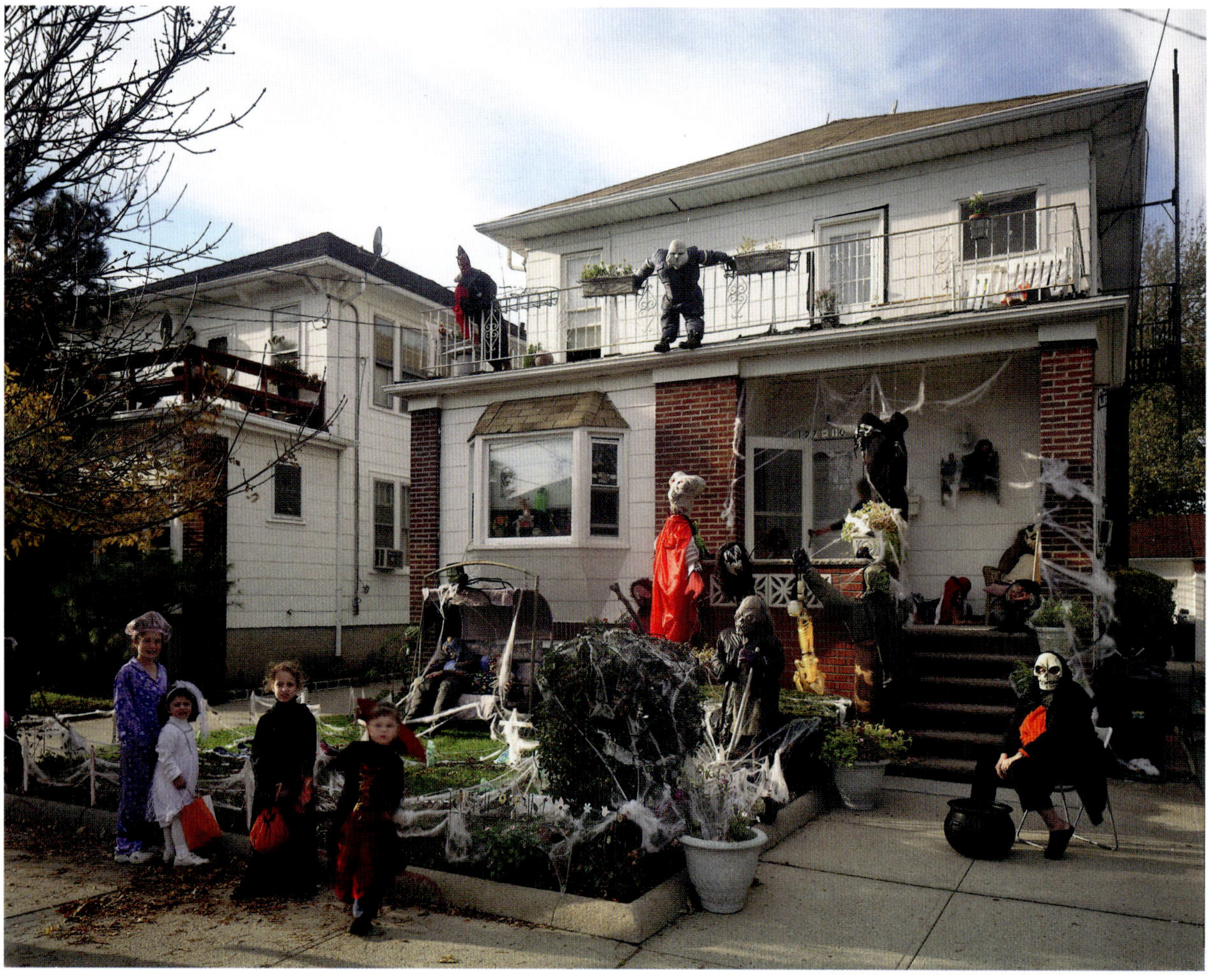

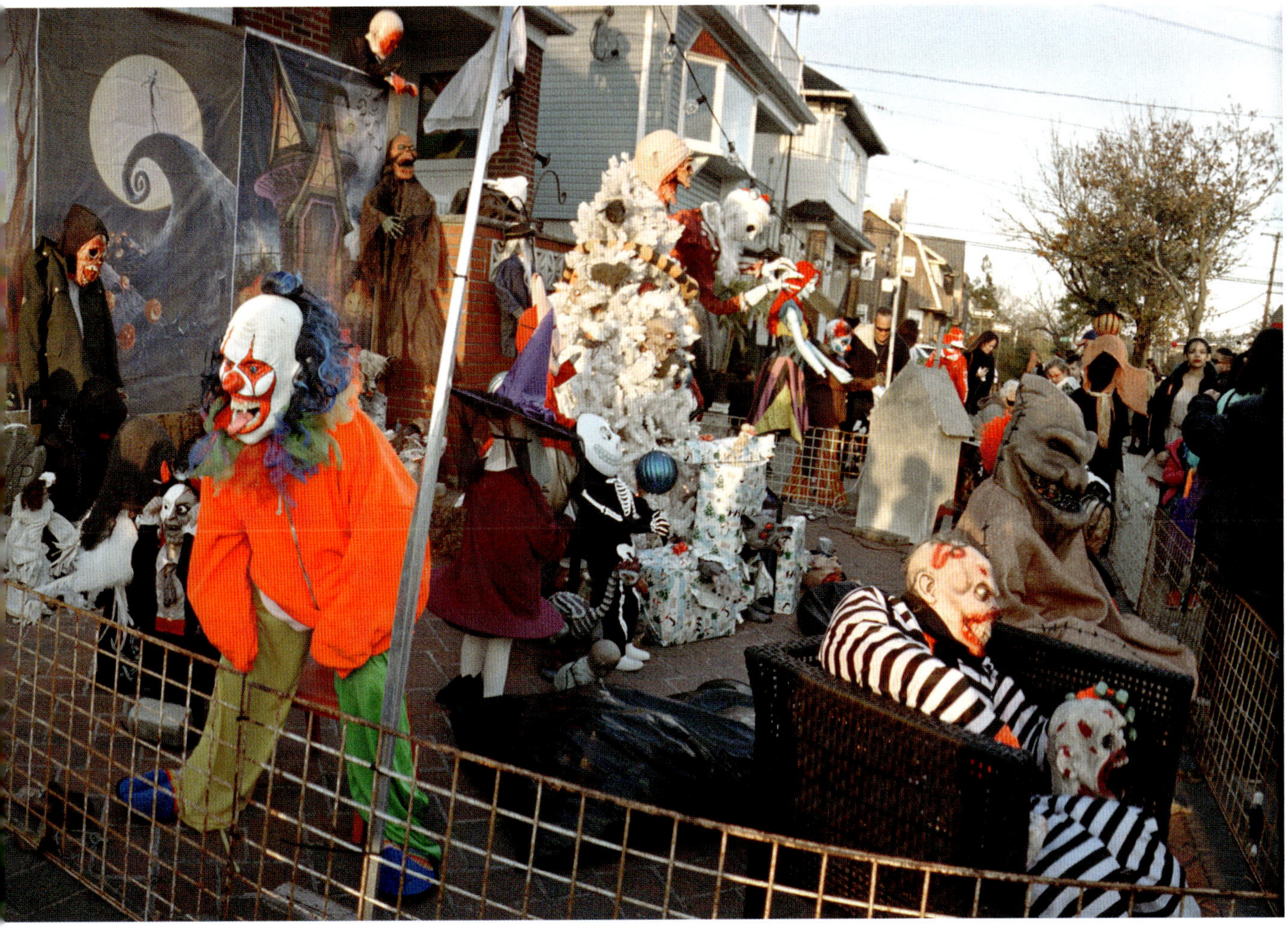

In 2003, a local family set up a haunted house on Newport Avenue in Rockaway. From then on, I only had to walk a few blocks from my home to join a procession of strange creatures on their way to this central source of Halloween activity. Ghosts and goblins, superheroes and vampires, angels and devils across the Rockaway Peninsula gathered here. Eventually, the family added robotic creatures to further enchant the growing crowd of trick-or-treaters. Except for a few very particular parties, I concentrated most of my Halloween photography here through 2024.

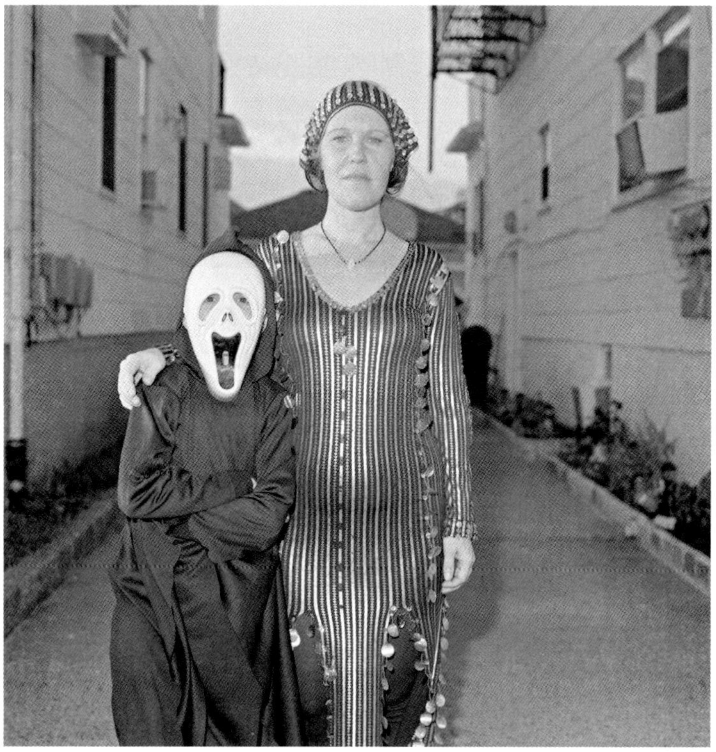

Mother and Ghostface,
2018, Queens.

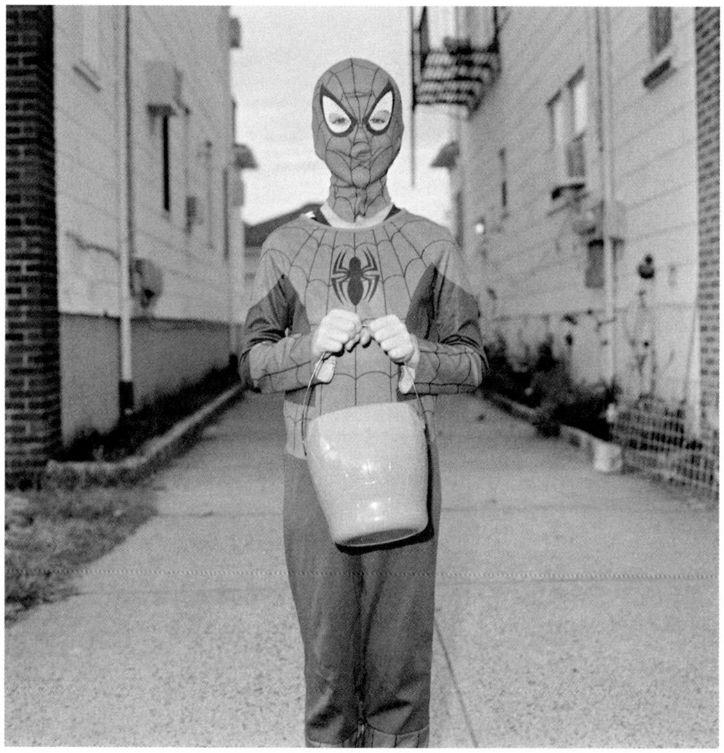

Spiderman, 2022, Queens.

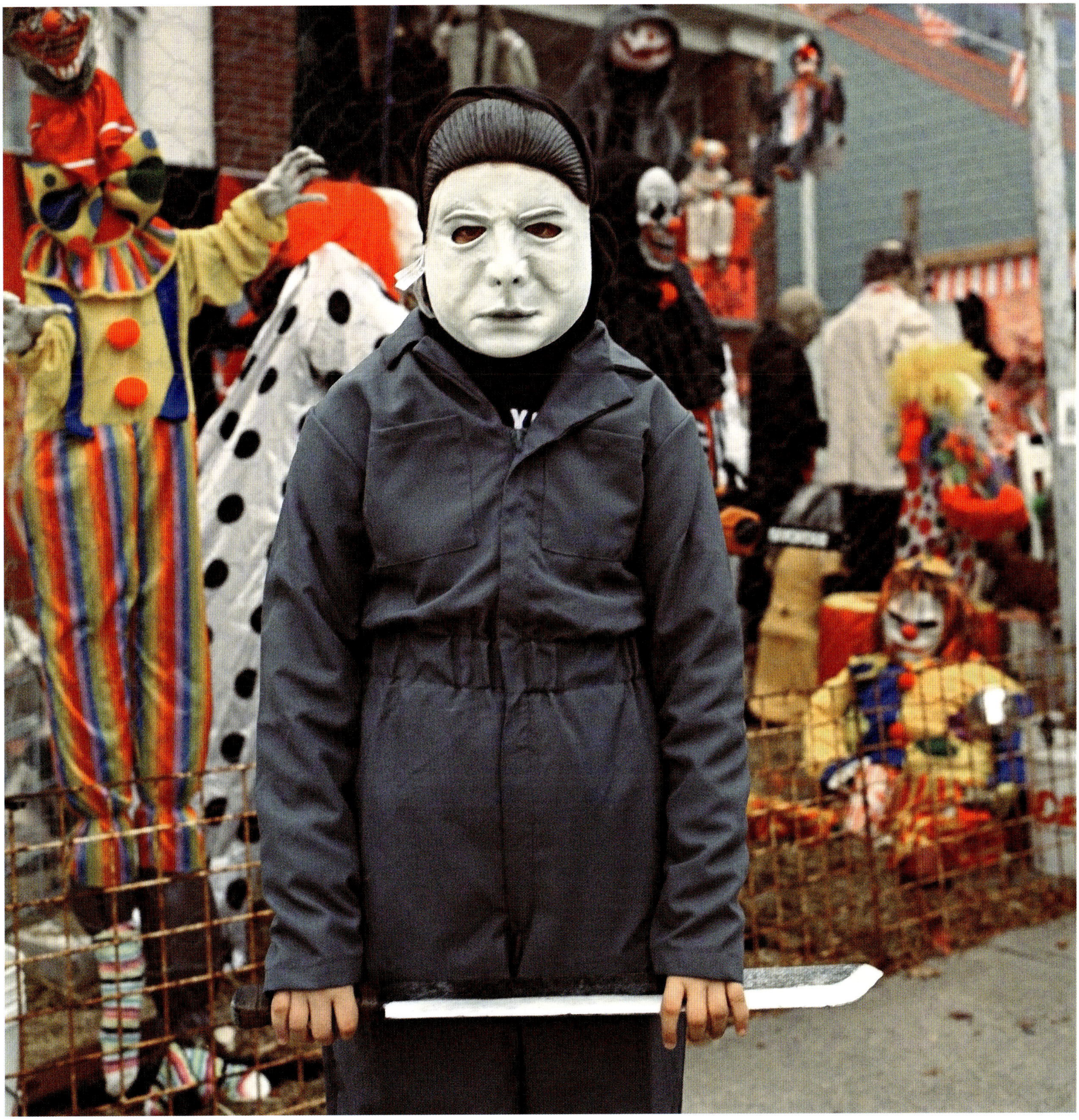

Somber swordsman,
2023, Queens.

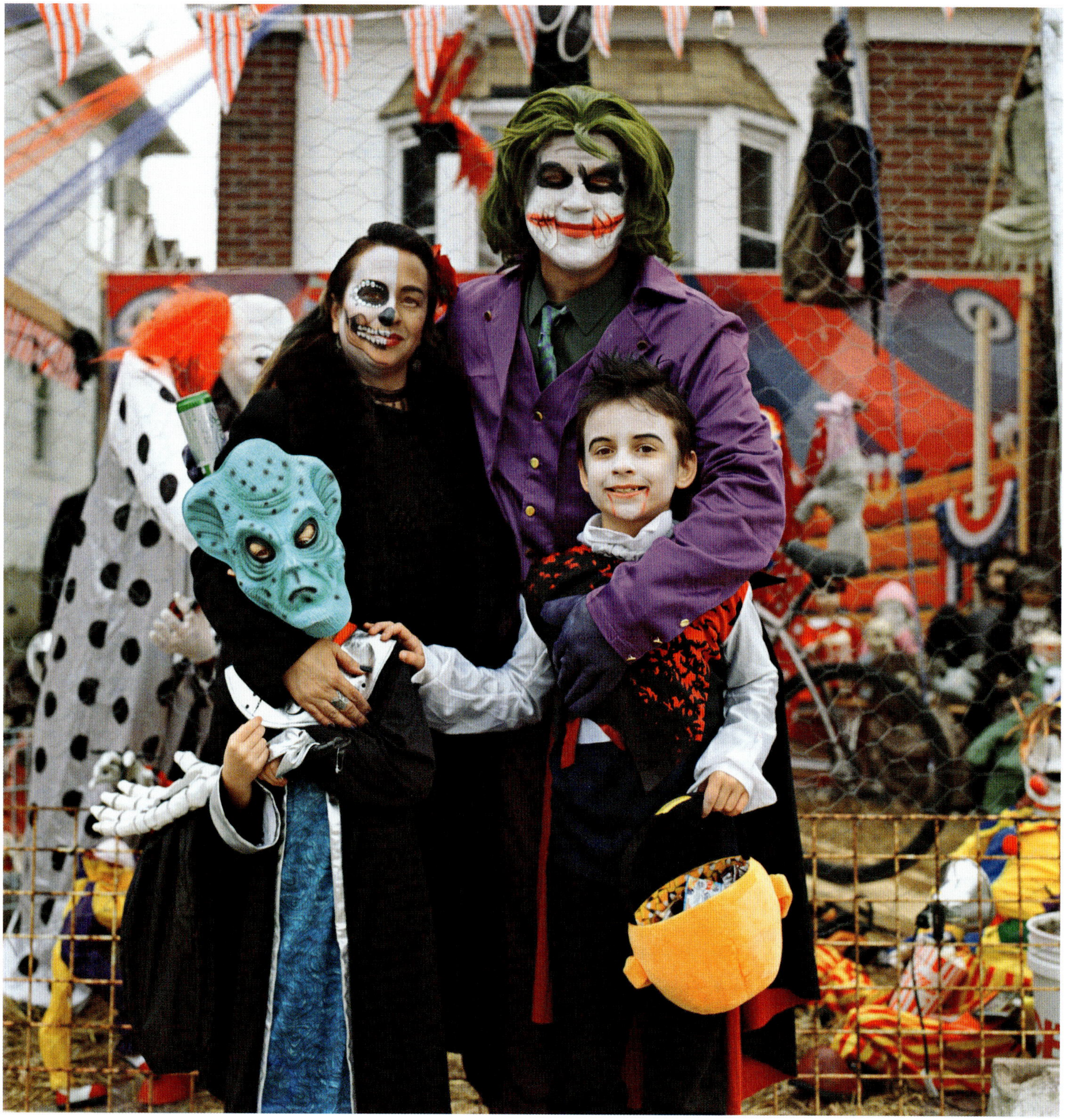

Joker family, 2023, Queens.

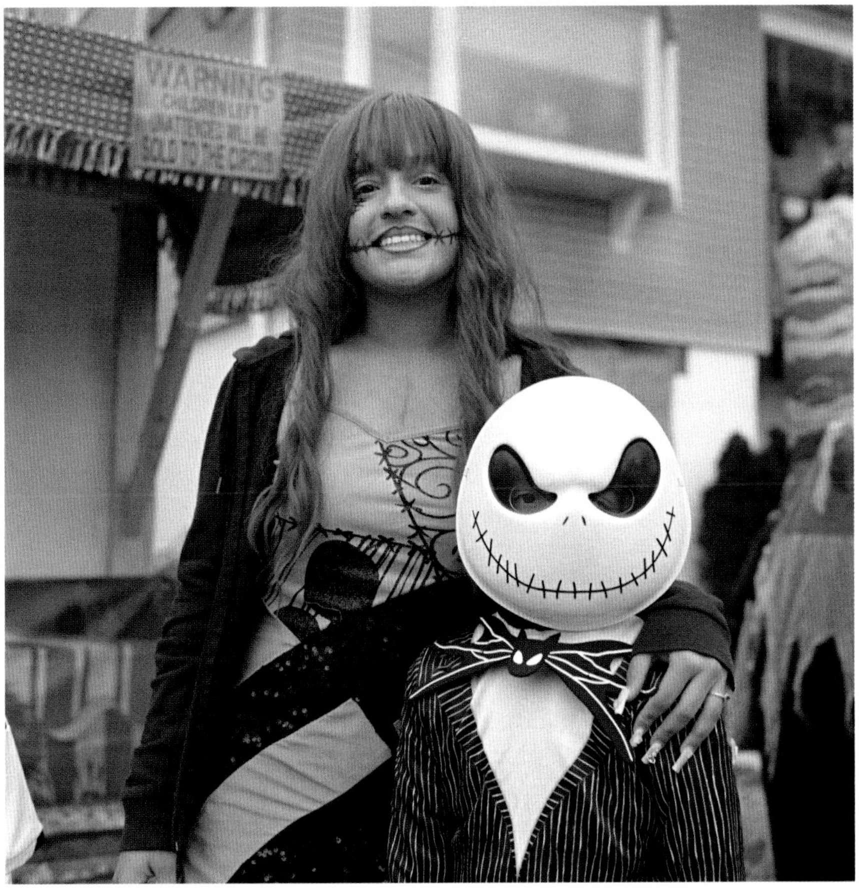

Sally and Jack,
2023, Queens.

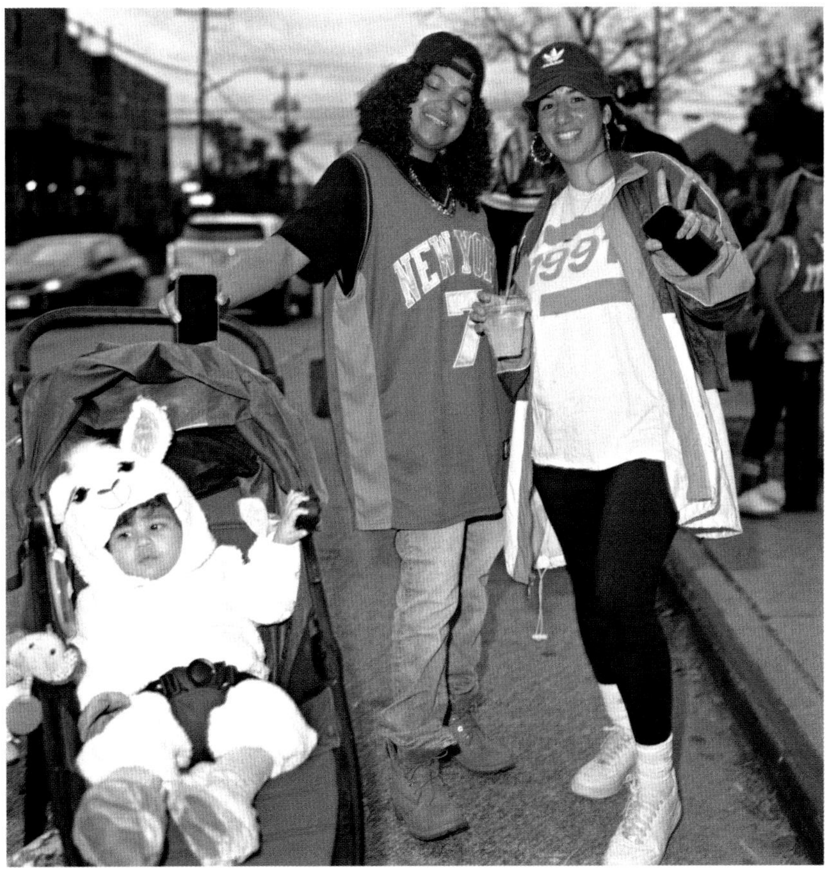

Two women and
bunny, 2021, Queens.

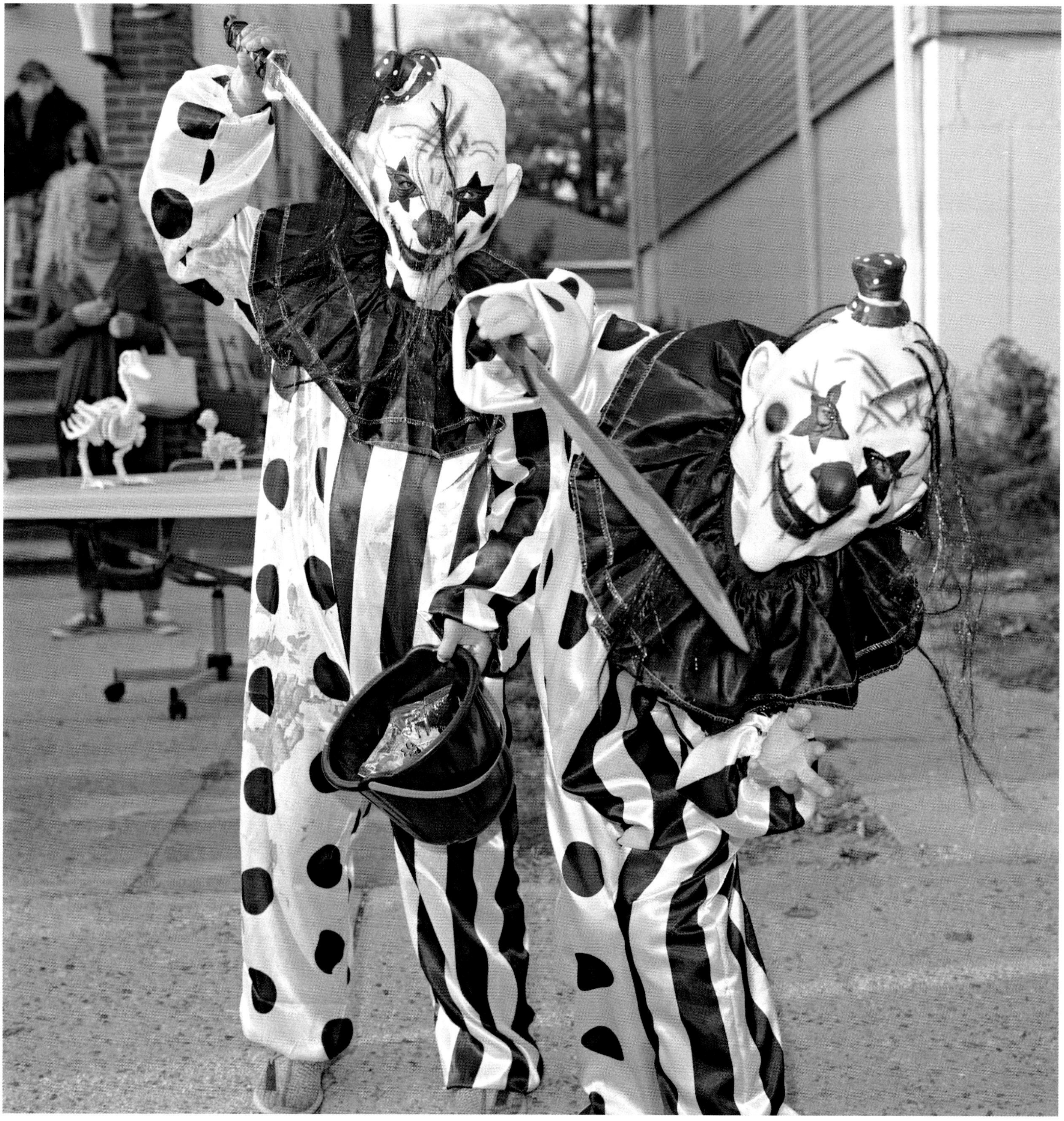

Two clowns with swords,
2022, Queens.

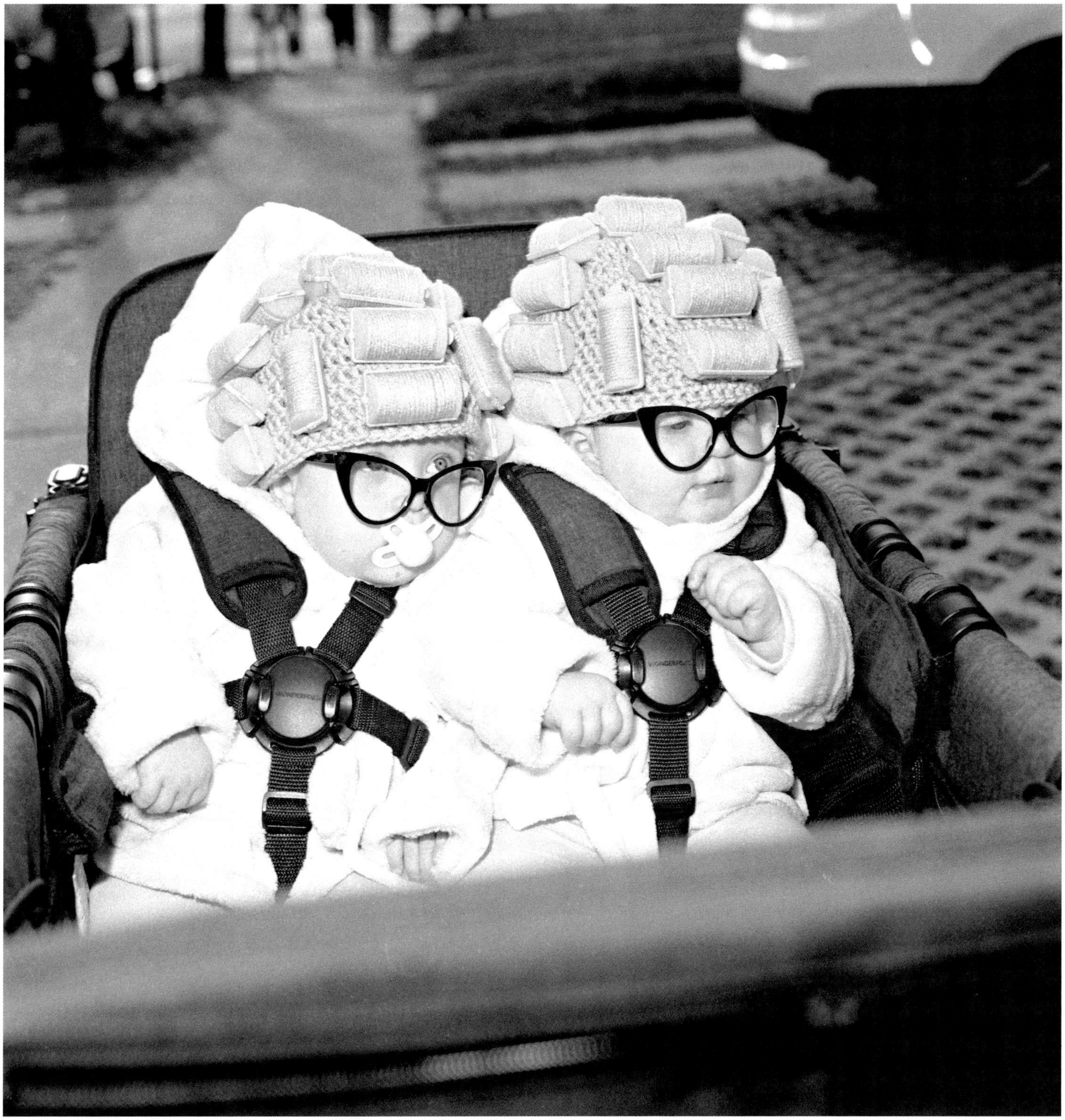

Baby carriage grandma
twins, 2022, Queens.

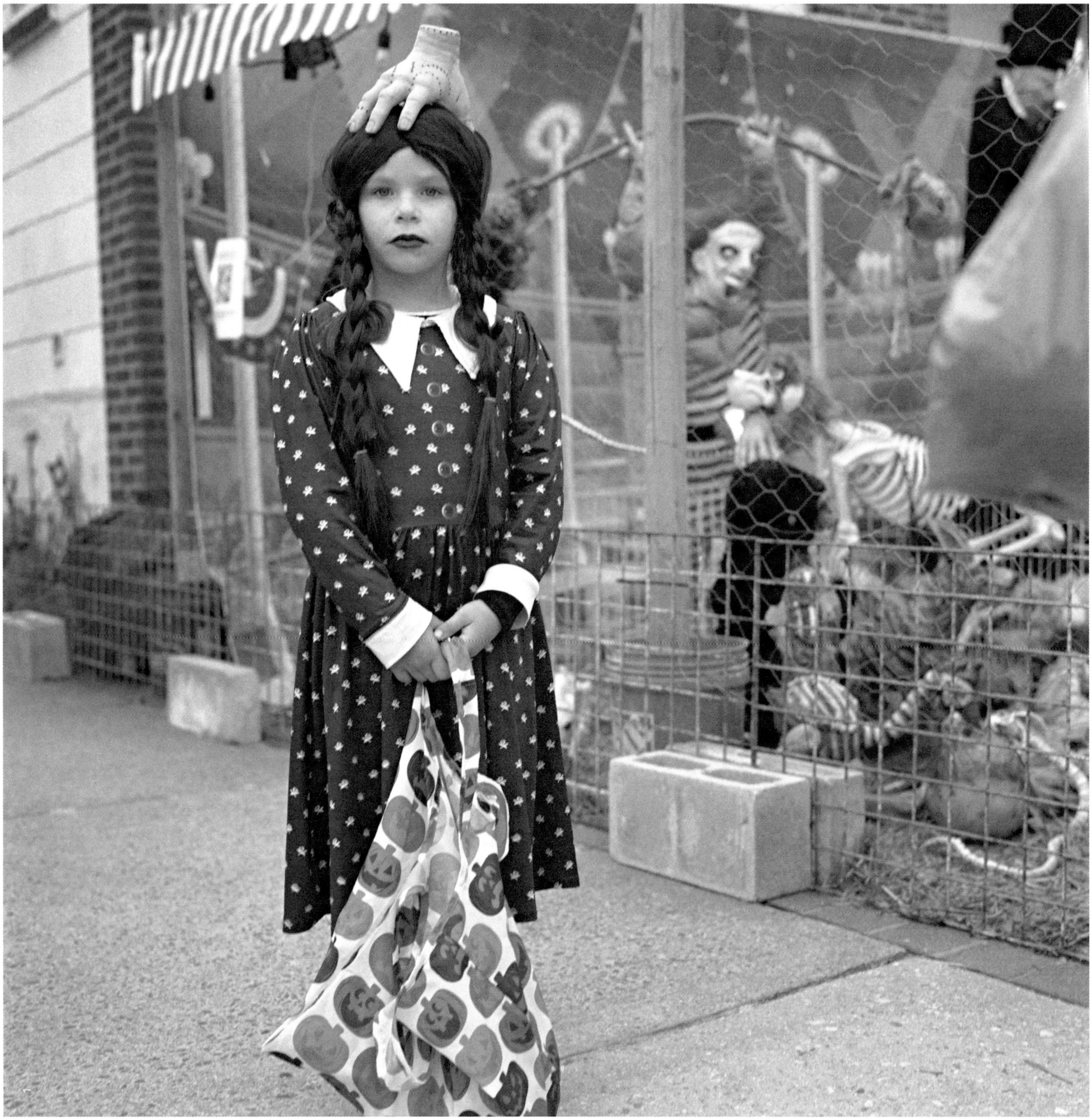

Wednesday,
2023, Queens.

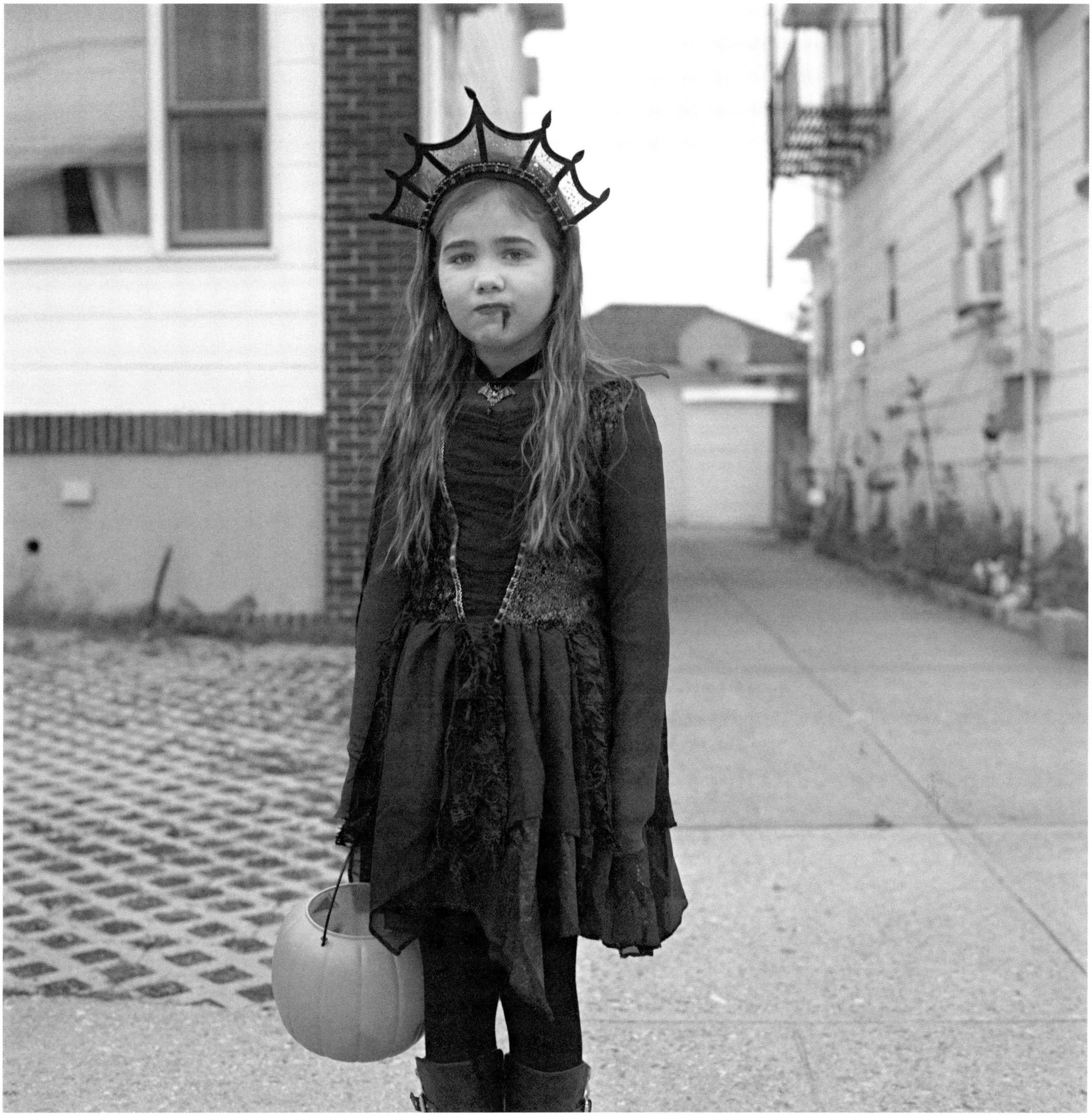

Girl with bloody lip,
2023, Queens.

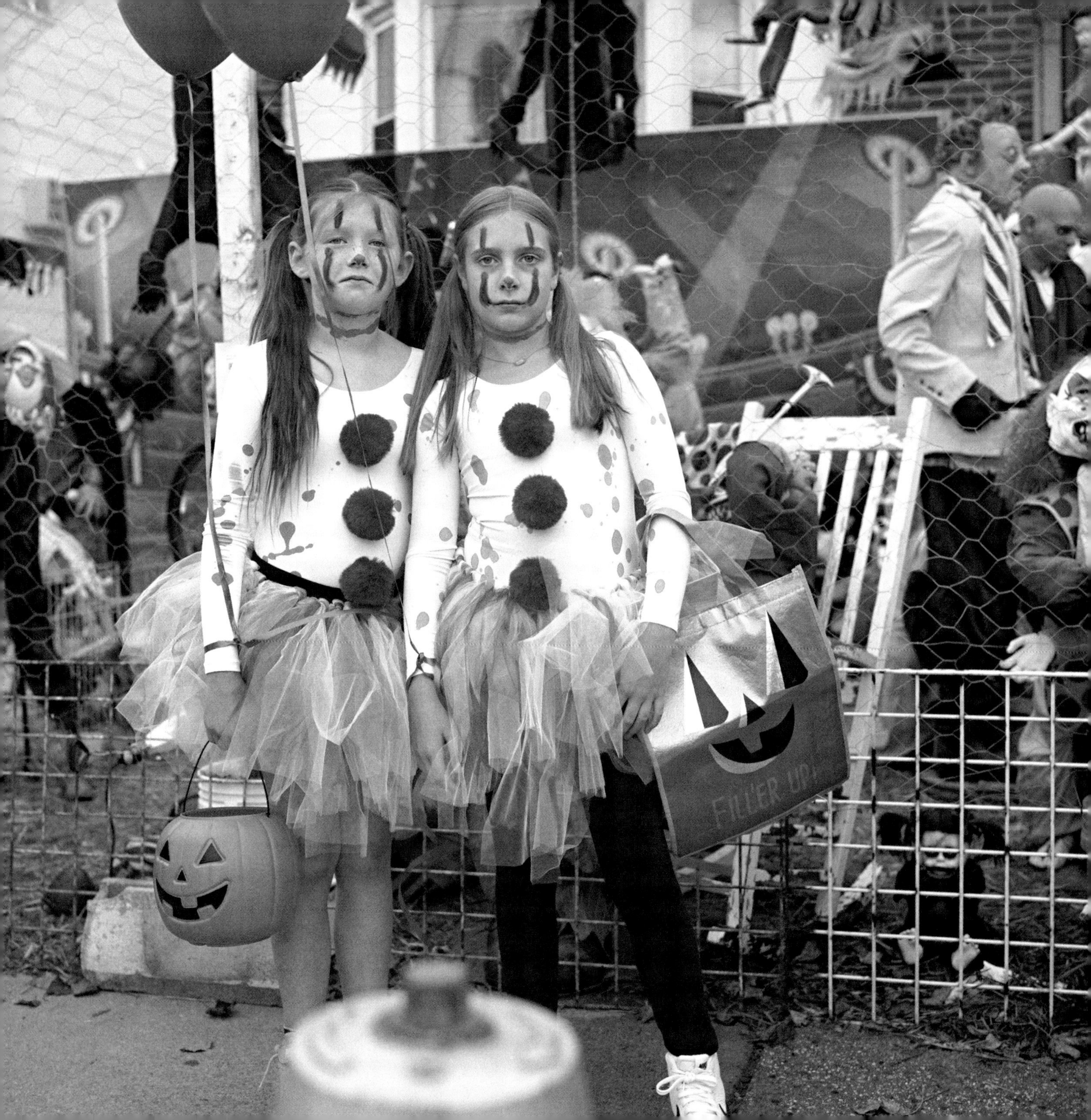
FILL'ER UP!

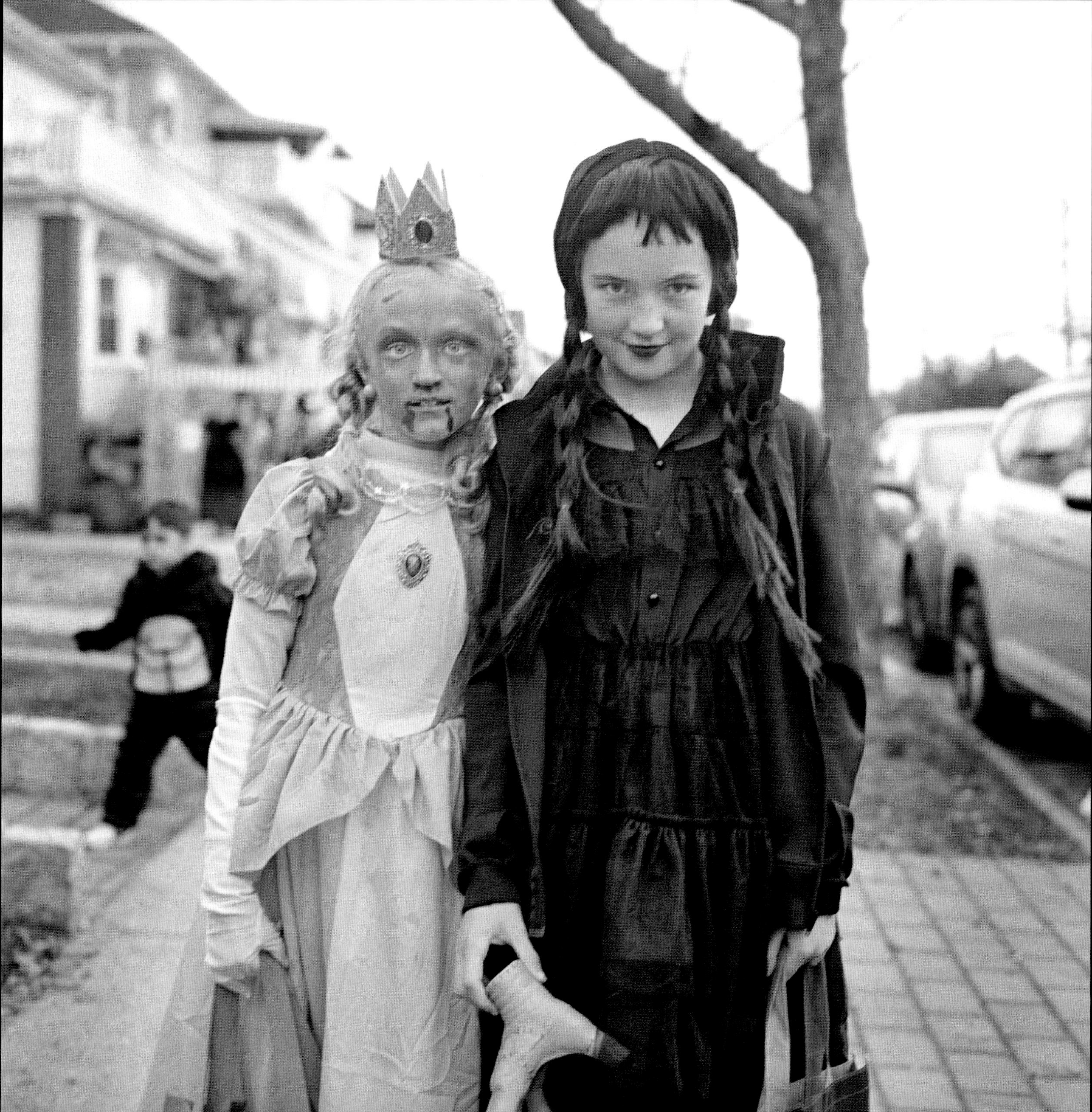

Two costumed girls,
2023, Queens.

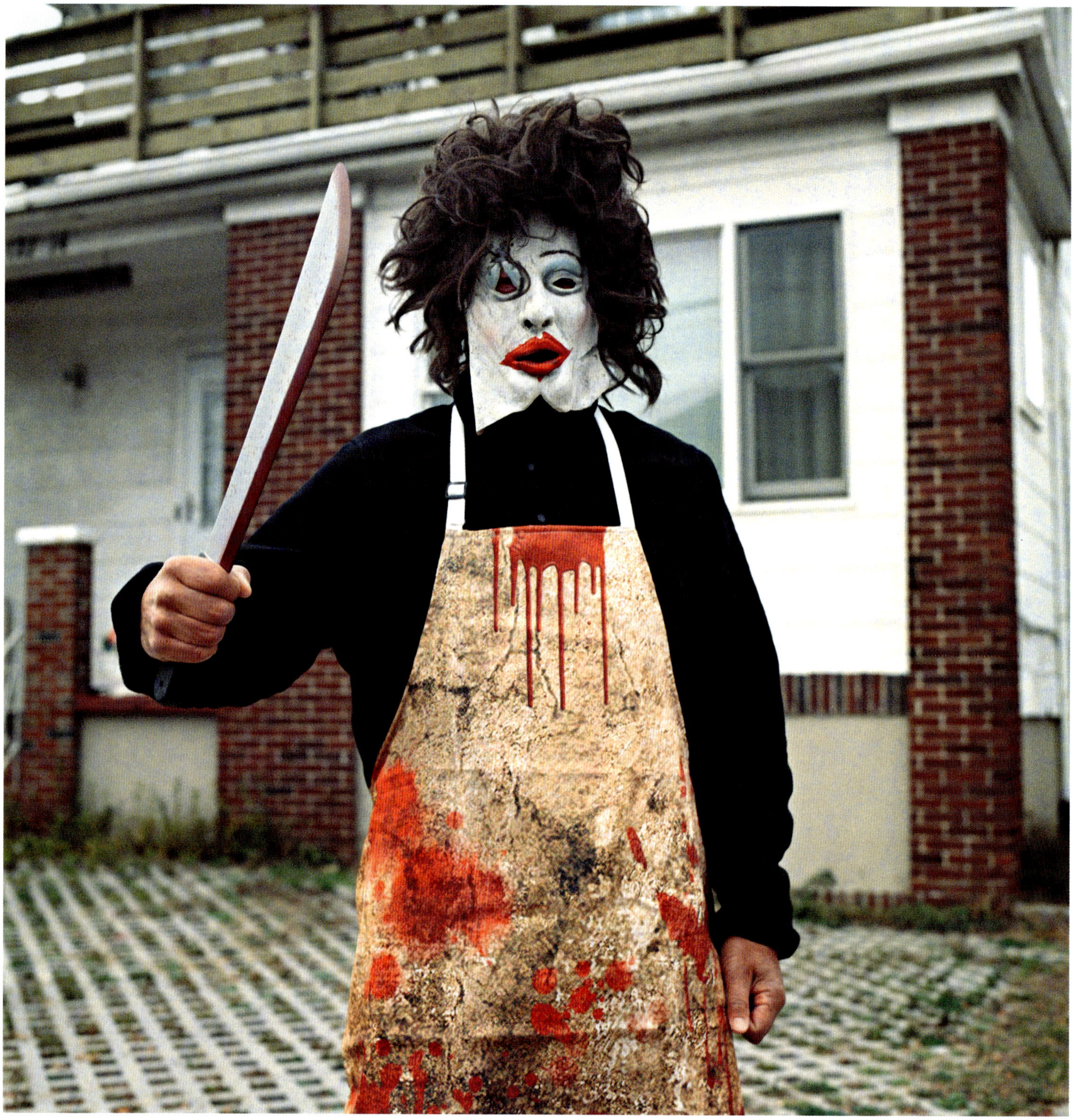

Bloody boy with knife,
2023, Queens.

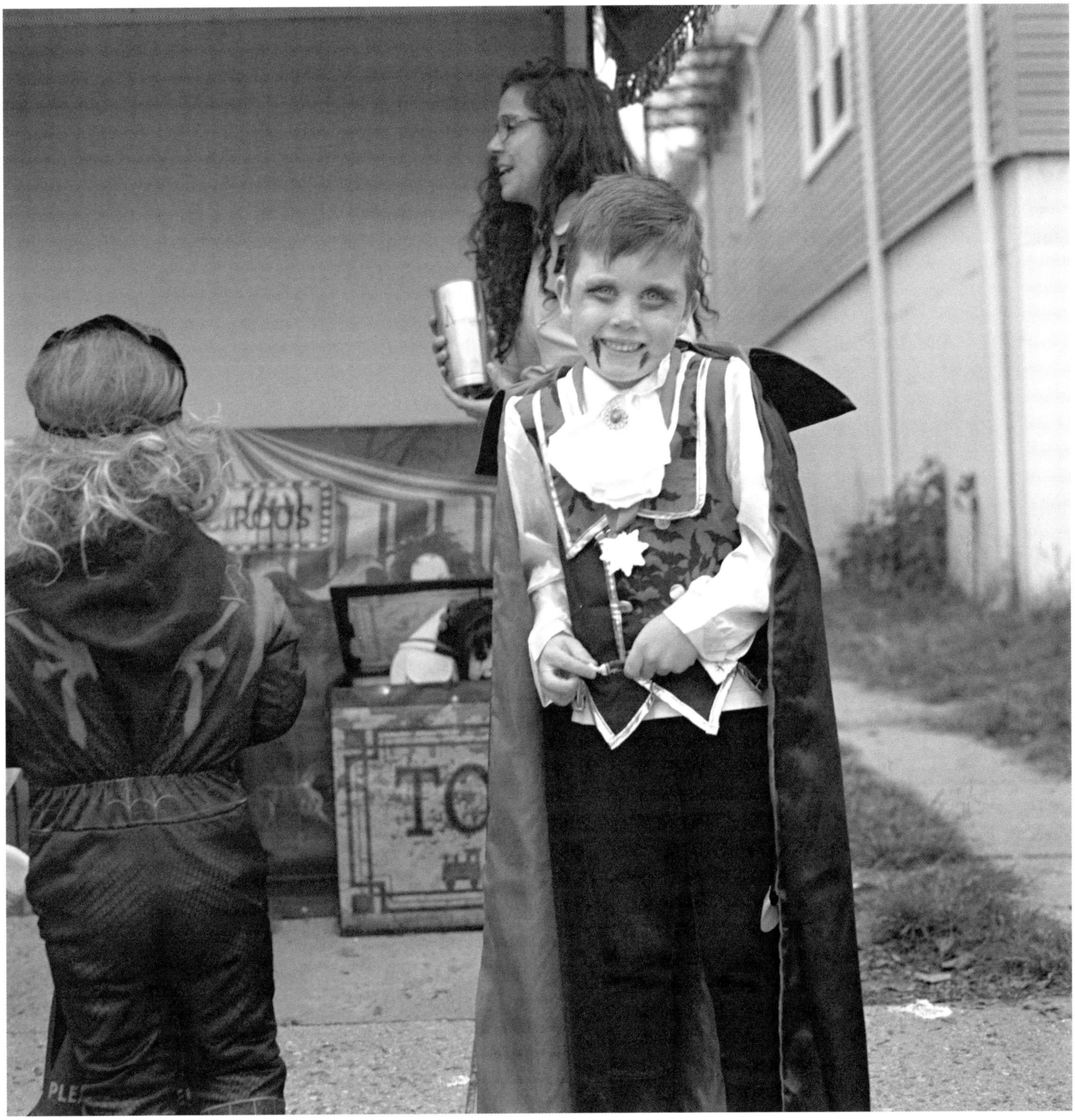

Nervous vampire,
2023, Queens.

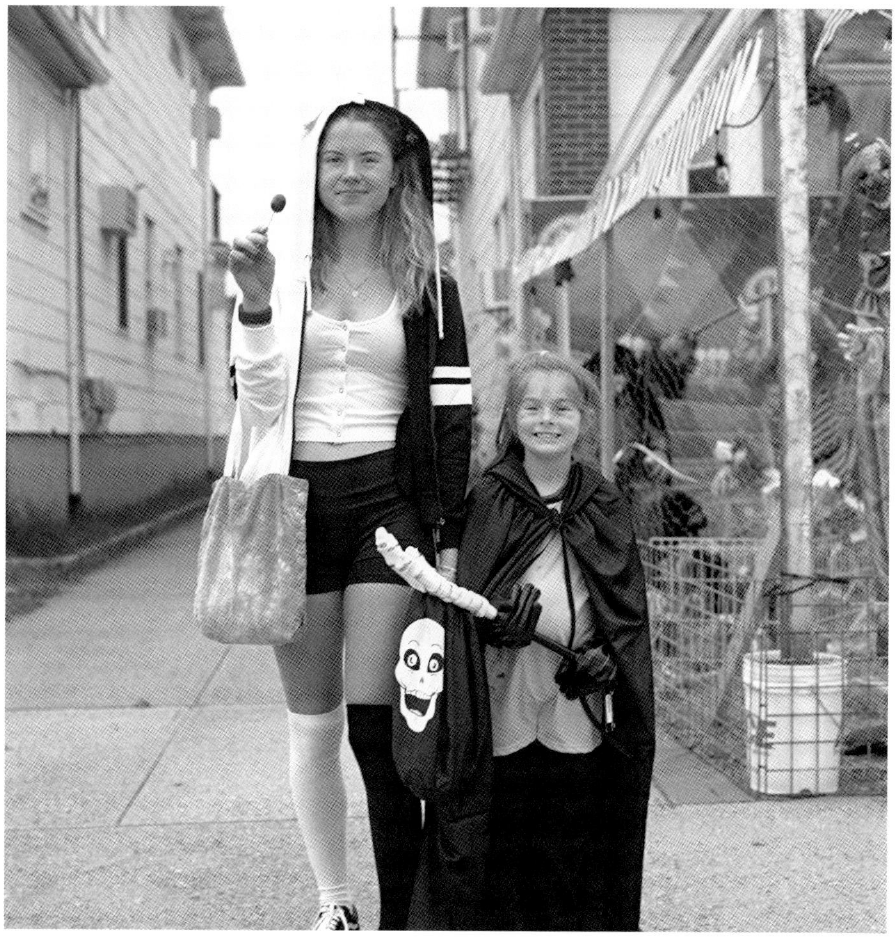

Left: Two girls, one lollipop, 2023, Queens.

Opposite: Boys with $ bag, 2014, Queens.

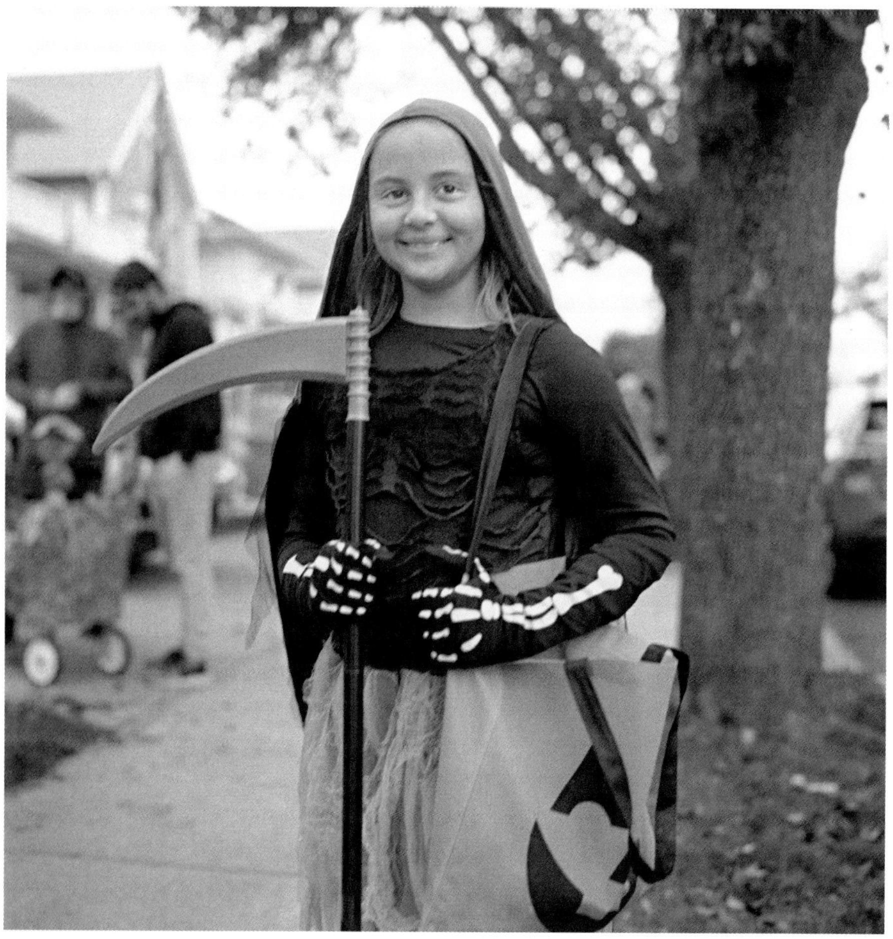

Girl with scythe, 2023, Queens.

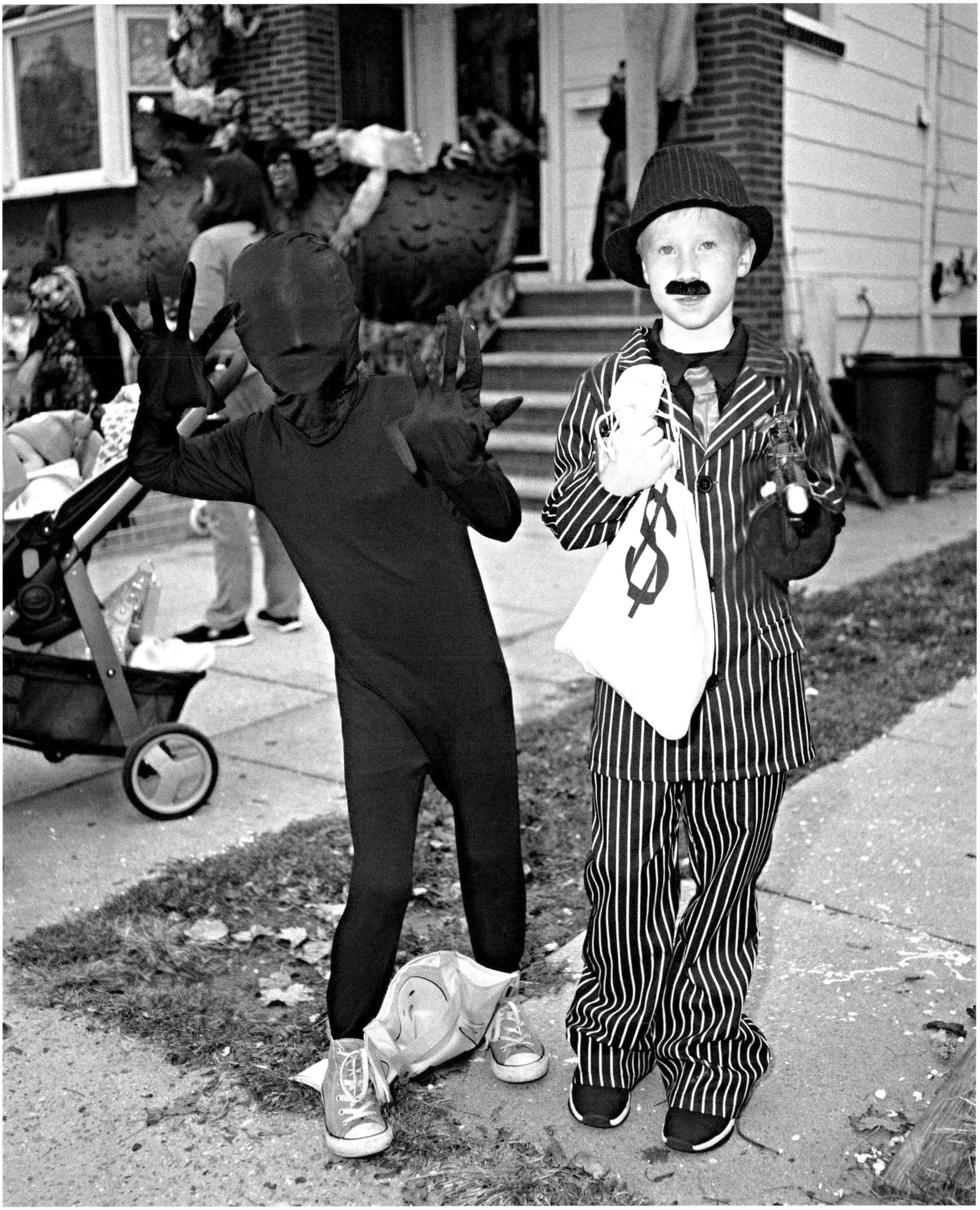

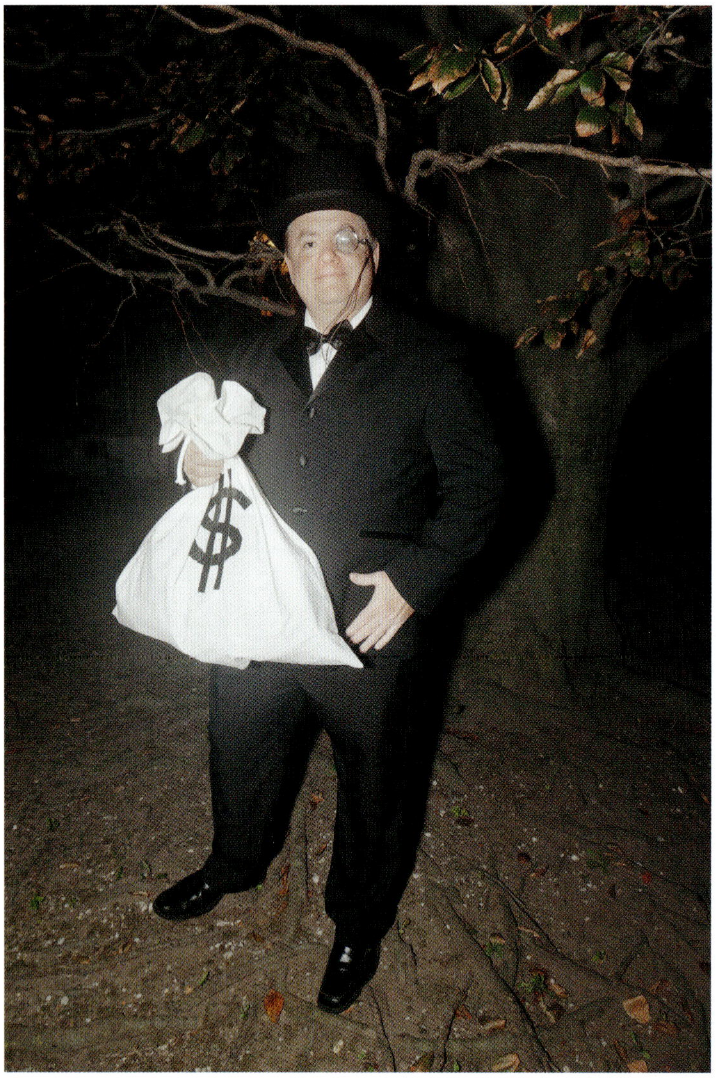

Monopoly man at Marie's party, 2017, Queens.

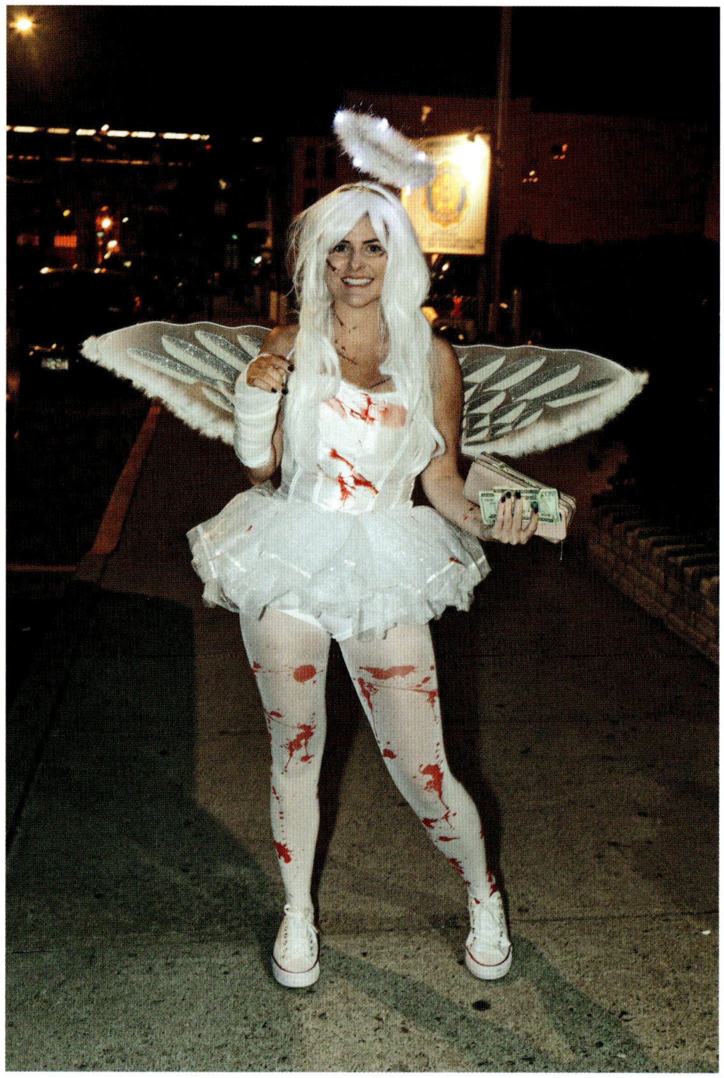

Above: Bloody angel at Bingo party, 2019, Queens.

Opposite: Two girls, 2008, Queens.

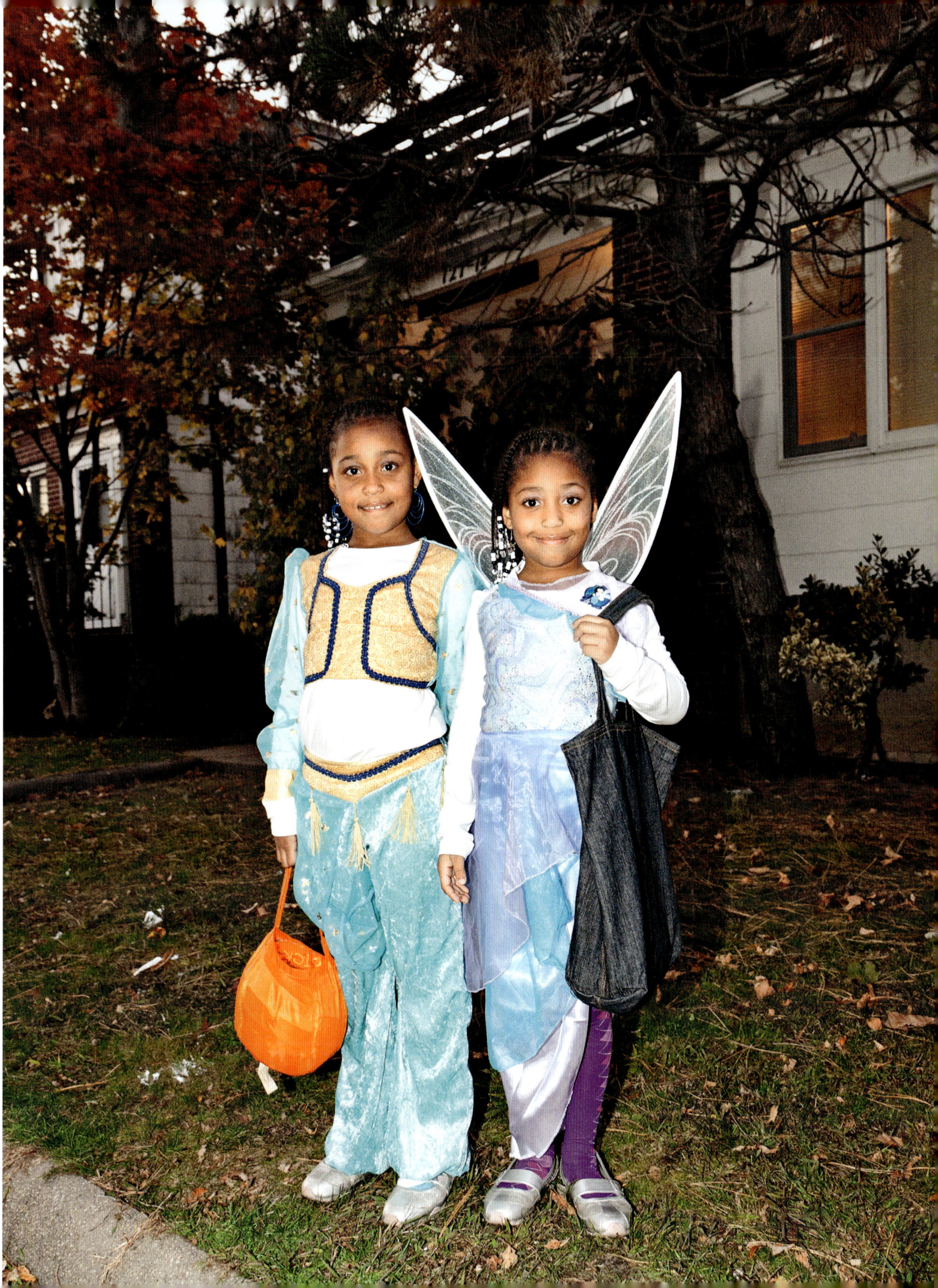

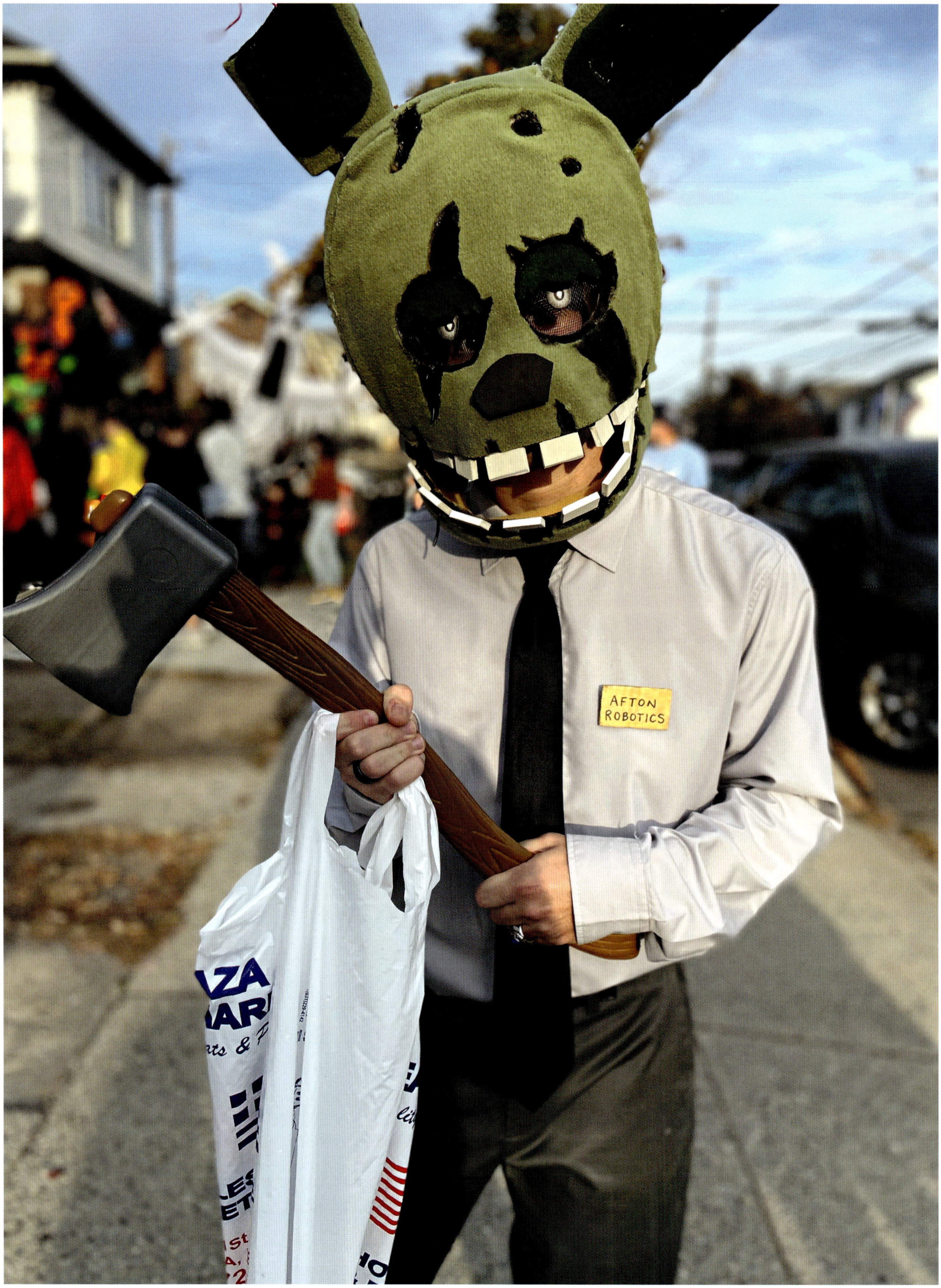
AFTON
ROBOTICS

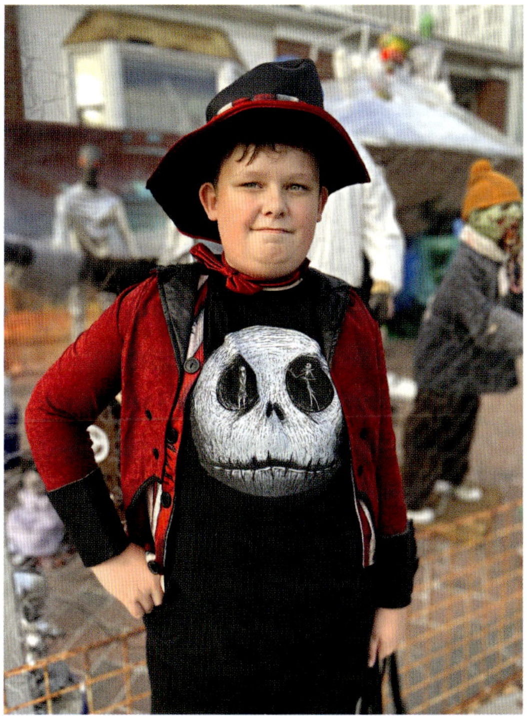

Left: Boy with cool shirt, 2024, Queens.

Opposite: Afton Robotics, 2024, Queens.

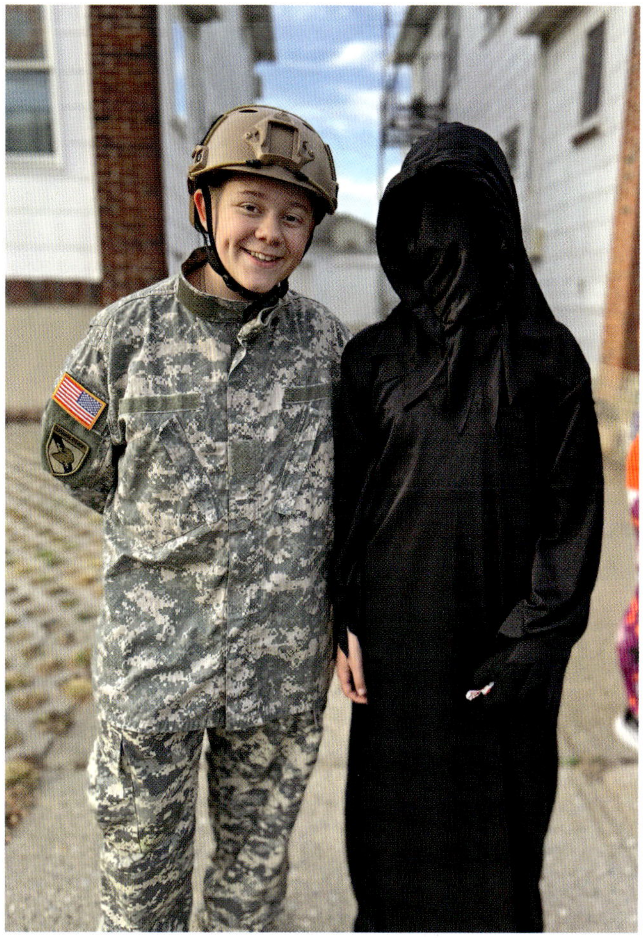

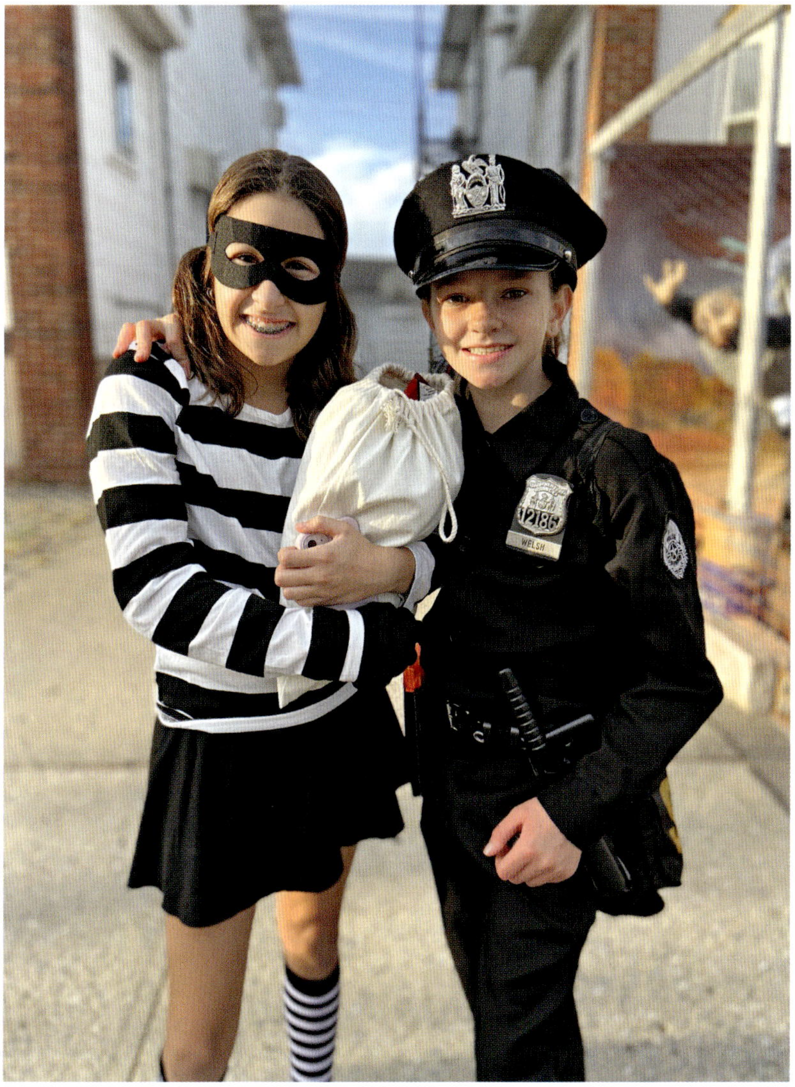

Above: Soldier and grim reaper, 2024, Queens.

Left: Cop and robber, 2024, Queens.

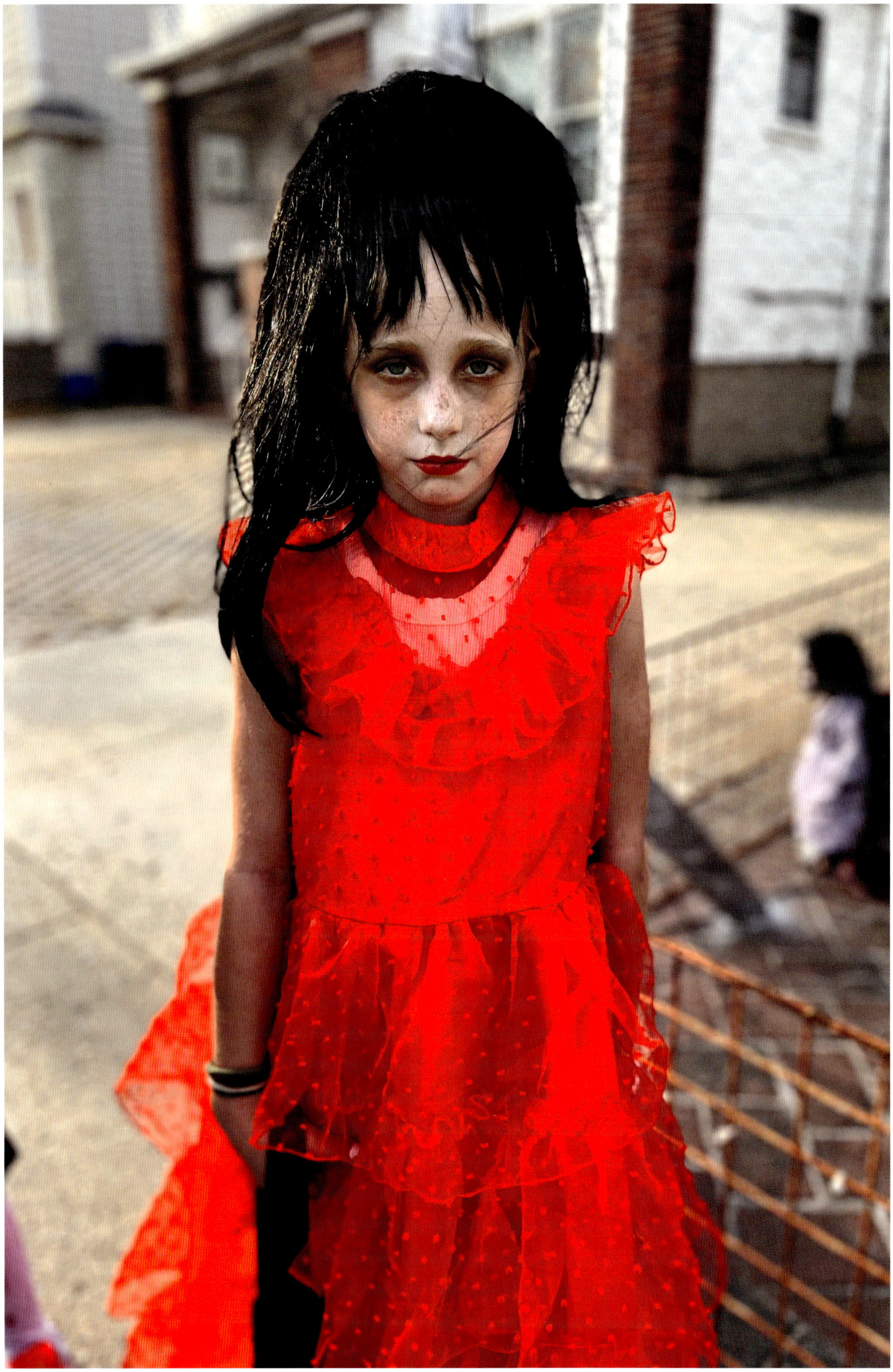

Lydia Deetz,
2024, Queens.

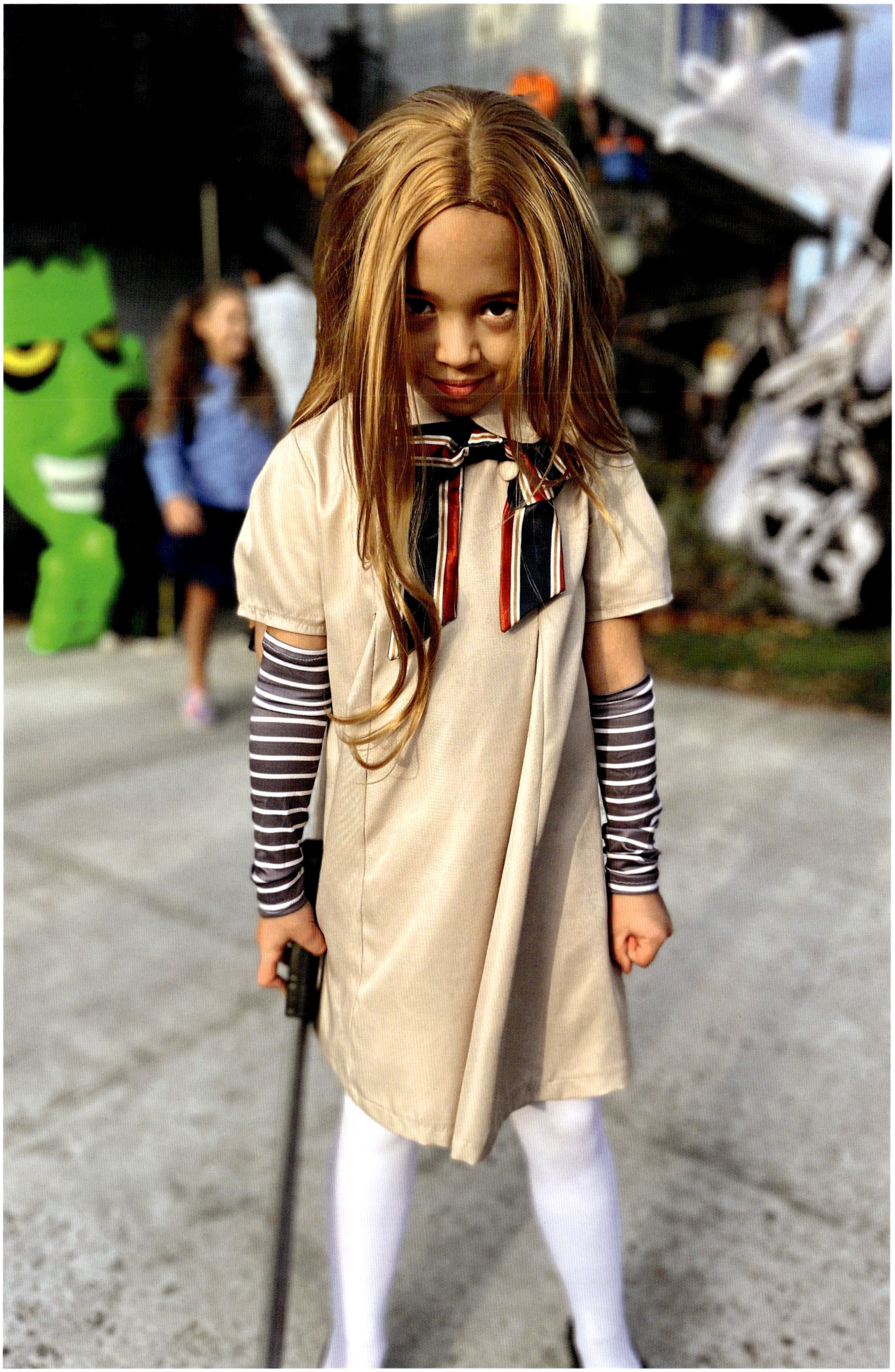

M3GAN, 2024,
Queens.

In 2008, I photographed at a strange office party in Manhattan.

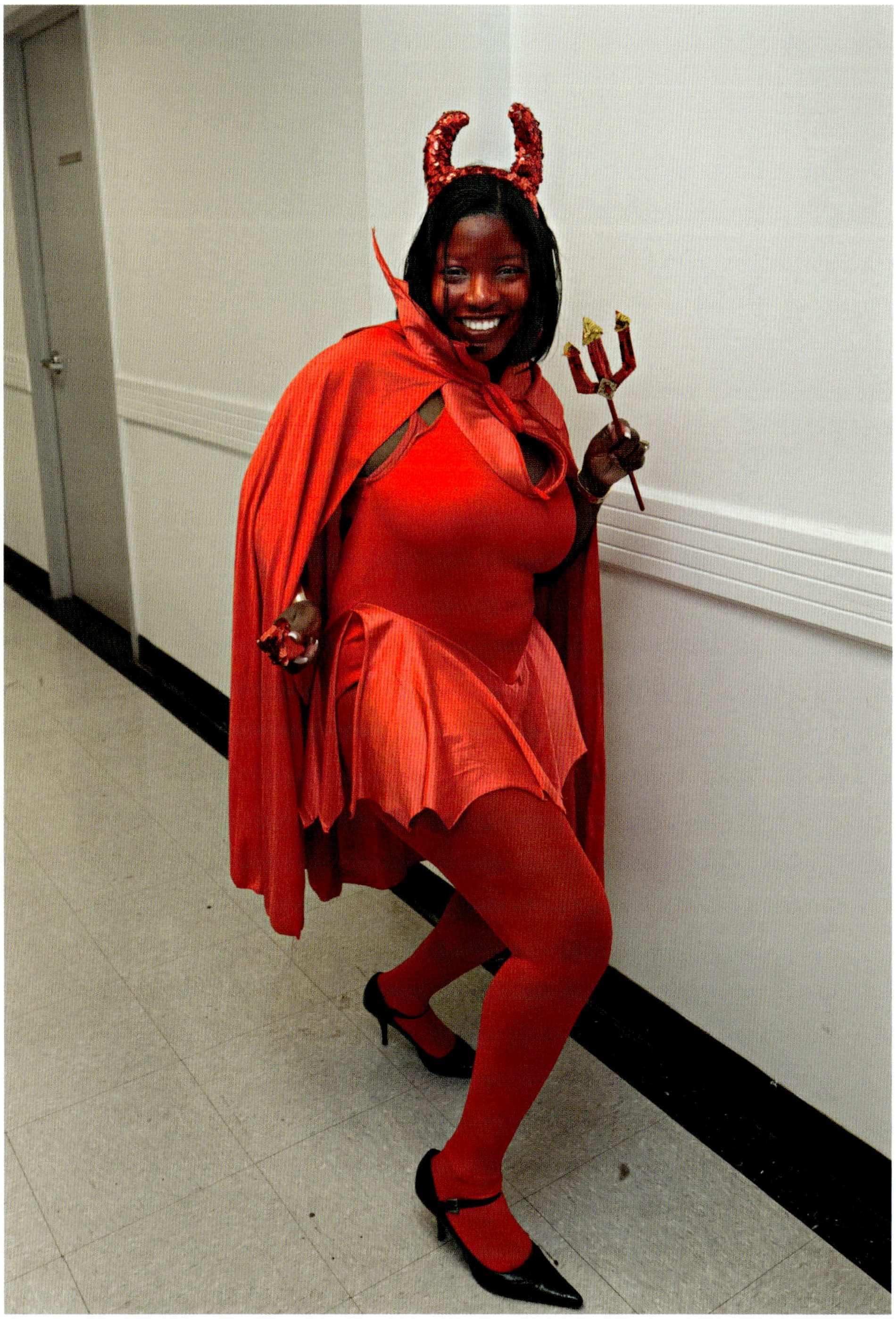

Red devil, 2008, Manhattan.

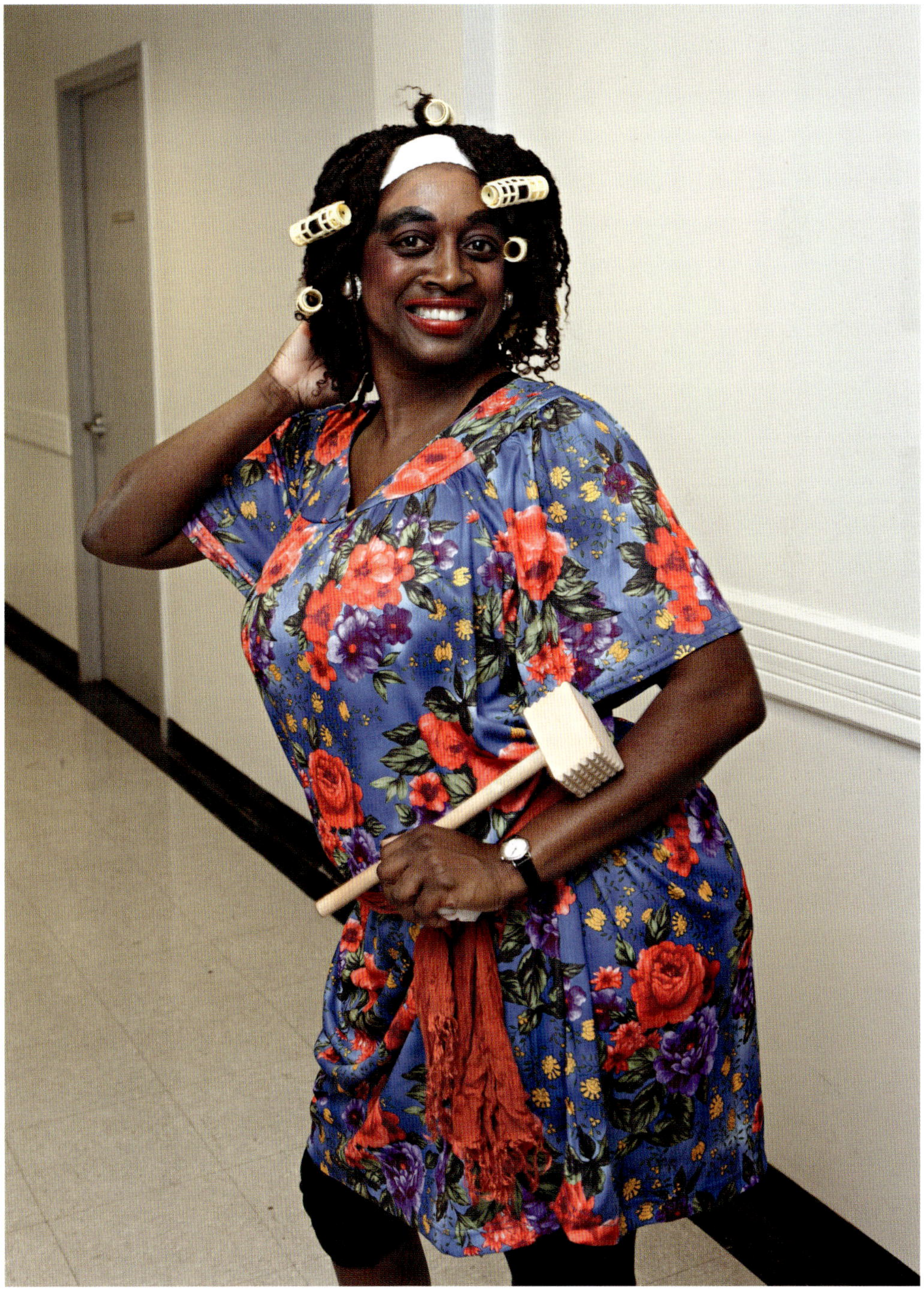

Housewife, 2008,
Manhattan.

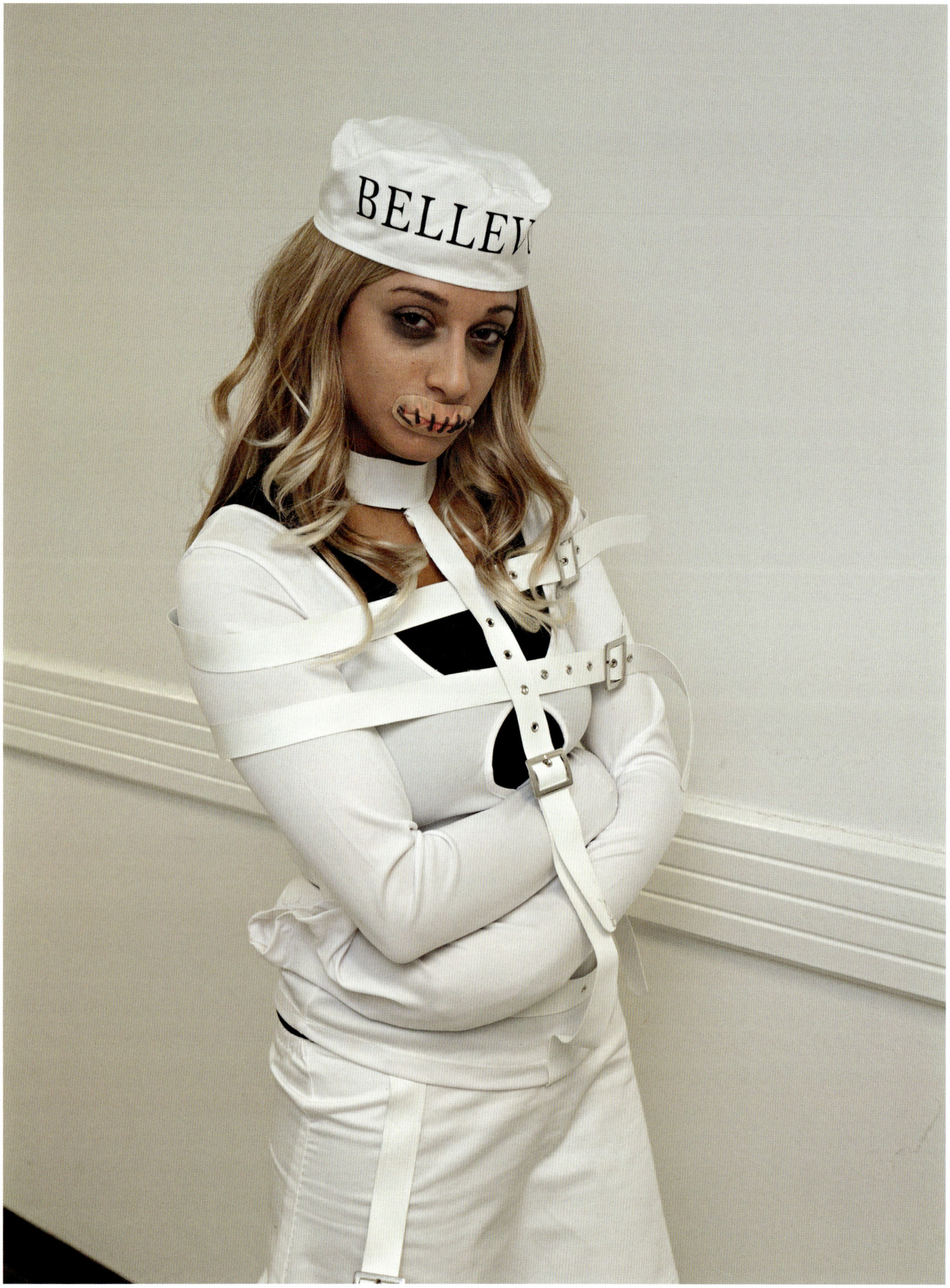

Mental patient, 2008, Manhattan.

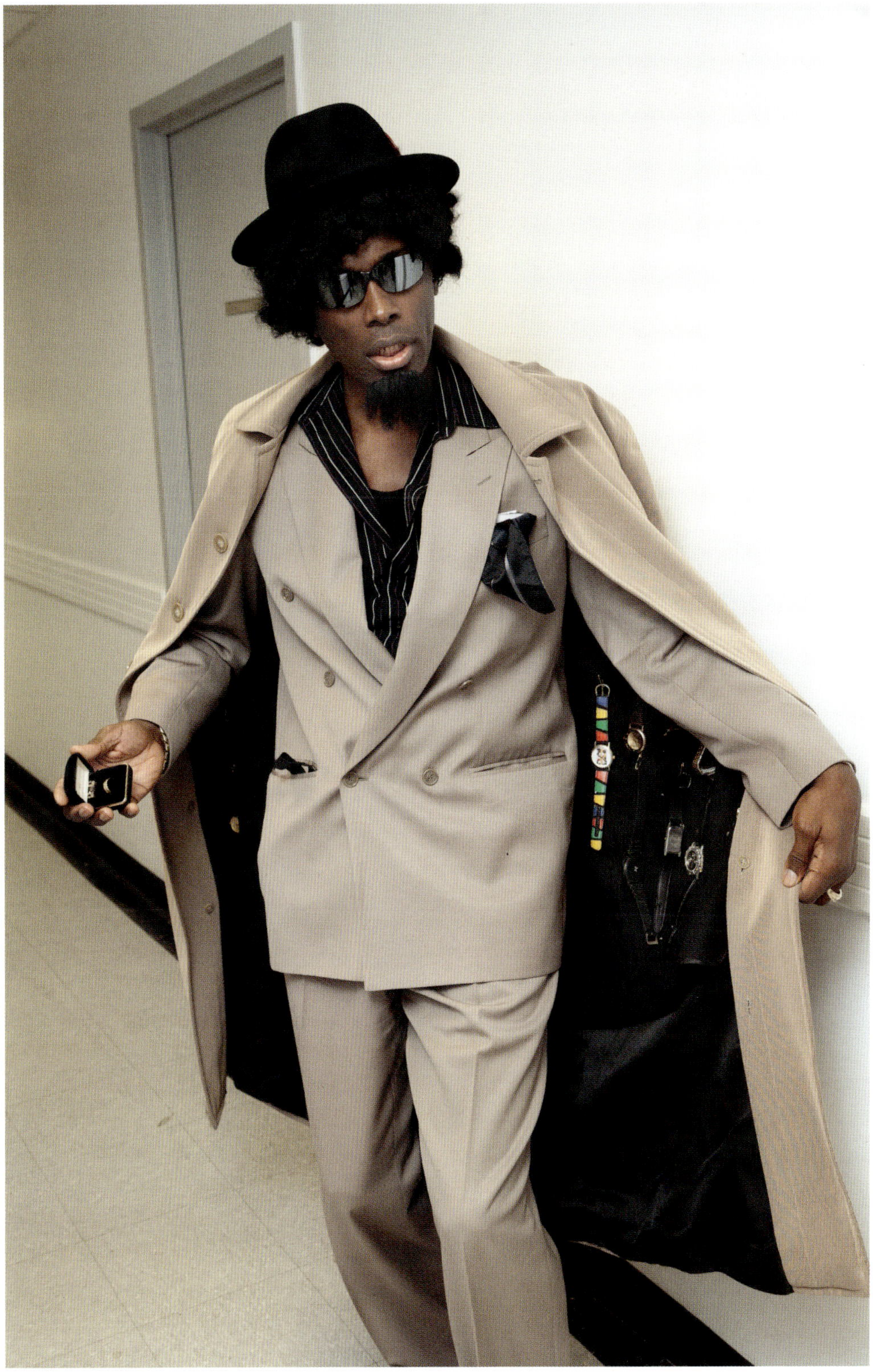

Hustler, 2008, Manhattan.

Vampire family,
2011, Brooklyn

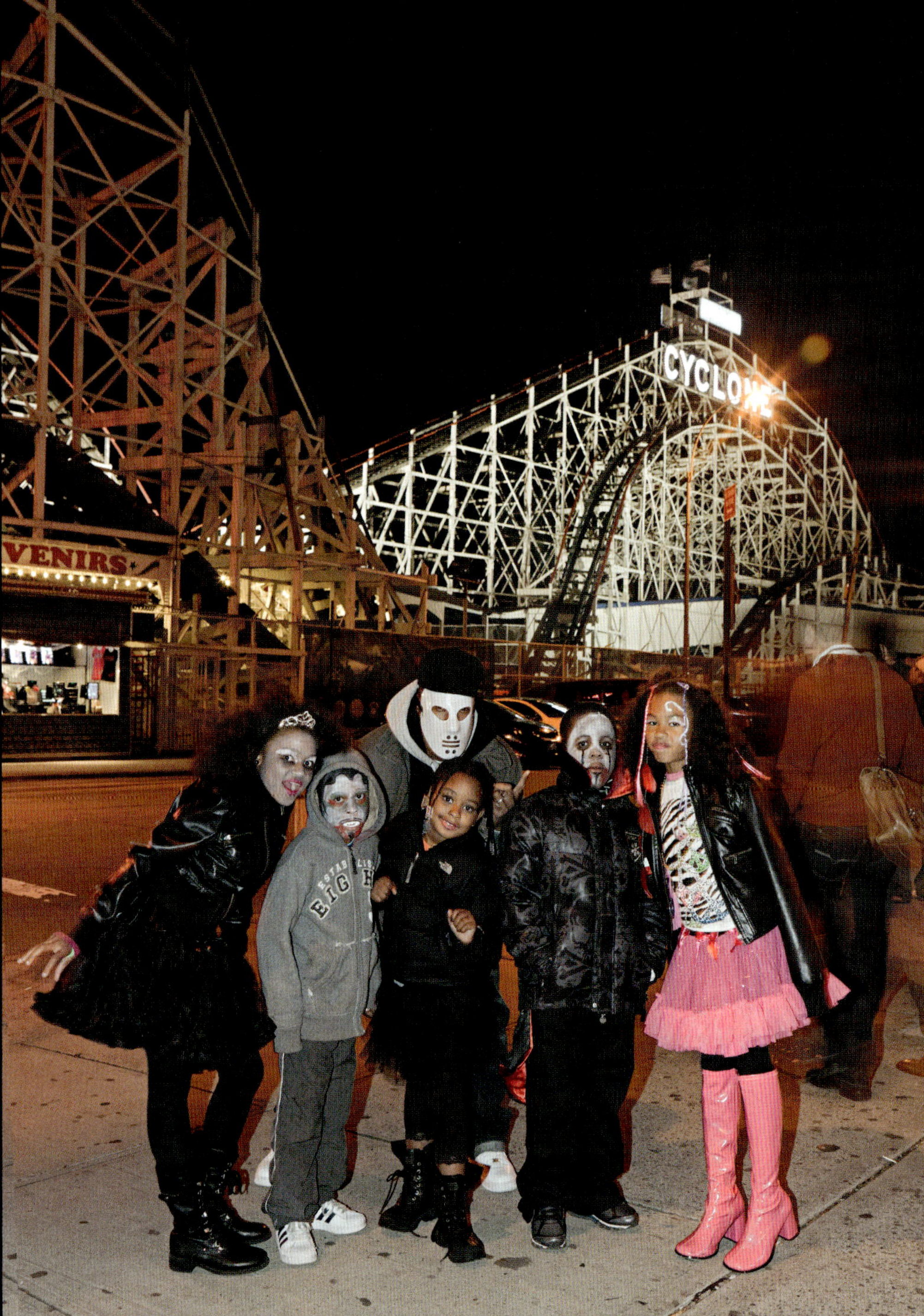

In 2011, I photographed at Luna Park in Coney Island, Brooklyn,

Father and son,
2011, Brooklyn.

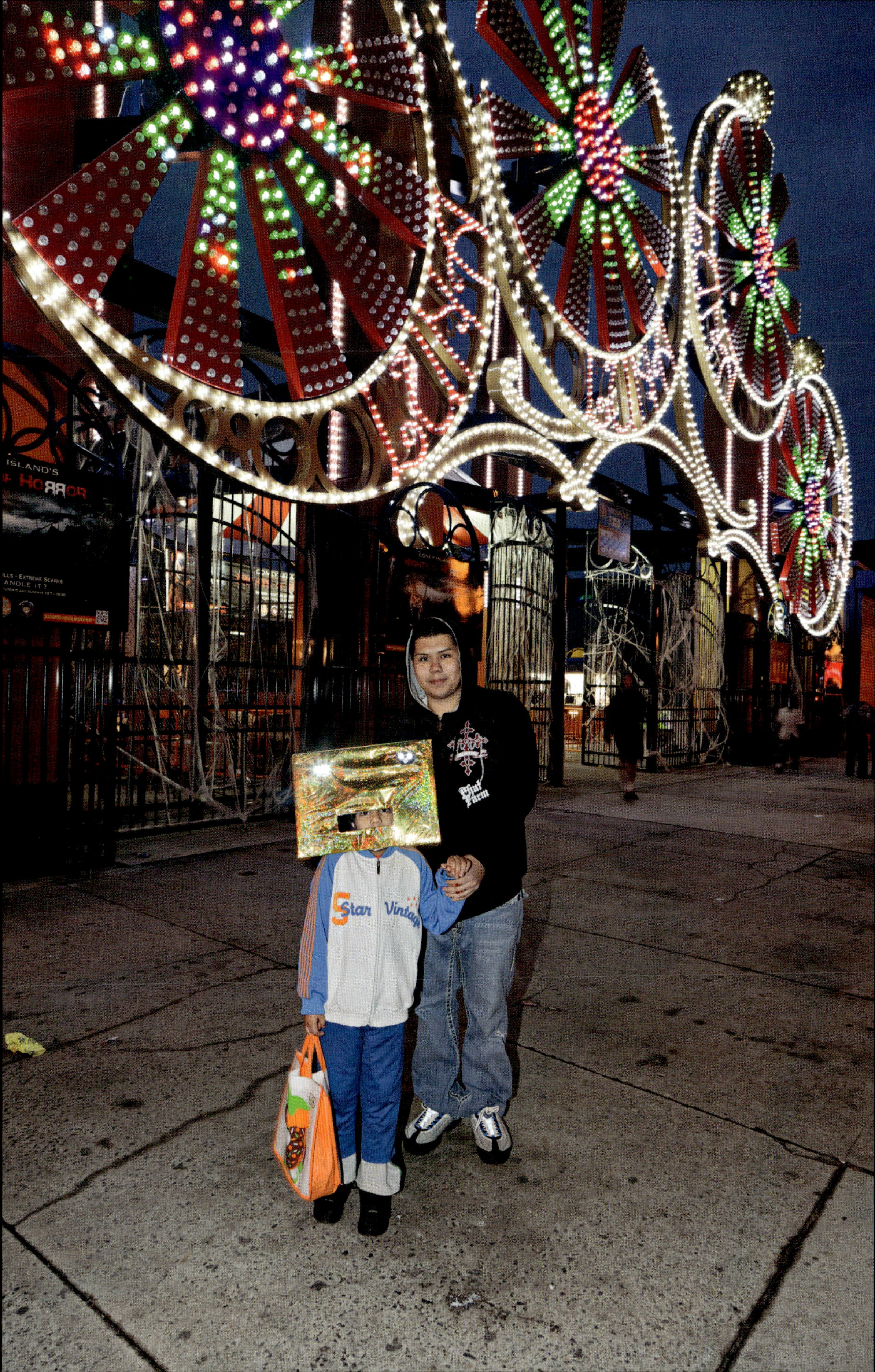

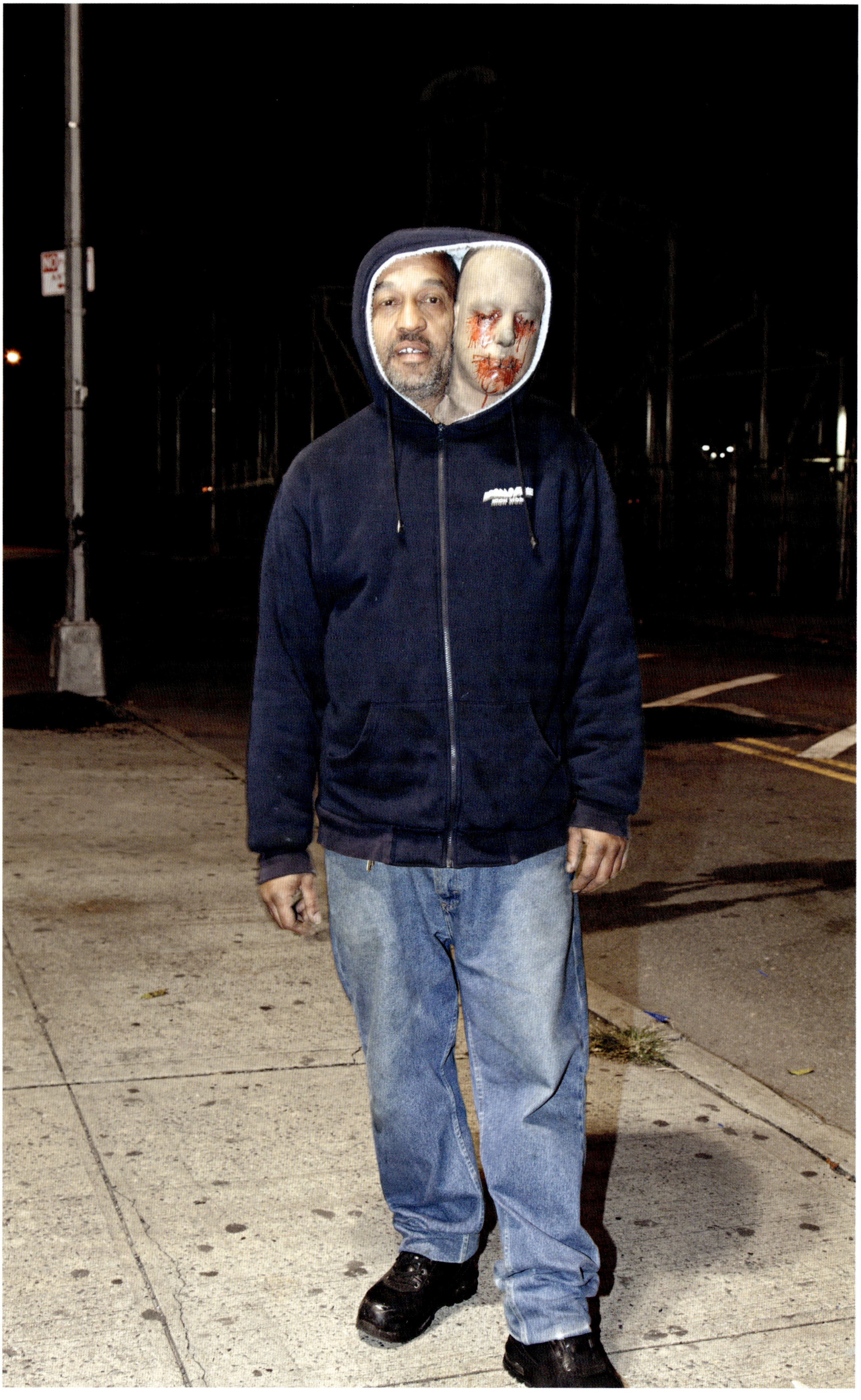

Two-headed man,
2011, Brooklyn.

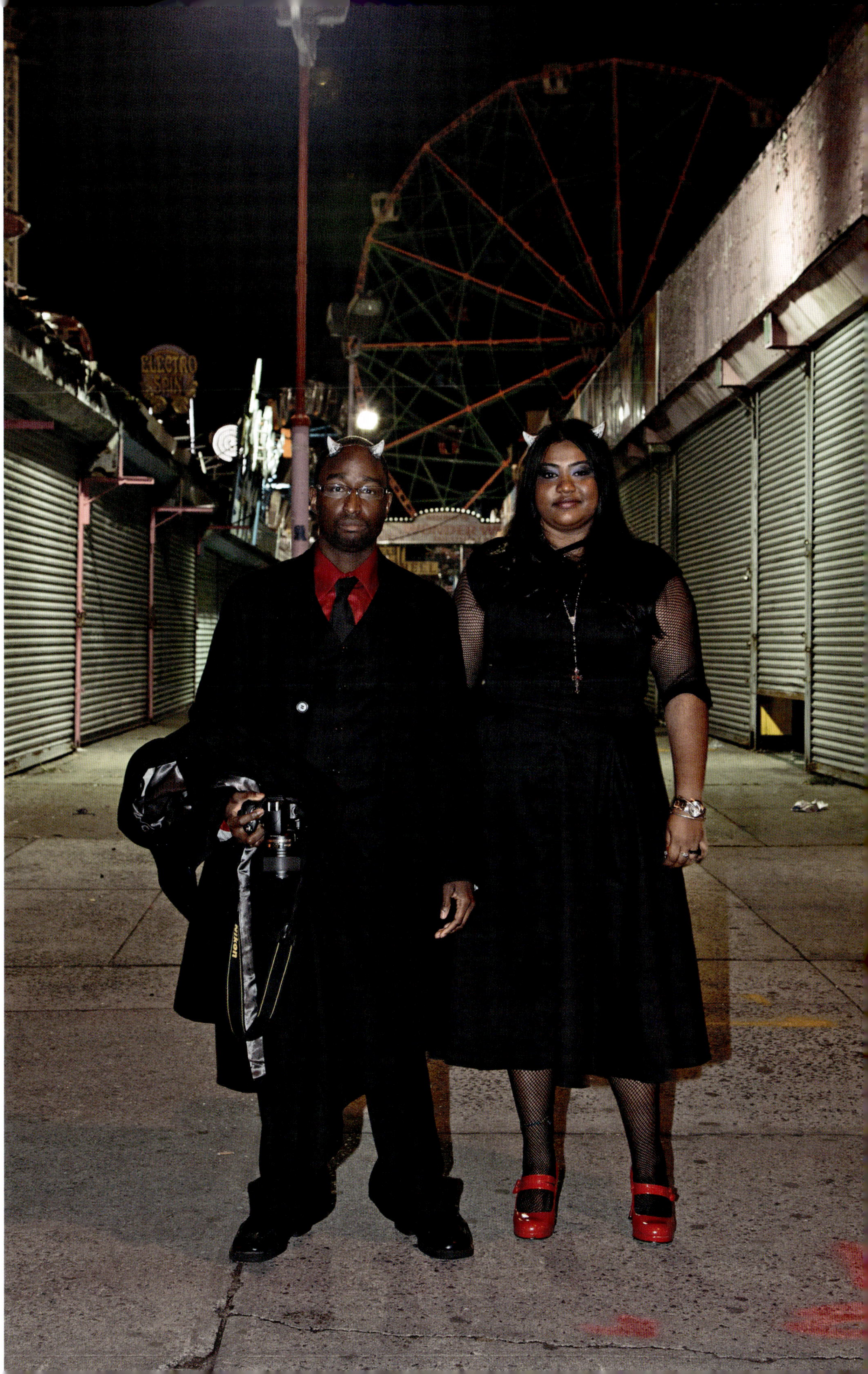

Cool couple,
2011, Brooklyn.

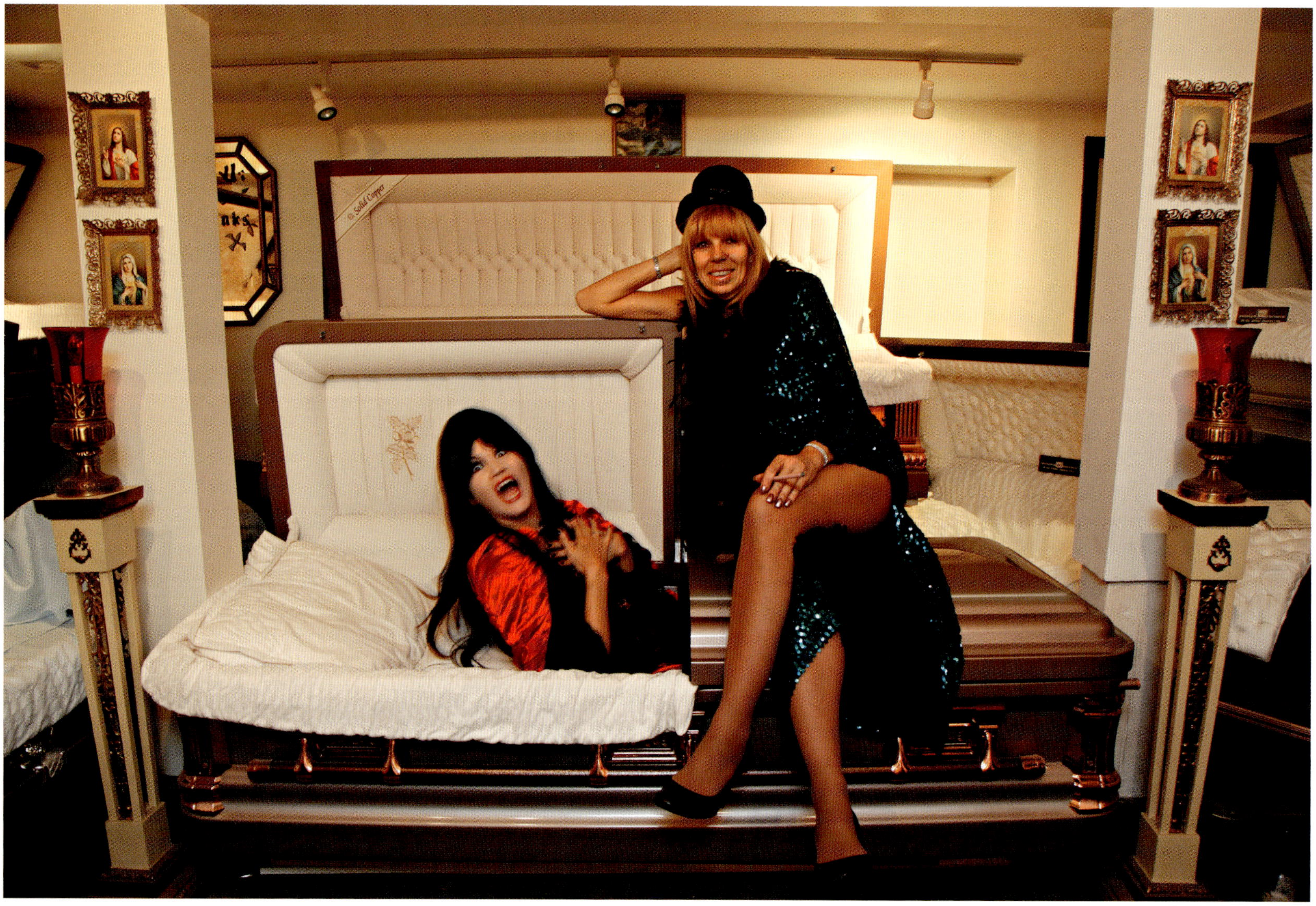

Doris and a vampire,
2013, Brooklyn.

In 2013 and 2014, I photographed at two interesting Brooklyn locations. The first was Jurek Funeral Home, whose owner hosted an annual Halloween party.

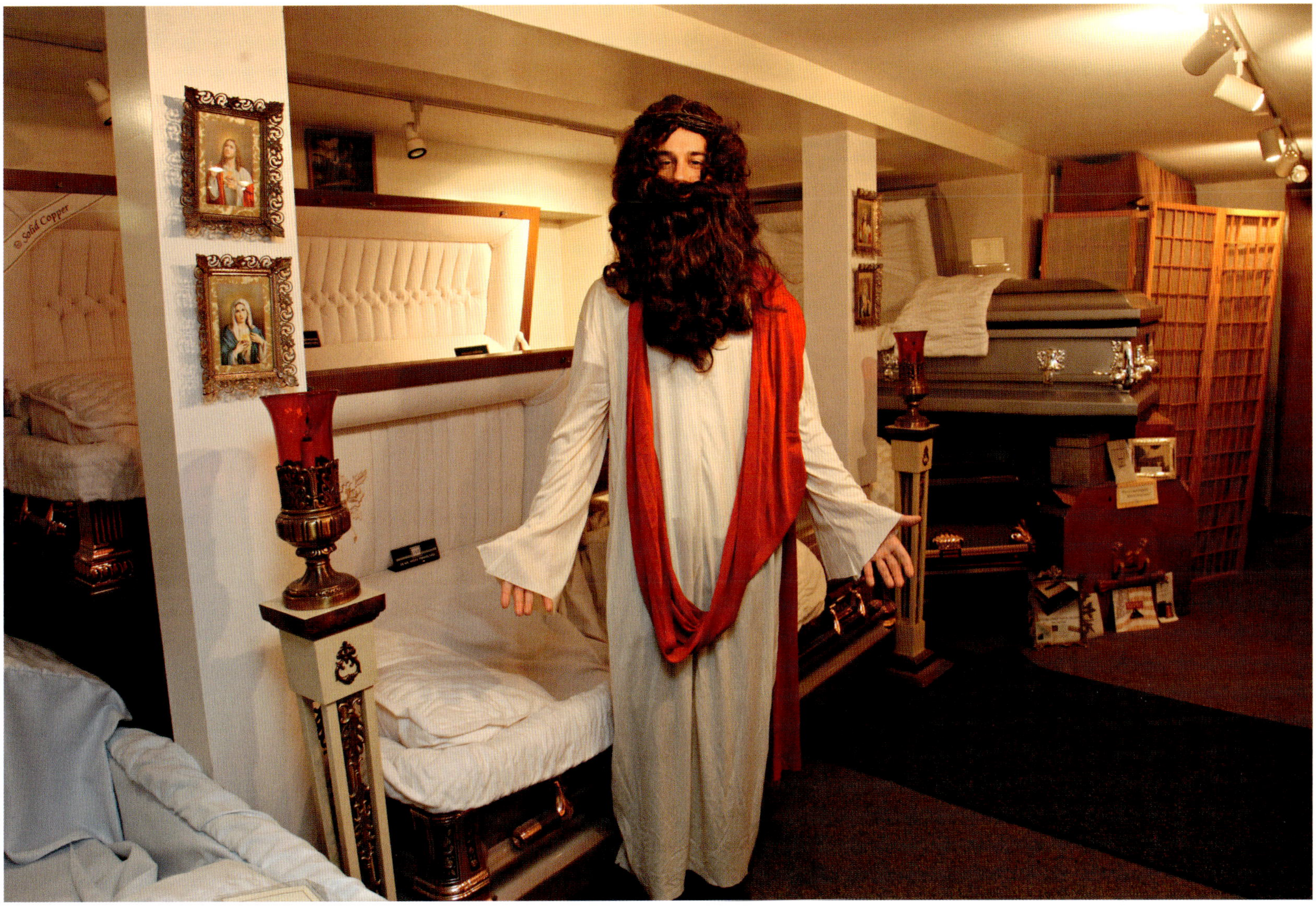

JC and coffins,
2013, Brooklyn.

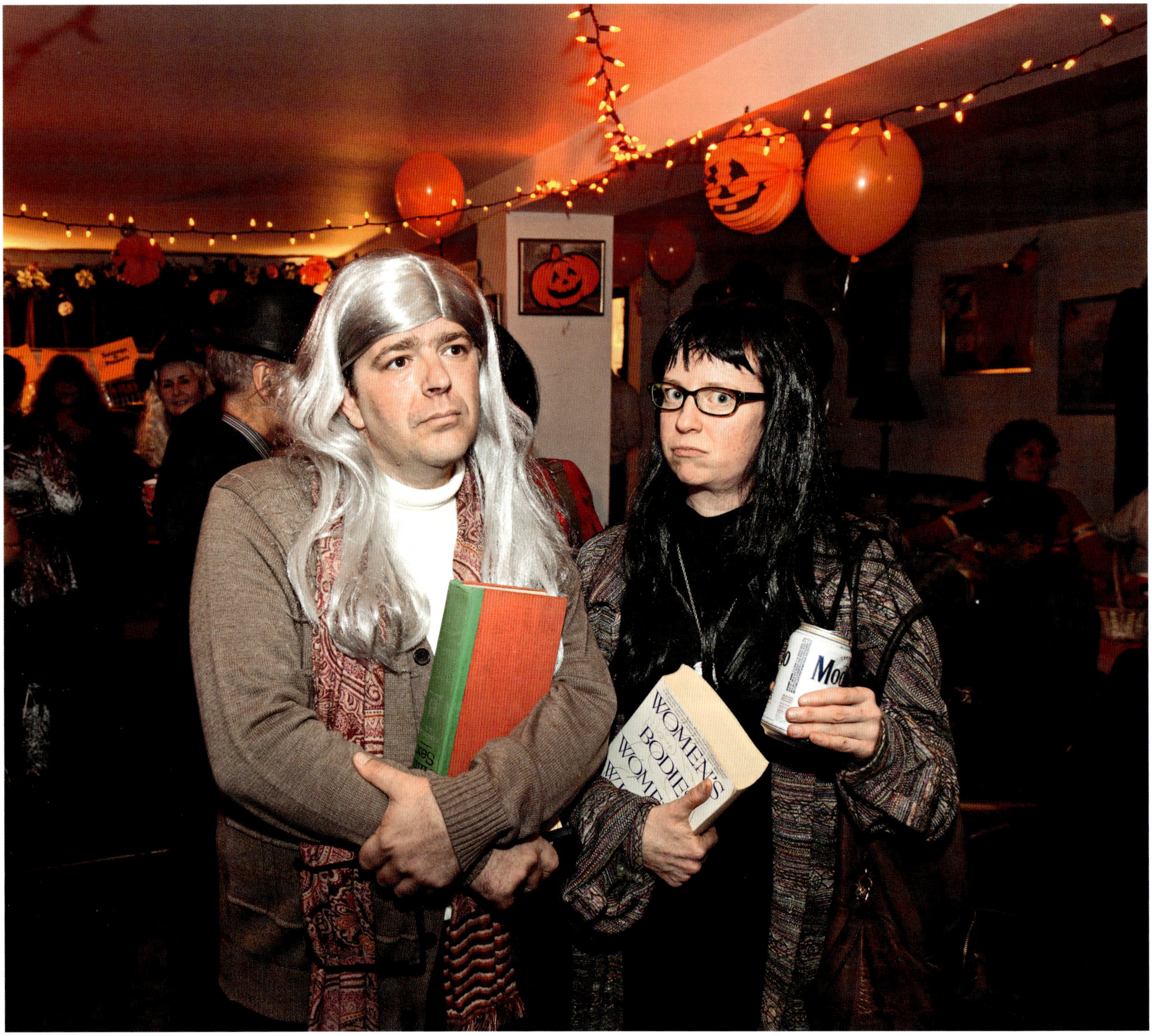

Portlandia couple,
2013, Brooklyn.

Weeping Angel and Dalek, 2013, Brooklyn.

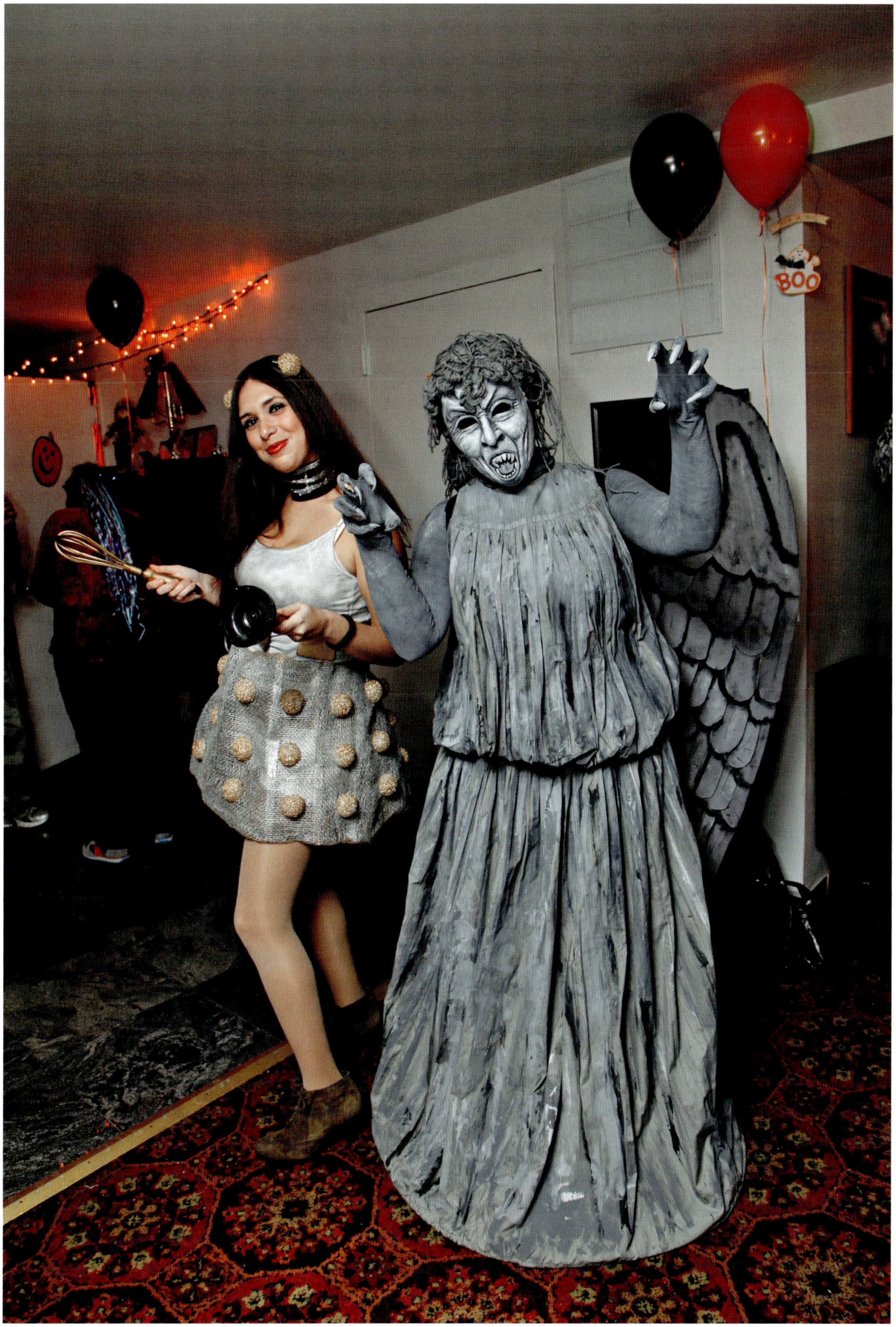

The second was the Leatherneck Tattoo Parlor.

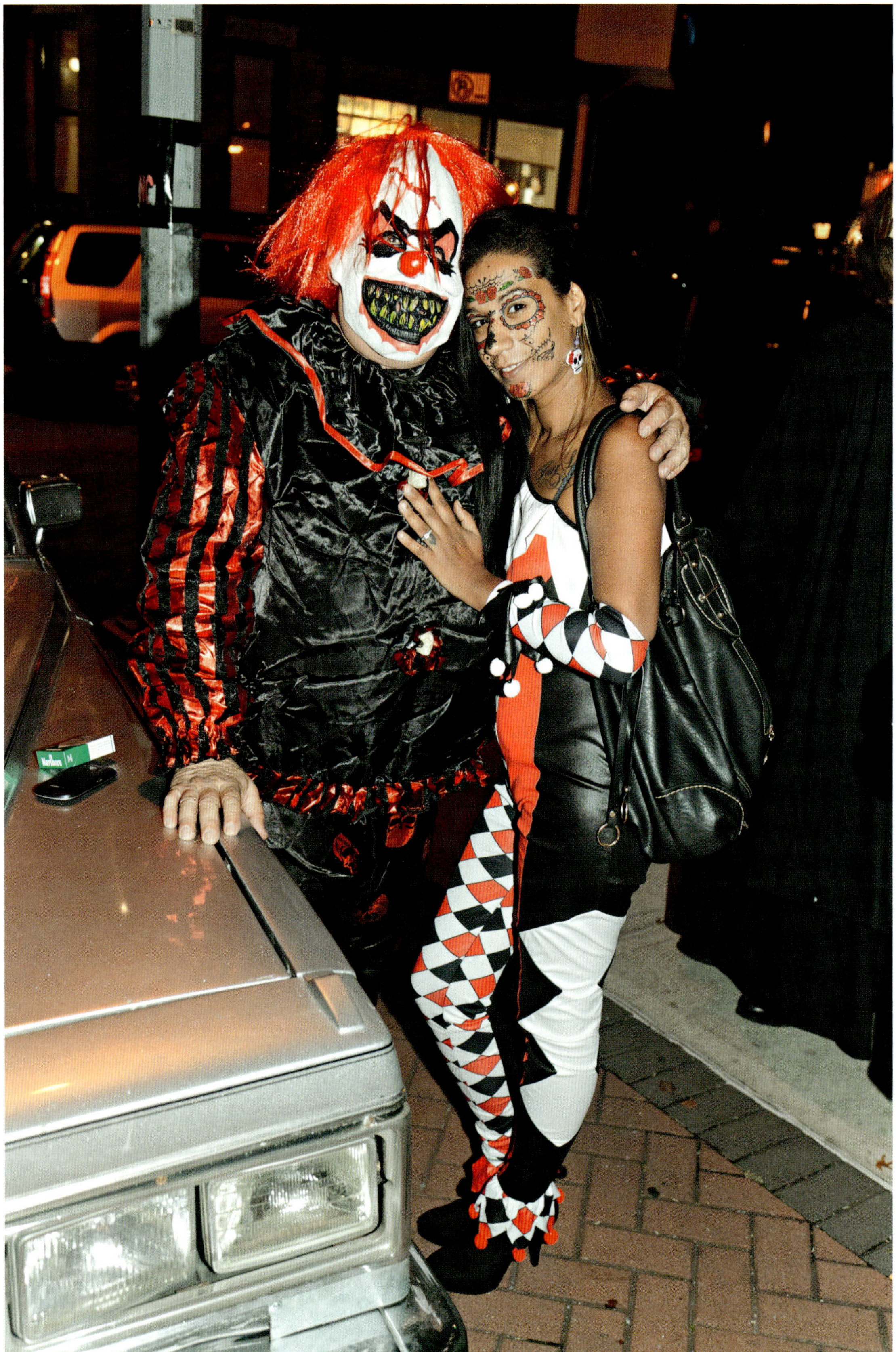

Clown and woman in harlequin outfit, 2014, Brooklyn.

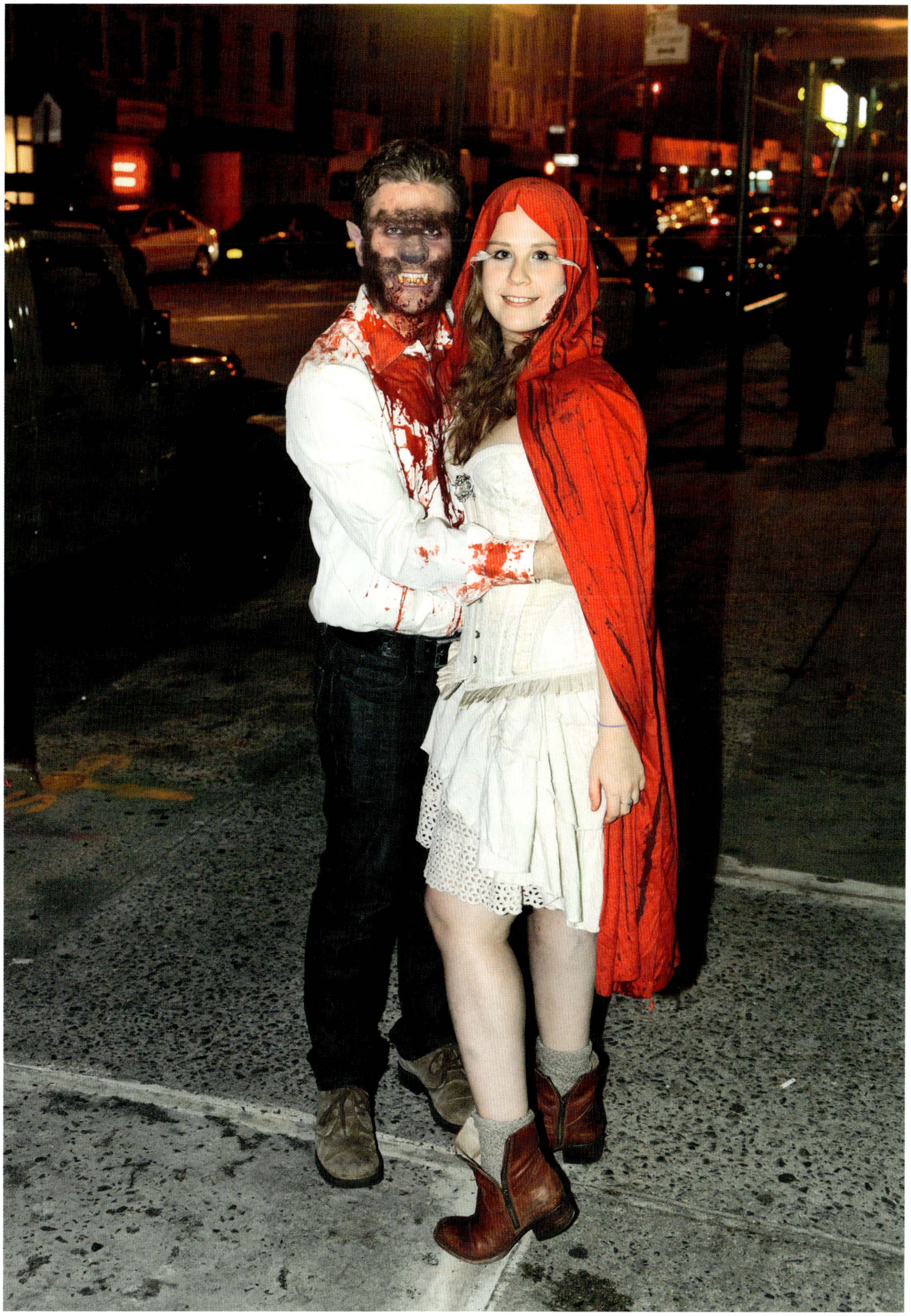

Little Red Riding Hood and the Big Bad Werewolf, 2014, Brooklyn.

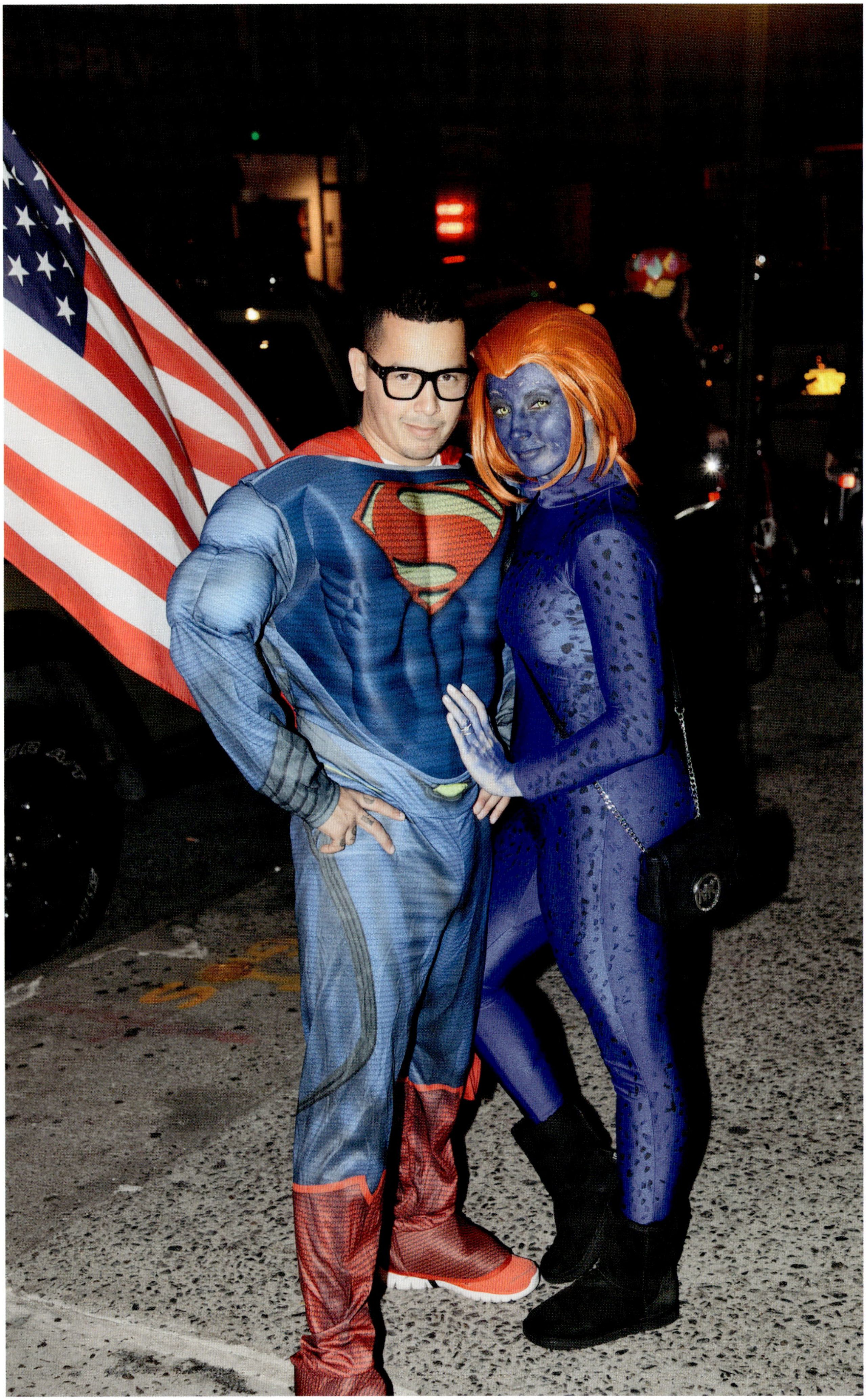

Left: Superman and Mystique, 2014, Brooklyn.

Opposite: Popeye and Olive Oyl, 2014, Brooklyn.

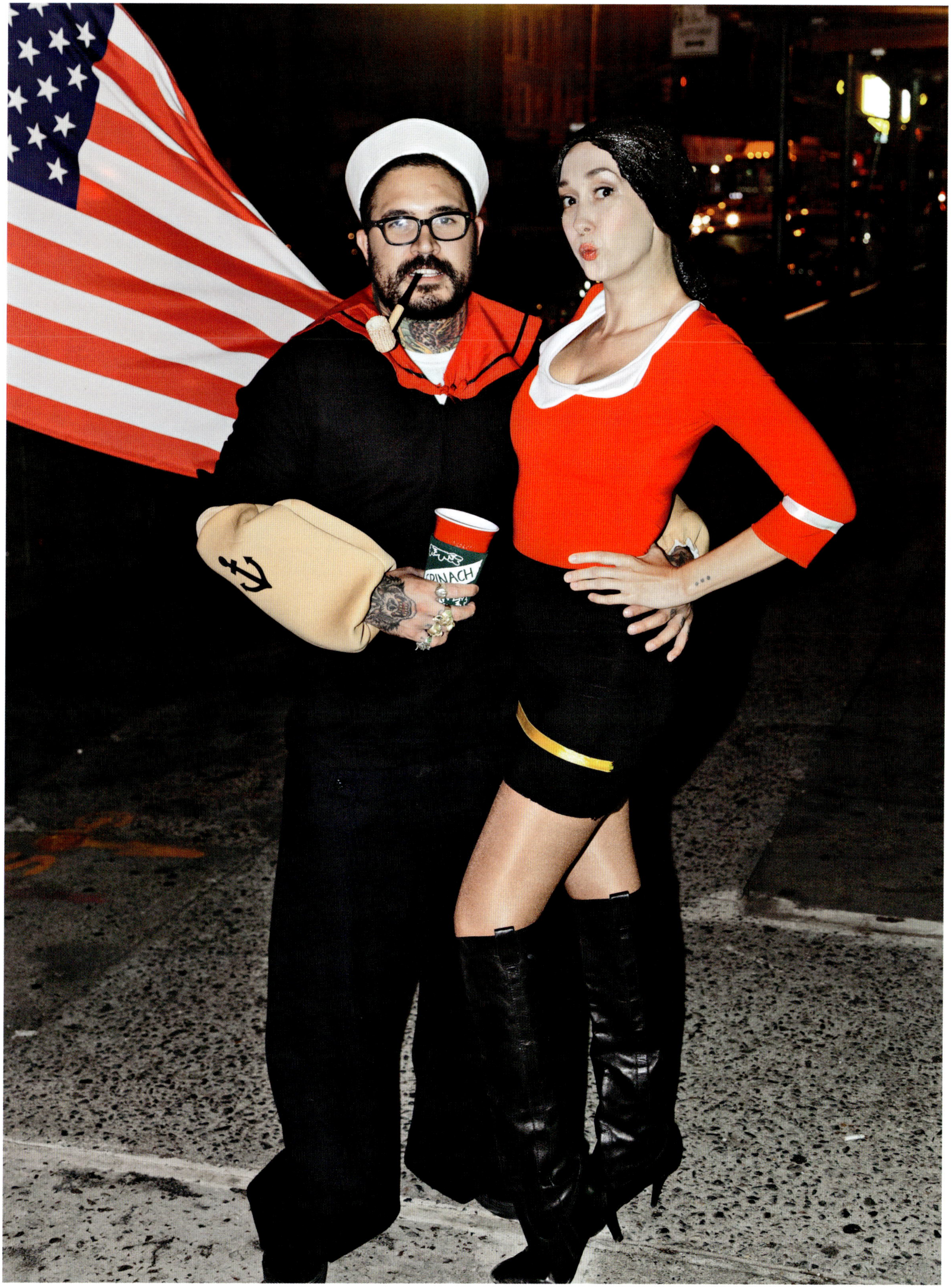

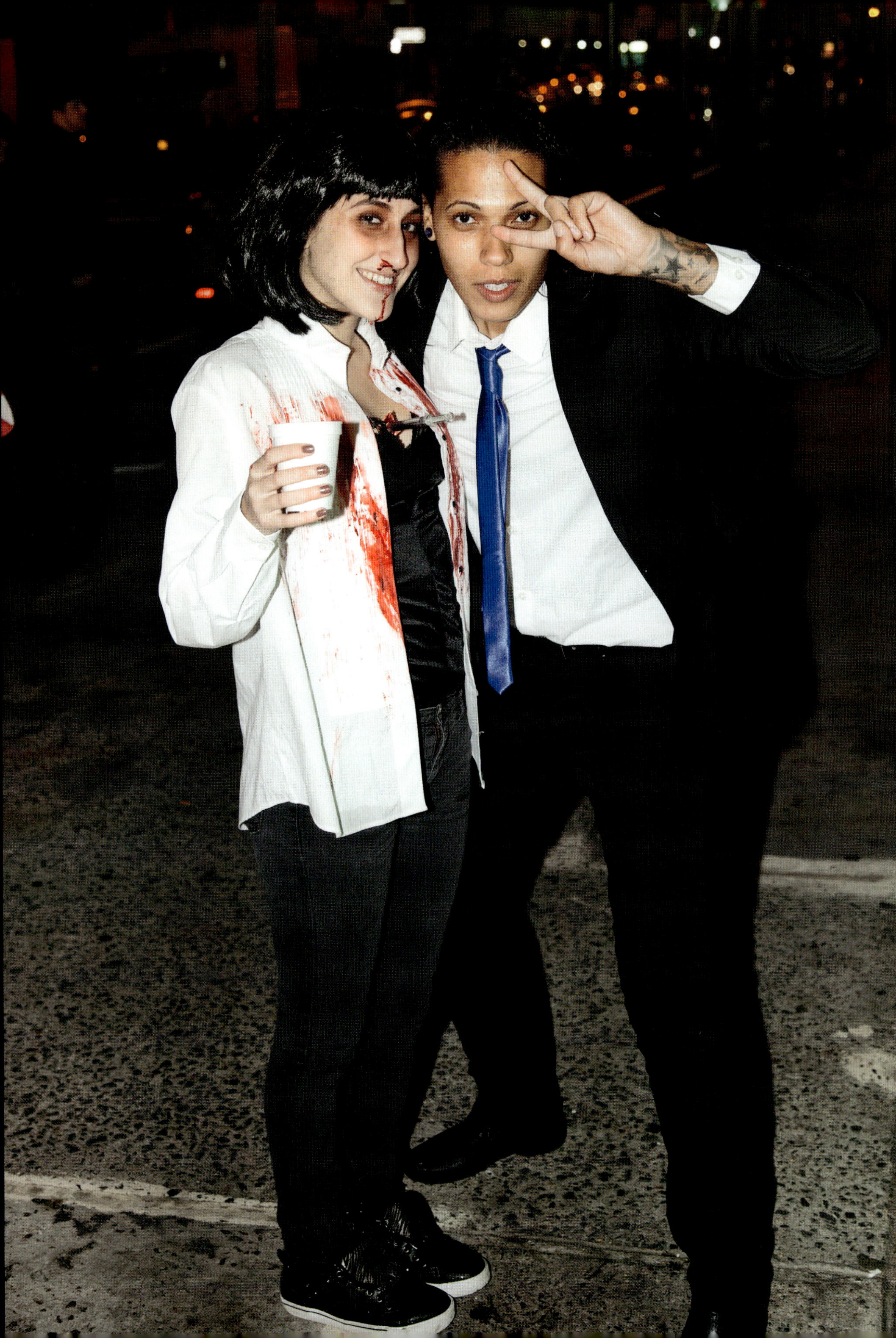

Pulp Fiction characters, 2014, Brooklyn

Forrest Gump characters,
2014, Brooklyn.

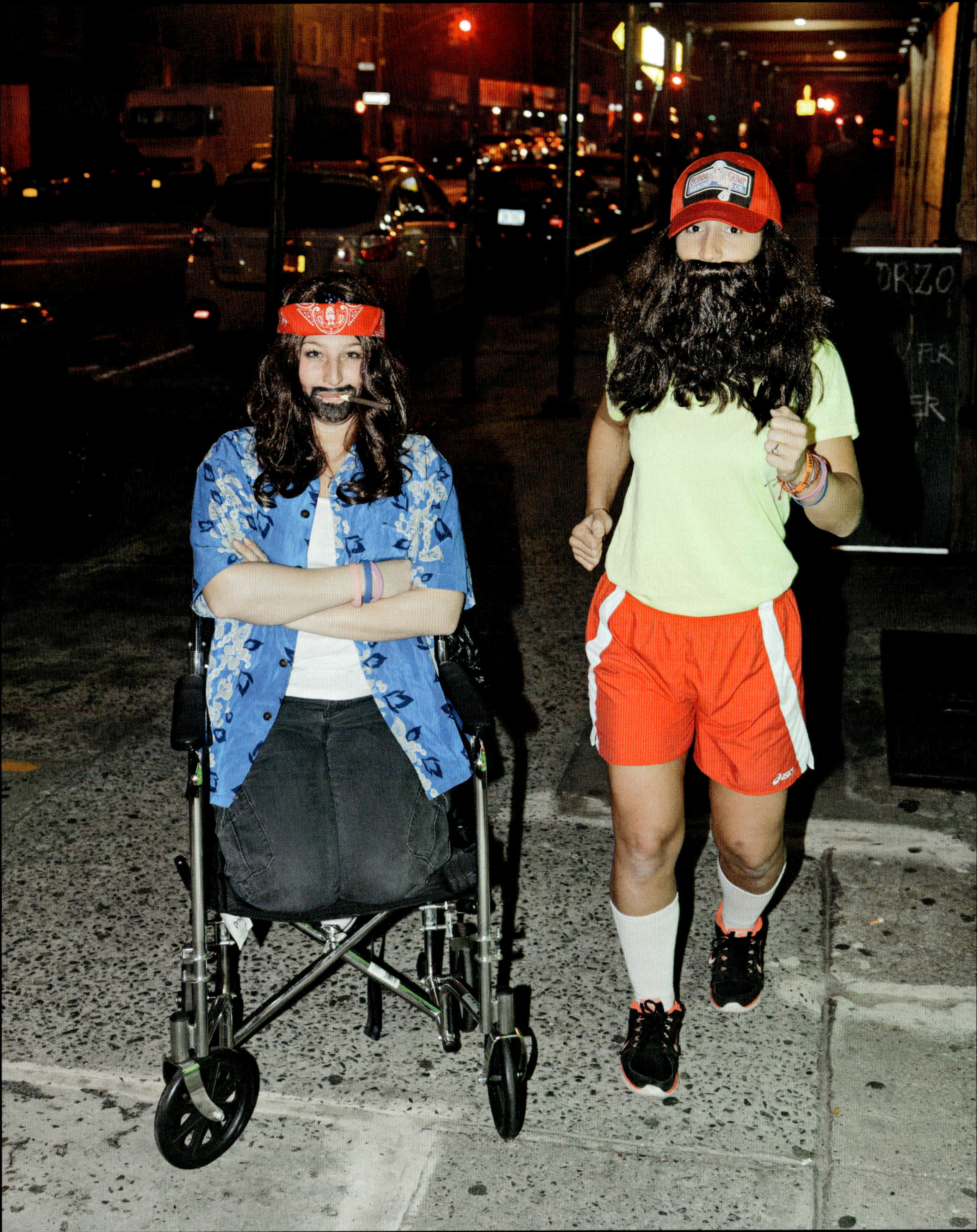

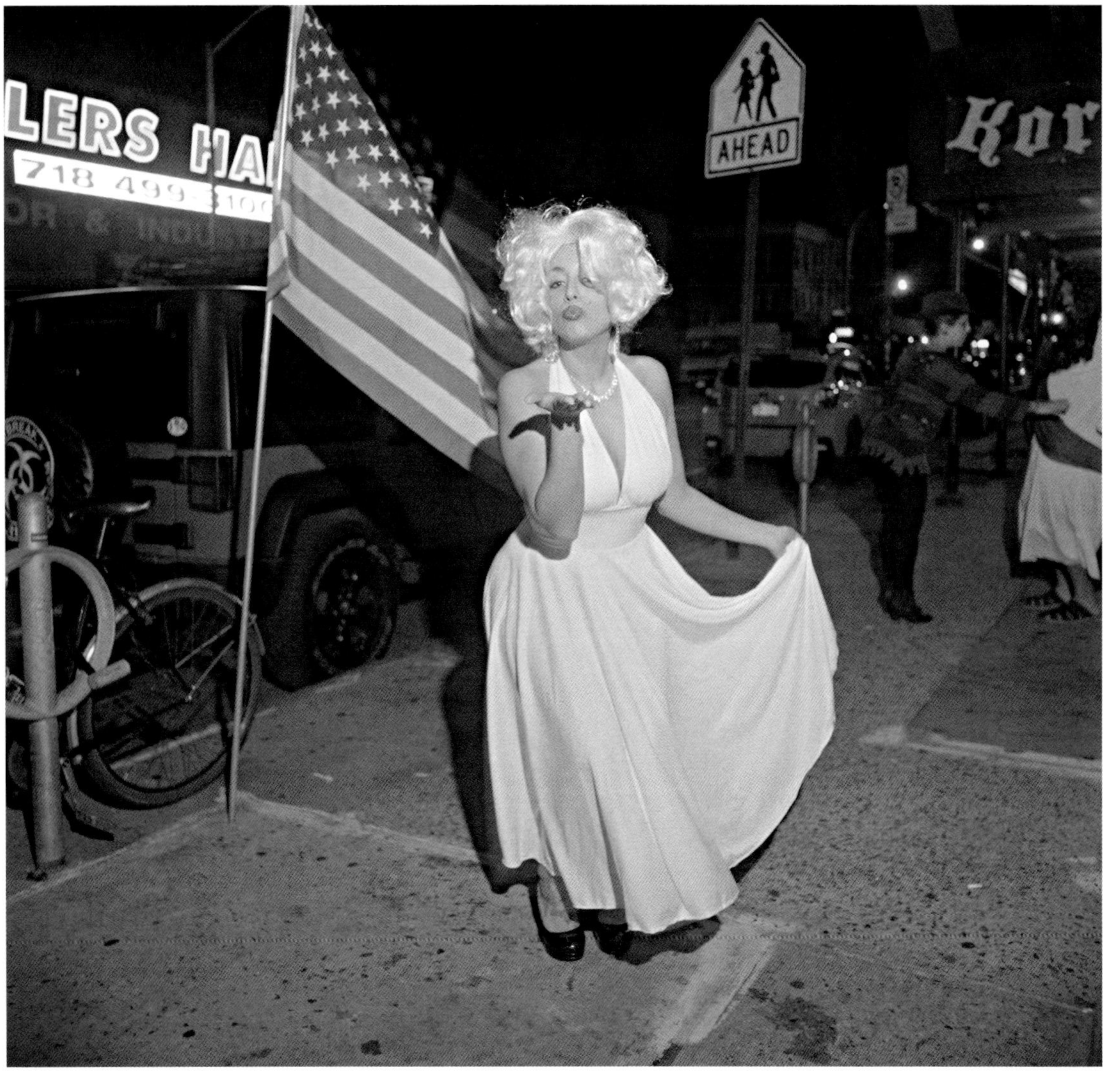

Marilyn Monroe, 2014, Brooklyn.

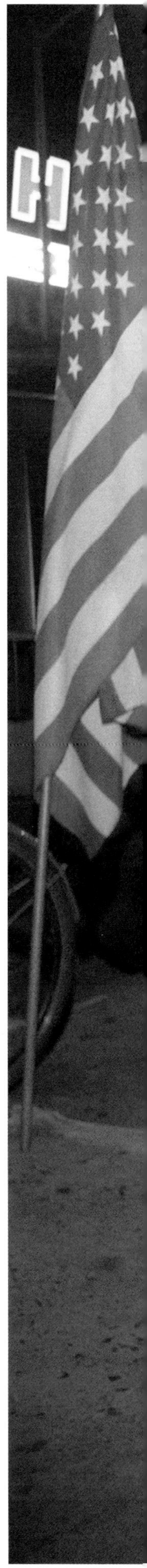

JC with hammer and nail, 2014, Brooklyn.

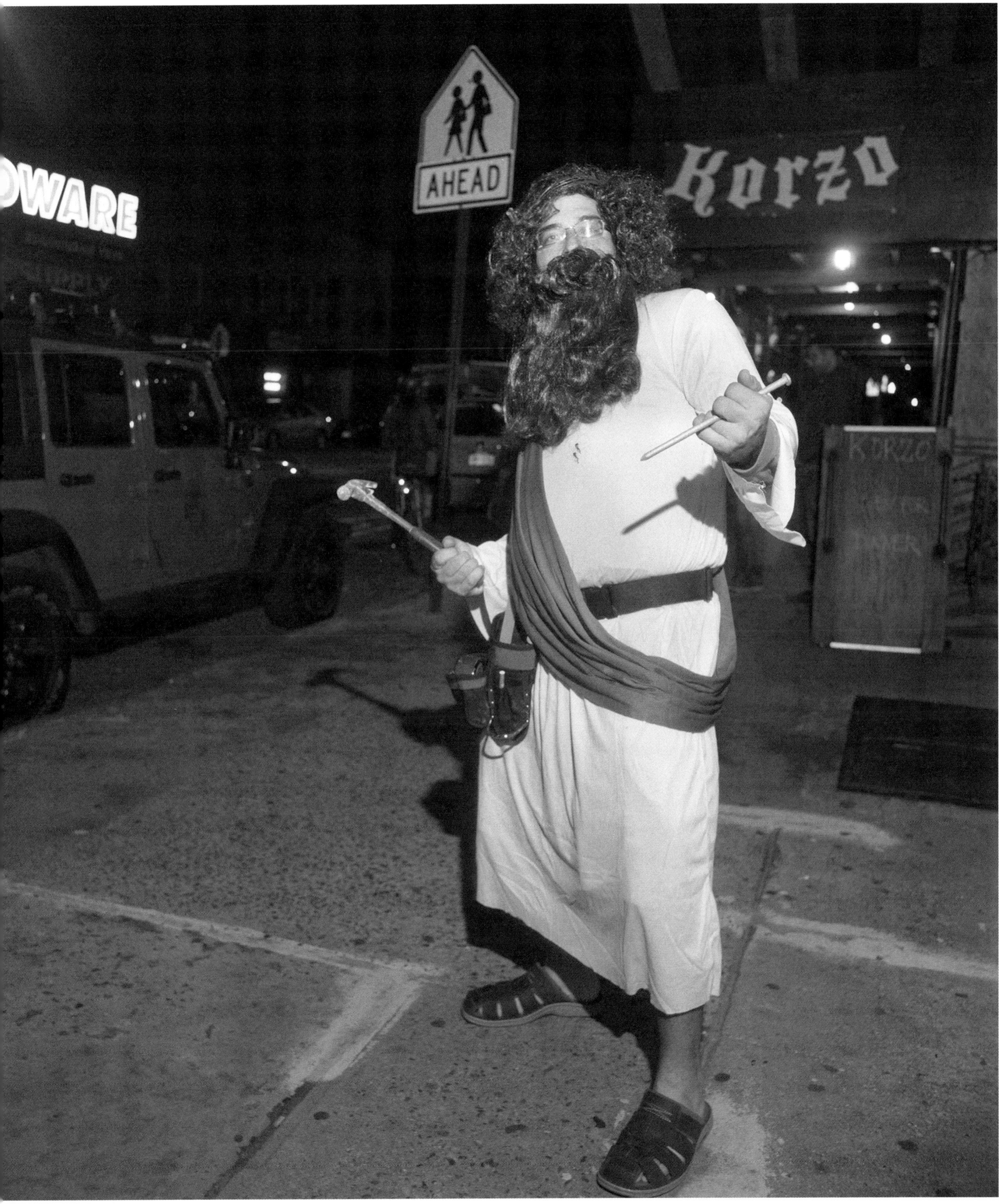
AHEAD
Korzo

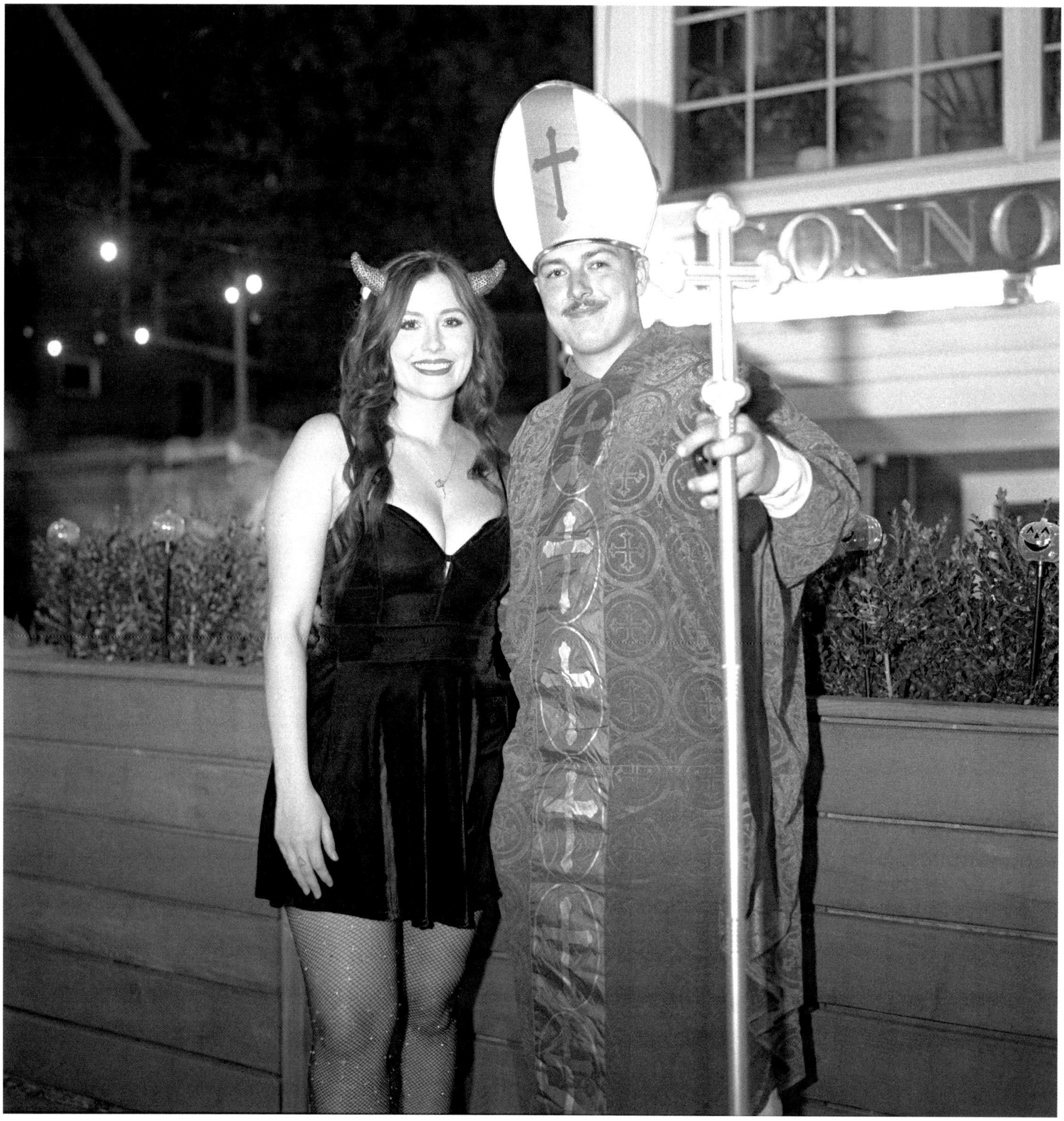

The Pope and the
Devil, 2023, Queens.

In 2023, I photographed a Halloween party at Connolly's Bar in Rockaway.

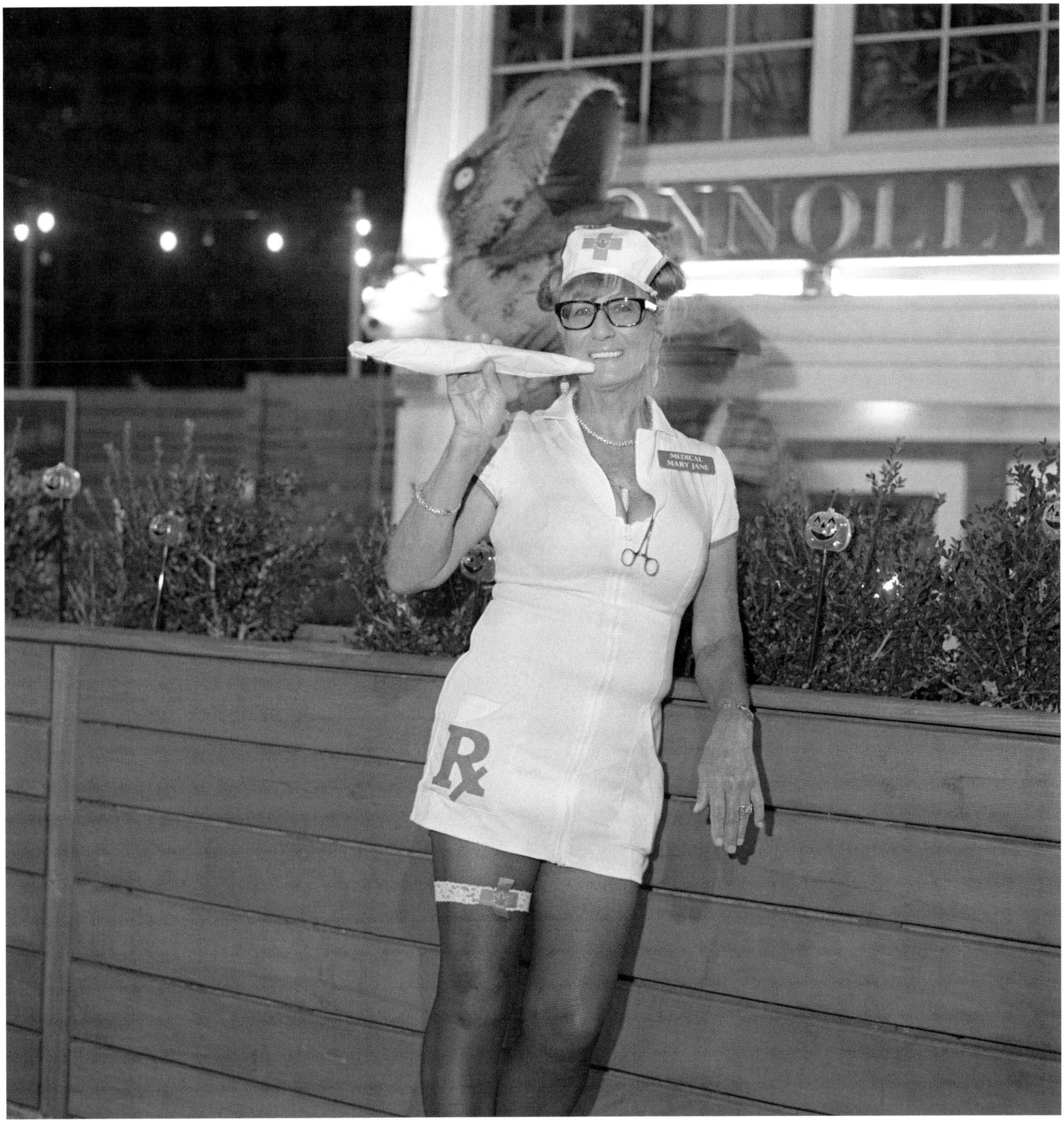

Nurse with blunt,
2023, Queens.

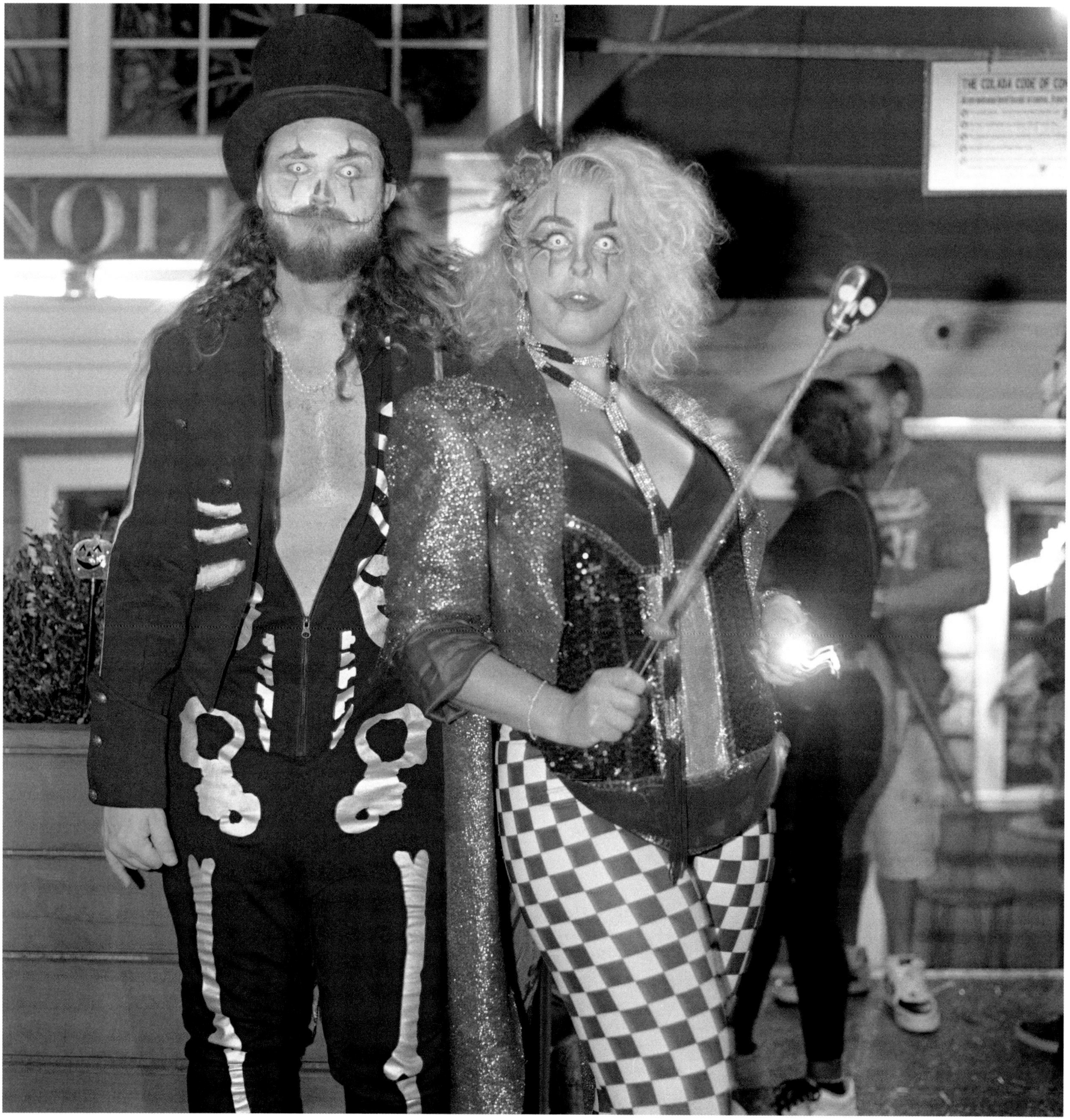

Bright-eyed couple,
2023, Queens.

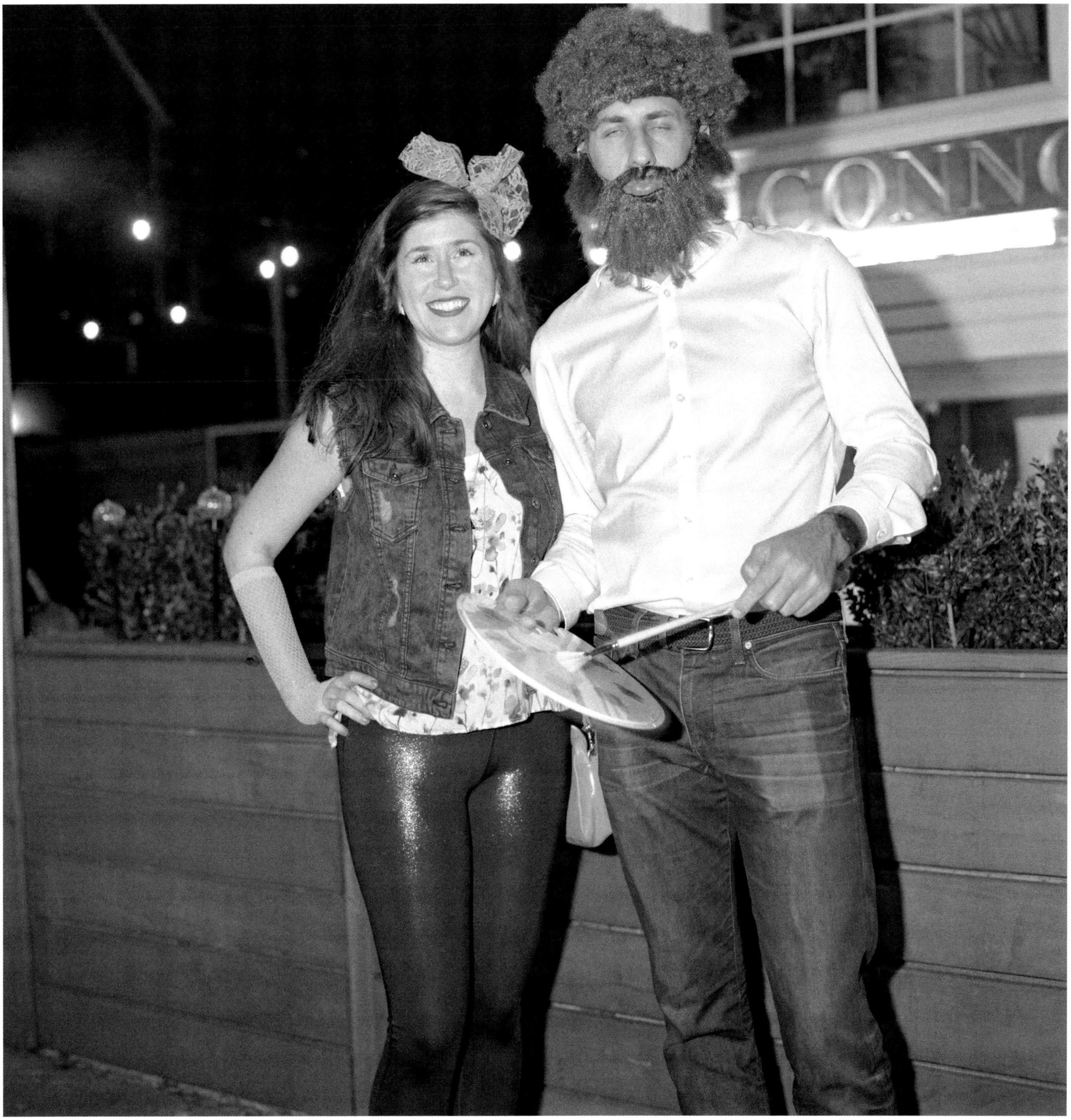

Bob Ross and friend,
2023, Queens.

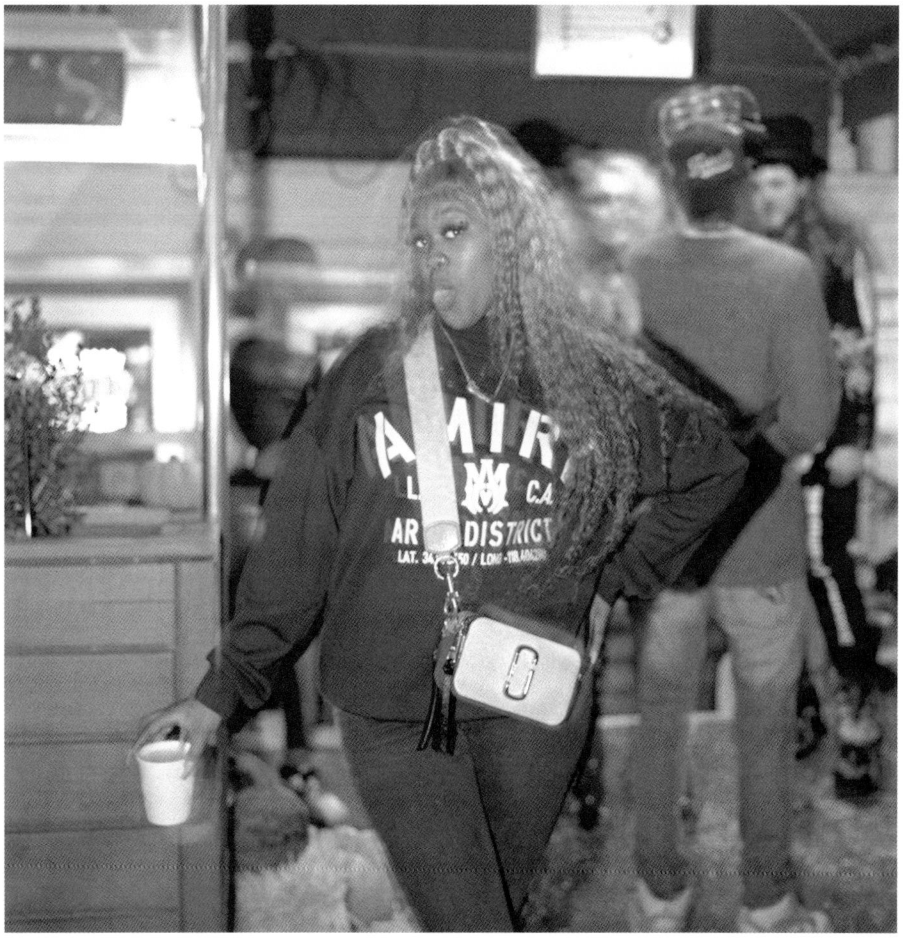

Woman with beer cup, 2023, Queens.

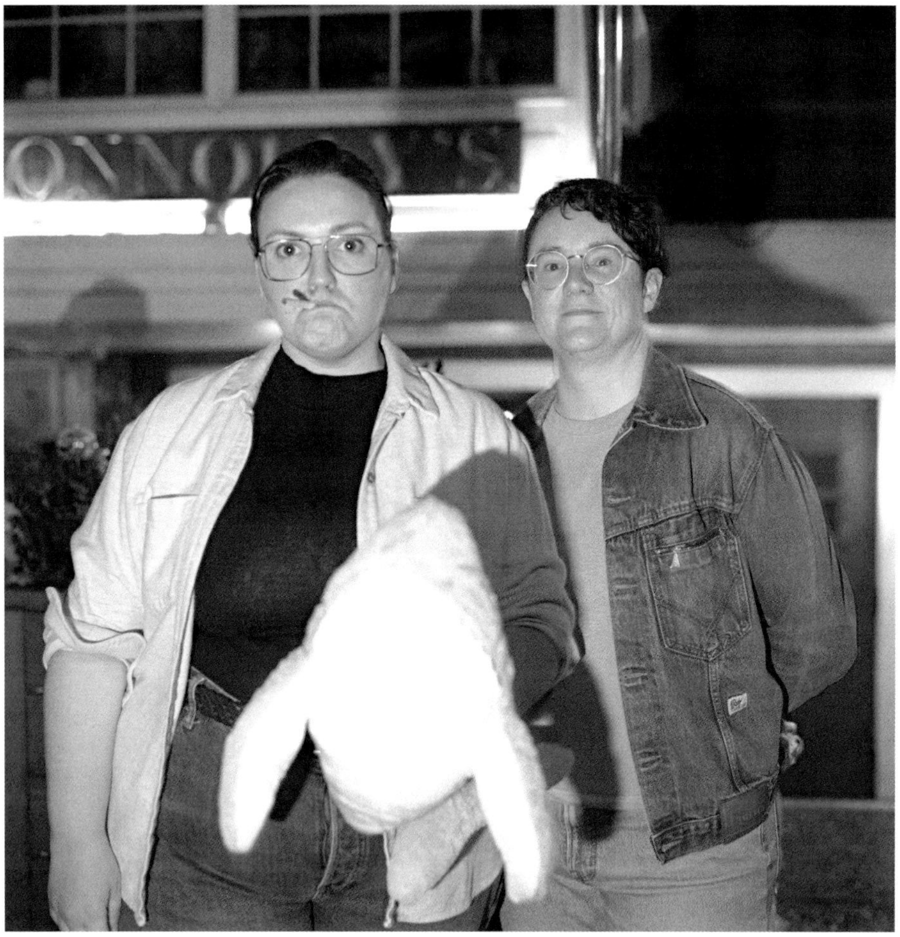

Two toughies and bunny, 2023, Queens.

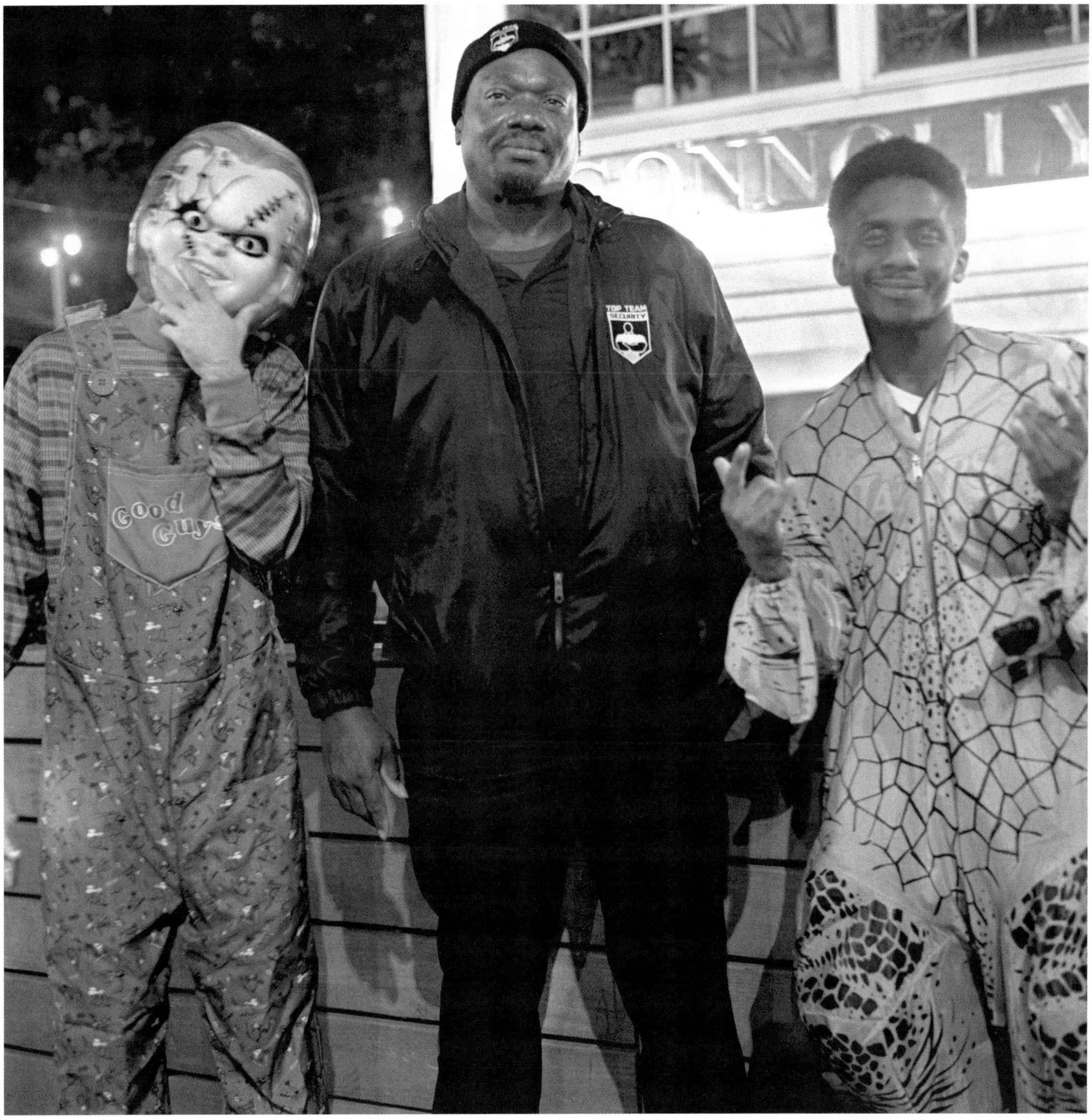

Bouncer and guests,
2023, Queens.

TECHNICAL NOTES: HOW TO MAKE A CHALK SOCK

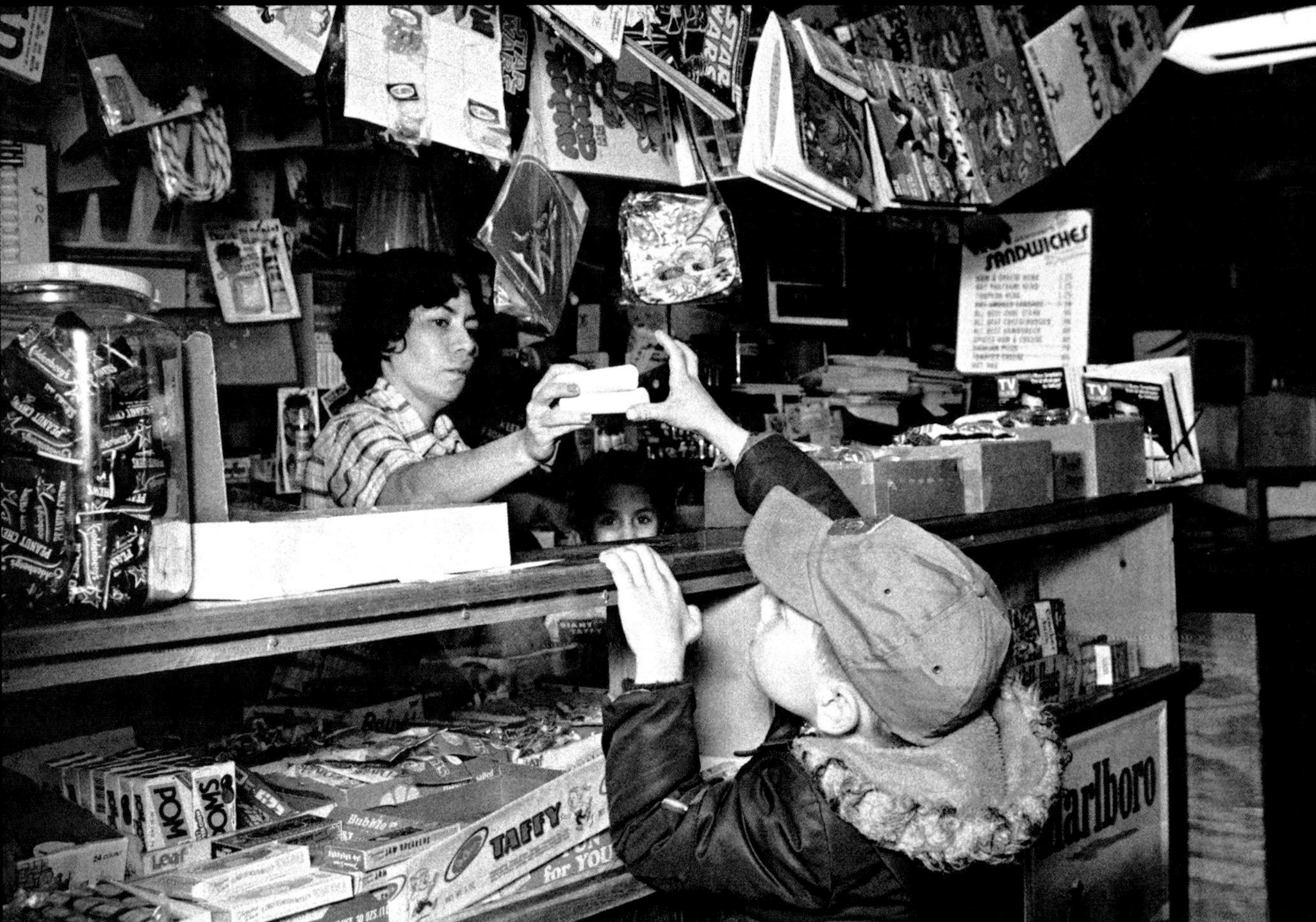

1. Buy two pieces of large colored chalk.

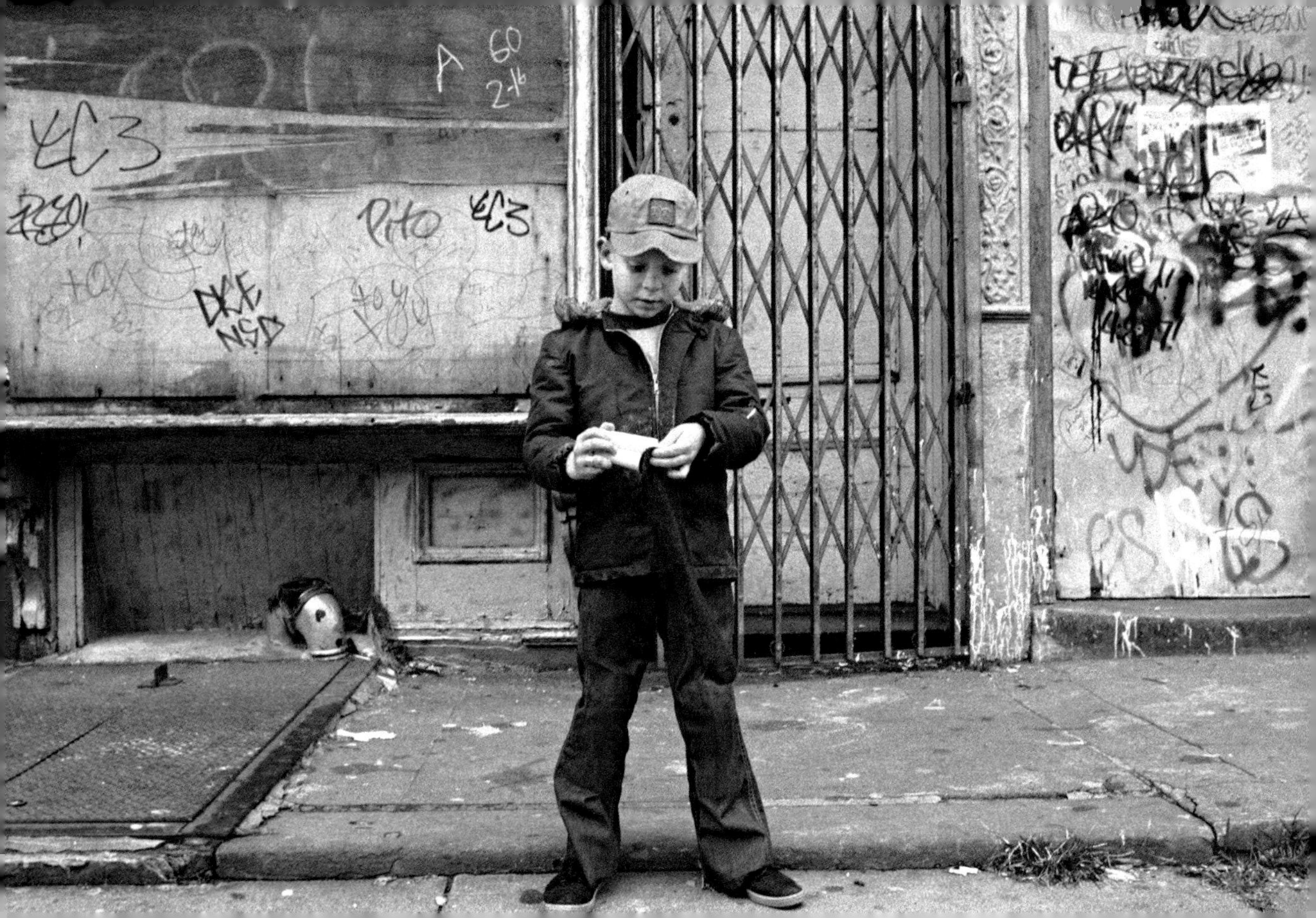
A 60
2-16

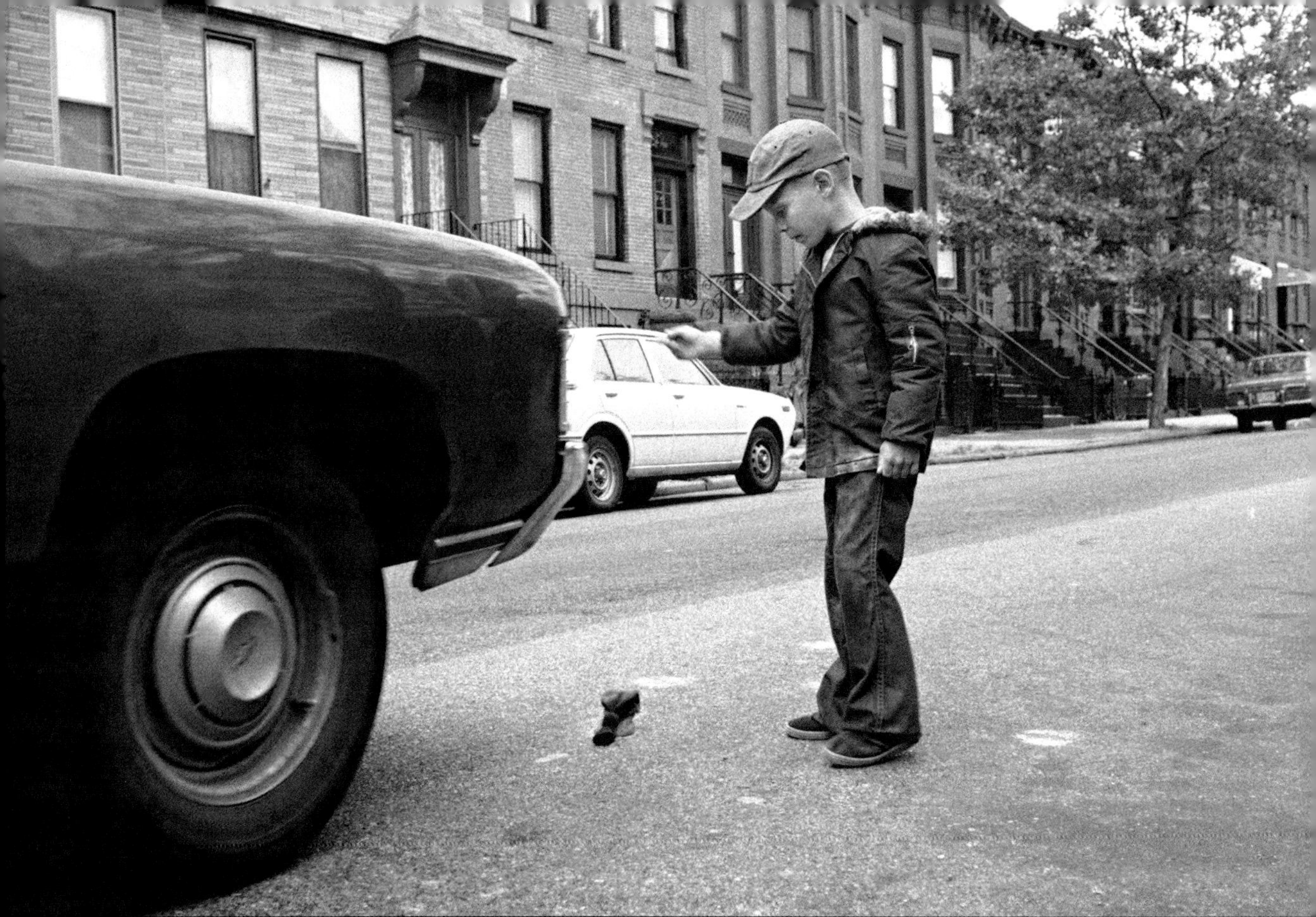

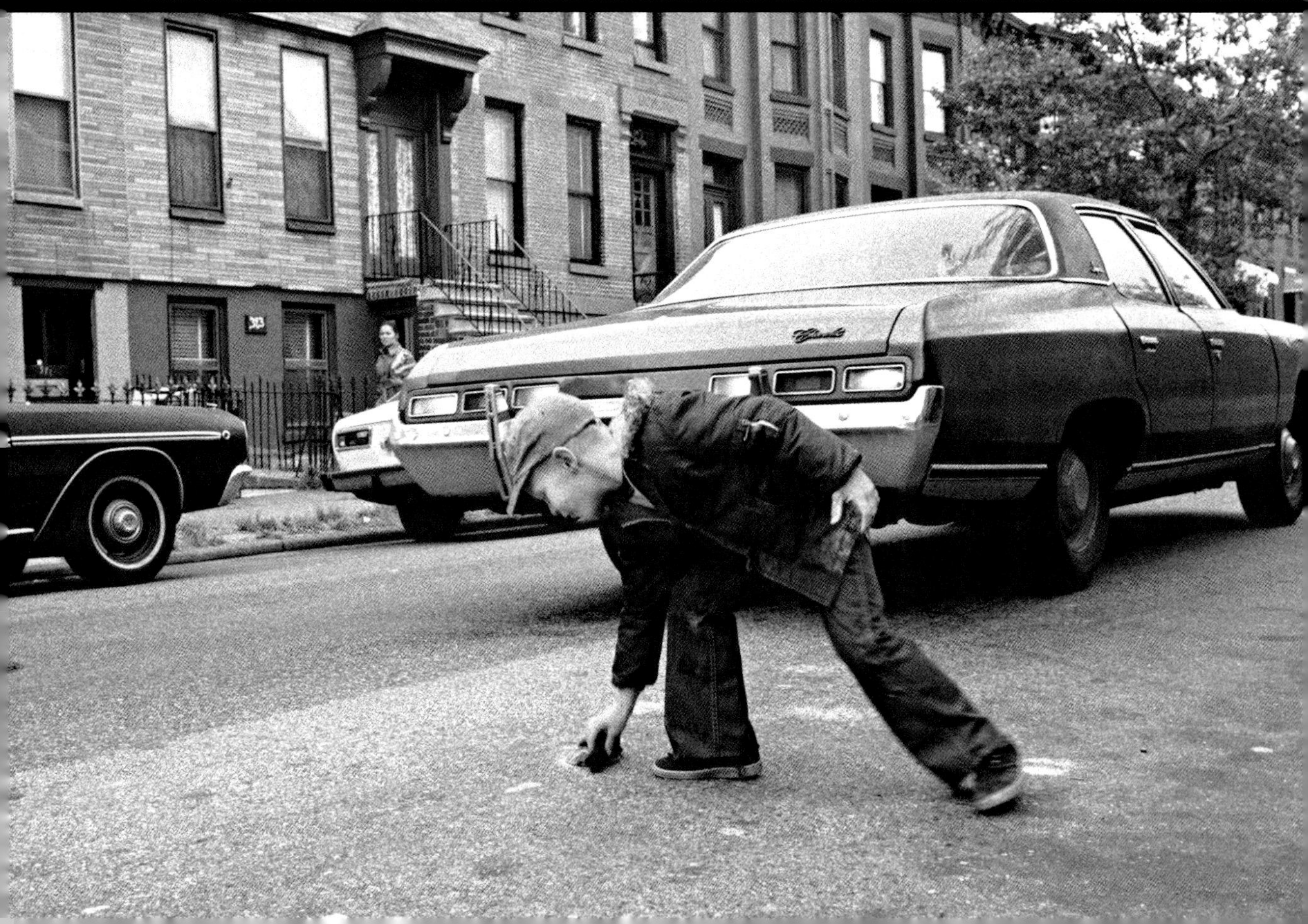

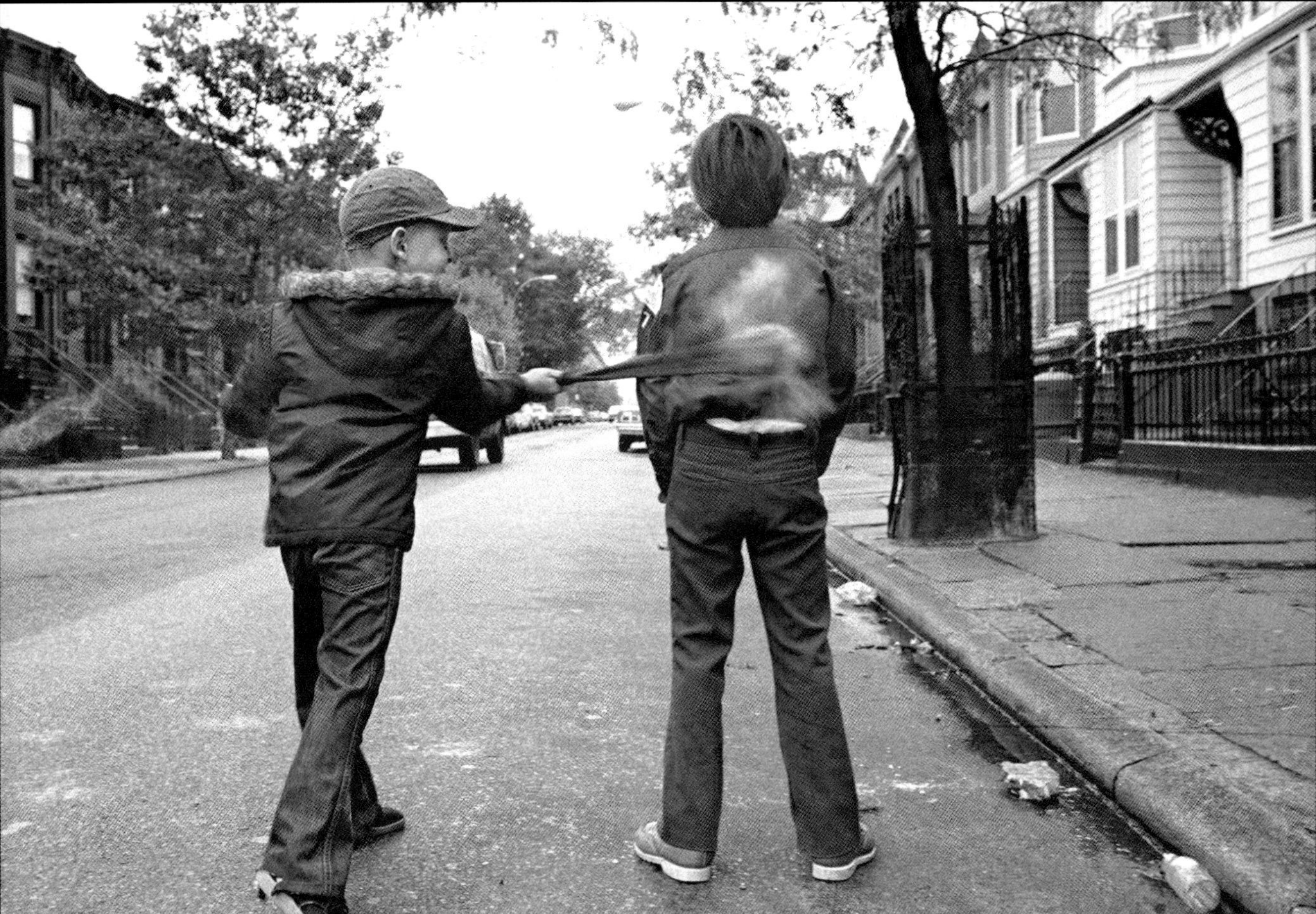

3. Toss the sock under a moving car to crush the chalk to powder. (Repeat if necessary.)

4. Pick up the sock and make sure it is now filled with powder.

EPILOGUE

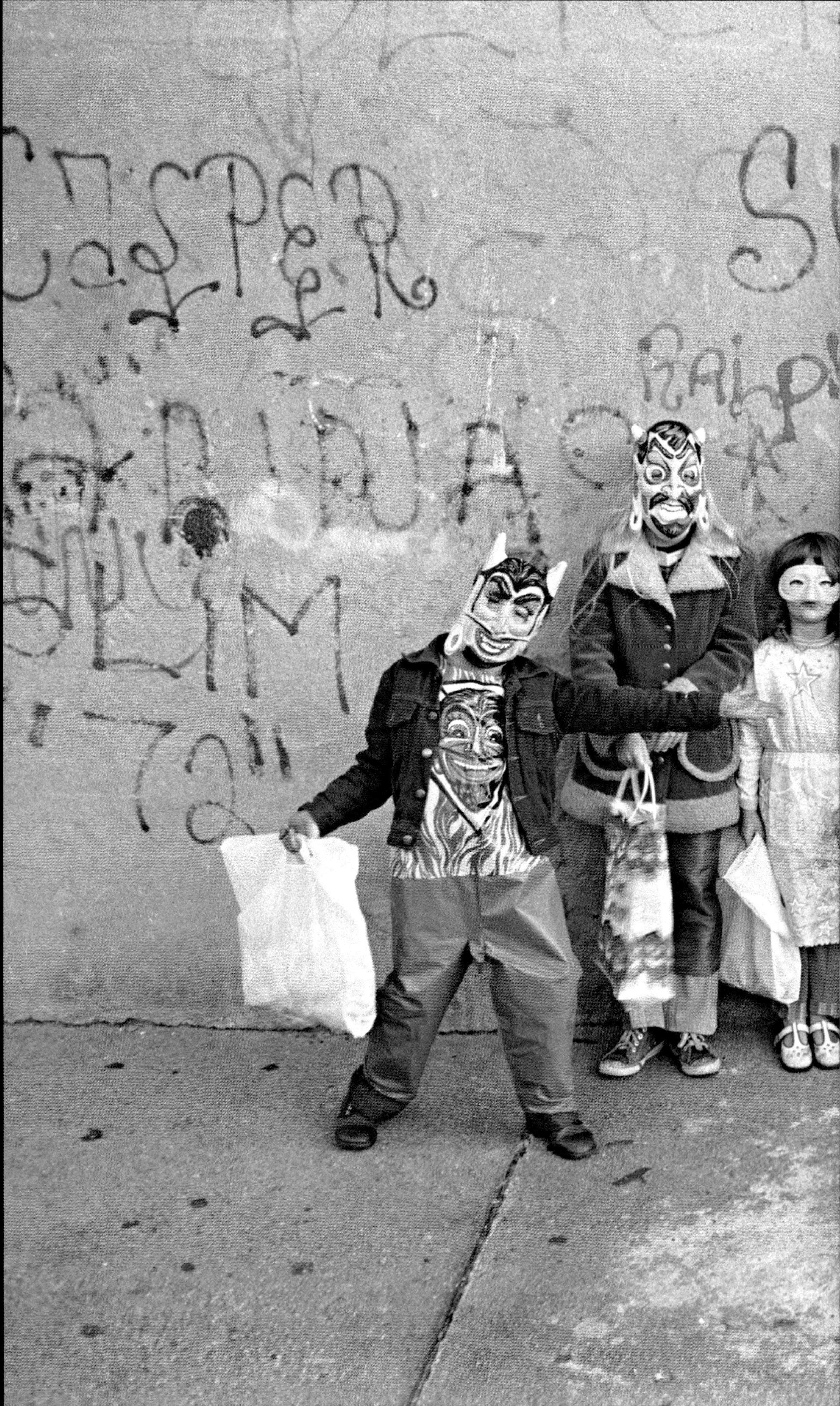

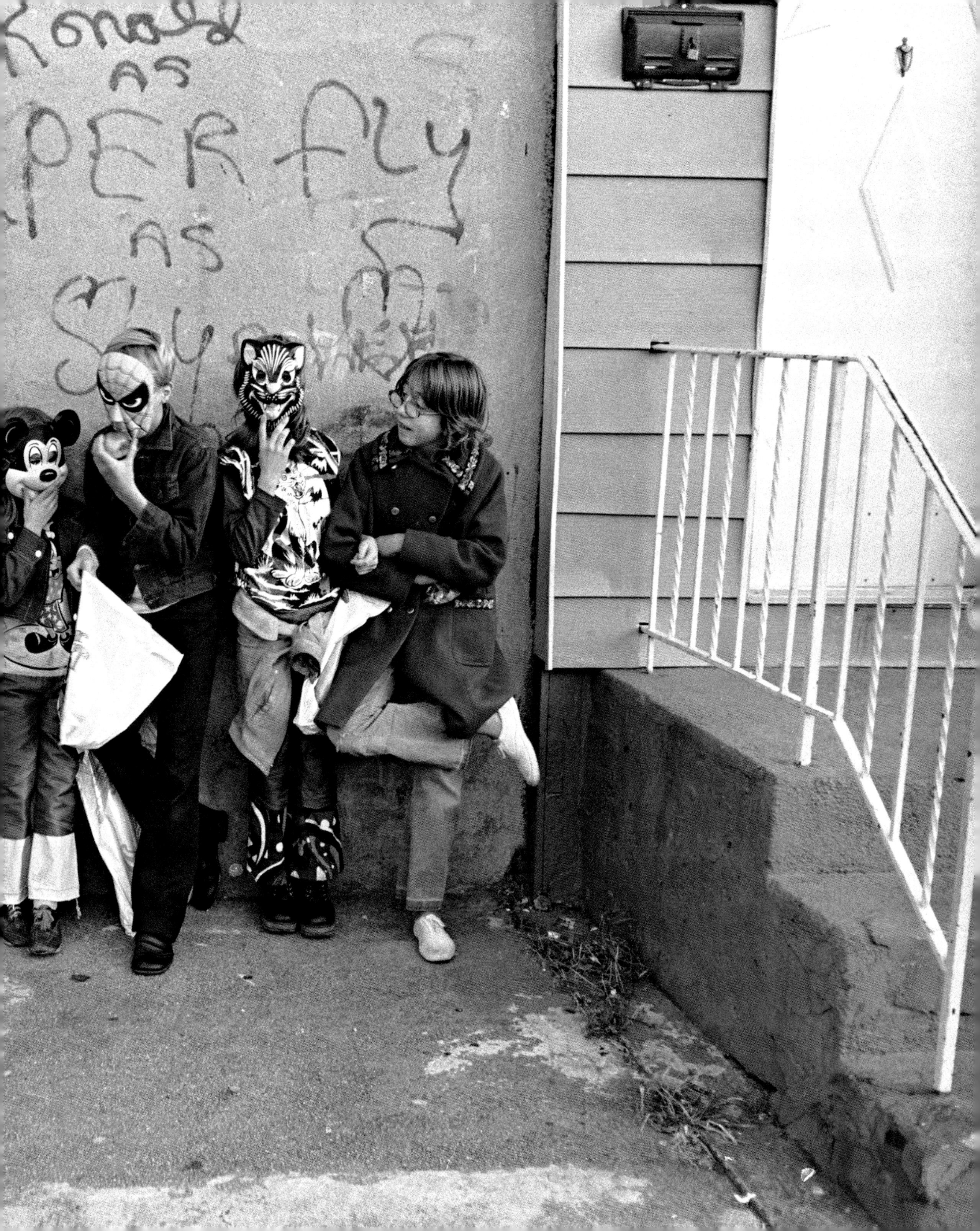

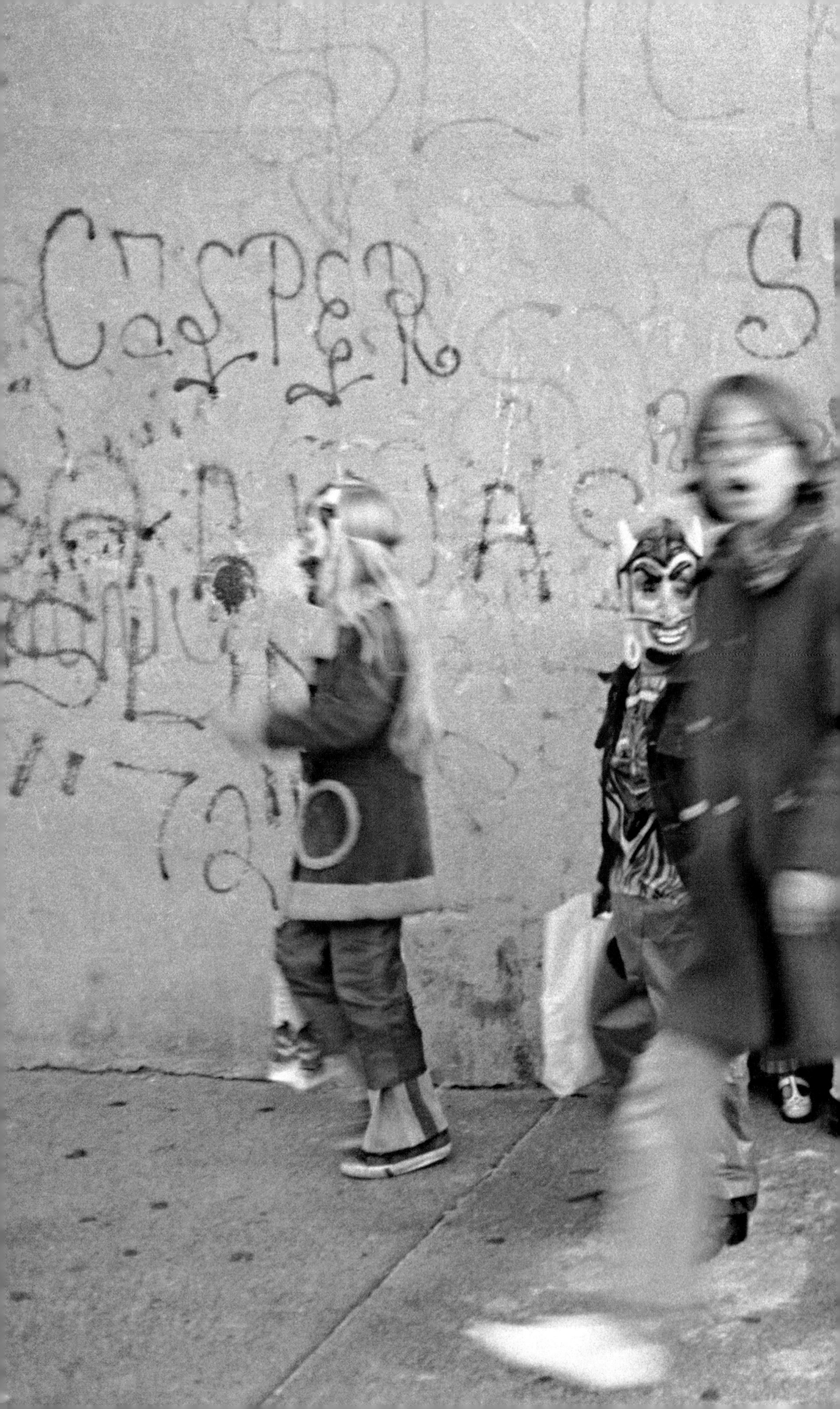
CASPER

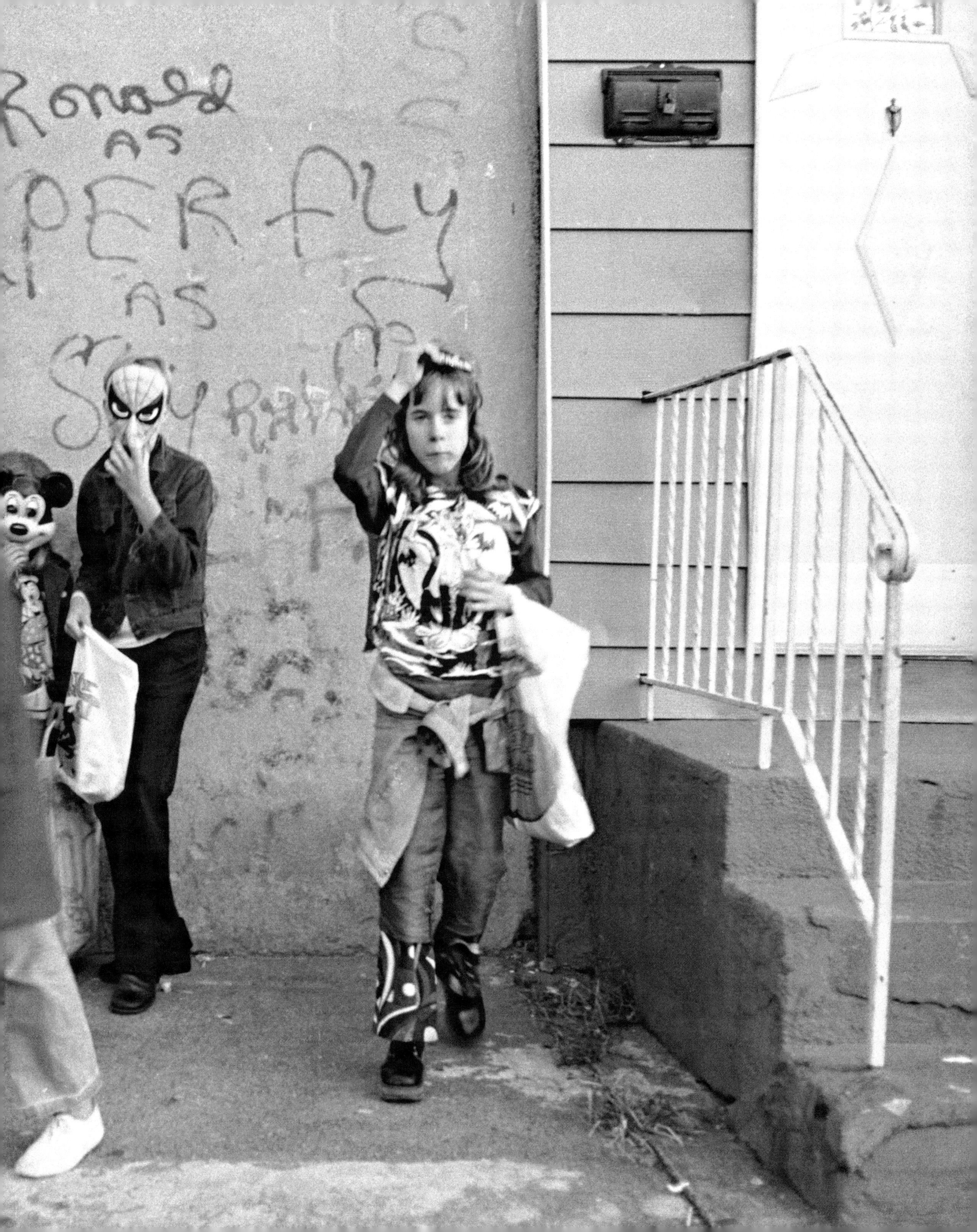
Ronald
AS
PER FLY
AS

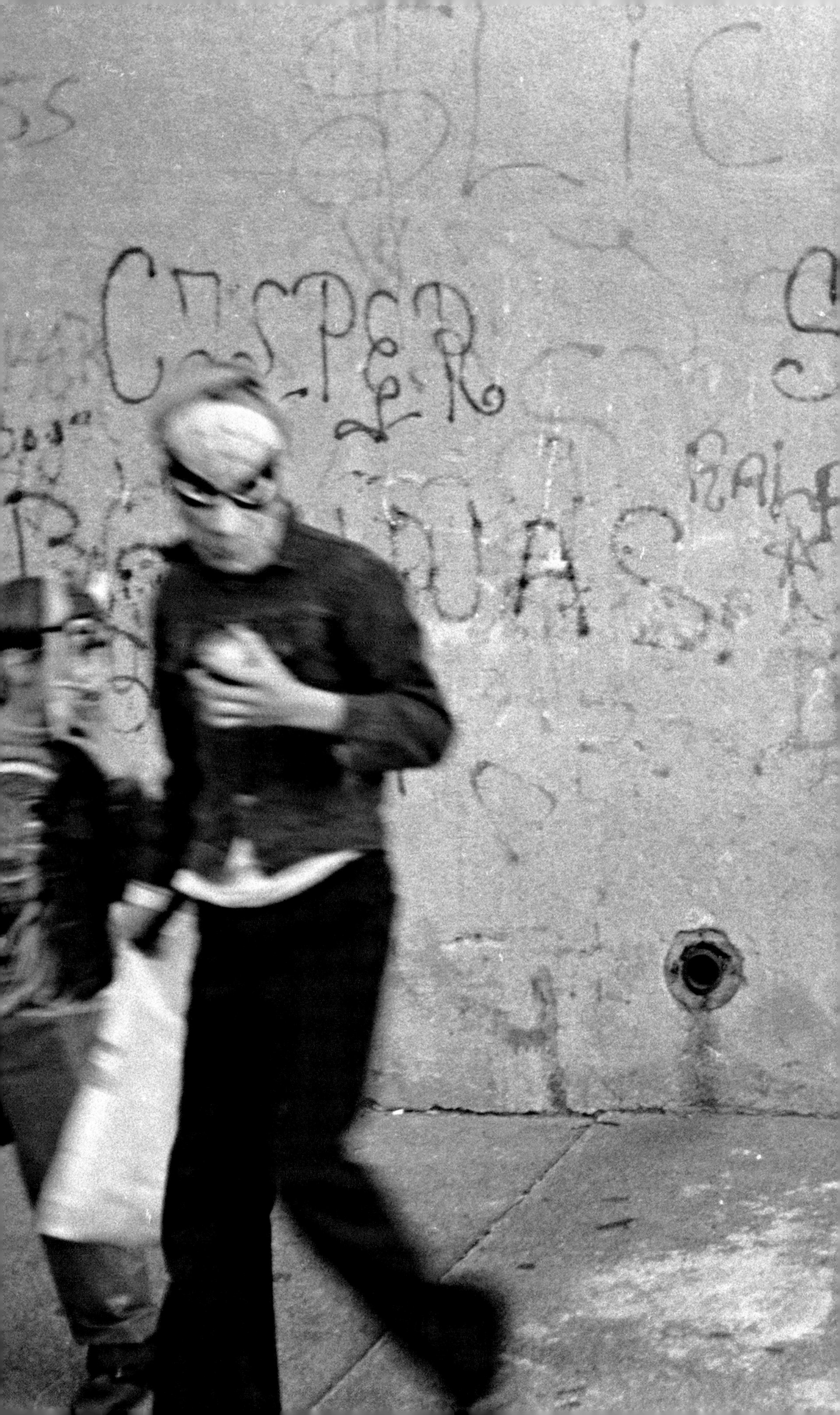

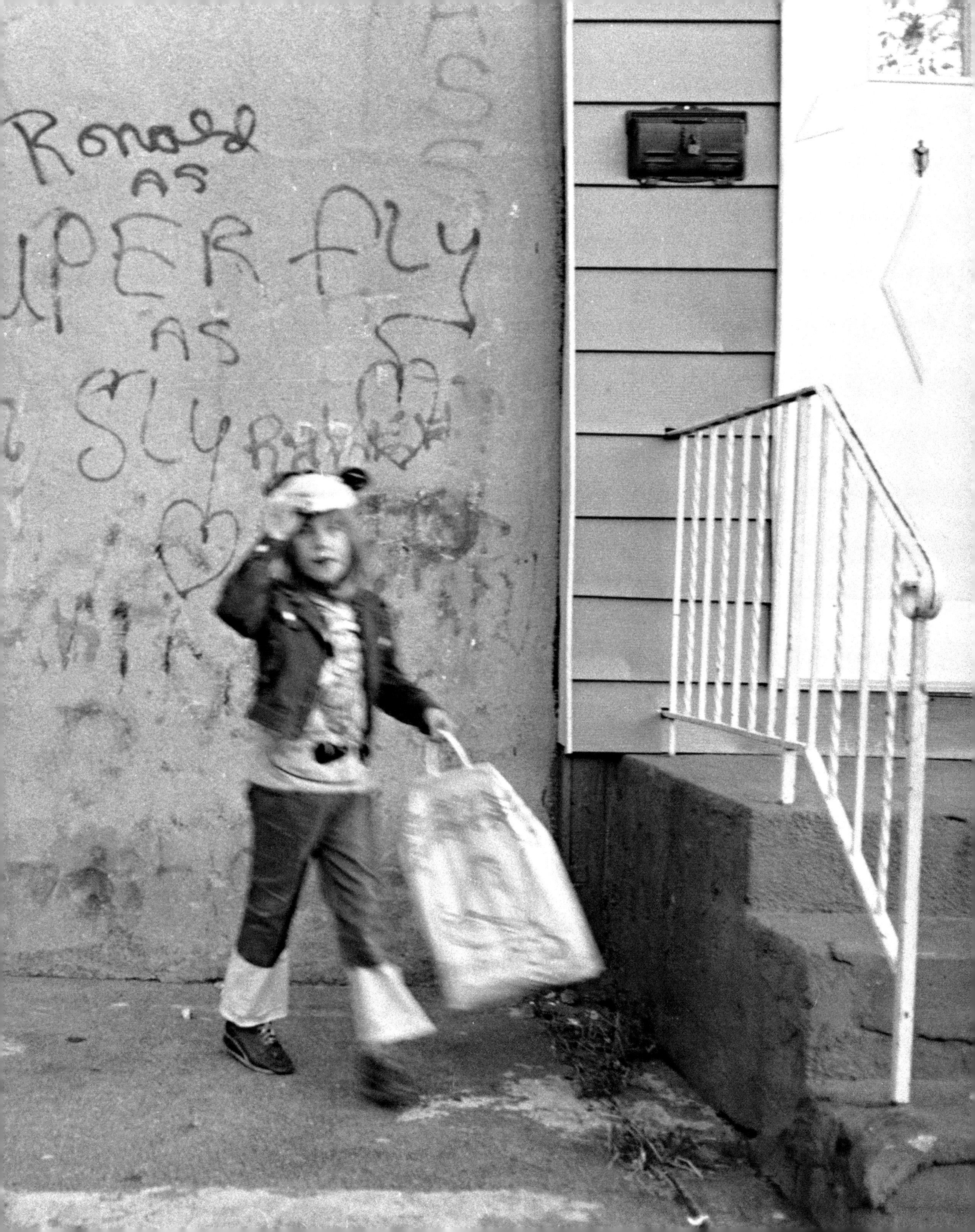
Ronald
AS
PERFLY
AS
SLY

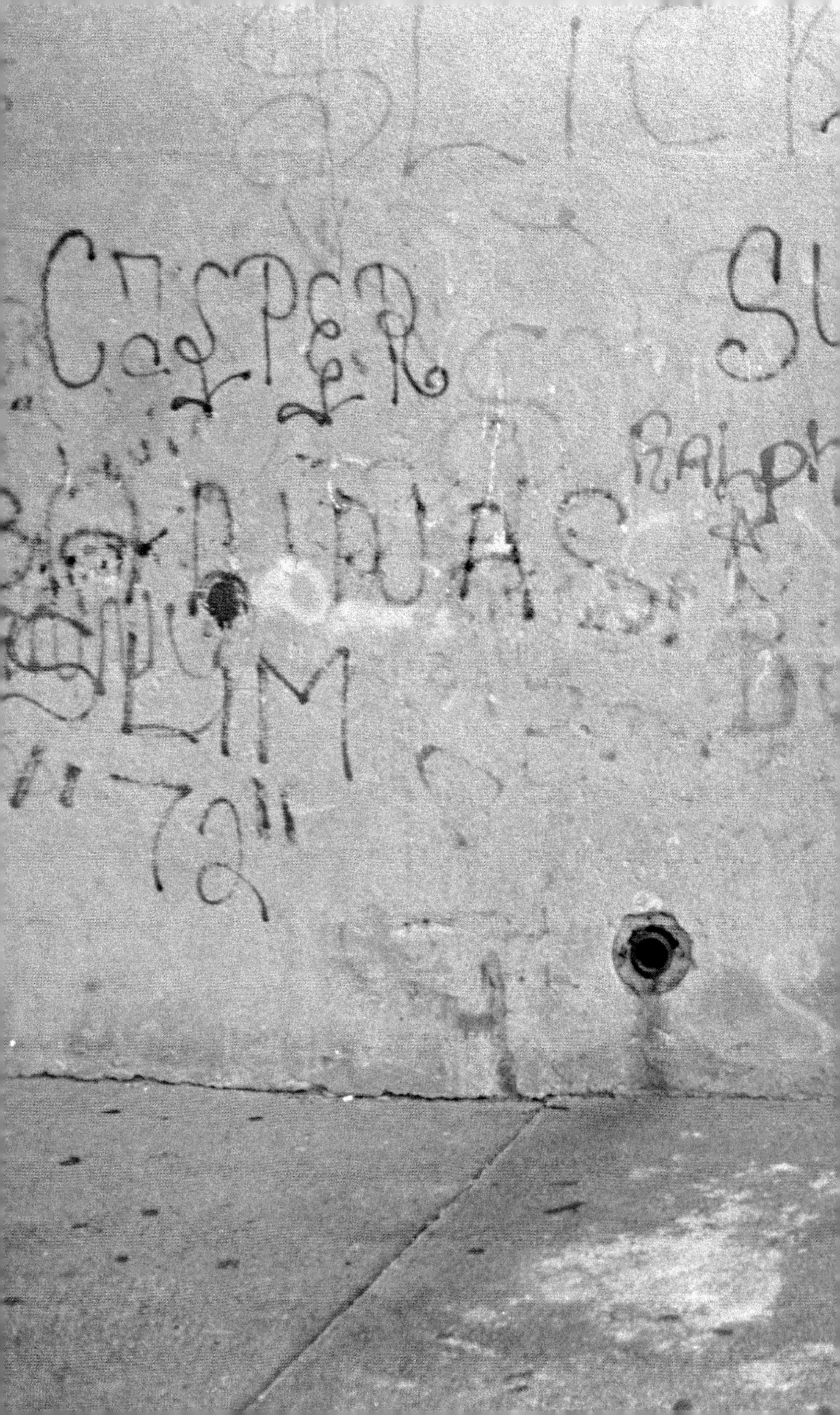
CASPER

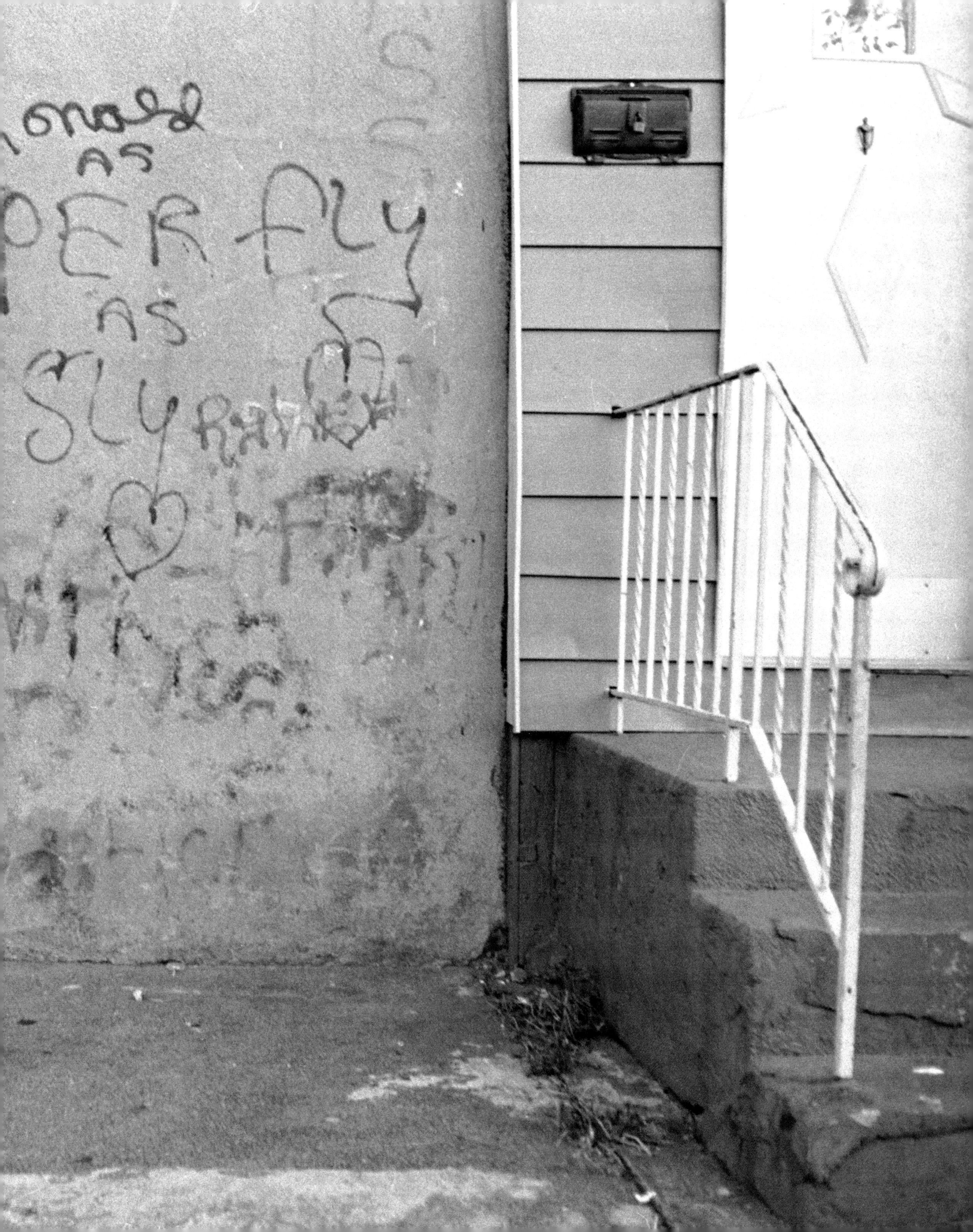
AS
ER fLY
AS
SLY

ACKNOWLEDGMENTS

Special thanks to:

My wife, Barbara Cannizzaro, for her insightful, long-term review of my Halloween photographs.

Francesca Richer for her perceptive design advice.

Erin Canning and her colleagues at The Quarto Group for an excellent edit and design of a large body of photographs.

The ghosts and goblins, angels and devils, vampires and witches, Wonder Women and Supermen, and all the masked and costumed characters who graciously allowed me to take their photographs in so many places over so many years.

ABOUT THE AUTHOR

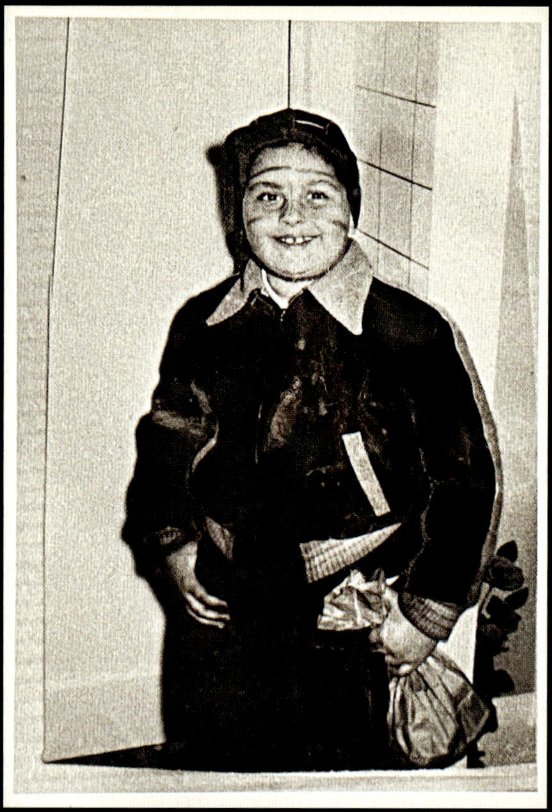

Larry as a trick-or-treater
with a paper bag of candy, c. 1957.

Larry Racioppo was born and raised in South Brooklyn and has photographed New York City since 1971. He was a VISTA Volunteer and a participating artist in the Cultural Council Foundation's CETA Artist Project. A Guggenheim Fellow and former staff photographer for NYC's Department of Housing Preservation and Development, his work is held by the Museum of the City of New York, the Brooklyn Museum, El Museo del Barrio, the Center for Brooklyn History, and the National September 11 Memorial & Museum. Recent books include *Memorial '76*, *Here Down on Dark Earth: Loss and Remembrance in New York City*, *Coney Island Baby*, and *Brooklyn Before: Photographs 1971–1983.*